Prussian Poland in the German Empire (1871–1900)

by Richard Blanke

EAST EUROPEAN MONOGRAPHS, BOULDER
DISTRIBUTED BY COLUMBIA UNIVERSITY PRESS
NEW YORK

1981

EAST EUROPEAN MONOGRAPHS, NO. LXXXVI

Richard Blanke is Associate Professor
of History at the University of Maine
at Orono

Copyright ©1981 by Richard Blanke
Library of Congress Card Catalog Number 81-065162
ISBN 0-914710-80-X

Printed in the United States of America

TO ANN

Table of Contents

Preface v
Introduction: Prussian Poland and the Prussian State to 1871 1
I: The *Kulturkampf* and Prussian-Polish Relations 17
II: From *Kulturkampf* to *Nationalitätenkampf* 39
III: The Anti-Polish Offensive of 1886 55
IV: Polish National Solidarity under Attack 93
V: An Era of Reconciliation 121
VI: The Populist Revolt and the Failure of Loyalism 147
VII: Prussian Polish Policy at the Crossroads: the Hohenlohe Era 177
VIII: The Triumph of Nationalist Enmity 209
Bibliography 239
Maps 261
Index 265

Preface

This is a study of two parallel developments: the evolution of Prussian Polish policy, 1871-1900, and the simultaneous evolution of the Polish minority in Germany. During this period, Prussian Polish policy underwent an important transition from the comparatively modest desire for political tranquility, without special regard for ethnic assimilation, to attempted denationalization and serious socio-economic discrimination. Prussian Poles, particularly the articulate and politically interested element among them, underwent an equally important change in national outlook: from a traditional nationalism, noble-dominated and retrospective, to a "modern" national movement, broadly based and ethnically defined. One can view these developments as distinct, each evolving according to its own internal logic (most of the existing literature focuses almost exclusively on one aspect or the other). This study, however, focuses on their interdependence: the impact of Prussian policies and the German context in general on the particular direction taken by Polish nationalism (and Prussian-Polish society) and the way an evolving Prussian-Polish society both called forth and largely frustrated various government measures.

It is probably unnecessary to justify to even the most present-minded the devotion of attention to the problem of German-Polish relations. The origin of World War II and the expulsion of the population of entire provinces after 1945 point to the unprecedented intensity which national differences reached in the German-Polish borderlands, and thus to the fateful role of the Polish dimension in German history. Yet this dimension has been widely neglected by historians of Germany and the Polish problem as a factor in the history of the German Empire underestimated. Poles were by far the largest ethnic minority in post-1871 Germany: they constituted 6% of the Empire's population and 10% of the population of the Prussian State. They were a majority or sizable minority in four eastern provinces and a prominent element in Berlin and the Ruhr as well by 1900. Among the commonly cited "*Reichsfeinde*" they were outnumbered only by Catholics during most of the period under study here, yet a glance at frequently used textbooks and general surveys of German history shows widespread omission of the Polish aspect.

First of all, therefore, this study is an effort to fill a fairly large gap in the historical literature: the absence of a treatment (comprehensive and up-to-date or otherwise) of the German-Polish problem in English. Recent German-language writing on this question has tended to consist of narrowly defined monographs and general surveys based on the same traditional secondary accounts. Much important work has been done in Poland in recent decades, but this is not easily accessible to most English-speaking scholars. Originally this study focused on Prussian Polish policies, but it soon became clear that one cannot study the way Prussia/Germany handled her Poles without examining the object of these policies: the Prussian Poles themselves. Indeed, an obvious explanation for the general failure of Prussian Polish policy is that the government in Berlin had no real understanding of the people it was trying to manipulate or assimilate. This is not to say that Polish nationalism itself was irresistible, but there were other factors of an economic, social, demographic, or local-political nature which decisively affected the success or failure of Prussian policies. Only attention to the population of Prussian Poland can help to explain why these policies missed their mark so badly. Of course, this means being drawn inevitably into the realm of provincial or even local history and politics, but I have tried to include such material here only when it seemed essential to the larger picture.

This work tries to retain the qualities of a monograph, making the widest possible use of primary sources, but also (at the risk of falling between two chairs) treats in comprehensive fashion the broadly-defined problem of Prussian-Polish relations over a fairly long and significant period. There are some aspects of this problem where I add little to the findings of earlier scholars and have been content to incorporate these here (*e.g.*, the work of Witold Jakóbczyk on "Organic Work," Lech Trzeciakowski on the *Kulturkampf* in Poznania, Helmut Neubach on the expulsions of 1885, and Rudolf Korth on school policy). Selective use of the huge secondary literature on Bismarck and the Second Empire was also necessary (the Bibliography includes only those works which pertain in some way to the Polish problem). Otherwise, this study is based on all the pertinent archival and printed primary sources which were available to me. This includes the major archives of West Germany and Poland (but not those in East Germany, to which access has repeatedly been denied). Government policies are generally better documented and have been easier to reconstruct than the Polish side of this problem, for which there are few unpublished sources; much of the latter aspect has necessarily been based on newspapers and government reports. The dates in the title (1871-1900) define the period which has been explored on the basis of primary sources. The evolution of this problem obviously began well before 1871, however, and its immediate effects continued at least until after World War I. In fact, aside from the largely symbolic redefinition of the sovereign power in Prussian Poland as "German-national" (rather than "Prussian-state"), 1871 did not mark a major change in this relationship. The Polish question remained a primarily state (vs. Imperial) problem and was thus little affected by the unification of Germany per se. (Of course, the Kulturkampf which followed was of fundamental importance.) Similarly, 1900 did not see the conclusion of much aside from Hohenlohe's chancellorship; but for the desire to keep this work of manageable size, it could easily have been extended to 1914. As for terminology, "Prussian Poland" is most likely to need special definition: the maps at the back of this study suggest some of the ways one can define the geographical context (and even these categories were in a state of constant flux in the Nineteenth Century); most of the time, Prussian Poland is defined "politically" (Map #3), because this is where the national-political activities and organizations were concentrated.

In terms of theoretical context, this work is essentially a study of nationalism (or rather two competing and occasionally contrasting nationalisms). While I have incorporated theoretical concepts from time to time, this is not primarily a case study, however, nor is it couched in the terms or context of any particular theory or definition of nationalism. The general (theoretical) literature on nationalism seems a long way still from the facts of the Prussian-Polish problem. Perhaps this account of one particularly significant national conflict will contribute to a more useful and realistic theoretical framework as others seek to fit the Prussian-Polish situation to a more universal context. Unlike so many works with nationalist subjects, this study is not a morality play, with a good and a bad side to it; indeed, the two nationalisms featured here are not really that different from each other. Germans and Poles both adhered in growing numbers to their nation during this period, investing more and more of their individual identities in their respective supra-individual entity. Growing numbers on both sides felt called upon to defend this entity against the alien competitor, against which they harbored various collective grievances of a cultural, economic, and political nature.[1] Both national movements were well established by 1871 and by

1900 presented similar, "modern" typologies: morally ethnocentric, relying on organization, indoctrination, and stereotypes of the opposition, complaining of economic discrimination, etc.[2] Neither movement could be reduced in Marxist fashion to the aspirations of a single social class; in both cases, leadership was in the hands of an "intelligentsia" of diverse background, allied (in the German case) with the organs of a semi-feudal state and in the Polish case itself largely of gentry origin. Both movements (especially the Polish but even the German on the local and provincial level) defy analysis from the standpoint of social science theories which view nationalism in the context of industrialization or "modernization;" the Prussian-Polish borderlands at this time were little affected by industrialization and in the Polish case pre-industrial classes were clearly in control.[3] It is similarly difficult to fit either of these nationalisms into the "six basic types" suggested by Carlton Hayes. Neither can be called "humanitarian/cosmopolitan" after 1871, nor can they be described as predominately "economic/protectionist" (though economic issues were an important part of the overall struggle by 1900). Nor can these two movements be put into neat political categories: neither qualifies as "liberal/English;" neither was "radical /Jacobin" (using nationalism as a cover for a generalized attack on a conservative status quo); neither was strictly "conservative/traditional," (though individual Polish leaders might fit this pattern). Prussian Poles and Prussian Germans exhibited a similar or analogous political spectrum, *i.e.*, neither people was clearly to the right or the left of the other. Finally, neither form of nationalism can be described accurately as "integral/totalitarian." To be sure, they were both "integral" by design, but in a clearly pre-totalitarian sense. Perhaps the best term to apply to German and Polish nationalism during the 1871–1900 period is "lapsed liberal;" politically ambivalent and morally inconsistent, integral in a quasi-legal sense, predominately (but certainly not exclusively) middle-class in social coloration. But this is a stage or manifestation of nationalism which has not yet found a very prominent place in the theoretical literature.

There are also important differences between the German and Polish nationalisms treated here. Polish nationalism at this time was the nationalism of the underdog, voicing the hopes and fears of a minority people without political power. Though traditionally of the historical or territorial type, it was largely transformed during the period under study here into the ethnic or "objective" type, with language the chief criterion.[4] German nationalism, on the other hand, was the sentiment of a majority people in power, presuming superiority over a "lesser" people on the basis of a perceived *Kulturgefälle*. In contrast to the Polish case, German nationalism had previously been primarily of the ethnic/

objective type (in response to the absence of political unity and natural frontiers which rendered the territorial/historical/"subjective" nationalism of western Europe inappropriate).[5] But with the achievement of the nation-state in 1871, German nationalism changed. Exhibiting little of the satisfaction and repose one might expect, it continued to make demands, switching now to a political/territorial rationale (trying to equate nation with state rather than with language and culture). For the most part, this effort to secure the conformity of non-Germans in the Empire was unsuccessful. Perhaps it was too late to create the kind of subjective national consciousness that the English and French achieved among ethnic minorities in their much older states. Perhaps also, as the following study suggests, German leaders simply took the wrong approach. There are certainly no compelling reasons for accepting as inevitable the victory of the kind of nationalist thinking and feelings portrayed here; language differences alone have not always led to political hostility, even in central Europe (and the objective cultural differences were present long before the appearance of serious national conflict involving the mass of Germans and Poles after 1871).[6] Thus this study presumes a fair amount of freedom on the part of the principal actors, concentrating on the choices they made (and the alternative choices they might as well have made).

* * *

Thanks should be expressed to a large number of persons and institutions who have aided this study. To cite only a few: the Fulbright Commission and the Research Funds Committee of the University of Maine, Orono, for the financial support necessary to conduct research in Europe; the Russian and East European Center at the University of Illinois, Champaign-Urbana, for the summertime use of its fine library; Harvard University, which has also been generous in allowing visiting scholars access to its library; the very friendly Raczyński Library in Poznań; above all, the Herder Institute in Marburg/Lahn, which has the best single collection of literature on this problem. Thanks also to individual archivists who helped with the use of materials at Bonn, Koblenz, Berlin-Dahlem, and Poznań; to my PhD advisor, Prof. Wolfgang Sauer, who has continued to provide many useful suggestions; to Gotthold Rhode, Helmut Neubach, Richard Breyer, Witold Jakóbczyk, and others who were kind enough to discuss this project with me at one stage or another. As for the East German Interior Ministry, which so carefully restricts access to that country's archives: thanks for nothing. Finally, thanks in advance to those who will point out to me the inevitable errors and shortcomings of the work which follows.

Notes

1. Eugen Lemberg, *Nationalismus*, 2nd edit. (Reinbek b. Hamburg, 1967), I:20; K.R. Minogue, *Nationalism* (Baltimore, 1970), p. 25.
2. Anthony Smith, *Theories of Nationalism* (New York, 1971), p. 171.
3. *Ibid.*, p. 127.
4. *Ibid.*, pp. 124, 211ff.; Lemberg, I:100; Konstantin Symmons-Symonolewicz, *Nationalist Movements* (Meadville, 1970), pp. 52ff.
5. Smith, pp. 132, 204; Minogue, p. 64.
6. Lemberg, I:86ff.

Introduction: Prussian Poland and the Prussian State to 1871

There was little indication in 1815, when Prussia resumed rule of her share of the defunct Grand Duchy of Warsaw, that this area would become the scene of a fierce national struggle by century's end. The liberal, cosmopolitan values of her reformist leaders and the felt need to justify her possession of this area in the first place combined to create reasonably conciliatory conditions. The Prussian government issued broad promises of respect and support for the majority Polish nationality; according to the Russian-Prussian pact of May 3, 1815, Poles were to receive "those institutions which assure the preservation of their nationality by means of those forms of political existence which each of the governments to which they belong judges it convenient to grant them."[1] King Frederick William III assured the inhabitants of Poznania:[2] "You too have a fatherland and therewith a demonstration of my respect for your devotion to it. You are being incorporated into My Monarchy without having to deny your nationality. . . . Your language is to be used along with German in all public transactions."[3] A member of the Radziwiłł family, Prince Antoni, became Poznania's first governor (*Statthalter*); Polish became indeed the second official language and the Polish nobility enjoyed the same rights and privileges as Prussian Junkers. On the whole, they continued to dominate the province's social, economic, and local-political life much as they had done before the partitions.

Government hopes that Polish leaders would respond loyally to conciliatory conditions were only partially realized. It proved difficult to reconcile Polish patriotism with active participation in the Prussian state; aside from a few who served as *Landräte* and judges, most Polish nobles remained aloof from the Prussian bureaucracy and army.[4] During the *Vormärz* period, however, the government seemed satisfied with passive political loyalty and did not demand active participation or ethnic conformity from its Polish population. During these first decades after 1815, it held to the belief that the advantages of Prussian order and German material culture would be decisive in the long run and the Poles would eventually resign themselves to the new situation. Attempts to accelerate this process of political assimilation were considered unnecessary and might even prove self-defeating. In so far as one can speak of an active "Polish policy" prior to 1830, it consisted of efforts to improve conditions of life in a way that would enhance the appeal of the Prussian system in Polish eyes. Major emphasis was placed on the improvement of education; between 1815 and 1848 the percentage of Poznanian children who attended school increased from 22% to 70% and the number of secondary schools increased from three to ten.[5]

Such efforts during the *Vormärz* period were still very much in the spirit of bureaucratic cosmopolitanism; the expanded school system was not merely a Germanizing instrument and the language and religion of the Poles were respected. The prevailing attitude was expressed by Culture Minister Altenstein in 1822:

> Religion and language are the holiest treasures of a nation, in which its entire world of convictions and concepts is bedded. An authority which recognizes, respects and values these may be sure of winning the hearts of its subjects; one which shows indifference toward them however, or even permits attacks against them, embitters and degrades that nation and creates for itself disloyal or bad subjects. . . . The education of an individual and of a nation can only be achieved by means of the native language. . . . If one really wants to see successfully to the education of the Polish nation, this will always take place most dependably by means of their own language. The interests of the government will be sufficiently taken care of as long as the German language is established as a subject in every Polish school and one sees to it that the children become fluent in it before leaving school."[6]

Prussia pursued something of a zig-zag policy toward her Polish population in the Nineteenth Century, characterized by a number of sharp policy shifts, but overall the trend was away from this kind of rationalist, nationally tolerant approach. A first such shift followed upon indications of Prussian-Polish involvement in the 1830 uprising in the Congress Kingdom (Russian Poland.) Radziwiłł was replaced as Poznania's governor by a German, Eduard von Flottwell, who began to pursue a policy of "Germanization" (though, to be sure, what he understood by that term was still a far cry from what it later came to mean.) Poznanian county estates (*Kreistage*) lost the right to propose *Landrat* candidates and the office of prefect (*Vogt*), traditionally held by local estate-owners, was replaced here by appointed district police commissioners.[7] Flottwell's most ambitious project was the establishment of a "Fund for Estate Management" (*Güterbetriebsfonds*) to buy up as many Polish estates as possible. This Fund bought up about 10% of the land owned by Polish nobles in Poznania (1833-43); the proportion of land owned by Poles fell from 79% to 68% during his tenure, due to these purchases but even more so to his ability to interest Germans to buy into the province as individuals.[8] Flottwell's policies doubtless were a factor in causing a trend away from the gradual integration of the Polish nobility into the Prussian state, which they increasingly saw as a threat to their nationality and social position. By the end of the 1830s, Poznania was the scene of growing conflict between the Prussian state on one side and the Polish nobility and (for other reasons) the Catholic Church on the other.

The accession of King Frederick William IV in 1840 reversed this trend temporarily. The "Flottwell Era" came to an end when Flottwell was dismissed and his Fund dissolved. An amnesty was issued for Prussian Poles involved in the 1830 uprising, an extradition arrangement with Russia was ended, and Poznania's Credit Institute, run by Polish nobles, was refinanced by the state.[9] The King reaffirmed the promises of 1815: "It was the intention (of the Vienna settlement) to value and respect the praiseworthy love of every noble people, including the Poles, for its language, customs, and its historical memories; under Our government too, respect and protection for these things is to be provided."[10] School policy guidelines outlined by Culture Minister Eichhorn in 1842 accepted the bi-lingual character of Poznania and required that the language of instruction in each elementary school be that of the majority of pupils.[11]

Frederick William IV reflected a romantic cultural nationalism as well as a specific sympathy for things Polish which many German contemporaries shared. But his sympathies did not include things outside the cultural sphere, e.g., Polish "separatism," and most Polish nobles in Prussia were still as opposed to political assimilation as they were fearful of cultural Germanization. They demanded autonomy for the Grand Duchy and continued to see a unitary Prussian state, even one which did not seek to denationalize them, as their chief adversary. Thus it was only a matter of time until Prussian-Polish relations soured again. In 1846, a major conspiracy by Poznanian Poles to aid the Polish uprising in Austrian Galicia was uncovered. In 1848, Prussian Poles played a prominent role in the revolutions which almost toppled the monarchy. Aided by General Mierosławski's 20,000-man armed force and the support of German liberalism, which was generally sympathetic to Polish national aspirations even vis-à-vis Prussia, Polish nationalists were able to seize control of most of Poznania for several months.[12] The new liberal government in Berlin sought at first to appease the Poles by reorganizing Poznania and turning the clearly Polish part over to them. But the idea of dividing up the province (approximately ⅔ Polish and ⅓ German)[13] on ethnic grounds was hopelessly impractical, especially in light of the growing nationalist self-interest of the German inhabitants. By the time the third and final demarcation line was determined in Berlin, Polish Poznania was left with only a small fraction of Prussia's Poles and with scarcely enough territory for a *Regierungsbezirk*. Both Poles and Germans remained dissatisfied with this and in October 1848 the partition idea was overruled by the Landtag, which reasserted the indivisibility of the Prussian state and its individual provinces.

From this time on, Prussian Poles became aware of two separate factors standing in the way of their aspirations: the conservative Prussian state and German liberal nationalism. In the short run, the Prussian state seemed to present the greater problem, at least for those nobles who still looked to the restoration of an independent Polish state. The 1850s saw increased political repression in Poznania (and throughout Prussia), with strict censorship, manipulated elections, and a growing distrust of the Polish nobility by the state bureaucracy. But in nationality matters it remained official policy to maintain a neutral stance. "The spreading of German nationality. . . . is a task that the government cannot undertake. If the German nationality needs the protection. . . . of administrative officials in order to assert itself, then it has no future to look forward to anyway."[14] To be sure, the neutrality of the Prussian state in national matters was never that convincing in Polish eyes. There was a growing discrepancy between such principles and bureaucratic practice as the earlier faith in the peaceful Germanizing potential of order and prosperity declined. In addition, German nationalist ideas were finding their way into this same bureaucracy, with new emphasis on German language and culture as unifying factors required by the state. Nonetheless, as long as Prussia remained in principle a dynastic-territorial rather than national state, there were grounds for hoping that a *modus vivendi* with her Polish population might be found, in spite of the feelings of the gentry nationalists. In the long run, it was the other adversary, German nationalism, which proved to be the more serious and aggressive rival, with which coexistence ultimately proved impossible for Prussian Poles.

While German nationalism was moving from the liberal opposition into the higher echelons of the Prussian state, an analogous diffusion of national consciousness from the Polish gentry to the mass of Prussian Poles began to take place. Whereas in Germany (and elsewhere in western Europe) the growth of nationalism was associated with the rise of the middle classes and expressed by a "bourgeois" intelligentsia, in Poland and other parts of eastern Europe, still little affected by liberalism and industrialization, nationalism was mainly a matter of the gentry and an intelligentsia of gentry origin appealing to a largely peasant popula-

Introduction   5

tion. In Prussian Poland, a conscious effort by progressive gentry to "raise" the national consciousness of the peasantry can be dated from the 1840s and became a prevalent concern after 1848. For one thing, the beginnings of parliamentary-political life in Prussia in 1848 encouraged Polish leaders to devote more attention to the mobilization of a mass base. For another, the positivistic idea of "Organic Work" (*praca organiczna*) came to rival and then replace the romantic reliance on conspiracy and insurrection as the strategy of Polish nationalism, an obvious consequence of the failure of the latter approach in 1830, 1848, and finally 1863. Organic Work meant, among other things, efforts to build up a middle class amidst a still semi-feudal agrarian society, beginning with the creation of a pragmatic intelligentsia of professional and business people. The major vehicle of this effort was Karol Marcinkowski's "Society for Academic Aid to the Youth of the Grand Duchy of Poznania," funded by nobles and by the Catholic Church. From its founding in 1841 until World War I, it sponsored the education of some 3500 young Poles, most of them becoming teachers or priests.[15] Organic Work also sought to further the economic development and modernization of Polish society by stimulating trade and urban crafts; the "Central Economic Society" of 1863 and several dozen "agricultural circles" founded in the 1850s and 1860s sought to encourage better agricultural practices. Aside from the tangible benefits of such efforts, they also proved an effective means of integrating the Polish masses into the noble-led national movement and helped the nobility to retain its direction of Prussian-Polish society. In West Prussia, for example, a relatively small number of nobles who were socially most prominent and politically most influential also ran the largest bank, the provincial press, and chaired most of the new economic organizations.[16] Care was taken that the organized peasant and urban-middle classes would remain under noble tutelage and not develop separate class interests or outlooks of their own. A corollary of Organic Work was the concept of "National Solidarity," which suggested that good Poles could only feel one way about the significant issues and such feelings were best expressed in unison by the traditional noble leadership in close alliance with the Church.

It should be stressed that the nationalism of the Polish nobility at this time was based less on objective characteristics, e.g., language and religion, than on the common historical experience of and devotion to the Polish Commonwealth, a multi-national empire which had evolved with little concern for ethnic factors. Indeed, in the 1860s Prussian Poland defined as Prussia's share of the 1771 Polish state (see Map 1) was only about 43% Polish-speaking.[17] Thus Polish gentry nationalism was essentially of the subjective, territorial type; it was strongly voluntaristic, defined by some in terms of the unwillingness to accept the loss of independence.[18] Continued loyalty to the Commonwealth, and its resurrection if possible, was a matter of historical rehabilitation for the class which had run this "nobles' republic" and remained so closely identified with it.

But the mass of Prussian Poles in the early-Nineteenth Century lacked the subjective national consciousness of the gentry; there was little about the old Commonwealth which could appeal to them or cause them to desire its return. Thus another aspect of the changed approach of Polish leaders after 1848 was an emphasis on the objective criteria of nationality (language and religion), which they had in common with the masses. By building their movement around these factors, the masses might be integrated into the national movement and the society itself made better able to resist perceived Prussian pressures toward assimilation. The simultaneous extension of education under the rationalist Prussian bureaucracy, with the resultant growth of literacy and the press, helped create the most important conditions for the spread of national consciousness from the gentry to the rest of Prussian-Polish society. Even at a time when cultural Germanization was not yet a state policy, the tendency of such a rationalist bureaucracy to foster the use of a common German language as a convenient tool of administration served to provoke (as Emperor Joseph II of Austria discovered) some nationalist reaction among Poles and contributed to the nationalist mobilization of Prussian-Polish society.

There are indications of heightened involvement by the Prussian-Polish masses in the national movement after 1848 (e.g., in 1863), but such involvement remained very much at the instigation, and under the direction, of the nobility.[19] For the most part, however, and certainly compared to what was to come, relations between the Prussian state and its Polish minority remained relatively quiet during the 1850s and 1860s. The lot of the Polish peasantry had clearly improved under Prussian rule and for a long time this tended to make this crucial class somewhat immune to agitation by the gentry. Only the Church seemed to have the ability to move the peasantry, but until the *Kulturkampf* it showed littled inclination to do so in a nationalistic direction. With the Church and peasantry not yet heavily engaged in the nationalist movement, and with no more than a small, incipient urban middle class, the Polish movement remained dependent upon the energies and devotion of the nobility. And even the nobility seemed at times to be losing its fervor. The influence of Pan-Polish emigres in Prussian Poland waned, especially in the wake of the unsuccessful 1863 insurrection. The resultant loss of hope of renewed national independence caused attention to shift to economic or local-political concerns within the partitioning powers and to political goals which might be achieved within the confines of the existing political framework by the new titular leaders of Prussian-Polish society: the twenty-odd representatives to the Prussian Landtag. True, the official position of these representatives remained one of adamant opposition to their situation, but their protestations began to take on a routine, *pro forma* coloration. Some discovered common political and economic interests with Prussian conservatives or shared at least an aversion to liberalism and secularism, which again provided some grounds for anticipating the eventual defusing of Polish disaffection with their Prussian context.

But this apparent trend was interrupted and reversed by several developments of the 1860s: on top of the diffusion of nationalist attitudes into the Prussian state apparatus and the German and Polish populations at large came Bismarck's rise to power in Prussia, the unification of Germany, and the nationalization of German liberalism. In particular, it required the religious and national policies of Bismarck after 1871 to truly energize Polish society in a nationalist direction. From his appointment as Prussian Minister-President in 1862 until his dismissal as German Chancellor in 1890 (and to some extent long after that), he was the determining factor in the development of Prussian-Polish relations. For this reason it might be worth while to examine his attitudes toward this problem, based on the large body of published documentation by or about Bismarck.

The impression which emerges is that Bismarck adhered to a number of highly subjective, sometimes idiosyncratic views regarding the Polish question. It seems also that he was more wont to give free rein to these personal feelings in his Polish policy than in other areas. Certainly it seems clear that Bismarck, from the beginning of his political career and by any comparative measure, was notably hard on the Poles and their aspirations. In 1848, in the midst of the polonophilia sweeping much of Germany, he spoke up almost at once against the Poles, giving them much of the blame for the revolutionary disturbances and opposing the concessions which the King and German liberals were willing to make to them.[20] He denounced the liberal illusion that "the Poles could be anything else but our enemies as long as they were not in the complete frontiers of 1772, with West Prussia and everything else."[21] In a long letter to the *Magdeburger Zeitung*, dated April 20, 1848, he spelled out his views on the Polish question: "The national development of the Polish element in Poznania can have no other reasonable goal than to help prepare the establishment of an independent Polish empire." Even were the Poles to be given control of Poznania, "they would remain our sworn enemies as long as they had not conquered" the rest of pre-1772 Poland, and Upper Silesia as well. "Prussia's best sinews would be cut and millions of Germans turned over to Polish arbitrariness." Better that Prussia should remain on friendly terms with Russia than permit the rebirth of an independent Polish state of any kind.[22]

During the following years, when he was occupied with diplomatic matters in Frankfurt, St. Petersburg, and Paris, and not directly involved with domestic Polish policy, Bismarck still did his best to encourage a hard line against Polish aspirations by other powers. When there was talk of restoring an independent Polish state as the result of Russian defeat in the Crimean War, Bismarck registered his strong opposition: "These gentlemen do not know Poland and do not know that an independent Poland could only then cease to be Prussia's determined enemy if we outfitted her with lands without which we could not exist, like the lower Vistula, all of Poznania, and whatever speaks Polish in Silesia. And even then we would not be sure of peace with her in a pinch."[23] As Prussian ambassador to Russia, he came close to unwarranted interference in the internal affairs of his host country in his efforts to dissuade Tsar Alexander II from making concessions to the Poles.[24] When he was transferred to Paris, he took up the same refrain with Napoleon III.[25]

No sooner had Bismarck become head of the Prussian government than the Polish question erupted again in the form of the 1863 Russian-Polish uprising and reports that Poland might be restored, if not by her own strength then with the help of the western powers. Bismarck did his best to discourage Britain and France from such a course. When the British ambassador to Prussia complained about the Alvensleben Convention (by which Bismarck agreed to seal the Prussian border against the Polish insurgents), Bismarck made it clear that he could not permit an independent Poland to emerge on his eastern frontier. Even if the Poles should be successful against the Russians, "then we would have to try to occupy the Kingdom ourselves." In response to the British ambassador's warning that the other powers might look askance at this, Bismarck suggested that he would just have to take that risk: "For us the suppression of the uprising is a matter of life and death."[26] He ordered his representative in London to make the same point there:

> "It is a political necessity for us that the insurrection be suppressed and generally not achieve its aims. The restoration of an independent Polish state between Silesia and East Prussia, with the resultant desire for Poznania and the mouth of the Vistula, indispensable to an independent Poland, would constitute a permanent threat to Prussia. . . . We could

never satisfy the demands which this new neighbor would raise at our expense."

Even were Russia voluntarily to give Poland her freedom, Prussia would have to seriously consider whether to accept this or "forcibly occupy the Kingdom ourselves."[27]

Bismarck always maintained that this strong opposition to any kind of Polish independence, even when it did not directly involve Prussian Poland, stemmed from the likelihood that any change in the status quo regarding Poland would be a change for the worse. Unlike German liberals and Austrians, he was never seriously interested in using the Poles against the Russians; for the reasons suggested above, he preferred that the Russian Empire, however powerful, be his eastern neighbor. To side with the Poles against the Russians, even if it culminated in a successful war, could only lead to the acquisition of more Polish-speaking subjects and thus exacerbate the domestic Polish problem. As he said on a later occasion, in response to the rumored willingness of Russia to cede some of her Polish areas in exchange for a free hand against Austria: "We already have more Poles in Prussia than we can use."[28] Bismarck also refused to consider the use of Prussia's Polish possessions as bait in this way. Poznania and West Prussia were not only nationally heterogeneous but strategically indispensable to Prussia in a way that Galicia and the Congress Kingdom were not to the other eastern empires. In short, he doubted that the 1815 division of Poland, whatever its shortcomings, could realistically be improved on from Prussia's point of view. As for one such shortcoming, Polish national aspirations, he was left with no choice but to combat them; "Polish nationalism (*Polonismus*) cannot be judged humanistically and impartially by us, but only antagonistically."[29]

Decisive for Bismarck's conduct of domestic Polish policy in Prussia was another underlying conviction: that there was a necessary connection between the way the partitioning powers treated their Poles and the way they felt about each other. When one of them, e.g., Austria, began to make concessions to its Polish population, this was a clear sign for Bismarck that she feared or planned on war with one of the other partitioning powers.[30] He was sure that any relaxation of Prussian Polish policies would be read as a hostile act by Russia, whereas a hard line here was an important foundation of the good relations which he always sought to maintain with that power. Thus he approached Prussian policy toward her Polish population less as a domestic question than as a foreign-policy matter of considerable importance.

It is not always easy to differentiate between those aspects of Bismarck's Polish policies which were part of such convictions, based on a rational understanding of underlying realities, and those which were in fact determined more by his personal animosity toward things Polish. For while some of his generally hostile approach to Prussian Poland can be explained with reference to perceived dictates of foreign policy or geopolitics, other evidence suggests that he also bore a good deal of animosity toward Poland and the Poles even where such foreign-policy rationales were lacking. There is certainly little doubt about his low opinion of and dislike for the Polish noble leadership. From his first contacts with Polish nobles as a university student, he seems to have reacted negatively to their allegedly flamboyant, extravagant manner. He was never tempted to participate in the polonophilia of the 1830s and 1840s.[31] As Prussian Minister-President, he was from the beginning harsh and abrupt toward Polish petitions and parliamentary complaints. He categorically denied any feeling of obligation toward them based on the 1815 settlement or royal proclamations (cf. above) and typically parried such complaints by denouncing conditions in the old Commonwealth. He denied the right of the gentry representatives to speak for a Polish nationality in Prussia: "You have no people behind you; you have nothing behind you but your fictions and your illusions."[32] At times he described the Polish nobles as the most reactionary figures in creation; at others he imagined them in collusion with the revolutionary Left all over Europe. He accused them of harboring an "impenetrable hatred of things German" and desiring above all "to free themselves from the German Empire and the Prussian monarchy."[33] He apparently had this noble leadership group in mind in 1861 when he wrote: "Hit the Poles so that they despair of their lives! I have full sympathy for their position, but we can do nothing else but exterminate (*ausrotten*) them if we want to endure."[34] To be sure, these last words, the harshest recorded statement by Bismarck about the Poles, appear somewhat out of the blue and out of context in a letter to his sister devoted otherwise to trivial matters; perhaps they should not be taken too literally. On the other hand, aside from a couple of Polish nobles who were apolitical or assimilated, he never found it possible his whole life long to say anything good about this class or its individual members.

Toward the Polish masses, on the other hand, Bismarck always tried to avoid such expressions of hostility. He was convinced that the Polish peasant masses were filled with a "grateful affection" for the Prussian state and, unlike the nobility, had no desire to return to the serfdom, corruption, and economic backwardness of the Polish Republic.[35] From their participation in the wars of unification, he concluded that the Polish masses had "sealed with their blood, and with the courage characteristic of their nationality, their loyalty toward the King on the

Danish and Bohemian battlefields."[36] When Bismarck used the term "nationality" in this context, he referred only to a linguistic-cultural category; he denied that the bulk of Prussian Poles constituted a separate political nationality. He enjoyed telling a story from his youth about a Kashube who had come to blows with a German who called him a "Polak," insisting that, "no, I am a 'Prussak' like you."[37]

Bismarck, it might be noted, had acquired some ability in conversational Polish and enjoyed demonstrating this in personal encounters with lower-class Polish subjects. He even tried (unsuccessfully) to get Crown Prince Frederick to learn some Polish, and to make sure that his son William, the future Emperor, did the same, perhaps as a means of reaching the trustworthy Polish masses over the heads of the recalcitrant gentry.[38] Even towards these loyal Polish masses, however, Bismarck's attitude was essentially paternalistic and condescending. He would go out of his way to secure a Polish-language prayer-book for a wounded soldier, but not permit him to read a Polish newspaper. He frequently expressed his respect for the Poles as soldiers and found them to be "well-behaved people," provided, however, that "one can teach them that it is nice to wash oneself and that one should not take things."[39] One cannot know for sure to what extent this somewhat ambivalent affection for the Polish masses as opposed to the nobility was genuine, or merely a politically and rhetorically useful distinction which ceased to apply to such Poles as acquired a political and national consciousness of their own. But this was a distinction which Bismarck adhered to rigidly throughout his career, long after it had ceased to accord with any Polish reality and long after his own policies could any longer be reconciled with a desire to benefit even the loyal Polish masses.

In spite of Bismarck's strong personal views on the Polish question, his accession to power in 1862 saw no immediate turn in domestic Prussian Polish policies. He was obviously preoccupied with more important issues during the 1860s and primarily concerned just to keep things quiet in the Polish provinces. The Agricultural Bank for Poznania, from which Polish estate-owners stood to benefit most, was approved by him in 1865, with the hope, to be sure, that this would be "of great significance for the gradual Germanization of the Grand Duchy of Poznania, which is so desirable from a political viewpoint."[40] In spite of Polish suspicions to the contrary, they continued to have access to judgeships and other state offices; Justice Minister Leonhardt assured the Landtag in 1868 that it was not state policy to exclude Poles from such positions and announced the following year that "in the course of this year not fewer than nine judges of Polish nationality have been transferred back to or hired in the province of Poznania."[41] On occasion, Bismarck even took up a position against those who favored stronger actions against the Polish national movement; when Poznanian *Oberpräsident* Horn came into conflict with Poznanian Archbishop Ledóchowski in 1868-9, it was the former who had to go.[42]

There were, of course, points of dispute, but these stemmed mostly from the perceived political unreliability of the Polish provinces rather than any concerted attempt to Germanize them in the 1860s. For example, Poznania was excluded from some of the self-government privileges enjoyed by the other provinces; local estate-owners were denied the right to propose *Landrat* nominees and county committees were appointed rather than elected.[43] Interior Minister Eulenburg acknowledged that his government did not yet feel that it could trust its Polish subjects, but promised to reconsider "if you could convince the government in some clear way that it could say of the province of Poznania: in essence and feelings, this is a Prussian province."[44] There were also frequent Polish complaints about the schools, but Eichhorn's 1842 regulations remained in force. On the whole, however, the 1860s were a relatively quiet period before the storm in Prussian-Polish relations; the Prussian state and German nationalists were preoccupied, the Polish noble leadership seemed to be moderating or losing heart, and the Polish masses were not yet fully involved in the national movement.

This situation changed sharply following the transformation of Prussia into part of a German nation-state in 1867 and 1871. One can argue whether this was more than a superficial alteration of the Poles' situation; they continued to be ruled more by the state than by the German Empire, after all, and the Prussian state was little changed internally by the unification of Germany. But the Poles themselves took this change very seriously and protested against what they saw as the "annexation" of Poznania and West Prussia (previously outside the German Confederation) into a formally German political unit for the first time in 1867. As Kazimierz Kantak argued, the Poles, if forced, could conceive of themselves as part of a Prussian "nation," defined as a political rather than an ethnic entity, but they could not see themselves as part of a "North-German" people. When the 1867 constitution of the North German Confederation was approved by the Landtag, the Poles denounced it as an "act of force" and demonstratively laid down their mandates (which the new constitution had just terminated anyway.)[45] They repeated this ceremony, minus the resignations, with the creation of the German Empire in 1871, demanding that "Polish territories under Prussian rule" be excluded from the new state in accordance with their interpretation of the 1815 treaties and guarantees.[46]

More important than this formal change of political status was the change in the national attitudes of German liberalism, especially with regards to the Polish question, which accompanied it. Prior to this time (e.g., during the "constitutional conflict"), German liberals had been fairly close allies of Prussian Poles. The liberal-dominated Landtag voted 246:57 in opposition to Bismarck's "tilt" toward Russia in 1863 when the Alvensleben Convention became public.[47] As late as 1869, the Poles were able to get the liberal Landtag majority to pass (168:165) a resolution that Polish-language *Amtsblätter* be printed for the Kashubian areas of West Prussia and that these in effect be recognized as part of "Prussian Poland."[48] As is generally known, however, precisely during these years German liberals were shifting from their earlier cosmopolitan, occasionally even polonophile, position toward a more self-centered German nationalism. Herder's reverence for ethnic-cultural entities was giving way to Hegel's reverence for the state, now that the Germans had a nation-state of their own.[49] Russian friendship having been a key to the creation of this state and apparently a long-term pillar of its foreign policy, the need to cultivate the Poles faded. When it came time to create a structure for the new German Empire, German liberals began to surpass even Prussian conservatives in their zeal for centralization and uniformity. One of their first acts after 1871 was to join with Bismarck in an attack on the religion and nationality of the Poles: the *Kulturkampf*.

Notes

1. Art. III, para. 2, quoted in Rudolf Korth, *Die preussische Schulpolitik und die polnischen Schulstreiks* (Würzburg, 1963), p. 35; similar promises are contained in the Vienna Final Acts, June 9, 1815, Art. I, para. 2, *Ibid*.
2. The bulk of the newly incorporated Polish lands were designated the "Grand Duchy of Poznania." This became the principal component of Prussian Poland but the two terms are not synonymous; other Polish- (or Kashubian-) speaking lands were part of West Prussia and had been part of Prussia continuously since 1772; still other Polish-speaking lands (Upper Silesia and Masuria) had not been part of a Polish state since the Middle Ages. While the Kashubian areas can be seen as part of the Polish national movement in the late-Nineteenth Century, Masuria and (with minor qualifications) Upper Silesia cannot; thus "Prussian Poland" refers here to the bulk of Poznania and the Polish/Kashubian districts of West Prussia.
3. May 15, 1815, quoted by Korth, p. 35, from the Prussian *Gesetz-Sammlung*, 1815, p. 47.
4. Manfred Laubert, *Die preussische Polenpolitik 1772-1914*, 3rd edit. (Krakau, 1944), p. 54.

5. Siegfried Baske, "Praxis und Prinzipien der preussischen Polenpolitik vom Beginn der Reaktionszeit bis zur Gründung des Deutschen Reichs," *Forschungen zur Osteuropäischen Geschichte* 9 (1963):143; similar results were achieved under Theodor von Schön in West Prussia, cf. Peter Böhning, *Die nationalpolnische Bewegung in Westpreussen 1815-1871* (Marburg, 1973), p. 45.
6. Reskript dated December 23, 1822, cited by Laubert, p. 63, and by Władysław Niegolewski in the Reichstag, January 20, 1875, *Stenographische Berichte Uber die Verhandlungen des Reichstags* (hereafter *Reichstag*) and Ludwik Jażdżewski in the Landtag, January 25, 1888, *Stenographische Berichte über die Verhandlungen des preussischen Hauses der Abgeordneten* (hereafter *Abgeordnetenhaus*).
7. Korth, pp. 3ff.
8. Oswald Hauser, "Polen und Dänen im Deutschen Reich," in *Die Reichsgründung 1870/1*, ed. T. Schieder & E. Deuerlein, p. 295; Böhning, p. 56.
9. Baske, p. 15.
10. From an 1841 speech, cited by Florian Stablewski, February 7, 1882, *Abgeordnetenhaus*.
11. cited by Korth, p. 38 from *Verfassung und Verwaltung des Preussischen Staates*.
12. Laubert, p. 96.
13. Jerzy Kozłowski, et al., *Niemcy w Poznańskiem wobec Politiki germanizacyjnej 1815-1920*, ed. L. Trzeciakowski (Poznań, 1976), p. 21.
14. Minister-President Manteuffel in 1850, cited by Kazimierz Kantak, April 1, 1886, *Abgeordnetenhaus*.
15. Witold Jakóbczyk, *Studia nad dziejami Wielkopolski w 19. wieku*, 3 vols. (Poznań, 1951-67), II:11, III:38.
16. Böhning, pp. 110, 138f., and *passim*.
17. Lech Trzeciakowski, *Kulturkampf w zaborze pruskim* (Poznań, 1970), p. 23.
18. John Kulczycki, "Social Change in the Polish National Movement in Prussia before World War I," *Nationalities Papers* 4(1976):18.
19. Böhning, p. 179.
20. Hans Wendt, *Bismarck und die polnische Frage* (Halle, 1922), p. 4; *Die politischen Reden des Fürsten Bismarck*, ed. H. Kohl (Stuttgart, 1892), I:49.
21. Letter to his wife, April 3, 1848, *Fürst Bismarcks Briefe an seine Braut und Gattin*, ed. H.v. Bismarck (Stuttgart, 1900), p. 112.
22. Johannes Penzler, *Die Jugendgeschichte des Fürsten Bismarck*, 2 vols. (Berlin, 1907), II:224f.; this letter was not actually published by the paper until 38 years later (January 5, 1886), when its author was better known and German liberal journalism less well disposed toward the Poles.
23. Bismarck to Manteuffel, February 23, 1854, *Die Gesammelten Werke*, 3rd edit., 15 vols. (Berlin, 1824-32), I:430.
24. Reports by Bismarck from St. Petersburg, March 12 and April 4, 1861, *Die politischen Berichte des Fürsten Bismarck aus Petersburg und Paris*, ed. L. Raschdau, 2 vols. (Berlin, 1920), II:30ff., 52ff.; report from St. Petersburg, November 8, 1861, *Gesammelte Werke*, III:279.

Introduction 15

25. Bismarck report from Paris, June 6, 1862, *Politische Berichte*, II:199.
26. Bismarck and Andrew Buchanan, February 11, 1863, *Fürst Bismarck und die Diplomaten, 1852-1890* (Hamburg, 1900), pp. 38f.
27. Bismarck to Bernstorff, February 17, 1863, *Gesammelte Werke*, IV:59ff.; a similar message went to Ambassador von der Goltz in Paris, February 23, 1863, *Ibid.*, IV:63ff.; see also Bismarck's speech to the Herrenhaus, November 19, 1863, *Politische Reden*, II:208ff.
28. Report of Lt. Lignitz in the German embassy in St. Petersburg to Bismarck, June 6, 1885, quoted in Helmut Neubach, *Die Ausweisungen von Polen und Juden aus Preussen 1885-6* (Wiesbaden, 1967), appendix #19.
29. Bismarck to Bernstorff, November 25, 1861, *Bismarck-Jahrbuch* ed. H. Kohl, (Berlin, 1899), VI:113f.
30. E.g., his interpretation of the inclusion of a nationalistic Pole in Beust's Austrian cabinet in 1870: "This collusion with Polish revolutionaries and the hostility toward Russia which comes thereby to light constitutes a considerable barrier to good relations with Austria, in that we must at the same time see therein hostility towards us." Moritz Busch, *Tagebuchblätter*, 3 vols., (Leipzig, 1899), I:191, entry of February 12, 1870.
31. Wendt, p. 2.
32. E.g., his speech of April 1, 1871, *Reichstag*.
33. Busch, II:313; speech of February 9, 1872, *Abgeordnetenhaus*.
34. Letter to sister Malwine, March 26, 1861, *Briefe Otto von Bismarcks an Schwester und Schwager*, ed. H. Kohl (Leipzig, 1915), p. 120.
35. Bismarck to Frederick William IV, *Gesammelte Werke*, II:84, dated December 21, 1855; Busch, I:554.
36. speech of March 18, 1867, *Reichstag*.
37. *Busch, I:554.*
38. *Ibid.*
39. *Ibid., I:466, 554;* a similarly derisive reference appears in an 1847 letter to his wife from "close by Poland. . . . where each night one hears the wolves and the Kushubes howling.", Penzler, II:167.
40. Bismarck to Finance Minister Bodelschwingh, January 29, 1865, *Gesammelte Werke*, V:69f.
41. speeches of December 1, 1868, and November 16, 1869, *Abgeordnetenhaus*; Kantak's reply for the Poles: "We acknowledge completely his actions with respect to us."
42. Bismarck to Culture Minister von Mühler, February 27, 1968, *Gesammelte Werke*, VIa:283; Wendt, p. 37.
43. speeches by Kantak, December 3, 1868, and Szuldrzyński, October 19, 1869, *Abgeordnetenhaus*.
44. speech of October 19, 1869, *Abgeordnetenhaus*.
45. Kantak speeches of March 18, April 10, and April 16, 1867, *Reichstag*; Żółtowski took a similar position in the Landtag, May 6, 1867, *Abgeordnetenhaus*.
46. Speeches by Żółtowski and Krzyżanowski, April 1, 1871, *Reichstag*.
47. Józef Buzek, *Historya polityki narodowościowej rządu pruskiego wobec*

Polaków 1815–1908 (Lwów, 1909), p. 124.
48. Action taken January 15, 1869, *Abgeordnetenhaus*.
49. Theodor Schieder, *Das Deutsche Reich von 1871 als Nationalstaat*, (Köln, 1961), p. 26.

Chapter I:
The *Kulturkampf* and Prussian-Polish Relations

The struggle between the Prussian State and the Catholic Church in the 1870s was accompanied by increased friction between the State and Prussian Poles as well. In many ways, the *Kulturkampf* ushered in a new era in Prussian-Polish relations, turning a Polish problem defined largely in terms of a recalcitrant nobility into one involving the Polish population as a whole. The extent to which this was an inadvertent consequence of the Church-State struggle, as opposed to the view that the Polish problem was an important motive behind the *Kulturkampf* in the first place, remains a matter of some debate. Heinrich Bornkamm describes the Polish problem as "the most convincing, indisputable motive;" Lech Trzeciakowski also takes the anti-Polish motivation of the *Kulturkampf* seriously.[1] But a larger number of historians have tended to discount the Polish aspect as a primary factor. Hans Rothfels doubts that Bismarck intended to launch an attack on the Poles at this time, citing his alleged aversion to ethnic nationalism and the worsening of the Polish problem as a result of the *Kulturkampf*, suggesting that its impact on the Poles was due to the influence of his National Liberal partners. Some Polish historians (e.g., Jerzy Krasuski, who attributes only a marginal role to the Polish issue in the genesis of the *Kulturkampf*) have also been persuaded to this effect.[2]

As for Bismarck's own version, the following statement is to be found in his memoirs:

"The beginning of the *Kulturkampf* was determined for me mainly by its Polish aspect. Since the renunciation of the policy of Flottwell and Grolman, since the consolidation of Radziwiłł influence with the King[3] and the establishment of a 'Catholic Section' in the Culture Ministry, statistical data established beyond a doubt the rapid advance of the Polish nationality at the expense of the German in Poznania and West Prussia, and in Upper Silesia the hitherto firmly Prussian element of the *'Wasserpolacken'* was polonized. . . . In Poznania and West Prussia, according to the testimony of official reports, thousands of Germans and entire communities, which in the previous generation had been officially German, were educated as Poles and officially designated 'Poles' through the activity of the Catholic Section."[4]

Of course, these words were written long after the period under discussion, and Bismarck's memoirs have not generally been considered a very reliable guide to his actual thinking and motives. But in this case he made the same points on many occasions while still in office. He justified the exclusion of Church influence in the schools "because of the expansion which the Polish element in Poznania has experienced due to the agitation of the clergy; I had to save the German element."[5] "That the *Kulturkampf* has gone so far, I have essentially the Poles to thank . . ."[6] In a talk with the Bishop of Trier in 1881, Bismarck "put the entire blame for the *Kulturkampf* on the Poles."[7] Again in 1884 he asserted that he had undertaken the *Kulturkampf* because "Polonization was taking place under the direction of the clergy, namely in West Prussia but also in Silesia. . . . It was impossible to cut off this Polonization without removing its root, the Catholic Section."[8]

In fact, if one examines the beginning of the *Kulturkampf* from this point of view, focusing on the Polish aspect, one can find a good deal of contemporary evidence to support Bismarck's own later version. While acknowledging the other important factors involved, more attention perhaps should be paid to the important role of the Polish problem. For example, in the Prussian cabinet's formal request to the Emperor for those measures which initiated the *Kulturkampf*, one finds prominently mentioned among the "internal motives:" "In the Polish-Catholic parts of the Monarchy, the Germanization task of the elementary schools has been pushed into the background (and) German language instruction neglected, while at the same time the Polish language area is growing."[9] Poznanian *Oberpräsident* Horn complained in the 1860s that Poles were not learning German very well and that German Catholics were being Polonized by the clergy who supervised their schools.[10] A report from West Prussia described a "continuing Polonization of the western and southwestern regions of this regency."[11] In 1872, Bismarck claimed that the "prevention of the continuing Polonization of three provinces" made his steps against the Church necessary.[12] He made the same point the following year, citing reports that "for the last decade the Polish element in Poznania and Polish Silesia has made the most colossal advances."[13]

That most *Kulturkampf* measures were directed toward the Catholic Church generally, and not just its Polish component or the Polish national movement directly, may be due in part to Bismarck's long-standing suspicion that it was Catholic policy to halt, and if possible reverse, the centuries-old trend of German advances vs. the Poles in the Prussian East. He also saw the Church in Polish areas as an integral part, if not indeed a controlling force, in the Polish national movement. He now described the Polish faction in the Landtag as representative of the Church as well as of the nobility (but still not of the Polish masses.)[14] One of Bismarck's first steps as Minister-President in 1862 was to put the Pope on notice that good relations with Prussia would depend upon how well he kept the Poznanian Church in line. He expected that, "if the Archbishop permits himself to be misused by a political party, or if he mixes religion and politics on his own volition, he will find no protection or encouragement in Rome."[15] He complained several times during the 1860s that the Polish hierarchy and clergy were exerting Polonizing pressures on the Catholics under their control.[16] Reports reaching him from West Prussia claimed that the Church and Church-controlled school teachers were actively supporting Polish candidates to the Reichstag and that "an artificial agitation is constantly fostered among the Polish population, *e.g.*, efforts toward a better instruction of school children in the German language are frequently presented as being against the Catholic Church."[17] When the Pope's jubileum was celebrated with Polish speeches and banners at the German-language Pelplin Seminary, provincial officials interpreted this as additional "evidence of the Polish tendencies of the Catholic hierarchy."[18] Continued use of the title "Primate of Poland" by the Archbishop of Gniezno-Poznań was still another reason for Bismarck to distrust the Church. When he found in 1872 that this "vice-king" title had been bestowed "secretly" by the Pope, he charged that this amounted to Papal "connivance in the restoration of the old Poland."[19]

In 1870, Bismarck notified his ministers: "It has been presented to me from different sides that in the predominantly Polish communities of West Prussia not enough is being done for school instruction in the German language, so that even children of German parents must do without it." Existing provisions aimed at providing all Prussian citizens with some knowledge of German were running up against "the opposition of the Polish-Catholic clergy functioning as local school inspectors." Though the Polish language in West Prussia lacked the legal protection still to be found in Poznania, "the Polish language was moving ahead at the expense of the German."[20] Following the conclusion of the Franco-Prussian War, he returned to this theme, denouncing the role which "ultramontane, anti-Prussian aspirations" played in the public schools, particularly in Polish areas, and urging that more be done by the state for "our interests and our language."[21] Soon thereafter, after additional reports from Upper Silesia that German was being taught half-heartedly in favor of relying on Polish, Culture Minister von Mühler announced a special visitation of the schools there.[22] Among Bismarck's objections to the Catholic Section (the dissolution of which began the *Kulturkampf*) was that its head, Krätzig, was a former employee and under the influence of the Radziwiłłs. He often expressed an exaggerated fear of the influence which this magnate family exerted in Berlin; Emperor Wilhelm had been romantically involved with a daughter of this family earlier and apparently only political considerations kept them from marrying. Bismarck saw Radziwiłł influence behind the successful careers of her brothers in the Prussian state service and in the opposition of the Empress and the wife of Culture Minister von Mühler to his abolition of the Catholic Section.[23]

In addition to these various objections to the Church's role domestically, Bismarck also questioned its loyalty to Prussia during the Franco-Prussian War. A "report of the general mood of the population" (*Stimmungsbericht*) from West Prussia described a "suspiciously agitated mood" among Poles, who seemed to pull for a French victory because they had been told by their priests that this would be a victory for Catholicism; "war enthusiasm is quite general, except for the Polish population."[24] Another such report complained that "a large part of the Polish population, in spite of all the successes. . . . persists in its cool, suspicious attitude; even now hopes for the success of French arms are audible from these circles."[25] Bismarck indicated at this time some concern about a possible coalition of defeated Catholic powers (Austria-Hungary and France) against him, in which case Prussian Poles might become security risks. In a talk with Mainz Archbishop von Ketteler, he insisted that questions of domestic Church-state relations and dogma were relatively minor issues, that his real concern at the outset of the *Kulturkampf* was ultramontane plotting which opened Germany up to the threat of an Austrian-Polish coalition.[26] He warned Interior Minister von Eulenburg in 1872 that "in our Polish areas the ground under us, while it is not yet actually wavering, is nevertheless so undermined that could collapse as soon as a Polish-Catholic policy develops."[27] Thus the Church was a problem in two ways in relation to the Polish question: it sought to frustrate the policy of gradual political assimilation of Prussian Poles and it seemed to be the potential medium for an anti-German coalition of Catholic powers.

With the inauguration of the *Kulturkampf* in 1871, Bismarck began simultaneously to tighten domestic Polish policies. The "School Supervision Law" (*Schulaufsichtsgesetz*) was the first major legislative project; it put all schools, public and private, under the supervision of the state; all school inspectors were to be appointed by the state, which meant that they would no longer tend to be Polish priests in Polish areas as had been the case.[28] At the Prussian cabinet meeting where this proposed law was given its final form, Bismarck accused school administrators of not opposing "more energetically the Polonizing influence of the clergy in the schools." So heavy was his emphasis on the Polish motivation for the new law that some ministers suggested that it be limited to the Polish areas, since this was obviously where the problem lay. Bismarck rejected this suggestion, for appearances' sake and because it might make the law unconstitutional, but the cabinet approved the bill on the assumption that, while theoretically covering the whole state, it would be applied primarily to the Polish areas.[29]

During the following months, Bismarck became increasingly active on the Polish front. At the end of 1871, he asked Eulenburg to investigate the Polish national movement, e.g., its organization, press organs, and the role of refugees from the Paris Commune in it.[30] In February, 1872, he asked him to expel all non-citizen Catholic priests (mainly Galician Poles) from Upper Silesia.[31] Two days later he again approached his Interior Minister, this time in a more agitated frame of mind, complaining of his previous passivity toward the Polish problem and urging him either to address it more energetically or he would find someone else to do so. He demanded that Eulenberg support him in his determination "to proceed against the Polish undermining of the foundations of the Prussian State, which has been prospering for ten years."[32] On this occasion Bismarck also proposed the expulsion of tens of thousands of non-citizen Poles from his Empire, making this the most radical suggestion to surface during this flare-up of activity against the Poles in the early 1870s. He wanted the expulsion "in principle of *all* Poles not entitled to live here, aside from the exceptions that the government grants of its own volition."[33] A week after this, Bismarck circulated his ministers again, urging greater use of German in schools and churches, the purging of anti-Prussian elements from the state bureaucracy in Polish areas and their replacement by carefully selected officials, and the stationing of all Polish recruits in German-speaking areas so that army units in Prussian Poland would be 100%-German.[34] On the same date an order was issued over Emperor Wilhelm's signature urging Silesian officials to "take up energetically" the problem of clergy trying to Polonize the eastern part of their province.[35] Four days later followed still another order to Eulenburg, this one ordering the expulsion of alien journalists from Upper Silesia.[36] In March came an order for the expulsion of members of all clerical orders from Poznania, on grounds that they were a principal factor in the Polish national movement having assumed "an intensity and significance unknown earlier . . . and coming to light ever more blatantly."[37] The "May Laws" of 1873 applied to Prussia generally, but several provisions had a special impact on Prussian Poland: all holders of clerical offices had to have German citizenship, a German university education, and a state examination in German history and culture; teachers at the seminaries were to be "German" as well.[38]

Along with these moves aimed more or less directly at the Catholic Church, the *Kulturkampf* included also attacks on the position of the Polish language in the schools (difficult as this would appear to be to fit into a definition of the *Kulturkampf* as a Church-state conflict.) Previously, courses in Religion [at the secondary level] had been taught in Polish to Polish students; now they were to be taught in German along with all other subjects.[39] The government overruled Archbishop Ledóchowski's contention that it was up to the Church to decide the language in which it gave its religious instruction. Culture Minister Falk argued that, since all Poles had supposedly been taught in German at the elementary level, they could be expected to handle instruction in that language at the secondary level.[40] Also at this time, Eichhorn's 1842 regulation allowing for the use of the mother tongue in elementary schools was overturned. German was made the sole language of instruction in all subjects in Upper Silesia (September 20, 1872); the same followed (June 24, 1873) for the province of Prussia (West Prussia became a separate province only in 1877). The new policy for Poznania, dated October 27, 1873, required the use of German for all subjects except Religion and Hymn Singing, which could still be taught in Polish in the first three grades under Church auspices.[41] In justifying these new regulations, Falk and his assistants refused to admit before the Landtag that nationalistic motives were involved; instead they argued various "objective," pedagogical grounds: "The main motive, which has guided the state government . . . is definitely not political, not directed against the Polish nationality, but precisely a pedagogical one."[42] They claimed only to be concerned that all pupils became fluent in German, whereas "little or nothing had been achieved in the study of German in the past" in the Polish-language elementary schools.[43] It made no sense to put off exposure to the language that they would eventually have to learn in anyway. Though official statistics indicated that 83% of Polish children in Prussia had no acquaintance at all with the German language when they began elementary school, these officials maintained that these children could learn in German if they only tried.[44]

Along with this lessening of the place of Polish in the schools went the transfer of many Polish-speaking teachers to other parts of Prussia; the number of such teachers in Poznania fell from 1854 in 1872-3 (vs. 4715 Germans) to 1310 in 1881-2. At the Mary Gymnasium in Poznań, the most prominent Polish secondary school in Prussia (and according to Falk "a center of unwarranted Polonism"), the number of Polish teachers dropped from twenty-three (out of twenty-eight) in 1872-3 to only five in 1884.[45] Falk acknowledged that these transfers were the policy of his Ministry, though he assured the Landtag that the teachers had been sent to "better places," often at better pay.[46] Perhaps as a consequence of these transfers, there was also a drop in the proportion of Polish students in the secondary schools. Though the Polish population was growing more rapidly than the German, its share of secondary school students fell from 28% (1872-3) to 20% (1881-2.) Trzeciakowski suggests a concerted effort to keep Poles away from an education that seemed only more likely to lead them into the national movement, though evidence for such intent on the part of the government is lacking.[47]

Aside from the church and school policies, the most important areas of contact between Prussian Poles and their government, there were other kinds of increased pressure on the Poles in the 1870s. For example, Polish regions were excluded from the self-government provisions of the 1872 *Kreisordnung* and the 1875 *Provinzordnung*. Eulenburg denied that this exception was directed against the Poles (while at the same time attributing it to the "national tensions" in Poznania); he did accuse them, however, of being Poles first and Prussians only second, if at all: "all of their convictions are nothing more than national convictions and they come before everything else," thus making it impossible to grant them provincial self-government.[48]

The government also moved against Polish economic organizations. Such organizations as the "Agricultural Central Association," regardless of their previously apolitical stance, were refused the state financial support which went as a matter of course to German counterparts. In the opinion of Agriculture Minister Friedenthal, all Polish-language organizations were "particularistic;" by using a language which few Germans understood, they were effectively excluding them from participation and thus not deserving of state support. Eulenburg charged that "in your entire economic and political life the desire to emphasize the national-Polish aspect continually prevails, and in such a way that we must view it from the Prussian and German standpoint as hostile to the state;" even Polish agricultural associations were assumed to "carry on Polish politics."[49] The government suggested either changing the official language of such organizations or joining with Germans in a single agricultural association, both of which suggestions were rejected by the Poles.[50] In the meantime, teachers and other public employees were prohibited from belonging to organizations where Polish was the official language.[51]

Another major step was taken against the Polish language, affecting its use outside the schools: the Official Language Law of August 28, 1876. German was declared to be the sole official language in Poznania (and elsewhere in Prussia where other languages had enjoyed some limited official recognition.)[52] Eulenburg, who had the task of justifying this measure to the Landtag, argued that every state needed an official language; German was a more precise and better developed language, better suited to legal and administrative technicalities, or at least so it seemed to him. He insisted that even this law did not mean that the government was trying to make the Poles into Germans; it only wanted to give them the "consciousness of being citizens of a German state."[53] This law had its most immediate impact on relations between Poles and the state bureaucracy, e.g., in the courts, where the proportion of Polish judges was low (30 out of 242 in Poznania, none in West Prussia) and declining. It meant also the disappearance of bi-lingual signs in Poznań and other towns.[54] Polish place-names were regularly changed into German, with fines for those who did not adopt the new forms; the government denied that more than a few hundred place-names were changed following the new language law, and these only where the "Polish-sounding name was exceptionally difficult for the German tongue . . . and created difficulties for the German-speaking population."[55] In some cases even Polish family names were altered to suit state officials; (one local official tried to compel a Polish parliamentarian to change the name of his estate from Władysławowo to Althütte, meaning "old cottage," but here the courts ruled against the government).[56] Eulenburg's attempts to apply the Official Language Law to the meetings of Polish organizations met the same fate. He had reasoned that as long as the government had the right to proctor such meetings, it could also insist that they be conducted in a language that the (German) proctor could understand. When challenged about the legal basis for such an interpretation, he replied that it was sometimes necessary to "supplement the law through 'practice.'" But in 1876 the *Oberverwaltungsgericht* forbade the closing of Polish meetings for this reason.[57]

In sum, when one pulls together the medley of anti-Polish measures cited here, it seems clear that the anti-Polish thrust of the *Kulturkampf* was an integral part of Bismarck's efforts during these years, and not merely one of the inadvertent side-effects. The rationale for these measures differed somewhat, judging from the statements of Bismarck and his ministers, reflecting perhaps the transition from a Prussian-state to a more German-national context. Culture Minister Falk maintained a fairly rationalist, bureaucratic approach, generally free of nationalist rhetoric; his school policies were intended to prevent Germans in Poznania from being "limited" or segregated from the Poles, while seeing to it that the Poles considered themselves "in every direction members of the state, which just happens to be a German one."⁵⁸ Puttkamer, his successor, was more like Bismarck, a state-oriented conservative who saw in the Poles primarily a threat to the political status quo; once they were ready, he promised, "to subordinate themselves to the laws of the land . . . (to see) themselves and their province as an integral part of the Prussian Monarchy, as bound to her indestructably, unalterably, then they would certainly find the desirable degree of accommodation by the government in all the areas where they now complain of oppression."⁵⁹ Eulenburg however, while also a Bismarckian conservative, betrayed the ambivalence of Prussian nationality policy at this time when he declared: "We must work to make the Poles first Prussian and then German, but they must become Prussian *and* German."⁶⁰

Even if one takes the continued lip-service paid to the ideal of Prussian neutrality in ethnic-national matters seriously and the repeated disavowals by Prussian ministers of a desire to denationalize the Poles at face value, there remains a large gap between proclaimed ideals and historical reality. The ultimate effect of the measures undertaken by the Prussian government at this time was to move the Prussian State (perhaps because it was now part of the German Empire) into a position of suppressing not only the organized political subversion by a nobility loyal to another state idea but the nationality (expressed in apolitical linguistic or religious terms) of the Polish population as a whole. Not surprisingly, the anti-Polish aspects of the *Kulturkampf* had a major impact on the development of Prussian-Polish relations and on the internal development of Prussian-Polish society as well. The most prominent of these results deserve some closer attention.

The *Kulturkampf* helped first of all to enlist the Catholic Church of Prussian Poland in the Polish national struggle. Despite Bismarck's charges to the contrary, this had not always been the case previously, at least not as far as Polish nationalists were concerned. Niegolewski and Kantak bemoaned the fact that the Church in Poznania had never been as nationally apathetic as it was in the 1860s.⁶¹ The leader of the Poznanian Church, Archbishop Ledóchowski, was a cosmopolitan diplomat who had previously shown little Polish nationalism; according to Bismarck, he could no longer even speak the language very well (which did much to recommend him for the archbishop's position.)⁶² During the 1860s it seemed that Bismarck had made the right choice; Ledóchowski urged his clergy to stay out of politics and banned the traditional patriotic hymn "Boże coś Polską" from the churches. He was publicly committed to loyalism and to the monarchical idea; he even kept his priests out of some of the Organic Work organizations, thereby earning the growing criticism of the nationalist press.⁶³ Bismarck described him in 1870 as "an excellent man who keeps the Poles in order for me and on whom I can rely."⁶⁴ With the *Kulturkampf*, however, relations between the Prussian State and the head of the Poznanian Church worsened rapidly. Ledóchowski responded to the new measures by urging all Catholics in his diocese to vote for the candidates of the *Koło Polskie*, the Polish Party so-called. He responded to the changes in the language of instruction in the schools by trying to organize a private instruction system (which was outlawed almost at once by Falk, however).⁶⁵ Like most of his fellow Church leaders, he defied the May Laws, incurring a conviction and a heavy fine and losing state support payments for the Church when he refused to pay it. In November 1873, Bismarck and Falk decided to take steps to remove him from office. After Emperor Wilhelm's half-hearted efforts to effect a compromise had failed, and Ledóchowski refused to step aside "voluntarily," he was arrested in February 1874 and imprisoned at Ostrów for two years.⁶⁶ He was elevated to the rank of Cardinal during his incarceration and went into exile in the Vatican upon his release in 1876. He continued to ignore the verdict of a Prussian ecclesiastical court deposing him, so that the archbishop's chair in Poznania remained vacant for the next ten years (with an inevitable rise of ill feelings among the Polish-Catholic population).⁶⁷

Overall, the *Kulturkampf* led to a harsher treatment of the Church in Prussian Poland than elsewhere in the state. Trzeciakowski has reckoned that while about 20% of the clerical positions in Prussia as a whole were vacant, this was true of 30% of those in Poznania. Due to the shortage of priest-teachers acceptable to the state, Religion was taught in only seven of the province's twenty secondary schools; many of the state priests were Germans who found little acceptance among their parishioners.⁶⁸ As a consequence, the Poznanian Church became more clearly committed to and identified with the Polish national cause. One indication of this growing commitment was the expanded role of clergy in Polish economic or other self-help organizations. (These organizations themselves witnessed rapid growth during the 1870s, perhaps another side-effect of the *Kulturkampf*.) In 1871, there were about 25 credit co-operatives; only one of these was headed by a priest and two others had clergy in other leadership positions. Five years later, twenty of the (by now) 87 credit co-ops were led by clergy and many of the rest had a priest in at least one leadership position. This trend continued during the following decades until by the end of the century there was approximately one priest leader per credit co-op and clergy were a major support of the economic self-help organizations which were themselves a major support of the Polish national movement.[69]

A second major result of the *Kulturkampf* was the imposition of a certain political unity upon Prussian-Polish society. As this struggle began, there were indications of a potentially serious split between Prussian Poles who belonged to the generally dominant ultramontane category and others who were nationalists of a more liberal or secular type. This incipient liberal opposition was associated with the most influential newspaper in Prussian Poland, *Dziennik Poznański*. Established in 1859, this paper took one of its first editorial stands in favor of Italian unification and the primacy of the national idea in general, even where this had to be realized at the expense of Church interests (as in Italy). The controversy was sharpened when Franciszek Dobrowolski became editor of *Dziennik Poznański* in 1871 and began to insist upon the possibility of conflicting interests between Nation and Church, in which case the former had to come first. This position was attacked by the ultramontanes, including Archbishop Ledóchowski and also most of the nobles who held parliamentary seats; they argued either that Church interests should come first or, more often, that there was no necessary clash of interests.[70] When a moderately anti-clerical critic of the Archbishop, Józef Kraszewski, was nominated for a parliamentary seat in 1871, the dominant clerical faction in the *Koło Polskie* imposed a requirement that all of its candidates take a loyalty oath to the Church, whereupon Kraszewski withdrew.[71] These liberals were clearlly the weaker party at this time; they drew some support from the educated gentry and the small urban bourgeoisie, but lacked the support of the rural or lower-middle class population. The clericals, on the other hand, were strongly supported by the newly activist Church and the most influential nobles and had virtually the entire rural population behind them.[72]

In any case, these differences failed to develop into a real split; as the *Kulturkampf* intensified, they were submerged in the name of "national solidarity," an ideal which actually seemed to be realized for a time in the 1870s and 1880s. The participation of German liberals in alliance with Bismarck also hurt the liberal cause in Prussian Poland; in the words of one Polish parliamentarian: "If they approve the war of extermination which is being conducted against us . . . we want nothing to do with such liberalism."[73] Niegolewski, a nationalist of the more secular type, announced in 1871 that he had won election against the opposition of the Poznanian Church, but within a year or two he spoke out as frequently for Church as for national interests and led Polish opposition to the expulsion of the Jesuits.[74] As the priest Ludwik Jażdżewski claimed with considerable justification in 1874: "All the parties in our province have united . . . all hostilities have subsided and (society as a) whole is today stronger than ever."⁷⁵ Essentially, this unity was achieved by liberal acquiescence in the clerical position as the national movement came increasingly under Church auspices in the 1870s.

A third result of the *Kulturkampf*, of some importance at least in the short run, was the alliance formed between the Poles and one of the largest German parties, the Catholic Center. Beginning with common positions on issues affecting the Church, it led to Center support for a number of Polish national aspirations as well. For example, the Center supported an 1875 Polish motion to guarantee their "rights of nationality and language" and an 1876 motion to give Polish equal status with German in Poznanian courts.⁷⁶ The leader of the Center, Ludwig Windthorst, stated his position on the Polish question in a way that curiously combined support for better treatment of the Poles with the possibility of their eventual Germanization: "The Poles are not given to us to be Germanized, but that we treat them (legally). Now, if one has the desire that they be Germanized, then you can be sure that they will be Germanized much sooner and much more through the most careful consideration for the rights which have been provided them than through a measure like this (Official Language Law), which must make the blood boil in the veins of these people."⁷⁷ A Polish spokesman noted the new situation in 1873: "We have so far been alone in the struggle for our nationality and its rights, with the exception of the often platonic sympathies directed toward us by a few noble men." As a result of the *Kulturkampf*, however, "we will have all the Catholics with us."⁷⁸ The same point was made by Jażdżewski: "At least our co-religionists feel for us, and the strength which we gain through this relationship benefits us also from our national standpoint."⁷⁹ The Center and Poles began to support each other in election campaigns, informally or by means of election alliances.⁸⁰ There were even suggestions that the Poles ought to simply affiliate with the larger German-Catholic party, but they resisted this idea and tried to avoid the impression that they were merely a Polish version of the Center. Jażdżewski, though a priest himself, stressed that the *Koło Polskie* was first of all the Polish national party.⁸¹

In general, Polish representatives did not make it easy for even well-intentioned Germans to support them. The gentry parliamentarians remained adamant on the national question, regardless of the ineffectiveness of such a posture and its effect on the sensitivities of German parties which might have been useful to them politically. For example, they opposed a resolution applauding the new Empire and one spokesman expressed doubt that his co-nationals could ever show "spontaneous, direct participation" in the state which was, after all, the culmination of the national dreams of most Germans.⁸² While Prussian

Poles were no longer involved in revolutionary conspiracies to any extent, they refused to abandon (in the Prussian and German parliaments) their hopes for the restoration of a Polish state which would include a part of the new German Empire. Niegolewski was even coquettish about the willingness of the Poland of which he dreamed to do without East Prussia.[83] The reacquisition of Alsace-Lorraine by Germany after so many years served the Poles as an analogous promise that their national hopes might also be realized in the however distant future.[84] This nationally unyielding stance continued throughout the *Kulturkampf,* even when it threatened to undermine the support of the Center. Kantak, the chief spokesman for the Poles in the Landtag throughout this period, acknowledged (or claimed) in 1877 that "all Poles hope and expect national independence;" he added later: "We believe in, we hope for, and we pray for the restoration of Poland, for Poland is our faith, our hope and our love."[85] The *Koło Polskie* refused to see itself as just another political party in the legislative bodies: "We are no party; it is the national position which we represent. . . . We are strictly the representatives of the Polish people, which has sent us here."[86] "We Poles stand equally distant from every (German) party."[87] "We do not represent Prussian, not German, but only Polish interests."[88] Thus Polish representatives accepted no responsibility to represent the Germans in their districts and denied the right of German representatives from Poznania and West Prussia to speak for the Poles in their districts.[89] In spite of such statements, however, the Center generally supported the Poles into the 1880s, its parliamentarians and especially its large national press giving Polish complaints an exposure they would not otherwise have had. And along with the gentry nationalists cited above, there were now influential priests in the Polish faction who believed strongly in Catholic solidarity across national lines and took greater pains to keep the alliance with the Center alive.[90]

A fourth consequence of the *Kulturkampf* was logically the growth of Polish resentment and the heightening of friction between Prussian Poles and their government. Official reports from the provinces clearly reflect this: "The repeated elections and the determined actions of the royal state government in the conflict with the Catholic hierarchy have intensified the national and confessional differences more and more and now have stretched them to the extreme . . . (leading to) great anger and agitation among the Catholic people."[91] This was also apparent in the increasingly agitated speeches of Polish parliamentarians, who found themselves frustrated in their efforts to counter Bismarck's measures against them. *Koło Polskie* called for maximum aloofness from and strict opposition to the government, with involvement by Polish representatives only when

Polish interests were directly at stake. During the 1870-1 session of the Landtag, only five Polish representatives were moved to speak at any time; after a couple of years of *Kulturkampf* they began to take a more active part in deliberations and a dozen or so typically took the floor in a given session. But their attempts to introduce amendments or resolutions were usually stymied, in spite of Center or Progressive support.[92] They circulated petitions against the school language regulations (which attracted 160,000 signatures) and against the Official Language Law (which received over 300,000 signatures), but these had little impact on Bismarck's government.[93] They also periodically reminded the government of the 1815 treaties and royal statements, again to no effect.[94] All in all, aside from the Center support (which fell to them almost by default), the gentry leaders of the *Koło Polskie* found no effective strategy for dealing with the anti-Polish measures in conventional, parliamentary fashion.

Thus they gave vent to their anger and frustration in increasingly emotional denunciations of Bismarck's policies, which at the same time appear to reflect accurately the mood of their constituents. Jażdżewski was relatively moderate when he warned: "It is no wonder that the national differences today emerge more sharply than ever before. . . . State officials are doing everything to offend and incite us. . . . (Existing policies) necessarily encourage this internal aversion and this bitter feeling, which we feel every day in this state, to become ever greater and cause our hearts to turn away from a state which distresses and torments us in an unnecessary and unjustified manner."[95] Another parliamentarian accused the government of "inflicting injustices, trampling on state treaties, violating natural rights, vulgar derision of the most solemn promises of your kings, and then demanding of us that we should kiss the hands of the intruders!"[96] A third spokesman described Bismarck's policies as "nothing more than a system of neglect (*Verkümmerung*), persecution and oppression . . . a national-political war of extermination. . . . (But) we are not redskins; . . . we have steadfastly survived worse persecution in the past."[97] In particular, the word "extermination" (*ausrotten*) came to be used regularly by Polish spokesmen to describe their impression of the government's intentions: "The extermination of our nationality is their aim;" "The extermination of the Polish language and nationality is being pursued."[98] Bismarck cannot of course be seriously accused of seeking the extermination or even denationalization of Prussian Poles as an ethnic-linguistic group. On the other hand, he would apparently have been quite happy to see the Polish nobility and the politicized Polish clergy disappear altogether. What he apparently did not realize was that in attacking the latter groups he alienated also the Polish masses and turned them from a passive ethnic group into a national-political movement under the noble-clerical direction. His policies helped very much to turn the despised Polish gentry from ineffective generals without an army into the leaders of a formidable, because broadly based, national movement.

This brings up a fifth result of the *Kulturkampf*, perhaps the most important of all in the longer run: the extension of the Polish national movement both socially and geographically. Kantak was quite right when he proclaimed in 1877 that "the movement is rising ever higher and penetrating ever more deeply."[99] "Nothing has clarified and strengthened the Polish question as much as the *Kulturkampf*. Its primary contribution has been to unite all, from the poorest man to the wealthiest, and they in turn are united with the Church."[100] Polish representatives challenged Bismarck to visit Poznania and see for himself the extent to which his own policies had united and politicized the Polish masses whose loyalty and passivity he had so often praised.[101] Bismarck could also discern this from the reports of provincial officials, which told of an "intensive increase of Polish-national agitation" with growing involvement of peasants and clergy.[102] To a large degree, the apolitical stance of the Polish peasant, which Polish leaders had lamented as often as Bismarck had praised it, disappeared during the *Kulturkampf*. The smaller urban population also began to exhibit Polish national consciousness and play an active, if still subordinate role, in the national movement. One indication of this is the number of important new press organs which appeared during this period: *Orędownik* (1871), aimed at the urban population specifically, the ultramontane *Kuryer Poznański* (1872), and *Goniec Wielkopolski* (1877), the most radically nationalistic of all.[103] The mobilization of Polish society as a whole in the national cause, which progressive gentry had worked toward in earlier decades, began now to realize itself, again due as much to Bismarck's policies as to the propaganda and organizational efforts of the Polish nobles.

In addition to broadening the social basis of the Polish national movement, the geographical area in which it operated was similarly enlarged during the *Kulturkampf*. This movement had previously been limited pretty much to Poznania and the southern districts of West Prussia, i.e., areas with a large Polish nobility to carry the burden at a time when other classes were not involved. Even in West Prusisa, where Poles constituted only ⅓ of the population and owned only about 1/6 of the land, the movement was long dependent upon Poznanian support and direction.[104] The Kashubes who inhabited the northern part of that province, speaking a Slavic dialect more or less akin to Polish, had not participated in the general Polish national movement prior to the *Kulturkampf*. But the state attack on their Church and clergy caused many of them to overcome traditional anti-Polish feelings and enlist in a common cause, at first Catholic but then increasingly national-Polish.[105] More important still was integration of the more than one million Upper Silesian Poles into the national cause, though this was to be sure a much slower process. Upper Silesia had not been part of a Polish state since the Middle Ages and was politically almost completely in the hands of the German Center. This remained the case until after 1900; if anything, the *Kulturkampf* here may have helped strengthen the bonds between German and Polish Catholics under Center leadership. But here too, the 1870s saw the emergence of a Polish press, mass assemblies, involvement by the lower clergy in Polish national affairs, and other indications that the Upper Silesian Poles were responding to the government's attack on their Church and language by adopting a previously non-existent militancy in national matters as well.[106] Of the major Polish-speaking regions of Prussia, only Masuria remained truly aloof from the Polish movement, despite the proselytizing of Polish nationalists; the predominantly Lutheran confession of this region, which meant that it was less affected by the *Kulturkampf*, is the most obvious explanation for this.[107]

Thus in sum, while Bismarck's battle with the Catholic Church is often described as a draw at the national level, its impact on the nature of the Polish problem in Prussia was clearly contrary to the interests and expressed aims of his government. The Polish national movement was energized and supported by a more united society; it found the effective support of the Catholic Church, in Polish areas especially but to some extent in the rest of Germany as well; it was strengthened by the involvement of previously apathetic social classes and outlying geographical areas. In a sense, the movement was "democratized" during this period, and thus made better able to resist subsequent government attacks during the post-1885 period. Of course, this development was not inevitable; it was still possible in 1871 to foresee rather the revival of the Prussian supra-national tradition under Bismarck (who, after all, to that point had seemed to exploit nationalism rather than adhere to it). And it should be remembered that Prussia did successfully maintain the political allegiance of some of her non-German ethnic groups (Masurians, Lithuanians, and Upper Silesians to a considerable extent), which suggests that it was not beyond the realm of possibility in Poznania, with respect to the Polish masses if not the nobility.[108] Instead, during the *Kulturkampf* "the crucial error (*Sündenfall*) of the transition from the humanitarian state idea to constricted nationalist thinking, with the final aim of "denationalization" (*Umvolkung*) in the Polish-speaking areas, took place."[109] Prussian Poland, long the least restive of the three partitions of old

Poland, began now to evolve into the most assertive section, with a national movement which was the most effective because it was most deeply rooted in its society.

Notes

1. *Die Staatsidee im Kulturkampf,* 2nd edit. (Darmstadt, 1969), p. 52; Trzeciakowski, p. 86.
2. *Bismarck, der Osten, und das Reich,* 2nd edit. (Stuttgart, 1962), pp. 88f.; *Kulturkampf* (Poznań, 1963), pp. 20, 181; see also Georg Franz, *Der Kulturkampf* (Munich, 1954) and Erich Schmidt-Volkmar, *Der Kulturkampf in Deutschland, 1871-1890* (Göttingen, 1962).
3. see below, p. 20.
4. *Gedanken und Erinnerungen,* 2nd edit., 3 vols. (Stuttgart, 1922), II:149.
5. Bismarck to the Center politician Franckenstein, July 19, 1879, *Also Sprach Bismarck,* II:322.
6. Bismarck to a group of parliamentarians, March 8, 1881, *Fürst Bismarck und die Parliamentarier,* 3 vols. (Breslau, 1894), I:210f.
7. Karl Bachem, *Vorgeschichte, Geschichte und Politik der deutschen Zentrumspartei,* 3 vols., (Cologne, 1927), III:222.
8. speech of December 3, 1884, *Politische Reden,* X:287ff.
9. November 1, 1871, in *Die Vorgeschichte des Kulturkampfes,* ed. A. Constabel (Berlin, 1956), p. 142.
10. Korth, pp. 38f.
11. report from Danzig, February 1871, in Günther Dettmer, *Die ost- und westpreussischen Behörden im Kulturkampf* (Heidelberg, 1958), Anhang I.
12. conversation with Danzig *Regierungspräsident* Diest, February 22, 1872, *Also Sprach Bismarck,* II:157.
13. conversation with Johann Friedrich von Schulte, January 2, 1873, *Ibid.,* II:149.
14. speech of April 1, 1871, *Reichstag.*
15. Bismarck to Ambassador von Canitz in Rome, October 24, 1862, *Gesammelte Werke,* IV:5.
16. speech of March 18, 1867, *Reichstag;* Dettmer, p. 23.
17. reports from Danzig, March 1867 and February 1870, Dettmer, p. 23 and Anhang I.
18. report from Danzig, August 1871, *Ibid.*
19. Prussian cabinet meeting, March 3, 1872, *Vorgeschichte des Kulturkampfes,* p. 185; "Die Stellung des Erzbischofs von Posen und Genesen als Primus von Polen," I.A.B.g, Polen 14, *Politisches Archiv des Auswärtigen Amts, Bonn* (hereafter *PA Bonn*); Bismarck suggested joint action with Russia on this issue but nothing came of it apparently; Bismarck to Reuss, March 6, 1872, Trzeciakowski, p. 106.
20. memo of March 15, 1870, *Gesammelte Werke,* VIb:291.

21. Prussian cabinet meeting, October 13, 1871, *Vorgeschichte des Kulturkampfes*, p. 127.
22. Mühler to *Oberpräsident* von Stolberg, October 28, 1871, *Ibid.*, pp. 136ff.
23. *Gedanken und Erinnerungen*, II:149; conversation with Schulte, 1/2/73 *Also Sprach Bismarck*, II:149; Tadeusz Nowakowski, *The Radziwiłłs* (New York, 1974).
24. Diest to Eulenburg, August 2, 1870, *Vorgeschichte des Kulturkampfes*, pp. 19ff.; report from Danzig, August 1870, Dettmer, Anhang I.
25. report from Danzig, February 1871, Dettmer, Anhang I.
26. November 19, 1871, *Also Sprach Bismarck*, II:135f.; Ludwig Pastor, *August Reichensperger*, 2 vols. (Freiburg, 1899), II:49f.
27. Bismarck to Eulenburg, February 7, 1872, *Bismarck-Jahrbuch*, I:83ff.
28. Hauser, p. 302; Trzeciakowski, p. 85.
29. Prussian cabinet meeting, November 1, 1871, *Vorgeschichte des Kulturkampfes*, p. 136.
30. December 31, 1871, Laubert, p. 136.
31. memo of February 5, 1872, *Vorgeschichte des Kulturkampfes*, p. 170.
32. Bismarck to Eulenburg, February 7, 1872, *Bismarck-Jahrbuch*, I:83ff.
33. *Ibid.*; though this proposal was not implemented for thirteen years, Buzek cites it as the actual beginning of a policy of "extermination" of the Poles by Bismarck, pp. 132ff.
34. memo of February 13, 1872, cited by Laubert, p. 137, and Friedrich Koch, *Bismarck über die Polen* (Berlin, 1913), p. 75.
35. Trzeciakowski, p. 180.
36. memo of February 17, 1872, *Vorgeschichte des Kulturkampfes*, p. 179.
37. Eulenburg to Emperor Wilhelm, March 5, 1872, *Ibid.*, p. 187.
38. Dettmer, p. 43.
39. Laubert, p. 140; Tadeusz Klanowski, *Germanizacja gimnazjów w W.K. Poznańskim i opór młodzieży polskiej w latach 1870-1914* (Poznań, 1962).
40. speeches of February 25 and December 16, 1873, *Abgeordnetenhaus*.
41. Laubert, p. 140; Hauser, p. 302.
42. speech by Greif, June 11, 1875, *Abgeordnetenhaus*.
43. speech by Waetzoldt, January 31, 1874, *Ibid.*
44. speech by Stablewski, March 14, 1883, *Ibid.*
45. *Przegląd Polski* (Cracow), in *Wielkopolski (1851-1914)*, ed. W. Jakóbczyk (Wrocław, 1954), p. 148; Trzeciakowski, p. 199; speech by Niegolewski, January 20, 1875, *Abgeordnetenhaus*.
46. speech of January 30, 1874, *Abgeordnetenhaus*.
47. p. 199; see also Gossler speech of March 14, 1883, *Abgeordnetenhaus*.
48. speech of November 11, 1880, *Ibid.*
49. speech of February 25, 1876, *Ibid.*
50. speech by Agriculture Minister Lucius, November 27, 1880; reply by Kantak, same date, *Ibid.*
51. speech by Niegolewski, January 20, 1875, *Ibid.*
52. Laubert, p. 142; Hauser, p. 302.

53. speech of May 13, 1876, *Abgeordnetenhaus.*
54. Trzeciakowski, p. 203; speech by Kantak, December 2, 1879, *Abgeordnetenhaus.*
55. speech by Friedenthal, January 22, 1878, *Ibid.*
56. speech by Niegolewski, January 20, 1875, *Reichstag;* speech by Kantak, December 12, 1879, *Abgeordnetenhaus.*
57. speech by Eulenburg, March 21, 1876, *Ibid.;* Böhning, p. 157; Trzeciakowski, p. 233; the courts also ruled in favor of the Poles when the government claimed the right to proctor the meetings of the *Koło Polskie* and its local organizations (see speech by Ignacy Łyskowski, December 1, 1879, *Abgeordnetenhaus);* after these setbacks the government shelved plans to compel the Church to use the "official language" in Poznania; see speech by Florian Stablewski, February 20, 1877, *Ibid.*
58. speech of February 25, 1873, *Ibid.*
59. speech of June 28, 1879, *Ibid.*
60. quoted by Schieder, p. 25.
61. speeches of February 4, 1867, *Reichstag.*
62. Stefan Kieniewicz, Henryk Wereszycki, et al., *History of Poland,* (Warsaw, 1968), p. 538; William Rose, *The Rise of Polish Democracy* (London, 1944), p. 62; Richard Perdelwitz, *Die Posener Polen von 1815 bis 1914* (Schneidemühl, 1936), p. 71.
63. Lech Trzeciakowski, "The Prussian State and the Catholic Church in Prussian Poland, 1871-1914," *Slavic Review* 26 (1967):623; *Dziennik Poznański,* quoted in Trzeciakowski, *Kulturkampf,* p. 103.
64. Busch, I:6.
65. speech of 16, 1873, *Abgeordnetenhaus.;* Hauser, p. 303.
66. Trzeciakowski, *Kulturkampf,* pp. 112ff.; "Prussian State," p. 624; Hauser, p. 303; the suffragan bishops of Poznań and Gniezno, the Bishop of Kulm, and about one hundred other clergy were also imprisoned in Poznania.
67. Laubert, p. 143; Enno Meyer, "Die Polen im preussischen Staat von 1815 bis 1914," in *Deutschland und Polen,* ed. H. Fechner, (Würzburg, 1964), p. 59.
68. Trzeciakowski, *Kulturkampf,* pp. 125, 131, 197.
69. Alexander Szembek, *Les associations économiques des paysans polonais sous la domination prussienne* (Lille, 1909), pp. 92f.; Kieniewicz/Wereszycki, p. 538.
70. Perdelwitz, p. 60; Trzeciakowski, *Kulturkampf,* pp. 37, 53; *Wielkopolska,* p. xxxvii.
71. Trzeciakowski, *Kulturkampf,* p. 53.
72. This analysis by *Orędownik,* January 24, 1873, in *Poznańskie, Pomorze, Warmia i Mazury w latach 1864-1914,* ed. W. Jakóbczyk and J. Wiśniewski (Warsaw, 1960), p. 6.
73. speech by Wierzbiński, May 9, 1874, *Abgeordnetenhaus.*
74. speeches of April 1 and November 25, 1871, and June 17, 1872, *Reichstag.*
75. speech of May 7, 1874, *Abgeordnetenhaus.*
76. debates of January 20, 1875, and November 23, 1876, *Reichstag.*

77. speech of April 20, 1876, *Abgeordnetenhaus*.
78. speech by Chłapowski, February 27, 1873, *Ibid*.
79. speech of May 7, 1874, *Ibid*.
80. report from Poznań, November 8, 1884, describing Center leader Ballestrem's campaigning for a Polish candidate among German Catholics, #5964, Rep. 84a, *Geheimes Preussisches Staats-archiv, Berlin-Dahlem* (hereafter *GPSA Berlin*).
81. Bachem, III:190; speech by Jażdżewski, February 17, 1875, *Abgeordnetenhaus*.
82. speech by Szuman, January 19, 1871, *Ibid*.
83. speech of April 1871, *Reichstag*.
84. speeches by Żółtowski, April 1, 1871, and Niegolewski, May 20, 1871, *Ibid*.
85. speeches of November 8, 1877, and March 15, 1883, *Abgeordnetenhaus*.
86. Kantak speech of February 20, 1877, *Ibid*.
87. speech by Leon Czarliński, November 28, 1881, *Reichstag*.
88. speech by Wierzbiński, May 9, 1875, *Abgeordnetenhaus*.
89. Czarliński speech of January 27, 1882; *Reichstag*; Kantak speech of May 13, 1876, *Abgeordnetenhaus*.
90. e.g. Stablewski: "We are not only Poles, we are also Christians." February 11, 1879, *Ibid*.
91. report from Danzig, February 1874, Dettmer, Anhang I.
92. e.g., Łyskowski's efforts to amend the Official Language Law, May 13, 1876; Kantak's speech of May 20, 1876, *Abgeordnetenhaus*.
93. Trzeciakowski, *Kulturkampf*, p. 226.
94. Kantak speech of March 18, 1867; Kantak and Magdziński, May 13, 1876, *Abgeordnetenhaus*.
95. speech of January 10, 1879, *Ibid*.
96. speech by Wierzbiński, May 20, 1876, *Ibid*.
97. speech by Szuman, November 20, 1872, *Ibid*.
98. Taczanowski speech of January 20, 1875, *Reichstag*; Stablewski speech of January 17, 1879, *Abgeordnetenhaus*; Łyskowski speech of May 7, 1876, *Ibid*.
99. speech of February 6, 1877, *Ibid*.
100. speech by Czarliński, January 27, 1882, *Reichstag*.
101. speech by Magdziński, December 3, 1884, *Ibid*.
102. report from Bromberg, February 28, 1883, #5964, Rep. 84a, *GPSA Berlin*.
103. Trzeciakowski, *Kulturkampf*, p. 219;
104. Baske, pp. 74ff.; Böhning, *passim*.
105. Dettmer, p. 23; Böhning, pp. 190ff.; Friedrich Lorentz, *Geschichte der Kaschuben* (Berlin, 1926), p. 131; Dietrich von Oppen, "Deutsche, Polen und Kaschuben in Westpreussen, 1871-1914," *Jahrbuch für die Geschichte Mittel- und Ostdeutschlands* 4(1955):212.
106. Mieczysław Pater, *Centrum a ruch polski na Górnym Śląsku (1874-93)* (Opole, 1971), p. 304.
107. Tadeusz Grygier, "Sprawa polska w Prusach Wschodnich w latach

1870-1900 w oświetleniu władz pruskich," *Przegląd Zachodni* 7(1951):493-544.
  108. Schieder, pp. 22, 24f.
  109. Hauser, p. 302; Martin Broszat, *200 Jahre deutscher Polenpolitik* (Munich, 1963), p. 106.

Chapter II:
From *Kulturkampf* to *Nationalitätenkampf*

During the 1880s, Bismarck decided to settle with the Catholic Church and thus bring the *Kulturkampf* to a close. But this willingness to make up with German Catholics did not extend to their Polish co-religionists. According to Bismarck himself, he would have ended the *Kulturkampf* much sooner had he been able to have one policy toward the Church in German areas and another in the Polish provinces.[1] As many of the anti-Church measures were withdrawn, the anti-Polish aspects remained in place. While most of the principal German churchmen found their way back to their positions and normalcy returned to their dioceses, this was not the case in Poznania, whose archbishop was never permitted to return. Most of the Church's seminaries had reopened by 1885, again with the exception of the Poznanian diocese.[2] Polish journalists remained under close surveillance after the pressure on the major German-Catholic newspapers had eased. At one point in 1884, the editors of all but two Prussian-Polish newspapers were in jail under sentences totalling almost six years; the editor of the Church-controlled *Kuryer Poznański* spent over three years in jail, and the editor of the ultra-nationalist *Goniec Wielkopolski* two more, for violations of Prussian press laws.[3] Indeed, it was only at this time that many Poles became conscious of some of the measures taken against their nationality, previously overshadowed by those against their Church. Only now did it become clear that they were under attack primarily because of their nationality and not merely because of their religion. Thus the *Kulturkampf*, for all its adverse impact on Prussian-Polish relations, proved to be merely a preview of the much more intense national struggle which began in earnest in the 1880s.

This increased friction between Prussian Poles and their government took place against a background of intensified German nationalism in general, which was itself a parallel development to the intensified Polish nationalism generated by the *Kulturkampf*. This was not a case of an aggressive official nationalism forcing a struggle with a passive or helpless group (as was often the case in Russia), nor was it, on the other hand, a case of an aroused national minority pushing a more permissive than oppressive dynastic regime to the wall (as in Austria). What gave the German-Polish struggle in the Prussian East its special intensity was the collision of two fully developed, well organized, and by no means unequal nationalisms. The fact that the Germans had a powerful state apparatus on their side was not decisive (and, as will become evident later, may even have been a mixed blessing at times), whereas the Poles made up in single-mindedness what they lacked in state power. Perhaps this was the reason for the continued development of a German nationalism separate from, and with aims well in excess of, Bismarck's government. In any case, by the 1880s the liberal, externally-focussed nationalism of the previous decades seemed to give way increasingly to an authoritarian, aggressive type which kept at least one eye on alleged internal enemies (or *Reichsfeinde* in Bismarck's parlance). Aside from the Poles, this new type of German nationalism found various outlets, including anti-Semitism, imperialism, economic nationalism, and suppression of the cosmopolitan Social Democrats. There was also a stronger feeling by such nationalists that their new Empire ought to become ethnically, even religiously, more homogeneous. In party-political terms, this feeling was strongest among the National Liberals; it was given expression most prominently by Heinrich von Treitschke, who argued in 1882 that "we are a national state, and the disappearing minorities in our Empire who are not German by blood will have to show consideration for the great majority of their fellow-citizens."[4]

At first, Prussian Poles were a less important target of this nationalism than Jews and socialists. Bismarck's first efforts to make peace with the Church were accompanied by the anti-socialist laws and the closing years of the *Kulturkampf* coincided with the emergence of political anti-Semitism in Germany, (*e.g.*, the first Anti-Semitic Reichstag deputy was elected in 1884).[5] As opposed to the Poles, the Jewish element was more visible to most Germans; Jews lived in towns amidst other Germans, engaged in occupations which competed with them, and were more likely to be active politically. The Poles, on the other hand, (prior to their large-scale recruitment for mining and industrial jobs in Berlin and the Ruhr) kept largely to their own provinces, except in their role as seasonal agricultural workers. But the distinction between anti-Semitism and anti-Polish feelings was not always a sharp one on the level of popular nationalism; the former frequently antedated and shaded into the latter. For Bismarck, the Poles were certainly the greater annoyance; in fact, he may have done much to direct the attention of this resurgent German nationalism to the situation in the Prussian East. During the following decades, as the anti-socialist laws were withdrawn and political anti-Semitism fizzled out, pressure on the Poles by German society and government increased more or less steadily until by the end of the century they were the one remaining, unequivocal *Reichsfeind*.

A number of explanations for the particular development of German nationalism in the 1880s have been offered. Some have attributed it to liberal disappointment following the euphoria of the *Reichsgründung*, the failure of the new Empire to win more than a draw with the Catholic Church in its first major domestic struggle, and their own fall from Bismarck's grace. Hans Rosenberg has made a good case for seeing it in the context of the economic malaise which began to surface during the second trough of the "long depression" (1882-1886).[6] The immediate cause of its specifically anti-Polish aspect may well have been the publicity given to some disturbing demographic trends. In an 1883 article entitled "Germanization or Polonization," Friedrich Neumann (sic) presented a wealth of statistical evidence which seemed to indicate that the Germans were losing the upper hand against the Poles in the eastern provinces.[7] During the previous two decades, the German population of Prussia's eastern provinces, while still increasing in absolute terms, had begun to decline rapidly relative to the Polish rate of increase. In four regencies cited by Neumann (comprising Poznania, Upper Silesia, and eastern Pomerania), the Polish population had increased by 250,000 since 1871 and the German by only about 55,000. Poznania's German population increased by less than 5% during the 1871-1895 period while the Polish grew by 21.5%; during the 1881-1885 period, when German nationalist attention was attracted to Polish demographic advances, the German population of Poznania actually declined by some 5000 persons.[8] Interior Minister Robert von Puttkamer presented the following rates of increase for the 1871-1880 period to the Reichstag:[9]

Regierungsbezirk	*Polish increase*	*German increase*
Marienwerder	8.0%	3.4%
Bromberg	8.4	7.0
Poznań	10.9	1.9
Oppeln	10.5	9.0

Until 1890, the Prussian State collected figures only for "confession," not for nationality or language; thus all of these numbers are the result of extrapolation and subjective judgments based on confessional statistics. Assuming that about 10% of the Catholics in Poznania were German and about 25% in West Prussia, Lech Trzeciakowski has more recently computed the following figures to illustrate the relative German decline in these two provinces (1860-1890):[10]

Regierungsbezirk	Percent German 1860	Percent German 1890
Poznań	41%(?)	34%
Bromberg	53	50
Marienwerder	63	61
Danzig	75	72

These trends were all the more disturbing to German nationalists because they pointed to an abrupt reversal of historical patterns. Until the unification of Germany, during decades when the government did little purposely to alter the national balance in its Polish provinces, the German percentages increased steadily; the German proportion of Poznania's population reached its historic peak in the 1860s.[11] Continued German advance was taken for granted by Germans, and apparently conceded by many Poles as well. As Józef Kraszewski observed in 1868: "For one who has witnessed somewhat earlier times, the progress of Germanization is visible and undeniable."[12] Roman Szymański noted in 1870: "The German element in the towns is making significant progress and expanding constantly, supported not only by political but also by economic conditions advantageous to it."[13]

In attempting to account for this relatively sudden reversal of German demographic fortunes, some observers focused on the legendary Slavic birth rate. During the 1824-1873 period, the annual increase of births over deaths was actually somewhat higher for Protestants (1.05%) than for Catholics (.97%); while Catholics had a higher birth rate, it was negated by a higher infant mortality rate and higher death rates generally. But after 1871, with improvements in hygiene, this situation changed; by 1900, the Catholic rate of natural growth in Poznania stood at 2.25% annually, as opposed to 1.3% for Protestants.[14] Others cited the alleged "Polonization" of Germans, e.g., the Polonizing influence of Polish clergy over German Catholics in Poznania.[15] Most likely however, these demographic trends were a logical consequence of economic conditions in the Prussian East and of the different ways Germans and Poles reacted to them.

Poznania and West Prussia were (along with East Prussia) the most rural provinces in Prussia; they were economically most dominated by agriculture and had the lowest standards of living; only Silesia (also ethnically mixed) had lower average wage scales.[16] In Poznania, previously significant domestic and artisanal industries had been gradually displaced by the products of western factories. The proximity of the rather tightly closed Russian frontier had crippled this province's traditional transit-trade activities. Such large-scale industry as did exist was devoted to the processing of agricultural products and more likely to be situated in the countryside than in the still-small cities, which remained almost exclusively administrative and mercantile in character. And even these agriculture-based industries (wool, spirits, wood) were in decline after 1871.[17] Such an economy was unable to absorb the growing population, so that the Polish provinces remained plagued by problems of rural overpopulation and emigration, (such as had been characteristic of the rest of Germany earlier in the century). In spite of above-average birth rates, Prussia's eastern provinces did not keep up with the rest of the country in terms of population growth. While the population of Prussia as a whole increased by 45.2% (1867-1900), that of Ostelbia grew by only 21.5%; while Prussia's urban population doubled during this period, Ostelbia's cities grew by only 20%.[18] The "flight from the land," which in western Germany usually meant migration within a larger region, meant in the Prussian East a move out of the region altogether. Upper Silesia, whose rapid industrialization during this period supported a rapidly growing population, was an exception to this rule; it was, of course, the lack of industrialization which was primarily responsible for the low rate of population growth elsewhere in the Prussian East.

Being so dependent upon agriculture, the Polish provinces also suffered from the general agricultural slump which saw German farm prices fall by 20% during the decade after 1876.[19] Many large landowners responded to their financial straits by hiring their workers from across the Russian border, where labor was ample, cheap, but (usually) also Polish. From a nationalist perspective, these landowners might have been persuaded instead to raise their wages and working conditions so that the local population of Poles and Germans would stay instead of seeking better jobs in the West, thus eliminating the need for imported labor. But even Bismarck did not feel for many years that he could demand this of the powerful agrarian interests. Instead, many residents of Poznania and West Prussia, Polish and German alike, chose to seek work elsewhere, or were compelled to do so by the competition of these *Gastarbeiter*. Some found permanent jobs in industry; the less fortunate took seasonal jobs in agriculture (*e.g.*, in the sugar-beet fields of Saxony, whence the generic term for seasonal farm workers [*Sachsengänger*] is derived).

At this point, one can differentiate between the normal behavior of the two nationalities. Poles, working in alien German-speaking areas where it was difficult for them to feel at home, typically went west only to earn enough money to return home and perhaps buy some land of their own.

Alternatively, they worked seasonally in the West, but retained their main residence in Poznania or West Prussia. Germans, on the other hand, were obviously in a better position to adjust to life among co-nationals in the West and thus constituted a disproportionate share of those emigrating permanently to the West from the Polish provinces.[20] For other reasons, they also participated disproportionately in the heavy emigration overseas from these regions during these years.[21] Thus, though the average annual excess of births over deaths for Protestants in Poznania was about 9,000 in the 1880s, the net increase was only about 2500 annually because of this heavy emigration. In the agricultural sector alone, emigration actually exceeded by about 20% the excess of births over deaths for Poznania's Protestant population during the last two decades of the Nineteenth Century.[22]

Reinforcing the above trends was the rapid decrease of the Jewish population of the Polish provinces. The Catholic population of Poznania increased by 33.5% (1849-1885); the Protestant growth was not that much lower: 30.2%. But the Jewish population declined by 33.7% during this period and, since Jews were normally considered part of the German nationality, this meant that the rate of growth for the German (Protestant+Jewish) population was only 20.3% during this 36-year span.[23] In Poznań regency, the Protestant population remained little changed during this period (c. 31%); the increased Catholic (Polish) share of this region was largely at the expense of German Jews, who were especially heavily represented in the movement westward and whose share fell from 6% to 3%. Poznania's Jews lived mainly in cities and towns; many county seats had Jewish populations approaching the 50% mark in the 1840s, though they had fallen to the 4-7% level by 1900. Thus the vacancies created by the Jewish exodus meant an increase specifically in the urban Polish population, with political consequences which will be treated below.[24]

In sum, after decades or even centuries during which gradual German advance was taken for granted, the attention of German public opinion and of the Prussian government was drawn to these disturbing demographic trends in the 1880s. Bismarck himself tended to attribute them to relatively unimportant but tangible factors: Polonization of Germans, the role of the Church, and various kinds of conscious effort by the Polish national movement. He apparently failed to comprehend fully the economic or social causes and his measures in response were therefore largely ineffective. Among German nationalists the feeling that existing policies were not making much headway, neither pacifying nor assimilating the Poles, continued to grow. They argued that the Polish problem could no longer be counted on to solve itself, that a more active state policy was necessary before the situation got further out of hand.

One expression of this new mood was an article by Ernst von der Brüggen in *Preussische Jahrbücher,* the traditional voice of German national liberalism, introducing *Lebensraum* concepts into the Polish question. Brüggen pointed to the "right to light and room" of the 400,000 newly-born Germans each year, room for which could only be found in the Prussian East. "We have no higher duty to Poznania than to Germanize it by peaceful means . . . to have the immigration of Germans especially to Poznania encouraged by the state."[25] A more prominent representative of this new German nationalism (at once assertive and defensive) as it related specifically to the Poles, was Eduard von Hartmann, a moderately successful philosopher of strongly anti-clerical opinions. In a January 1885 article entitled "The Decline of the German Nationality," Hartmann popularized the idea that the German nationality had been forced onto the defensive, that the German ethnic frontier was contracting in many areas to the east and south of the new *kleindeutsch* Empire.[26]

Hartmann attributed this decline to several factors. First was the growth of national consciousness among the Slavs and other eastern peoples. They were becoming more assertive, unwilling to live under an often-German leadership class. He cited also the economic and cultural development of these peoples (noted already among Prussian Poles) which many Germans refused still to acknowledge. A second reason for this alleged decline was the unwillingness or inability of the German nation-state to do anything for Germans who did not belong to it. It was Bismarck's policy, of course, to avoid friction with his eastern neighbors by denying any interest in the fate of their German minorities. As a result, Hartmann perceived a lamentable lack of national consciousness among these stranded Germans and a tendency either to move west or to give up their nationality without a struggle. Finally, Hartmann dwelled on the alleged animosity of the Catholic Church toward Germany and the German nationality.

Hartmann argued that the government of the Prussian-German Empire ought to compensate for these losses by seeing to it that the ethnically mixed areas under its control became homogeneously German. He urged a policy of rigorous Germanization and did not shy away from use of the term *"ausrotten"* to describe the approach to be adopted toward Prussian Poles. He proposed several immediate steps to deal with the Polish problem. One of these, an all-out war with the Catholic Church and the purging of non-Protestants from the state apparatus, was politically anachronistic at a time when Bismarck was trying to come to terms with the Church. His suggestion that the Polish agricultural population be encouraged to emigrate to the newly acquired tropical colonies was impractical and economically senseless. But his third proposal apparently had some impact: he suggested a program of expropriating large Polish (and German) estates in the Polish provinces and colonizing these with German farmers from the West. Hartmann's article was apparently read by several of the Prussian ministers responsible for the Settlement Law of 1886, which strongly resembled his proposal and of which he may be considered the spiritual father.

Inside the Prussian government, this new sense of urgency regarding the Polish question was expressed most clearly by Culture Minister Gustav von Gossler. He focused on the Polish danger more consistently than previous ministers and introduced an aggressive tone into his public statements which exceeded even Bismarck's. He felt himself confronted by a Polish national movement, which "has developed with growing force, . . . (aiming at) the liberation of the Polish fatherland (in the pre-1772 frontiers). . . . steadily growing extensively and intensively (e.g., in Upper Silesia)," aided by a network of organizations which, however apolitical outwardly, were "drawn completely into the circle of Polish agitation" and by the Polish-Catholic clergy, "associates and directors of the Polish national movement."[27] Gossler's tenure in office (1881-1891) witnessed the conclusion of the *Kulturkampf* and the reestablishment of relations with the Catholic Church, but also a simultaneous escalation of measures directed at Prussian Poles. He was supported by provincial officials who had come to similar conclusions about the need to confront the Polish problem. Christoph von Tiedemann, previously head of Bismarck's Imperial Chancellory, became *Regierungspräsident* in Bromberg in 1881 and quickly advocated a hard line against the Poles. To help the government keep better track of the Polish national movement, he began to prepare and circulate translations of the more nationalistic statements to be found in the Polish press.[28] Arthur von Posadowsky, future Imperial minister then serving as *Landrat* in Rawicz, also urged that more attention be paid to the Polish national movement and that steps be taken to protect the German language and nationality in the East. He branded as an illusion the notion that "consideration for the religious . . . or national feelings of the Poles will meet with any kind of appreciation on their part."[29]

Finally, spokesmen for the German minority in Poznania and West Prussia also began to make themselves felt as a factor in the new climate of anti-Polish sentiment. In the Landtag, German representatives from the two "Polish provinces" were not actually a minority, holding a 2:1 edge over Polish representatives with the help of the three-class voting system. They were invariably in the forefront of those disputing Polish claims and complaints and trying to pressure Bismarck into harsher anti-Polish measures. They even opposed the extension of provincial self-government to Poznania for fear that the Poles would dominate it and open the German population up to "Polish terrorism."[30] They frequently complained that the Germans of Poznania were being thrown onto the defensive as a result of German-Catholic support for Polish aspirations, the Polonizing efforts of the Catholic clergy, and the intermarriage of Germans with Polish women. In the words of their spokesman, "any German is lost when he marries a Pole, . . . (for) the Polish nation is distinguished by great personal charm."[31]

The first apparent major response to the Polish problem in its newly threatening demographic dimensions came in March 1885. Bismarck ordered the expulsion of more than 30,000 Russian subjects living in Prussia as resident aliens. This was not actually a new idea, having been first proposed by Bismarck himself in 1872 (see above, p. 21). He returned to this idea in 1881-2, ordering a precise count of these aliens and tighter measures against new entrants, but still nothing was done for a number of years, mainly because of the strong opposition of agrarian interests to the prospects of losing their supply of cheap farm workers at a time of falling farm prices and rising German wages.[32] Interior Minister von Puttkamer, who was in charge of this issue, was himself a West Prussian estate-owner and sympathetic to these concerns. But in 1885 the fear of rapid Polish advances in the Prussian East finally got the upper hand over agrarian interests. Bismarck and Gossler concluded that, "despite our acknowledgement of agriculture as the most important industry of all, we still consider it to be a lesser evil for a few areas to have a shortage of labor than for the state and its future to suffer." They dismissed Puttkamer's argument that most of the aliens were not only economically useful but well-behaved politically and not a burden to society: "Those aliens of faultless behavior, who are troublesome neither for the police nor for the welfare system, are often the most dangerous politically."[33]

In spite of its chronological proximity, it is not entirely clear that this expulsion measure was originally meant to be the beginning of the more comprehensive anti-Polish program launched the following year. Not only had this step been long in preparation, but it was not directed exclusively, perhaps not even primarily, at Prussian Poles. The expulsion measure, like the general climate of nationalist opinion in the early 1880s, was apparently as much anti-Semitic as anti-Polish. In so far as there was popular or local pressure on Bismarck to take action against the aliens, it came from small towns, whose citizens complained of unfair

Jewish economic competition. Of the 30,000-plus persons of Russian citizenship cited in Puttkamer's study of the problem, only about 60% were Catholic and presumably Polish, whereas some 30% were Jewish and 10% Protestants (presumably Germans or Balts).[34] The expulsion order, though opposed by Puttkamer and West Prussian *Oberpräsident* von Ernsthausen, was supported by many other eastern officials, themselves agrarians or close to agrarian interests, who apparently anticipated being rid of the economically or politically bothersome Jewish traders and artisans while hoping to retain the Polish farm workers.[35] In other words, this seems to have been a long-contemplated, one-shot measure, (undertaken in a vaguely nativist rather than specifically anti-Polish atmosphere) rather than the opening gun in a comprehensive anti-Polish campaign.

The Russians, who were asked to take back a large number of less-than-desirable subjects on very short notice, reacted mildly to the Prussian expulsion order. Considering the strained Russian-German relations which existed already (due to tariff and other economic differences), it is surprising that more friction was not generated. True, Russian consent followed only upon protracted negotiations, but these were caused mainly by fear that political subversives might be returned along with the expellees. The transient camps at the Russian border, to which the expellees were quickly transported (with, at most, a month's notice), were soon overcrowded as the Russians sifted slowly through the returnees. Some were refused by the Russians unless the Prussians had proof of their Russian citizenship, but by mid-summer 1885 the process was functioning smoothly. Actually, many Russian subjects, particularly those who had left in the first place to avoid conscription, chose not to return and migrated to the United States instead.[36] In July 1885, a second order was issued, affecting mainly Galician Poles; Austria, like Russia, made little effort to oppose Bismarck's will, despite the greater political weight of both Poles and Jews in the Dual Monarchy.[37]

The expulsions lasted through 1887; by the end of that year about 29,000 had been expelled and 3,000 more cases were still pending. Another 10,000 aliens were permitted to stay for various reasons.[38] The government seemed satisfied with the results; Puttkamer reported to Bismarck that "the removal of the existing inconveniences . . . has been undertaken in the most effective manner."[39] There were fewer Poles (and Jews), the burden on local schools and other public services was lessened, and there was some hope that the vacancies left by the expellees might help slow down the westward movement of Germans.[40] Of course, there were also less happy results, aside from the disruption of the expellees' lives. The expulsions had no significant long-term impact on the national

From Kulturkampf to Nationalitätenkampf

balance in the Polish provinces. They had little direct bearing on the organized Polish national movement, since the affected Poles were normally peripheral to Poznanian/West Prussian society. Nationalist feeling among Prussian Poles understandably rose another notch, especially among the lower classes who suffered most from the measure. And, as feared, a serious shortage of farm workers soon developed in many frontier counties; six small counties in West Prussia experienced a sudden loss of at least 1000 farm workers as a result of the expulsions. Their former employers played at first with such fantastic schemes as the importation of Chinese workers, but then found ways to import the needed Polish workers illegally.[41] Despite increased border patrols, it was impossible to prevent concerted efforts to circumvent the new restrictions. The low wages which aliens received combined with the small fines assessed against those landowners who were caught to make it more profitable to continue using imported labor; the westward migration of Prussian natives quickly resumed.

For some months after the expulsions began, they failed to attract much public attention in Germany. The order itself was issued quietly, without the fanfare and nationalist rhetoric with which Bismarck accompanied his anti-Polish measures of the following year. He justified the expulsions on vague grounds of "the public welfare and the internal peace and security of the state."[42] In response to an interpellation in the Landtag (May 6, 1885), Puttkamer acknowledged some nationalistic motivation but defended the measure mainly on utilitarian grounds, citing the burden of the aliens on schools and public services and the depressing effect on local wages, which encouraged the continued heavy emigration from the Prussian East.[43] Little nationalist bitterness was evident on the part of either Puttkamer or the Polish spokesman, Ignacy Łyskowski, who spent much of their speeches reminiscing about earlier times when Germans and Poles in their common home province supposedly got along better together.

But as a better idea of the extent of the expulsions emerged, those groups most affected by them began to express their concern. Agrarian opposition was most adamant, but Upper Silesian industrialists affected by the later expulsion of Galicians protested too, unhappy over the loss of their "very easily satisfied, only very little rewarded" workers.[44] Mercantile intersts in Königsberg and other towns whose trade with Russia often depended upon Jewish middlemen also had reason to complain.[45] The expellees themselves usually left the country quietly, especially Polish farm workers who were there on short-term contracts anyway. Some of the Jewish victims, especially those with considerable financial interests at stake, pleaded their cases with the government, expressing their monarchist and German-nationalist sentiments in the most extreme terms. Their cause was not helped by provincial officials who insinuated (without foundation) that such Jewish aliens were as often pro-Polish as pro-German. But those who did have the determination and resources to fight their expulsion often succeeded, mainly by exploiting the ambiguous Prussian naturalization and residence laws or becoming naturalized by another German state.[46]

In November 1885, the Poles and the Center introduced another interpellation motion, this time in the German Reichstag (where opposition parties had been in the majority since 1881). This particular issue was well suited to bring the different opposition parties together, precisely because the exact motivation for the expulsions was still unclear at the time. The Center continued to see them as primarily anti-Catholic; Windthorst described them as "a new measure of the *Kulturkampf* type."[47] Progressives (*Freisinnige*) chose to focus on the anti-Semitic aspect; Social Democrats joined up against what seemed a gratuitous slap at helpless proletarians. Thus these major German opposition parties, which aside from the Center had not previously gone to any extremes to support strictly Polish aspirations, congealed into a Reichstag majority in opposition to the expulsions. As several strongly-worded resolutions of censure were introduced, Bismarck attempted to head them off by appearing before the Reichstag with a letter from Emperor Wilhelm insisting on the sovereignty of the Prussian state in this matter. Bismarck's apparent conversion to the states rights camp won him only derision from Windthrost and his allies, who had little difficulty demonstrating to the Reichstag majority that the expulsions related directly to civil rights and foreign affairs and were thus well within the Empire's competence.[48]

Thus Bismarck saw himself compelled to answer for his expulsion measures before a hostile Reichstag in January 1886. He responded to this challenge with an appeal to nationalism; only now did the expulsions assume a clearly anti-Polish coloration. Bismarck argued that Prussia, in her newly-defined role as a German national state, had the right and duty to "protect the German nationality, in its continuance and in its development, against any injury by foreign elements," thus the expulsions were necessary. What had earlier been presented as a measure against aliens generally and often Jews specifically, motivated by internal security or utilitarian concerns, now became a matter of defense against aggressive Pan-Polish designs on the Prussian East. "Polish nationalism and Polish propaganda were the reason for the expulsions," said Bismarck; it was a simple matter of wanting "to be rid of the alien Poles because we have enough of our own."[49]

Bismarck hoped to divide the opposition coalition by appealing to national feelings; he expected in particular that the Progressives would be vulnerable to such an approach. But, whereas historians have often seen an integral relationship between the expulsions and the anti-Polish measures of 1886-7, many contemporaries did not. The Progressives refused to be taken in by Bismarck's reinterpretation and continued to dwell primarily on the anti-Semitic aspect, charging the government with efforts to suppress Jewish economic competition and to weaken the potential constituency of their party. It was in fact difficult to accept a German-nationalist rationale for the expulsion of German-speaking Jewish aliens from such 100%-German cities as Königsberg.[50] Not even the Poles were inclined to see themselves as the sole intended victims; their parliamentary remarks were considerably milder than the denunciations of their German allies. They typically described the expellees as "Catholics" rather than "Poles" and agreed with Windthorst that the issue was one of religious more than national persecution.[51] In any case, the opposition coalition remained intact; Bismarck was unable to prevent the passage of a censure motion, authored by Windthorst, "expressing the conviction that the expulsions of Russian and Austrian subjects, decreed by the royal Prussian government, do not, in their extent and in their manner, appear justified and are not compatible with the interests of the citizens of the Empire."[52] This was actually the mildest of the resolutions offered, the only one not demanding the rescission of the expulsions altogether.

This was the first such rebuff to emanate from the parliament of the Second German Empire, and the only one dealt to Bismarck. Though the Bundesrat refused to ratify it a week later, and it never really threatened to interfere with his freedom of action in any case, it did come as a major annoyance and potential threat to Bismarck; it was probably decisive in his launching subsequently of an offensive against the Poles. For this reason the expulsions of 1885 were related at least indirectly to the subsequent campaign: it was the parliamentary reaction to them which prompted Bismarck to launch a series of wide-ranging and previously unplanned measures against Prussian Poles early in 1886.

Notes

1. speech of December 3, 1884, *Reichstag*.
2. Johannes Heckel, "Die Beilegung des Kulturkampfes in Preussen," in *Das blinde, undeutliche Wort "Kirche"* (Cologne, 1964), p. 549.
3. report from Poznań, May 22, 1884, *GPSA Berlin*, Rep. 84a, #5964; Hans-Wolfgang Wetzel, *Presseinnenpolitik im Bismarckreich (1874-1890)* (Tübingen, 1975), p. 232.

4. speech of November 30, 1882, *Reichstag;* cf. Feldman, p. 350.

5. Hans-Jürgen Puhle, *Agrarische Interessenpolitik und preussischer Konservatismus im wilhelminischen Reich (1893-1914)* (Hannover, 1966), pp. 298ff.; cf. Hans Schleier and Gustav Seeber, "Zur Entwicklung und Rolle des Antisemitismus in Deutschland von 1871-1914," *Zeitschrift für Geschichtswissenschaft* 9(1961):1593-7.

6. *Grosse Depression und Bismarckzeit* (Berlin, 1967), p. 56.

7. "Germanisierung oder Polonisierung," *Jahrbücher für Nationalökonomie und Statistik,* NF 7(1883):457-463.

8. Leo Wegener, *Der wirtschaftliche Kampf der Deutschen mit den Polen um die Provinz Posen* (Posen, 1903), pp. 31, 66f.; Perdelwitz, p. 74; Broszat, p. 109.

9. speech of May 6, 1885, *Abgeordnetenhaus.*

10. Trzeciakowski, *Kulturkampf,* pp. 26, 273; the German share of the population of Oppeln regency remained constant at 37% during this period, reflecting no doubt the ability of this rapidly industrializing region to attract new German immigrants. See also Richard Böckh, "Die Verschiebung der Sprachenverhältnisse in Posen und Westpreussen," *Preussische Jahrbücher* 77(1894):424-436; Paul Stade, *Das Deutschtum vs. die Polen in Ost-und Westpreussen nach den Sprachzählungen von 1861, 1890, und 1900* (diss. Berlin) (Berlin, 1908).

11. Baske, p. 22.

12. *Wielkopolska,* p. 138.

13. quoted in Trzeciakowski, *Kulturkampf,* p. 25.

14. Wegener, p. 34; While the Catholic vs. Protestant/Jewish figures do not correspond exactly to those for Poles vs. Germans, the confessional figures are more reliable for the pre-1890 period and more useful for comparative purposes. To be sure, about 11% of Poznania's Catholics were German, but these lived in peripheral areas along the Silesian border or in the Netze valley; when these areas are subtracted, the difference between Poles and "bi-linguals" (c. 71% of Poznania's population) and Catholics (72%) becomes quite small. *Ibid.*

15. Max Bär, "Die 'Bamberger' bei Posen," *Zeitschrift für Geschichte und Landeskunde der Provinz Posen* 1(1882):295-368, describes the Polonization over several generations of a large group of German-Catholic colonists from Franconia.

16. Wilhelm Vallentin, *Westpreussen seit den ersten Jahrzehnten die 's Jahrhunderts,* ed. F. Neumann (Tübingen, 1893), pp. 30, 60f.

17. Gotthold Rhode (ed.), *Geschichte der Stadt Posen* (Neuendettelsau, 1953), p. 129.

18. Peter Quante, "Die Bevölkerungsentwicklung der preussischen Ostprovinzen im 19. und 20. Jahrhundert," *Zeitschrift für Ostforschung* 8(1959):481f.; see also Heinz Rogmann, *Die Bevölkerungsentwicklung im preussischen Osten in den letzten 100 Jahren* (Berlin, 1937); Józef Szaflarski, *Ruchy ludnościowe na pograniczu polsko-niemieckim w ciągu ostatniego wieku* (Bydgoszcz, 1947).

19. Hans-Ulrich Wehler, *Das Deutsche Kaiserreich, 1871-1914,* 2nd edit., (Göttingen, 1975), p. 45.

20. Waldemar Mitscherlich, *Der Einfluss der wirtschaftlichen Entwicklung auf den ostmärkischen Nationalitätenkampf* (Leipzig, 1910), pp. 18f.
21. Böhning, p. 19; Wolfgang Kohte, "Zur Volkstumsentwicklung Posens und Westpreussens im deutschen Wirtschaftsgefüge des 19. Jahrhunderts," *Deutsche Zeitschrift für Wirtschaftskunde* 3(1938):172-187.
22. Wegener, pp. 25, 39.
23. *Ibid.*, Table V.
24. *Ibid.*; Johannes Guttzeit, *Die Geschichte der deutschen Polenentrechtung* (Danzig, 1927), p. 154.
25. "Die Kolonisation in unserem Osten und die Herstellung des Erbzinses," *Preussische Jahrbücher* 44(1879):33, 37.
26. "Der Rückgang des Deutschtums," *Die Gegenwart* 27(1885):1-3, 19-22; cf. Helmut Neubach, "Eduard von Hartmanns Bedeutung für die Entwicklung des deutsch-polnischen Verhältnisses," *Zeitschrift für Ostforschung* 13(1964):106-159; for similar sentiments by a German-Austrian nationalist, see Albert von Randow, "Die Landesverweisungen aus Preussen und die Erhaltung des Deutschtums an der Ostgrenze," *Jahrbuch für Gesetzgebung Verwaltung und Volkswirtschaft im Deutschen Reich* 10(1886):91-125.
27. speech of February 7, 1882, *Abgeordnetenhaus*.
28. Tiedemann to Poznanian *Oberpräsident* Günther, June 21, 1882; Puttkamer's reply, August 26, 1882, *GPSA Berlin*, Rep. 8 30 I, #693; report from Bromberg, November 20, 1883, *Ibid.*, Rep. 84a, #5964.
29. quoted in report from Poznań (*Zeitungsbericht*), May 10, 1883, *Ibid.*
30. speech by Tiedemann-Bomst, November 11, 1880, *Abgeordnetenhaus*.
31. speech by Tiedemann-Bomst (not to be confused with *Regierungspräsident* von Tiedemann or Heinrich von Tiedemann-Seeheim, founder of the later *Ostmarkenverein*), March 14, 1883, *Ibid.*
32. Bismarck to Puttkamer, *Gesammelte Werke* VIc:241, December 18, 1881; Neubach, *Ausweisungen*, p. 13.
33. quoted in Neubach, *Ausweisungen*, pp. 31f.
34. *Ibid.*, pp. 15, 31.
35. *Ibid.*, p. 37.
36. *Ibid.*, pp. 40, 64, 68f.; detailed accounts in *Archiwum Państwowe Wojewódstwie*, Bydgoszcz, Abt. des Innern, I 879.
37. *Ibid.*, p. 60; Adam Galos, "Rugi pruskie na Górnym Śląsku (1885-1890)," *Sobótka* 9(1954):56-107.
38. *Ibid.*, p. 130; Joachim Mai, *Die preussisch-deutsche Polenpolitik, 1885-7* (East Berlin, 1962), p. 98.
39. memo of January 21, 1886, "Massregeln zur Stärkung des Deutschtums in den östlichen Landestheilen," *GPSA Berlin*, 84a, #4066.
40. Neubach, *Ausweisungen*, pp. 131ff.
41. *Ibid.*, pp. 58, 133ff.
42. *Ibid.*, p. 30.
43. speech of May 6, 1885, *Abgeordnetenhaus*; The expellees were in fact concentrated in relatively few counties, where they sometimes amounted to 5% of the population and a much higher percentage of the school population,

Neubach, *Ausweisungen*, pp. 28f.

44. words of Oppeln *Regierungspräsident* von Zedlitz quoted by Neubach, *Ausweisungen*, p. 59.

45. *Ibid.*, p. 40; Mai, pp. 50ff.

46. *Ibid.*, p. 38; Mai, p. 58.

47. speech of May 6, 1885, *Abgeordnetenhaus*.

48. debate of December 1, 1885, *Reichstag*; the German constitution also gave jurisdiction over *Fremdenpolizei* to the Imperial government.

49. speeches of December 1, 1885, *Ibid.*, and January 28, 1886, *Abgeordnetenhaus*.

50. speech by Julius Möller, January 15, 1886, *Reichstag*.

51. speech by Jażdżewski, *Ibid.*

52. January 16, 1886, Reichstag; cf. document #45, *Anlagen*.

Chapter III:
The Anti-Polish Offensive of 1886

Bismarck was not the sort of politician, under the best of conditions, to take in stride a setback like the Reichstag's censure of his expulsion measures. The relatively insignificant domestic echo bothered him less than the presumed loss of face in the eyes of foreign powers, especially Russia. He felt a need, almost a compulsion it seems, to demonstrate quickly that he was still in control of a German Empire united behind him, an image which he considered vital to a successful foreign policy. Thus in January 1886, before the final vote on Windthorst's motion but with the outcome already clear, Bismarck determined to break up the opposition majority in the Reichstag by launching a nationalist campaign against the Polish minority in Prussia. There was little he could do about the make-up of the Reichstag itself; new elections would not have improved his position there. He turned therefore to the Prussian Landtag, where the three-class voting system provided a dependable majority; under the complicated Bismarckian constitution, the Landtag was to be "an important support for the government if a majority hostile to the Empire should be present sometime in the Reichstag."[1]

This campaign was inaugurated with a sentence inserted by Bismarck into the King's traditional opening speech to the Landtag, promising "measures for the protection of the German element in the eastern provinces against Polonizing efforts."[2] At the same time, he informed his ministers at the January 10, 1886, cabinet meeting that, "due to the aggressive behavior of 'Polonism,' which has appeared recently, especially because of the expulsions of foreigners over the eastern frontier, a more rigorous resumption of resistance to Polonization, even the encouragement of Germanization, is called for."[3] As noted previously, the Poles themselves had reacted relatively mildly to the expulsions; they protested, of course, as they had done for decades, but in a more or less formal manner. What disturbed Bismarck much more was the position of the larger, German opposition parties and the fact that for the first time the Poles had found support among them on an essentially Polish issue. He acknowledged in fact that "a special cause of this (new policy) lies also in the support which Center and Progressive parties have granted to the Poles."[4]

Bismarck intentionally fashioned his subsequent measures against the Poles in such a way that German Catholics and Jews would not consider themselves directly involved and German opposition parties might relax their support for Polish aspirations. Especially with regard to the Progressives, he was confident that their constituents, given the decline of liberal cosmopolitanism and the general growth of popular nationalism in the 1880s, "would not appreciate any further support for anti-German aspirations."[5] He hoped that the Center too, now that the *Kulturkampf* was over, would reflect the new nationalist sentiments. He tried, through his new relationship with the Vatican, to get the Pope to help bring the Center around to his way of thinking. In a letter to the German ambassador to the Vatican, he accused the Center of having participation in "a frivolous attack upon the Empire and the State" and gave that party much of the blame for the anti-Polish measures he was preparing. To make sure that the new measures would not be misunderstood in Rome, he emphasized that "the Polish question is solely one of nationality and has nothing at all to do with the position of the Catholic Church in the German Empire and in no way concerns German Catholics." As for Polish-Catholic priests, he "required worldly means of defense . . . against such embittered enemies of our state and our nationality as the Polish clergy. . . . We must remain in a position to intern Polish clerics who are dangerous to the state or be able to expell them from the country." He urged the Pope, as a "conservative and peace-loving" man, to keep the clergy out of leadership positions in the "Polish conspiracy against the state" and prevent them from "publicly . . . stirring up hate against the government of the King."[6]

Also at the cabinet meeting of January 10, Bismarck introduced a memorandum from his protegé, Christoph von Tiedemann, head of Bromberg Regency in Poznania. This memorandum, commissioned recently by Bismarck and received only two days prior to this meeting, was placed immediately at the head of the agenda.[7] Its contents reflected Tiedemann's (rather than Bismarck's) concept of the Polish problem. His first-hand experience in the Polish region had taught him some things about the Polish movement which Bismarck himself apparently was unaware of, or at least never acknowledged. For example, Tiedemann considered the rapidly developing Polish middle classes, "petty" and upper, urban and rural, to be the most "dangerous" (because economically most vigorous) segment of Polish society. He saw the growing Polish middle class as a chief cause (though it was more likely a result) of the westward emigration of Germans, especially German Jews, and the other adverse demographic trends which had appeared recently. He contended that the Polish problem was no longer simply a matter of the political opposition of the upper classes, of nobility and clergy; it had developed new demographic and economic aspects due to the relative growth of Polish numbers and the gradual "bourgeois" transformation of Polish society.

As for the Polish nobility, many of them were finding it more difficult than ever to maintain the economic underpinnings of their political and social position. According to Tiedemann, a significant part of the noble leadership was in a very precarious economic position, sliding deeper and deeper into debt due to the chronically low grain prices and other aspects of the "Long Depression." His memorandum contained a number of more or less standard political responses to the Polish problem, e.g., a special fund to grant bonuses to German civil servants and teachers in Polish areas, removal of the last traces of Polish as a second official language, complete state control to hire, fire, and transfer teachers in Polish areas, and the stationing of all-German army units in these areas. Most noteworthy, however, was Tiedemann's suggestion for an attack on what he saw as the economic roots of the Polish problem; he proposed that the government exploit the economic vulnerability of the Polish estate owners by buying out as many of them as possible. He proposed also that these estates be parcelled into homesteads and settled by German farmers from the West, thus helping to reverse the east-west population flow which was adversely affecting the national balance.[8]

The idea of buying up the estates of Polish nobles was not without precedent in Prussian history (see above, p. 2); Bismarck himself had considered it from time to time. But to parcel these estates and colonize them with Germans was new, as was the introduction of such economic weapons generally into the national struggle. Tiedemann (like Hartmann, by whom he may have been influenced), differed from Bismarck in his emphasis on economic weapons and his feeling that the Empire should be moving more rapidly toward ethnic homogeneity. Despite Bismarck's hostility toward the Polish national movement as represented by nobles and clergy, estate-parcelling and ethnic homogeneity were not part of his political outlook; he saw no need to involve the Polish masses in the national struggle, as Tiedemann's approach surely would. Thus one would expect Tiedemann's suggestions along these lines to have occasioned some opposition from Bismarck. Instead, on this particular occasion, he approved virtually all of his subordinate's proposals. Indeed, Bismarck even supplemented them by suggesting that the cabinet consider "whether the reestablishment of the penalty of property confiscation can be recommended for the provinces of Poznania and West

Prussia," an apparent preview of the most extreme manifestation of anti-Polish feeling under the Second Empire: the Expropriation Law of 1908.[9] Only the Emperor's opposition caused this idea to be dropped before it became public, but it suggests how far Bismarck was willing to go in 1886. It appears, in other words, that Bismarck, under the impact of the pending Reichstag censure, reacted impetuously, perhaps uncharacteristically, seizing upon previously alien ideas and taking them suddenly "very seriously" in order to counter the Reichstag.[10]

Bismarck's resolve to strike back at the Reichstag majority by means of a nationalist initiative in the Landtag came as a surprise to his fellow ministers and parliamentary allies. When he remarked casually (during the heated debate on the censure motion) that, with 100 million Marks, he could solve the Polish problem by buying up most of the Polish estates, the Reichstag took little notice and his allies assumed that he had been misunderstood.[11] At the January 10 cabinet meeting, his ministers apparently had no advance notice and, with Tiedemann's memorandum serving as a general guide, were given only fourteen days to prepare new decrees or legislative proposals directed at the Polish threat. When the cabinet convened two weeks later, it resolved to increase financial support for elementary schools, hire more nationally-minded German teachers, keep "anti-German" elements out of school administrations, improve national consciousness among judges and civil servants and give them salary bonuses for serving in Polish areas, and encourage the settlement of German peasants in the Polish provinces by buying up and parcelling large estates there.[12] The ministers of Culture, Interior, Justice, War, Agriculture, and Finance (*i.e.*, all those with even a marginal hand in Polish affairs) presented various proposals for combatting "Polonism." Not surprisingly, many of these were hurried and either impractical, picayune, or set aside because they failed to comply with the "positive" image which Bismarck desired; primarily "coercive measures," though he might be "generally in agreement with" them, should "not be put in the foreground." Bismarck wanted some measures with positive social side-effects, such as the settlement project, in order to secure the support of the National Liberals in the Landtag at a time when there was no apparent groundswell of support for an anti-Polish campaign among the German public at large. Puttkamer's proposal to restrict the use of Polish at public assemblies and Gossler's suggestion that the Catholic Church be made to conform to the state's official language regulations and use German publicly in the Polish provinces were examples of "negative" measures which were tabled for the time being.[13] For public consumption, the cabinet issued a general statement of its intention "to check Polish-national agitation in the eastern provinces through suitable positive measures and to intercede permanently, systematically, and with total determination for the preservation and strengthening of the German population and German culture in these provinces."[14]

Simultaneously, government supporters in the Landtag, using wording very similar to the cabinet's, introduced the so-called Achenbach Resolution:

> "1., to express satisfaction that in the speech from the Throne positive measures for securing the continuance and development of the German population and of German culture in these provinces are held in prospect, and 2., to declare the willingness to grant the necessary means for the implementation of such measures, especially in the area of school affairs and general administration as well as for the encouragement of the settlement of German farmers and farm tenants in these provinces."[15]

By this resolution, named for its Landtag sponsor but authored reportedly by Tiedemann,[16] Bismarck hoped to give the impression that his new policies were in part a response to parliamentary, popular wishes and that the legislators were not functioning merely as the passive instruments of his own desire for revenge. The discussion of this resolution also provided the occasion for a major "Poland debate" in the Landtag (January 28-9, 1886), during which Bismarck delivered the most extensive remarks of his career on the Polish question. Ranging far and wide over the history of Prussian-Polish relations, he hinted at pan-Polish plots against the Empire and all things German, described the plight of Germans in the Slavic East in the darkest colors, emphasized repeatedly the theme of Poles "pushing back" Germans, and on numerous occasions overstepped the line separating the conservative Prussian statesman from the common nationalist demagogue. The expulsion issue, the immediate cause of the present controversy, was pushed into the background as he concentrated instead on a variety of non-issues. He offered a long, emotional defense of the existing eastern frontier; he warned the Poles that, while he desired good relations with them, they should not expect him "ever to recognize the claims of our Polish colleagues to the restoration of any Polish empire within the Prussian frontiers," though this had not been seriously advocated for some time even by Polish nationalists. He denounced the Reichstag censure motion in the strongest terms, overlooking however the chief forces behind this setback (the German opposition parties) in favor of concentrating the full weight of his attack on the small number of conservative and probably bewildered *Koło Polskie* deputies seated before him. He asserted more bluntly than ever before that not only the expulsions but the entire *Kulturkampf* would never have been necessary but for the Poles and his need to combat "Polish-Catholic" (as opposed to German-Catholic) forces.[17]

What is remarkable about this two-day speech of January 28-9 is less the specific new policies it contained than the newly vehement anti-Polish tone. It was fair to conclude (as several Polish leaders did), that it amounted to a declaration of war by Bismarck's government against Prussia's Polish population, and thus marks the beginning of a new era in Prussian-Polish relations. In effect, Bismarck signaled an end to the previous attempts, however fitful, to win over the Polish popualtion to the Prussian state idea. He conceded that "the endeavor to win the benevolence of the Polish population, at least that of their leaders, the Polish nobility, for the Prussian state idea has been a mistake, an error . . . which we consider as our duty to our country and Germany to renounce." He no longer considered the international agreements which had accompanied Prussia's acquisition of most of the Polish lands even morally binding and would not "give a penny for any appeal to the (royal) proclamations of those times." He dismissed the likelihood that the new settlement project (announced here in outline form), *i.e,* state purchases of land for the settlement of Germans exclusively, might be contrary to the Prussian and German constitutions, striking a perhaps revealing analogy: "In war, too, some things happen whereby one completely loses sight of 'equality before the law.'"[18] These passages indicate pretty clearly that the period when Prussia, officially at least, viewed her Poles as fellow-citizens, however difficult and untrustworthy they might occasionally be, was now giving way to one in which they were viewed as enemy aliens in a state of permanent hostility toward the state and its German-speaking majority. To combat them, Bismarck was now prepared to go beyond previous precedents, using economic as well as political weapons, attacking the Polish population in general as well as the noble-clerical leadership.

During the following months, a large number of anti-Polish measures emerged, some the result of legislative action, others simply decreed by the competent ministers. The most important and best known of these was the Settlement Law (*Ansiedlungsgesetz*) of April 26, 1886. While Bismarck's decision to push this law through the Landtag was apparently sudden, a result above all of the Reichstag censure motion, the idea itself was of much older vintage. In fact, it was a merger of several disparate concepts, some analysis of which is crucial to an understanding of the exact shape of the Settlement Law and some of its later problems as well.

The first major component concept embodied in the Settlement Law was Flottwell's "Fund for Estate Management" of the 1830s.[19] This involved the use of state funds to buy out politically objectionable Polish nobles, eliminating them economically and (hopefully) politically from the province. Their estates were either to be sold to reliable Germans or (more often) kept in state hands and leased to German managers. To this extent, Flottwell's Fund served as a partial precedent for the 1886 law, except that it did not include the social-political aspect; it did not parcel estates, settle German farmers, or attempt seriously to alter the ethnic balance in Poznania.

The second major component of the Settlement Law might be termed neo-feudalist, associated as it was with conservative/agrarian efforts to circumvent the liberal-inspired 1850 law prohibiting hereditary lease (*Erbpacht*) contracts between landowners and tenants.[20] As industrialization surged and Ostelbian estate owners began to experience labor shortages, many of them saw the *Erbpacht* idea as a solution. Under this concept, an estate owner could set aside small parcels of land, each with a cottage and fair-sized garden. These parcels would be given to local farm workers on a permanent, hereditary basis in exchange for a money rent or labor for the landowner, or they might also be purchased outright by installment payments over a long period of time as an alternative. It was hoped that these parcels would be an incentive to such workers to remain in the East by giving them a greater feeling of security than was available to western industrial workers. The parcels would also give the farm workers something to live from during the time of the year when the landowner had no need to employ them.[21]

A third component was associated with prominent "social liberals" under the name *Rentengut*, or "property bought on the installment plan." Part of the *Erbpacht* idea at first, the *Rentengut* foresaw larger, economically self-sufficient farms instead of small farm-laborer plots. These farms were to be carved out of existing estates and domain lands throughout Germany, paid for in installments with the aid of low-interest loans from the state. *Rentengut* advocates included National Liberals like Johannes Miquel, Gustav Schmoller, Rudolf von Bennigsen and Max Sering, who desired the creation of a larger class of medium-sized farmers in the Prussian East for several reasons. It would help alleviate the labor shortage in Ostelbia by replacing large estates requiring hundreds of farm workers with supposedly more efficient independent farmers. Even for those large estates which remained, "where a medium-sized ownership class is present, the working class will also find itself better off and is more likely to remain . . . because it has hope of getting ahead. Thus the question of forming new, medium-sized farms is also connected very substantially with the labor and emigration questions."[22] *Rentengüter* would also help prevent the proletarianization of society, buttressing the idea of private property by making it easier for the non-propertied classes to acquire.

> "For the state it is a question of establishing in the interst of the whole a social order which softens the existing property differences and class conflicts and removes the cause of the depopulation of the eastern provinces with all its harmful side-effects. A system of steps should be established which makes possible a gradual rise by industrious elements. Only then does private property in land gain its full moral and economic value. . . . Such a middle class forms the firmest bulwark against all the cravings of misguided urban masses to destroy violently the state structure."[23]

Finally, in party-political terms this policy would not hurt either, since middle-class farmers were an important part of the National Liberal constituency.

Until 1886, each of these ideas had been around for some time but none of them seemed to be making much progress. A bill combining *Erbpacht* and *Rentengut* concepts managed to pass the Prussian lower house in 1874, only to be stopped in the upper house, where most members were still suspicious of any project involving the parcelling of estates.[24] Bismarck backed the *Erbpacht* idea for a time but later rejected it as "too medieval-feudal."[25] More recently, agrarians had turned increasingly to the use of alien farm labor from Russia and Austria, while the *Rentengut* idea seemed to languish. Despite support in academic circles, it failed to win the backing of Bismarck and others with political influence and its advocates were beginning to despair when Bismarck's new interest in the Polish problem gave their cause, as incorporated in Tiedemann's memorandum, new life in 1886.

The Flottwellian concept, with the state buying up Polish estates and selling them intact or merely holding onto them, also had its advocates before 1886. Bismarck occasionally touched on the possibility of resurrecting the Flottwell Fund, but he did not work for it consistently. In 1861, while trying to talk Alexander II out of making concessions to the Poles, he suggested that the best way to protect Prussia from the side-effects of such a policy was to encourage the "steady growth of the local German element," as he thought Flottwell had done.[26] In 1875, he asked whether "in case the parcelling of domain should be continued, the attempt should not be made to proceed, especially in the Polish territories of the provinces of Poznania, West Prussia and Silesia, to create German peasant homesteads."[27] In the early 1880s, Gossler seemed to conduct a somewhat lonely campaign in behalf of this idea. He reported in 1884 that he had used some "extra" funds under his administration to purchase a Polish estate in ethnically-mixed Fraustadt/Wschowa County. He knew of two other socially prominent Polish magnates who were then looking for buyers for estates they owned. He believed that this first purchase had already resulted in a "strengthening of German influence" locally and that additional purchases of this type could be very effective in a nationalist sense. On this occasion, however, scarcely a year before the introduction of the Settlement Law, this suggestion elicited little response and was simply passed over by the cabinet.[28]

In September 1885, after the expulsion measures had caused interest in the Polish question to rise, Gossler tried again, "reminding" his colleagues of his previous effort to draw their attention to the fact that "quite large estates belonging to Polish landowners are for sale and, through their purchase, the German element in the province of Poznania could be strengthened." He reported that he had used his ministry's funds to buy another estate and leased it out at a profit; he knew of at least twelve others, amounting to about 17,000 ha., up for sale by Polish owners. He wanted "at least to assure himself that the State Ministry is in agreement with him if he proceeds further in this direction." Bismarck was now more interested, remarking that he was "in complete agreement with the expediency of such a step, as long as the means are available." It might even be well to consider setting up a fund, similar to Flottwell's, "for the expressed purpose of Germanization."[29] Most likely, when Tiedemann was subsequently commissioned to draw up his memorandum, Bismarck expected a project along strictly Flottwellian lines, without the (for him) extraneous ideas of parcellization and settlement of German farmers.

In any case, the Settlement Law of 1886 grew out of, and contained within it, several different concepts which were not always mutually compatible. This perhaps explains why National Liberal leaders, when approached hesitantly in January 1886 about a modest project along Flottwellian lines, surprised Bismarck by their quick affirmative response. As Agriculture Minister Lucius recalled, Miquel was "all fire" when the subject was mentioned to him and urged that the law not be funded with a mere 20 million Marks (all that Bismarck felt he could safely request from the Landtag) but with 100 million Marks, or about $500,000,000 in today's terms.[30] Miquel was doubtless aware that the *Rentengut* concept, calling for heavy state investment in schools and similar amenities, with only slow capital return in the form of long-term installment payments, would be much more expensive than Flottwell's method of simply shifting ownership from Poles to Germans or the German state. National Liberal leaders probably understood that Bismarck had his own reasons for taking up the settlement project and his own ideas of how it should be done. They apparently hoped to slip *Rentengut* ideas into the new project; once tested in the Polish provinces it could then be extended throughout Prussia and Germany.

Bismarck was willing to let the liberals interpret his motives as they liked, as long as they supported his bills and let him deal with the Poles (and the Reichstag opposition) to his satisfaction. He may have been discomfitted when Tiedemann's proposal bore a closer resemblance to the *Rentengut* than to the Flottwellian concept, but he did not make an issue of it at first. In fact, he was not opposed to parcelling under all circumstances, but he wanted it along the lines desired by *Erbpacht* conservatives. He wanted smaller, worker-peasant plots, not the large *Rentengut* homesteads intended to provide a comfortable existence for farmers with higher expectations. His concept of the village idyll, as spelled out in the course of discussions of the Settlement Law, was far removed from that of German liberals:

> "Tenants and small cottagers, who manage by harnessing cows or a single horse, unless the opportunity (for supplemental income from) freight transport facilitates the wintering of several horses. . . . Farms of about eight hectares (20 acres) as the healthiest size for small agrarian holdings, where the peasant himself lends a hand to every job, keeps a farm hand only seldom, and does not have more than one horse; or (also) small plots for workers with their own house and garden property."[31]

Responsibility for drafting the Settlement Law was given to Lucius, since it seemed to fall within the sphere of the Agriculture Ministry. He produced a proposal vaguely entitled "For the Encouragement of Agriculture through the Founding and Preservation of Homesteads." It turned out that Lucius leaned even more strongly than his fellow Free Conservative Tiedemann toward the *Rentengut* concept. As recently as November 1885, he had presented a memorandum (which Bismarck apparently overlooked) urging favorable action on *Rentengüter*. Now, with only two weeks to work with, he seems to have simply imposed the settlement idea on a slightly altered version of his *Rentengut* plan. The greater part of his proposed law dealt with ways to help the peasant class compete with large estates and with detailed descriptions of *Rentengut* institutions. It was not limited to the Polish provinces and did not even mention the Poles specifically.[32] Bismarck and his fellow conservatives became concerned that *Rentengut* advocates were taking off in their own direction, ignoring the chief, anti-Polish purpose of the measure. Puttkamer insisted that "the state does not have the job, nor the ability, to readjust fundamentally the relationship between large and small landowners." He considered *Rentengüter* to be a dangerous experiment and wanted the purpose of the Settlement Law made clear: "to strengthen the Germans in the East, period." Bismarck also expressed his consternation that Lucius' draft "did not relate at all to the particular task of defending against 'Polonism'" and demanded major revisions. He insisted that the social-political, settlement and parcelling aspects of the bill remain strictly secondary to the primarily political purpose, namely the removal of the economic underpinning of the Polish noble leadership.[33]

The Settlement Law, revised with the help of Tiedemann, reappeared before the cabinet two weeks later as an essentially different bill. Its purpose was made clear: to increase the German population of the rural East, implicitly and inevitably at the expense of the Polish. The project was to be restricted to the Polish provinces and the state would retain control over the resale of any homesteads created under this law. Alongside the larger homesteads, which could be purchased outright through installment payments, provision was also made for the smaller farmer-worker plots which Bismarck preferred, as well as some parcels which would be subject to an annual rent not leading to eventual ownership. Steps were also taken to keep the operations of the Settlement Law fairly removed from public or Landtag scrutiny, aside from an obligation to present a single annual report to the Prussian parliament. For Lucius, the most painful revision was the removal of the project from his ministry and the creation instead of a special commission, the Settlement Commission (*Ansiedlungskommission*), to supervise it, answerable only to the cabinet as a whole. Though one of Bismarck's closer associates, Lucius apparently could not persuade Bismarck that he was the right man to direct a vigorous nationalist effort.[34] Bismarck intended to keep the project in the hands of people who shared his own views, more attuned to *Erbpacht* than *Rentengut* visions.

Bismarck was apparently never reconciled to the idea of creating a class of independent farmers on formerly Polish estates. For one thing, he had misgivings about getting the German public accustomed to having the state buy out estate owners for social purposes.[35] As *Germania* editorialized, following announcement of this project: 'Bebel and Liebknecht must be shouting for joy over this new confirmation of their concept and hope that with respect to property the state can and may do everything," a sentiment that was shared by many Germans on the government's side as well.[36] Bismarck wanted only to establish state control over as many Polish estates as possible. Otherwise, he claimed to be "as little enthusiastic about this colonization (at home) as he was about that overseas."[37] He found the *Rentengut* concept unsatisfactory also because it turned land over to individuals, whose ownership might make them feel too "independent," rather than to the state. If larger farms had to be created, then he preferred that the state lease the parcels at first, "in order to get to know the lessees," before permitting the reliable among them to acquire full ownership."³⁸

The Settlement Law even as revised was thus not entirely to Bismarck's liking. He went along at this time only because he wanted quick Landtag approval as an effective response to the Reichstag. When Wilhelm von Kardorff complained that, while the buying up of Polish estates was okay with him, "the way that is foreseen in the Settlement Law, settling German peasants on the acquired estates, was very dubious," Bismarck assured him that such reservations "correspond to my own view, (but) the National Liberal Party has made the settlement of German peasants a precondition of its support for the budget request and thus compels me to give in." He did not like the carving up of estates any more than other conservatives, he said, but in the wake of the Reichstag censure, he was determined to pay almost any price to achieve his "splendid satisfaction (*glänzende Genugtuung*)."³⁹ Actually, even fellow conservative ministers like Puttkamer doubted that impoverished or neo-serfdom conditions would help the German cause; "the most successful manner of settlement is the establishment of larger livelihoods with their own teams of horses and, if possible, within self-contained, completely German villages."⁴⁰

As eventually passed, the Settlement Law sought in effect to please everyone: it allowed for several types of land transfer, including outright purchase through installment payments and temporary and long-term leases; Miquel even succeeded in restoring the original *Rentengut* paragraphs deleted from Lucius' draft. As for the size of the parcels, the law was imprecise; Bismarck assured Miquel that they would be large enough to support a middle-class type of farmer, but the final determination here was left up to the Settlement Commission, over which Bismarck expected to have the prevailing influence.⁴¹ The law, as passed April 26, 1886, provded 100 million marks for "the strengthening of the German element . . . against Polonizing attempts by settling German peasants and workers." A Settlement Commission, composed of four ministers, four Landtag representatives, a chairman, and the Minister-President of Prussia, was established to administer the funds allocated. Bismarck chose Robert von Zedlitz-Trützschler, *Regierungspräsident* in Oppeln/Opole, to be chairman, though he does not seem to have jumped at the opportunity. In spite of the promise of direct access to Bismarck and near-cabinet status, the job was apparently not considered comparable to the presidency of a province or regency. Zedlitz agreed to take the job only when he was made *Oberpräsident* of Poznania as well, with the chairmanship of the Commission included among the regular duties of the provincial chief.⁴² Thus the Commission became part of the regular provincial bureaucracy instead of the independent agency Bismarck hoped to create. The 100 million Marks were to be spent to buy properties, carry out their amelioration and subdivision or resale, and cover whatever community costs might arise. Whether sold or leased, the state was to be assured of "appropriate indemnification" and any returns would flow back into the Commission's fund. In fact, this "indemnification" did not mean that the state would ever break even; losses of several million Marks annually were taken for granted if the state charged 2% interest to settlers but had to sell bonds which paid 4% to fund the law in the first place.[43]

Several basic rationales were cited to justify the Settlement Law in parliamentary debates and to appeal for support beyond the three-class Landtag to German public opinion at large. There was some effort by Lucius to sell the project as a "positive,' social-political measure with *Rentengut* coloration. He intimated that that high percentage of land in the form of large estates in Poznania and West Prussia (55% and 57% respectively) had played a role in the selection of these two (incidentally part-Polish) provinces to receive the benefits of the new law.[44] Greatest emphasis, however, was on the danger posed by an aggressive Polish movement and the need for this measure as a defensive reaction. According to Lucius' "Rationale" (*Begründung*), which accompanied the law:

> "The Polish nationality is notoriously seeking, and not without success, to extend itself more and more in certain eastern provinces, while displacing the existing German elements. Such advances, in important regions of the monarchy, by a nationality which, by language and custom, is fundamentally alienated from the life of the Prussian State, demand extensive defense measures in all areas of state administration . . . to protect the interests of the German population, to prevent the flooding of these regions by Polish elements, and to open the way more and more to German intellect and German culture."[45]

Actually, as figures collected by Gossler and presented to the cabinet during deliberations on the settlement project show, the Polish nationality measured in terms of land ownership was in steady retreat in Prussia. Even without help from the government, Poles had lost 24% of their 1860 land holdings during the following 25 years. By 1885, they owned only 34% of the privately owned land in "their" two chief provinces:[46]

regency	% land owned by Poles	% loss since 1860
Poznań/Posen	51%	23%

Bromberg/Bydgoszcz	42%	22%
Marienwerder/Kwidzyn	13%	30%
Danzig/Gdańsk	9%	28%

In other words, while Bismarck might use the specter of "Poles pushing back Germans" to stimulate the Landtag and German public opinion, the opposite was actually true. After years of agricultural depression, the Polish nobility (which accounted for the bulk of the above losses) was just then especially vulnerable to a state-sponsored attack on its economic foundations.

In fact, though Bismarck chose to focus his attack on the Polish nobility, it was the Polish peasant who constituted the real problem from his point of view. In Poznania, Poles still held 60% of the peasant-owned land (vs. 45% of the noble-owned land); Polish peasants were holding onto and even increasing slightly this share.[47] While the trend in estate ownership before 1886 was clearly in favor of the Germans, it was the tendency of the Polish peasant to increase his share of the land in the Polish provinces which formed the chief obstacle to the state's efforts to strengthen the German element there. Even conservatives came to realize that the Flottwellian concept was no longer enough, that one had to bring in German settlers and not merely get the estates into state hands. In Lucius' words, "the simple transfer of landed property, especially of larger estates, into German hands has by no means the Germanizing value that we must hope for from this proposal."[48]

For this reason, it was at least incongruous for Bismarck and his associates to uphold a dichotomy between the Settlement Law's effect on the Polish nobility and its lack of effect on the Polish masses. They argued that it was not directed against the Polish nationality as such, but rather against a certain type of political behavior practiced by Polish nobles and clergy. In fact, however often Bismarck might deny any intention to harm the Polish rural population, it was clear that if a Polish estate, worked primarily by Polish farm workers (90% of the farm workers in Poznania were Polish), were sold and parcelled out for German colonists from the West, these Poles would be without a basis for their existence and most likely forced out of the province along with the former estate owner. That is to say, the Settlement Law clearly implied the partial displacement of one rural group (Polish farm workers) by another (independent German peasants). Miquel's comment to the Herrenhaus to the effect that Poles who learned German well might be considered for homesteads[49] was without official effect and such Poles were never in fact given consideration under this law.

The Settlement Law passed easily (214:120) in the Prussian lower house, a foregone conclusion once the National Liberals were satisfied. Bismarck failed, however, to win over any of the groups which had joined to censure him in the more representative Reichstag, e.g., Center, Progressives, Social Democrats, or particularists. Though he got all the anti-Polish laws he desired from the Landtag, his "satisfaction" had to be less than complete as long as it remained clear that parties representing the majority of Germans were unpersuaded by his arguments and opposed to the stepped-up anti-Polish policy. Reaction from those European capitals on which he always kept one eye was also not very comforting. Russian reaction to his new measures against the Poles was largely negative and included threatened reprisals against the Baltic Germans on the part of opposition Pan-Slav groups and even the government. Austrian reaction was bound to be unfavorable; the Poles of Galicia were an important support of the Taaffe government and looked upon by some even as a third ruling nationality in the Habsburg Empire. As the Vienna *Neue Freie Presse* remarked:

> "Bismarck's hatred of this people (the Poles) is so great that his speech (of January 28-9, 1886) becomes an involuntary critique of our policy. . . . The position of the Poles (in Austria) becomes a wedge which threatens to break up the most powerful alliance. . . . Even more significant than his energy, tearing down all guarantees of civic equality, is the view from which it arises, the unbridgeable opposition that exists between the political motives of Prince Bismarck and those of our Empire."[50]

Austria-Hungary's Foreign Minister Kálnoky, while no friend of the Poles, refused to approve the expulsion orders and informed the German ambassador to Vienna that Austrians of all classes were upset by Bismarck's anti-Polish speech of January 28-9.[51] Some months later, an interpellation in the Austrian Reichsrat by German deputies asked seriously whether the alliance with Germany was still in effect.[52] Thus in the short run at least, Bismarck failed to find the hoped-for echo among either the Reichstag opposition parties or in major foreign capitals.

Returning to the settlement project itself, a number of important issues were not resolved in the law itself but were decided by the cabinet in subsequent months and years. For example, there was the politically sensitive question of whether to buy from German as well as Polish landowners, if the former volunteered their estates for sale. Some of the project's backers, including social liberals who hoped to stress social-political along with nationalist goals and who saw this as the first step toward an estate-subdividing program for the whole Empire, wanted German-owned lands included. Many German estate owners in the

Polish provinces, as close to bankruptcy as their Polish neighbors, felt that they ought to share in the "benefits" of the new law. On the other hand, conservatives from non-Polish areas feared that buying from Germans might awaken "socialistic" ambitions among the populace. The cabinet decided at first that the Commission could buy German estates if there was a chance that it would otherwise go into Polish hands, but that such purchases "should take place only as an exception and after previously acquired authorization from the State Ministry." And then it should concentrate its buying at forced sales (*i.e.*, from already bankrupt owners), and avoid "putting the desire to be kind to needy estate owners in the foreground."[53] Of course, it proved unwieldy for the cabinet to rule on each purchase from a German landowner and before long these decisions were made by Zedlitz and his officials in Poznań. Bismarck foresaw that German estate owners would not be above taking advantage of the new law; he cautioned Zedlitz that it would be better to let an occasional estate go to the Poles than let the Commission be coerced by intimations that this or that German was about to sell to a Pole if the Commission failed to meet his price. Within the year, the cabinet was compelled to issue tighter restrictions on the purchase from Germans:

> "As a rule, one should stick to the principle, approved by the royal State Ministry, that state funds provided by the law of 26 April 1886 should not be used for the purchase of properties from Germans, for the purchase of estates from Poles, available in a sufficiently large amount, is incomparably more important for the strengthening of the German element than the removal of the danger, which would occur through the purchase from a German, that this estate could be sold by the German owner to one or several Poles."[54]

Germans from Poznania and West Prussia, most notably Hermann von Kennemann and Heinrich von Tiedemann-Seeheim, among Poznania's largest landowners and best known as founders of the "Eastern Marches Society (*Ostmarkenverein*)" in 1894, continued to make no secret of their disappointment at being left out of a good thing. They were even a little envious of their Polish peers who enjoyed the "privilege" of having their failing estates purchased for a good price by the state.[55] But by 1888, the Commission was even less inclined to buy from Germans; it had by then been "approached about" buying 114 German estates at a time when the 102 Polish estates offered to it sufficed already to exhaust its original capital.[56] Only some years later, after a shortage of Polish estates began to develop and competition from Polish parcelling agencies arose, did the

Commission reconsider its policy and begin buying from Germans on a regular basis.

Another question which soon arose was whether to buy land from non-noble Poles, especially peasants. Bismarck insisted in the Landtag that he was not directing the Settlement Law at the Polish masses and had always had particularly high praise for the Polish peasantry. But buying from them was not "unconditionally excluded" by the cabinet. Such purchases could take place "only under special conditions," but these were fairly broad: where German peasants were already present in a given village, where forced land sales offered a "cheap buy," or (most significantly) in areas like Kashubia where there were no Polish estastes to speak of and the existing national balance could be altered only by buying from Polish peasants.[57] While Lucius cautioned that the Commission's funds ought not to be "frittered away by extensive purchases of peasant properties," the Commission did in fact from the beginning aid in the transfer of land from Polish to German peasants.[58]

With respect to the creation of new homesteads on the purchased estates, there was the question of accepting German Catholics as settlers. On one hand, their patriotism was still somewhat suspect and they were considered subject to Polonization by the Polish-Catholic Church. But Bismarck, determined to pry German Catholics away from their support of the Polish cause, "emphasized strongly that Catholic settlers were not to be excluded."[59] Lucius was able to announce in 1889 that about 15% of the settlers to date were Catholic.[60] Regarding the size of the homesteads to be created, there remained considerable difference of opinion between Bismarck and most of his colleagues. Lucius and other representatives of the *Rentengut* point of view objected to smaller plots which might create a class of dependent tenant or part-time farmers.[61] Bismarck, having included the parcelling and colonization elements in his anti-Polish program only to garner liberal support, was still not that interested in recruiting settlers in the first place. His position is clear from his comments in the margin of one of Zedlitz' submissions:

> "One finds more people to lease, fewer who have the money to buy.... As many and small as possible.... rather a lot of small peasants than a few large peasants, the latter take then Polish workers.... But slowly! In centuries.... The settlement overall must not be artificially forced, but rather the demand awaited. The main thing first of all is: removal of the *Polish nobility.*"[62]

He admitted in cabinet that "it was not the reasons advanced in the Landtag (i.e., the desire to create a large class of independent farmers in the eastern provinces) by which he was being guided, for he considered these to be impractical theories, and would recommend notifying (Zedlitz) of this."[63] While no one else in the cabinet seemed to share his preference for small worker-peasant plots, even as a minority of one Bismarck was a force to be reckoned with. It was decided to leave this matter to Zedlitz' discretion, which put him on the spot since he too did not share Bismarck's views. Only the difficulty of managing the purchased estates on an interim basis, and the surprisingly large number of German applicants with their own capital, caused Bismarck to drop his objections eventually. But from the start the Commission tended to drift, without a clear concept of the type of settler it was looking for and aware that Bismarck himself did not wholly approve of some of the aims of his own law.

Needless to say, had Bismarck had his way, had the "Settlement" Commission merely acquired Polish estates without rushing to divide them up among German farmers, his professions of friendship for the Polish masses would have been more credible. But if Polish estates were merely transferred intact to German owners or managers, the law's effectiveness from a nationalist standpoint would have been lost. The labor force available to work large estates, regardless of the nationality of their owners, was overwhelmingly Polish. During the preceding 25 years, during which German ownership of estates had increased steadily, the Polish population of *Gutsbezirke* (villages associated with a single estate and composed mainly of farm workers or tenants) had increased by c. 15% while the German population had declined by c. 10%. In 1895, the population of Poznanian *Gutsbezirke* was 85% Polish, though most of the estates themselves were owned by Germans.[64] Whether a German (or the German state) owned an estate had little effect on Germanizing the labor force; there were few Germans (and not that many Prussian Poles either) willing to remain in this low social and economic status in the midst of employment opportunities in the West.

Another problem soon faced by the Settlement Commission was the ambivalent attitude of the local German population. Aside from estate owners who wanted the option of selling out to the state and German farm workers or tenant farmers who hoped to acquire a homestead, the German population of the Polish provinces was not necessarily behind Bismarck's new project. Much of the urban population saw little benefit and much potential danger for themselves from the Settlement Law and the anti-Polish offensive generally. Their spokesmen argued that German strength in the East had always been based in the towns, not in the countryside; instead of trying to buck birth rates and the pull of western industries, the government ought to help reverse the commercial decline of the towns by reducing tariffs, especially with Russia.[65] The Commission attempted to mollify these Germans by concentrating some of its buying near towns where German tradesmen were having problems, locating settlers so they could keep the embattled German middle class supplied with customers.[66] At the same time, however, in order to make the settlers economically independent of surrounding Poles, it partially nullified this effort by encouraging a system of consumer cooperatives in the new settlement villages. The Jewish exodus continued; if anything it picked up steam after 1886 (the Jewish population of Poznania's towns declined from 10% to 4.5% during the following two decades.)[67] The German and Jewish middle classes were in a delicate position vis-à-vis their largely Polish clientele; they had little to gain and much to lose from a stepped-up national struggle with the people they relied on for apprentices, employees and especially customers.[68] Of course these burghers, who typically supported the Progressive Party politically, were at odds with the government on other grounds already; for this reason alone they were unlikely to cooperate with the new anti-Polish course against their better business judgment.

Thus from the beginning, aside from bucking several powerful economic trends, the Settlement Commission was hampered by a lack of clear policies and less-than-complete support from much of the local German population.[69] Before long, the many problems which were to plague the Commission and frustrate most of its efforts in later years began to appear. First there was the quick exhaustion of the supply of Polish estates for sale. The weakest Polish estates, those which had been skirting bankruptcy for years, were logically put up for sale during the first year or two of the Commission's operations. Once these were gone, the Commission had to pay better prices for whatever else was available. Its presence in the real estate market was a factor causing land prices to rise rapidly, which in turn provided additional credit cushion for the remaining Polish estate owners. In addition, the Commission was unlikely to come into possession of the better lands at forced sales. The Polish provinces lagged already in technology, upkeep, drainage, etc., and the lands which the Commission bought tended to be among the worst, neglected or overworked and requiring many years to make suitable for settlement.[70] Thirdly, even the all-German villages created by the Commission began to turn up sizable Polish populations.[71] Where the Commission gave the settlers enough land for a comfortable living, it also permitted them to hire outside help, which was invariably Polish. In this sense, at least, Bismarck's preference for smaller parcels and peasants unable to hire outside help was more realistic from a nationalist point of view.

The anti-Polish offensive of 1886 was characterized above all by the large number and variety of measures it contained. The Settlement Law was the most spectacular and highly publicized aspect, but it should not overshadow the rest. Bismarck launched a series of other, similarly unprecedented measures (many of them having greater immediacy for the Polish masses than the Settlement Law), which constitute an escalation of the national struggle on many fronts. This is especially true of the new school, Church and other policies initiated by Gossler, who, by virtue of his ministry's authority over school and Church-state matters and his ability to effect many changes by decree without legislative action, was second only to the Prussian Minister-President in his ability to influence the climate of Prussian-Polish relations. There were times (*e.g.*, under Altenstein and Eichhorn, or later under Zedlitz) when the Prussian Culture Minister was considered the Poles' best friend in Berlin. With Gossler in this post, however, the Culture Minister came to surpass even Bismarck as a target of Polish dissatisfaction. As noted above (p. 46f.), Gossler was among the most activist and nationalistic of Prussian culture ministers. He believed in keeping up a steady pressure on the Poles, often through small harrassing measures which did not even attract the attention of the German public. Before 1886, he regularly transferred Polish teachers to the West and began to offer bonuses to German teachers willing to replace them in Polish regions; he even made Polish students ineligible for various state scholarships. When Bismarck set out on his new course in 1886, Gossler was best prepared to come forward almost at once with a large number of new proposals to halt the "repression of the German element."

Ironically, such was the extent of Bismarck's determination to establish the Poles as a focus of public aggression that even Gossler proved at one point to be insufficiently nationalist. One of his proposals, calling for the expenditure of several million Marks to improve school conditions in the Polish provinces, was attacked because it failed to distinguish between German and Polish schools there. ("Polish schools" were those where Polish was still taught as a subject and used to instruct religion and hymn-singing.) There were many areas where one nationality was not sufficiently represented to warrant a separate school; German children attended a Polish-Catholic school with (in Gossler's view) a heavy risk of their Polonization. He sought to enable all German children to attend schools of their own; the money he requested was to build new schools, mainly but not exclusively German-Protestant ones, and hire additional German teachers.[72] Gossler expected this measure to serve a national purpose, for even Polish schools served as useful Germanizing agencies and provided the first contact of most Polish children with German language and culture. But Finance Minister Adolf von

Scholz, seeking perhaps to curry favor with Bismarck, criticized Gossler's proposal and the current ability of the elementary schools to Germanize effectively. In his opinion, it made no sense to spend money to improve Polish schools, since "the education of Polish children . . . just like the education of Polish teachers, only aids and abets Polish propaganda." Since the stated purpose of Bismarck's campaign was to protect those Germans living in ethnically mixed areas, he wanted the benefits from this proposal to go exlusively to German schools in the Polish provinces. "The improvement of schools in Polish regions, so far as it concerns Polish children, benefits 'Polonism'; only German schools should be improved."[73] Gossler appealed to the high marks which Tiedemann had given his school policies; he also had the support of all the other ministers who expressed an opinion, except for the most important one. Bismarck, when the matter came to a head in March 1886, sided with Scholz. He reasoned that, since "defense against 'Polonism'" meant in fact "protection of the German minority," so the term "elementary school" in Gossler's proposal should refer to the "German elementary school as the school one is trying to improve." In the bill to be presented to the Landtag, the term would remain "elementary school," but this was only to avoid controversy; it was taken for granted that Polish schools would not be favored with any of these funds. In Bismarck's opinion, emphasis should be put on the German schools in Polish areas; "for this purpose German teachers are to be brought in and, if necessary, new German schools established." Meanwhile, he did not strive for "a better education for Polish children nor for better training of Polish teachers; you will not win the former for the German nationality and with the latter you have only political opponents."[74] As the law was passed, 2.8 million Marks were to be used exclusively for the improvement and subsidization of German schools in Poznania and West Prussia.[75] Scholz may well have been concerned that Gossler's plan would cost more and cool off the "present favorable atmosphere" in the Landtag for such requests, but Bismarck's remarks suggest something of his growing single-mindedness with respect to the Polish question.

Another of Gossler's new measures met less opposition in cabinet but ran into some conservative opposition in the Landtag. It proposed that "the employment of teachers in public elementary schools in Poznania, West Prussia, and Upper Silesia belongs to the state alone;" existing authority to "hire, elect, or propose" teachers held by local school boards or (in *Gutsbezirke*) estate owners was abolished. Gossler's intention here was to remove such rights from Polish communities and estate owners, but it also affected a traditional right of German Junkers. The new law ended the special financial obligations of estate owners to support elementary schools in their estate-villages, but many conservatives did not consider this to be adequate compensation for their loss of effective control over local schools and teachers. They argued also that it made no sense from a nationalist standpoint, especially in Upper Silesia or Kashubia, where the nobility was virtually all-German. As with the expulsions, however, Bismarck's concern with the Polish problems overrode his regard for the interests of the Prussian nobility here too. He and Gossler wanted to tighten up the relationship between the state and public school teachers and free them from "unauthorized influences," i.e., Polish patrons and school committees which might use Polish-nationalist criteria in the supervision of their teachers. Gossler suspected that such local pressures had caused many teachers purposely to neglect their efforts in German language instruction.[76] With this law, he intended to improve the "political outlook" of those teachers having contact with Polish children, "strengthen the feeling that they are Prussian civil servants," make them independent of "influence on the part of the Poles," and make it easier to continue transferring unwanted teachers out of the Polish provinces altogether.[77]

This law was noteworthy also because for the first time Upper Silesia (i.e., the regency of Oppeln) was included in a strictly anti-Polish (as opposed to Kulturkampf) measure. This served to reinforce the lingering suspicion by Center leaders that Catholics in general were still under attack, since Upper Silesia was politically almost completely in the hands of that party. It regularly captured 11 of the 12 Reichstag seats here, excepting only the predominately Protestant county of Kreuzburg/Kluczbork; in 1890, it received 77% of all the votes cast, whereas the Koło Polskie was not even a factor until after 1900.[78] The inclusion of Upper Silesia in Gossler's bill also served to undercut Bismarck's contention that his campaign was directed exclusively at the political upper class of Poles. Upper Silesian Poles (who constituted almost 40% of the ethnic Poles in Germany!) had no nobility of their own and had previously resisted appeals to join in common struggles with the "real" Poles to the north, except during the Kulturkampf and then under Center Party direction. Karol Miarka, editor of Katolik and often cited as father of a discernible Polish movement in Upper Silesia, was closely allied with the Center. He saw no need for a separate Polish party, at least not while the Kulturkampf raged and the interests of the Catholic population were adequately represented by the Center.[79] The Center was a strong defender of Polish cultural rights, especially the use of Polish in the schools;[80] its delegation from Upper Silesia included a number of Poles, (e.g., Zaruba, who described himself in 1884 as a proud Prussian of Polish mother tongue).[81] As the Kulturkampf wound down and the government began to court the Center, there were efforts to set up a separate Polish-Catholic presence in Upper Silesia, but these efforts received little help from the Poznania-centered Prussian-Polish national movement. The *Koło Polskie*, essentially still an organization of Polish nobles, did not seem very interested in carrying the Polish national movement into Upper Silesia. Kantak did argue that Upper Silesians ought to have the same language rights as Poznanians; he rejected the notion that their dialect was a separate language: "Upper Silesian is one and the same Polish language as our own . . . (though) to be sure, they have preserved some archaisms."[82] But Franciszek Chłapowski, a Poznanian representative but a practicing physician in Upper Silesia, was the only *Koło* member to show sustained interest and became the unofficial *Koło* spokesman for Upper Silesia.[83] "No one among us has bothered about Upper Silesia until now. We hardly knew that over a million kinsmen lived there, whose language, customs, and traditions were the same."[84] But he too refused an appeal by the incipient national movement here to run against the Center candidate in an Upper Silesian district.[85] More representative of the prevailing *Koło* attitude was Jażdżewski; he referred to the Upper Silesians as merely one of the other peoples of the Empire, "tribes . . . . which likewise have quite separate national languages" which they ought to be allowed to use publicly.[86] Despite this typical abstinence of the Polish national movement from Upper Silesian affairs, government spokesmen remained suspicious; Puttkamer spoke of a "quite energetic action begun in recent times from Poznania in order to pull the ancient inheritance of the German nation . . . into the whirlwind of Polish aspirations," which he intended to stop through the "gradual conveyance into German culture through the schools."[87] But the reality was more as Chłapowski described it:

> "Persecution in the religious and especially in the linguistic sphere, in the schools and in the administration, has single-handedly united our interests, the interests of the Poles in Poznania and West Prussia, with those of the Upper Silesians for the first time, because our complaints have coincided. . . . No one has encouraged the feelings of national opposition, of poor disposition, of distrust in Upper Silesia more than the royal government in Oppeln itself through its unwise policies."[88]

Returning to the new education measures, a third law was drawn up aiming at "the Establishment and Maintenance of Extension Schools in the Provinces of West Prussia and Poznania" and called for compulsory attendance by all Poles under age 18 at "trade schools" to be established in the chief towns. At first glance this could appear to be a special effort by the state to improve educational conditions in the "disadvantaged" Polish provinces, except that the "trade school" designation was somewhat misleading. Not only was German to be the language of instruction but the chief subject as well. The real purpose of this law was to ensure that Polish adolescents remained in contact with the German language during the years when they had completed their eight years of elementary schooling but were not yet ready for induction into the army.⁸⁹ But on this occasion Bismarck was frustrated by the Prussian courts which refused several times to enforce attendance at these schools.⁹⁰

The most important and far-reaching of the new school measures appeared in September 1887. Gossler decreed (effective in the middle of the school year) that "the teaching of the Polish language is to be omitted in all elementary schools in the province of Poznania (having already disappeared from other Polish-speaking districts) and the classroom time which thereby becomes free is to be assigned to instruction and practice in the German language."⁹¹ This order meant a major change in the curriculum, since until then Polish had been taught for five hours a week in the lower grades and three hours weekly thereafter. This was also an example of the arbitrary authority which a Prussian culture minister enjoyed; as long as Bismarck approved, no other consent was necessary, and in this case he approved strongly. He was suspicious that the growing Polish national movement was aided by "the civilization which has been imparted to the teaching of Polish, by virtue of the excellent achievements of the Prussian school system." He did not want the state any longer to "promote learning, through the elementary and high schools, that will only be utilized in a sense that is inimical to it."⁹² When Poles sought to organize classes to teach their language on a private basis, Zedlitz effectively frustrated this by ordering that "approval is to be denied to applications by elementary school teachers for permission to give private instruction in Polish" or to use public school rooms for this purpose.⁹³

In the area of Church policy, also part of Gossler's ministry (official title: Minister of Ecclesiastical, School, and Medical Affairs), there were no direct attacks on the Polish-Catholic hierarchy. Archbishop Ledóchowski remained in exile in the Vatican; state control of church administration in his diocese remained unchanged from the *Kulturkampf*. Bismarck did not want to upset his fresh accord with the Vatican, covering Prussia as a whole, by taking additional measures. On the other hand, he could exploit the Church's own desire for good relations to get his way in the Polish provinces. For example, as part of his efforts to split German and Polish Catholics, he insisted on a German successor to

Ledóchowski. He decided as early as 1881 that "one cannot consider bringing a Pole into such a position in a region with Polish population."[94] The Pope tried for a long time to circumvent this demand; he offered Bismarck his way in the key Cologne diocese and proposed at least twelve different Polish churchmen for Poznań, all to no avail.[95] Bismarck proposed, among others, the distinguished archbishop of Mainz, Ketteler, who turned him down, however, reportedly on orders from the Vatican.[96] But Bismarck remained adamant, in no hurry to fill the position; in fact, he thought the chaotic condition of the church in Poznania might be in the state's interest if it lessened clerical influence there. "We cannot admit a Polish noble to the archbishopric of Gniezno-Poznań, even if the vacancy should last for generations. . . . The Polish population is more easily governed secularly without priests than with priests."[97] At last, in 1886, the Pope gave in and agreed to a German churchman, Julius Dinder, a native of East Prussia who spoke Polish fluently.[98]

By securing the appointment of a German to the position held by the "Primate of Poland" under the Commonwealth, Bismarck was setting up a situation where Poles would have to choose between religious obedience and national emotions at a time when the latter were getting stronger almost everywhere. This would hopefully lead to diminished sympathy by German Catholics for Polish aspirations. At first, this strategy seemed to pay off; the announcement of Dinder's appointment was greeted (according to local officials) with "bitter disappointment" in Polish quarters. There were petitions to Rome and statements of defiance in the press, leading to an open letter from Ledóchowski with a "most serious admonition" to accept Dinder, in view of his "superior priestly qualities," with "complete trust."[99] Gossler meanwhile moved quickly to exploit the advantages which he felt a German archbishop afforded. He intended to "show trust in him and give him a few presents, also let him see always that only he, and not a member of the Polish nobility, could have received such gifts."[100] He began to use more vigorously the means at his disposal to counter politically active priests, *e.g.*, having them transferred to less sensitive areas and using the government's approval right to ban Polish priests from predominately German areas.[101] In 1887, Bismarck ordered this latter policy applied to Reichstag districts where elections were typically closely contested between German and Polish candidates.[102] The government responded to Jażdżewski's role as the leading Polish spokesman in the Reichstag by first pressuring Dinder into withholding his appointment to a desirable parish, then persuading him to quit his parliamentary seat altogether.[103] Still Gossler was not satisfied: "It is recommended for now to gain further experience about the position which the Archbishop will take in the Polish-national question, whose importance and significance for the state goverenment is known to him . . . (for) it has repeatedly become apparent how very dependent the Archbishop is upon his Polonizing surroundings." While he had done what the government expected thus far, Gossler desired that "the pro-state sentiment find expression in still clearer manner through further actions." Until then, he would refuse to help Dinder financially, e.g., by making some necessary repairs to his residence. Unfortunately, Dinder was personally without the means to cover some of the expenses and obligations of his high office and this made him especially dependent upon Gossler's help and thus subject to his demands.[104] Actually he was not a very competent administrator either, but in Bismarck's opinion "an incapable German is nevertheless better than a capable Pole."[105]

When faced with a choice between Polish national interests and Church interests, Dinder opted logically for the latter, not unlike Ledóchowski in the 1860s. For example, when the government offered to reinstate religious instruction in German in the elementary schools (absent since 1872, when Ledóchowski refused to have this done exclusively in German), Dinder agreed, provided only that Polish be used as an aide where necessary.[106] He also kept his distance from the movement protesting the removal of Polish from the curriculum, though his own Polish-language religion classes would become less effective if Polish children were not taught to read and write their language. Even when Gossler sought to have Dinder restrain his priests, who were leading the opposition to the new school measures, Dinder obliged with a letter in which they were "seriously admonished to apply themselves to the exercise of their civil rights in the area of assembly and association with circumspection and reserve and to avoid all agitatory activity."[107] By the end of 1887, Gossler reported that the situation in Poznanian schools had found a "happy solution, completely in line with the state government," and that the state had every reason to be satisfied with its new archbishop.[108] Polish public opinion, on the other hand, became increasingly dissatisfied; all the newspapers except those controlled by the Church condemned Dinder's compromises with the government and saw them as proof of the harm a German archbishop could do to Polish interests. Even the clerical *Kuryer Poznański* warned Dinder that the Poles would not blindly follow him indefinitely if he turned against their nationality.[109] For Bismarck, these attacks on Dinder constituted "new proof for the well-known saying that for the Poles religion is only in second place and this only if it makes itself useful to Polish agitation."[110]

But as Gossler continued to apply pressure and make additional demands, he finally pushed Dinder too far. The Archbishop decided by

1888 that it was more important to retain the affection of his archdiocese than win that of the government through excessive concessions. When Gossler decided to have even religious instruction taught in German (thus removing the last official position of Polish in the schools), and began issuing orders to this effect prior to getting Dinder's approval, the latter refused to budge. Gossler was forced to rescind his orders: "The introduction of German as language of instruction for religion classes (should be) cancelled in those Catholic elementary schools . . . where the Polish language has been used."[111] Dinder also refused any longer to try to check the political activity of his priests; Gossler finally urged a more forceful intercession with the Pope to achieve this, but Bismarck, concerned about a revival of the *Kulturkampf*, urged him to proceed more slowly and use his prerogatives more discriminately.[112] Only after a long struggle was Dinder compelled, as the state's price for reopening his seminary, to permit the government a veto over the professors to be hired.[113] By this time it was the Prussian government's turn to be disillusioned with Dinder and disappointed in its hopes of controlling him, and through him the Poznanian Church. As even nationalistic Poles soon acknowledged, the replacement of Ledóchowski by Dinder had not in the long run helped Gossler achieve his aims in the areas of religious instruction and clerical political activity. This experience with Dinder perhaps explains the government's willingness eventually to let this position go to a Pole again upon Dinder's death in 1891 (see below).

A third subdivision of Gossler's ministry dealt with "medical affairs" and he felt obliged to offer the cabinet an anti-Polish proposal in this area as well. A law concerning the "Employment of Vaccinators in the Province of Poznania" gave the state the right to approve all new public vaccinators, ratify those already in office, and determine their fees. Gossler suspected that Poles, where they controlled the organs of local government, were favoring Polish doctors for these positions, which meant a very modest income supplement and supposedly some prestige. Tiedemann had determined that Polish physicians, "very clever agents," were "more and more the actual carriers of Polish agitation."[114] Gossler felt that these positions should go to German doctors, more of which might then be encouraged to work in Poznania.[115] Of course, apparently trivial measures like this contained an element of risk. They provoked derision in parliament and gave the impression that the government had run out of ideas which might have significant results and was now scraping the bottom of the barrel in its efforts to maintain an anti-Polish offensive.

While Gossler had worked pretty consistently on the Polish problem prior to 1886, and was therefore ready with a number of proposals when

Bismarck gave the signal, other ministers had to improvise quickly. Not surprisingly, many of their proposals were "make-laws" of dubious impact, brought forth only to appease Bismarck. Puttkamer's proposed redivision of the Polish provinces into a greater number of counties (creating 13 additional counties in Poznania and 5 more in West Prussia) seemed to fit into this category. This was originally part of Bismarck's scheme to abolish the province of Poznania altogether and divide it among neighboring provinces. He brought this idea up during the 1886 cabinet discussions of anti-Polish measures, but then pulled back in the face of Emperor Wilhelm's insistence on the inviolability of "historic entities."[116] This was one of the few cases where Wilhelm made his presence felt relative to the Polish question, though he did inject, in the midst of the wave of Bismarckian measures: "It seems to me very necessary . . . to emphasize from time to time that we do not aim at the extermination of the Polish language."[117] Puttkamer wanted to redraw the boundaries of counties in the Polish provinces in order to create safe German *Kreistag* majorities; the additional counties were simply an excuse to increase the number of *Landräte* and thus their ability to keep control of the situation locally.[118] Poles had long been excluded from such offices, traditionally filled by local nobles, but they had previously considered *Landräte* the least obnoxious of Prussian officials. But the new *Landräte* were often officials without local ties, entrusted by the government in Berlin "to raise and foster German national consciousness in all the counties with which they come into contact."[119]

In addition to the new decrees and laws of the 1886-7 period, provincial and local officials continued to do their part, aided less by the new measures than by the awareness that greater aggressiveness against the Poles now met with approval higher up. Examples in this category are too numerous to cite: university administrators banned Polish social fraternities; the annexation of suburbs by Poznanian towns was refused if this would dilute a German majority; a Polish teacher who complained to his *Landrat* about not being permitted to vote found that that official had recommended to his school board that he be disciplined on grounds that he would have voted Polish anyway.[120] The civil service was already largely off-limits to Poles, but upon discovery of a small number of low-echelon Polish court officials, it was decred that "Polish-speaking civil servants will not be hired in Polish regions." Those already employed had either to abstain from political activity or be transferred to other parts of Prussia; bonuses were arranged to persuade Germans to come in and take their places.[121]

Finally, the army too was involved in the 1886 campaign. It was already policy to station all-German units in Polish areas where possible, but about 12% of the forces in Poznania were still Polish. The army came in for some sharp criticism by Tiedemann for its alleged past failure to combat "Polonism;" that a mere regency president could put War Minister Bronsart on the defensive by accusing the normally sacrosanct army of "neglecting to counteract Polonizing endeavors" is a sign of Tiedemann's standing with Bismarck at this time. Bronsart did his part in coming forward with some trivial anti-Polish measures, *e.g.*, suggesting that retired non-commissioned officers get first crack at homesteads created by the Settlement Commission. Though it did not make good sense to him, he also promised to remove every last Polish soldier from the Polish provinces in order to ward off the threat of a regular civilian overview of the ethnic make-up of individual army units, as suggested by Tiedemann.[122]

Having looked at some of the chief elements in the anti-Polish campaign launched by Bismarck in 1886, one must examine the relationship of these measures to his professed position on the domestic Polish question (see above, pp. 10f.). Bismarck continued to insist that his adversaries were to be found among the Polish upper classes exclusively: "I am not directing all these measures . . . at Poles in general. On the contrary, I consider the Polish peasant to be a faithful Prussian subject if he is not artificially led astray . . . through other influences."[123] He admitted of only two major enemies within the Prussian-Polish population: the nobility and its following mainly . . . furnish the elements for the maintenance of agitation."[124] In his eyes, this class was thoroughly obnoxious, consisting of "intriguants, hypocrites, dishonest and undependable, completely incapable of maintaining a state . . . uninterruptedly out to proselyte politically.[125] As for the clergy, "the Polish clergy incites and stirs up the Polish population, urges them into insurrection as soon as the time for it seems to have come, tries through upbringing and ecclesiastical influence to make Germans into Poles, and preaches the most bitter racial hatred."[126]

At the same time, he continued to express his belief in the loyalty of the great mass of Prussian Poles. "The common man in Poland has himself no rebellious tendencies; on the contrary, he tends rather toward submissiveness; he is calm and gratefully recognizes the better condition, compared to earlier times, in which he now lives."[127] The Polish peasant "has proved to be a courageous soldier on our battlefields. . . . (He) does not desire a return to an independent Poland and to a nobles' republic. Thus he is always devoted, in the last resort, to his Prussian King and master. . . . He is quite satisfied with the advantages of German culture and only the nobles and priests are making a racket."[128] As late as 1894, Bismarck asserted that "the danger does not come from the lower classes of the population. . . . You can live with them and agitation will never come from them. They are not the sponsors of a movement hostile to us. . . . The Polish peasants are not dangerous and it is not decisive whether the workers speak Polish or German."[129]

The question is whether his treatment of the Polish minority in Prussia can be squared with these assertions. Bismarck notably refused to take any steps which might put his professed confidence in the Polish masses to the test, e.g.,by following Tiedemann's suggestion that county and local charters be amended to allow for greater peasant representation at the expense of the nobility in Polish areas.[130] And he was not frank about, or did not reflect very long upon, the actual impact of his own policies on the Polish masses. For example, he disclaimed any desire to harm the Polish language, wanting only to make sure that all understood German as a second language. It is doubtless true that he had no intention of stamping it out as a spoken idiom, but his government did almost everything short of that. Having earlier ended its use as a language of instruction in the schools for children who understood no other, he now made it most difficult for Poles to become literate in their language through either public or private instruction. Gossler's school policies also had their greatest negative impact precisely on the Polish masses who relied most heavily on public schools. In 1886 there were 11.1 schools per 10,000 Catholics in Poznań regency compared to 14.8 for the same number of Protestants; after fifteen years of the 1886 "School Improvement Law," the ratio for Catholics was unchanged while the Protestant ratio had improved to 19.3 schools per 10,000 population. By this time, Polish districts had the highest percentage of officially "overfilled" schools in Prussia; there were 202 one-room, one-grade schools with over 120 children each in Poznań regency, virtually all of these "Catholic."[131] Clearly the Polish population was discriminated against even in terms of access to schools whose purpose was Germanization. In linguistic, school, and other policies, there was thus an increasingly hollow ring to Bismarck's assertions that he was engaged in battle only with the noble political leadership.

Aside from the effect of his policies, Bismarck's view of Polish society consisting of perfidious leaders and loyal masses was anachronistic in any case. In his younger days it might have been tenable; the Galician uprising of 1846 certainly suggests as much. But it was no longer valid in 1886 and it seems that Bismarck himself must have known this, regardless of his public statements. The involvement of a growing cross-section of Prussian Poles, including peasants and townsmen, in national affairs was obvious from the response to his own measures, as relayed to him by his own ministers and officials. As Posadowsky wrote from

Rawicz, the Poles were improving their educational levels and the growth of the national idea among them was plain to all. "A Polish middle class has formed out of the impoverished nobility and the descendants of the peasantry and small-artisan class, which devotes itself to commerce, the medical profession, a judge's career and the law."[132] Puttkamer suggested that one should not take too seriously the government's contention that the Polish noble leadership lacked the support of other elements of the population: "This was a delusion; in the last decades, through . . . extremely smart calculation and application of all (possible) sources of power . . . a Polish middle class has indeed developed, . . . the product of a . . . systematically prepared and implemented movement, . . . a phalanx in permanent national opposition." The traditionally loyal Polish peasant had changed for the worse, "blindly following the endeavors of the Polish nobility. . . . It is a complete illusion to believe that, through any kind of measure, we can shove a wedge to our advantage between these compact groups of people."[133]

In fact, Bismarck was just about the only one in his government who still adhered to this distinction between Polish leaders and masses. There is evidence that even he was more aware of the changes in Polish society and the composition of the Polish national movement than he admitted publicly. While claiming publicly to be unaware of any middle class development among the Poles, he acknowledged in a memorandum to Gossler that, among the results of the Prussian school system was the creation of an "educated, Polish middle class, especially today's stock of doctors and lawyers, which was formerly not present in the eastern regions and now constitutes an essential factor among the elements resisting German nationality and the state government."[134]

In spite of the growing corpus of anti-Polish measures during Bismarck's tenure in office and their obvious impact on all segments of Polish society, some historians have still been inclined to take Bismarck at his word and to attribute the discriminatory aspects to other factors (*e.g.*, the National Liberals) or to his honest failure to recognize the impact of his policies. They emphasize the theoretical, ideological distinction between Bismarck and more nationalistic contemporaries, his continuing tendency to think in state rather than ethnic terms, and his lack of concern for ethnic homogeneity. Hans Delbrück, though a sharp critic of Prussian Polish policies, argued that "Bismarck himself was by no means an enemy of the Poles on principle; . . . (such an attitude) was thoroughly alien to his political thinking."[135] Laubert argued that Bismarck sought to Germanize only in terms of consciousness, not nationality, that he wanted well-behaved subjects regardless of their language or religion.[136] But the closer one looks at Bismarck's Polish policies, the harder it is to accept such an interpretation. As Hans Herzfeld noted, "the historically understandable idea of carrying on the struggle against the Polish nobility with the aid of the broad lower class of people had become an illusion."[137] Bismarck's unwillingness to recognize this was most likely wishful thinking, a myth which he found it personally and politically worthwhile to perpetuate. Needless to say, in the midst of such an unrealistic view of Polish society, it was unlikely that his government would devise very effective Polish policies.

Notes

1. Referring specifically to the controversy over his "measures against Polonization," *Gesammelte Werke*, VIII:865.
2. Council of Ministers meeting, January 10, 1886, *GPSA Berlin* Rep. 84a, #4066.
3. *Ibid.*
4. *Ibid.*
5. *Ibid.*
6. Bismarck to Kurd von Schlözer, January 31, 1886, *PA Bonn*, Preussen 2:1, vol. 1.
7. Adam Galos, "Utworzenie Komisji Kolonizacyjnej 1886 a sprawa wewnętrznej kolonizackji w Niemczech," *Prace Historyczne* 206 (1969):48; Mai, p. 102.
8. Council of Ministers meeting, January 10, 1886.
9. *Ibid.*
10. Robert Lucius von Ballhausen, *Bismarck-Erinnerungen* (Stuttgart, 1920), entry of January 10, 1886.
11. *Ibid.*, entry of January 14, 1886.
12. Council of Ministers meeting, January 24, 1886, *GPSA Berlin*, Rep. 84a, #4066.
13. Council of Ministers meeting, January 10, 1886; Gossler memorandum, January 23, 1886, *Ibid.*; with respect to the former proposal, however, Bismarck suggested only a few days later that, 'as a further repressive measure the exclusive use of the German language in all assemblies in which public matters are discussed is intended."*Gesammelte Werke*, VIc:328.
14. Council of Ministers meeting, January 24, 1886.
15. Document #22, January 23, 1886, *Abgeordnetenhaus: Anlagen.*
16. Johannes Behrendt, "Die polnische Frage und das österreichisch-deutsche Bündnis, 1885 bis 1887," *Vierteljahrsschrift für Politik und Geschichte* 7(1926):734.
17. speech of January 28, 1886, *Abgeordnetenhaus.*
18. *Ibid.*
19. See especially Puttkamer's memorandum, "Massregeln zur Stärkung des

deutschen Elements in den östlichen Landestheilen," January 21, 1886, *GPSA Berlin*, Rep. 84a, #4066.

20. "From now on, when land is transferred through inheritance only the transfer of full ownership is permissible." Brüggen, p. 41.

21. Arthur Aal, *Das preussische Rentengut* (Stuttgart, 1901), p. 33 and *passim*.

22. Speech by Miquel, quoted in *Zwanzig Jahre Deutscher Kulturarbeit*, ed. Prussian Abgeordnetenhaus (Berlin, 1907), p. 15.

23. Max Sering, *Die innere Kolonisation im östlichen Deutschland* (Leipzig, 1893), p. 8.

24. Aal, p. 36.

25. *Politische Reden*, VII:408f.; *Bismarck und die Parliamentarier*, I:288.

26. Bismarck, *Politische Briefe aus den Jahren 1849-1889*, 3rd edit., (Berlin, 1889), III:310f.; Bismarck to Rottenberg, head of the Imperial Chancellery, April 28, 1882, quoted by Galos, p. 45; Trzeciakowski, *Kulturkampf*, pp. 209f.

28. Council of Ministers meeting, December 16, 1884, *GPSA Berlin*, Rep. 84a, I.

29. Council of Ministers meeting, September 24, 1885, *Ibid.*.

30. Miquel's response: "Wenn schon, denn schon;" Hans Herzfeld, *Johannes von Miquel* (Detmold, 1938), II:77; Mai, p. 111.

31. Council of Ministers meetings, February 7, 1886, *GPSA Berlin* Rep. 84a #4066, and March 5, 1887, *Ibid.*, #4072.

32. Council of Ministers meeting, January 24, 1886.

33. *Ibid.*

34. Cf. Hermann von Petersdorff, "Lucius," in *Deutscher Aufstieg*, ed. H.v. Arnim & G.v. Below (Berlin, 1925), pp. 227-232.

35. Lucius, entry of February 7, 1886.

36. *Germania*, January 30, 1886, in *PA Bonn*, Preussen 4; speeches by Hermann von Kennemann, February 22 and April 6, 1886, *Abgeordnetenhaus*.

37. quoted by Herzfeld, II:78.

38. Council of Ministers meeting, February 7, 1886, *GPSA Berlin* Rep. 84a, #4067.

39. Heinrich von Poschinger, "Aus den Denkwürdigkeiten Wilhelm von Kardorffs," *Deutsche Revue* 33, no. 2 (1908):159.

40. Council of Ministers meeting, February 7, 1886.

41. Document #45, February 9, 1886, *Abgeordnetenhaus: Anlagen;* Herzfeld, II:80; Bismarck memorandum, February 12, 1886, *GPSA Berlin*, Rep. 84a, #4089.

42. Council of Ministers meeting, June 9, 1886, *GPSA Berlin*, Rep. 84a, #4089; *Bausteine zur Bismarck-Pyramide* (Berlin, 1904), p. 95; Robert Koehl, "Colonialism inside Germany," *Journal of Modern History* 25(1953):264.

43. Julian Marchlewski, *Zur Polenpolitik der preussischen Regierung*, 2nd edit. (East Berlin, 1957), p. 56.

44. Speech of February 22, 1886, *Abgeordnetenhaus*.

45. Document #45, *Ibid.*, *Anlagen*.

46. Gossler memorandum, "Massnahmen gegen das Vordringen des Polonismus," January 23, 1886, *GPSA Berlin*, Rep. 84a, #4066; speech by Lucius,

February 22, 1886, *Abgeordnetenhaus*.
47. Gossler memorandum, *Ibid.*; Broszat, p. 115, gives similar figures for 1878.
48. Speech of February 22, 1886, *Abgeordnetenhaus*.
49. Speech of April 15, 1886, *Herrenhaus*.
50. *Neue Freie Presse*, January 30, 1886, *PA Bonn*, Preussen 4, where the large sampling of foreign press reaction to the new anti-Polish measures suggests Bismarck's strong interest in the foreign reaction to them.
51. Reuss to Bismarck, February 4, 1886, *PA Bonn*, I.A. #79, vol. 1.
52. Behrendt, p. 744.
53. Council of Ministers meeting, February 7, 1886.
54. Puttkamer/Lucius to West Prussian *Oberpräsident* von Ernsthausen, November 5, 1887, *Archiwum Państwowe, Poznań* (hereafter: *AP Poznań*), XV A 51, vol. 4.
55. See their speeches of February 18, 1888, *Abgeordnetenhaus*.
56. Speech by Lucius, *Ibid.*
57. Council of Ministers meeting, December 23, 1886, *GPSA Berlin*, Rep. 84a, #4089.
58. memorandum, December 27, 1886, *Ibid.*
59. Council of Ministers meeting, December 23, 1886.
60. Speeches of February 18, 1888, and March 20, 1889, *Abgeordnetenhaus*.
61. Lucius memorandum, August 7, 1887, *GPSA Berlin*, Rep. 84a, #4072.
62. Marginalia on Zedlitz memorandum of November 10, 1886, *Gesammelte Werke*, VIc:328; Lucius, entry of June 7, 1887.
63. Council of Ministers meeting, March 5, 1887, *GPSA Berlin*, Rep. 84a, #4072.
64. Wegener, pp. 127, 138.
65. Moritz Jaffé, "Die wirthschaftliche Entwicklung der Posener Städte seit 1815 in ihren Grundzügen," in *Die Ostmark*, ed. W. Mitscherlich (Leipzig, 1911), p. 50.
66. *Deutsche Kulturarbeit*, p. 25.
67. Jaffé, p. 58; Franz Zitzlaff, Fritz Vosberg, & Karpiński, *Preussische Städte im Gebiete des polnischen Nationalitätenkampfes*, ed. L. Bernhard (Leipzig, 1909), p. xviii.
68. Wegener, p. 156.
69. The noble-dominated West Prussian *Landschaft* was not immediately willing, for example, to give up a major part of its local market and had to be pressured into ceasing sales to Poles: "From all corporations, especially those organizations endowed with state privileges, like the West Prussian *Landschaft*, it can legitimately be expected that they will decline to sell their landed property to Poles and that they will go to the extreme limits of the constitutionally permissible (to avoid doing so.)," Puttkamer/Lucius to Ernsthausen, November 5, 1887, *AP Poznań* XV A 51, vol. 4.
70. Sering, p. 202.
71. Laubert, p. 47.
72. Albrecht Wien, *Die preussische Verwaltung des Regierungsbezirks Danzig*

(1870-1920) (Cologne, 1974), pp. 46f.

73. Council of Ministers meeting, January 24, 1886; Adolf von Scholz, *Erlebnisse und Gespräche mit Bismarck*, ed. W.v. Scholz (Stuttgart, 1922).
74. Council of Ministers meeting, March 14, 1886, *GPSA Berlin*, Rep. 84a, #4067.
75. Gossler to Tiedemann, April 7, 1886, *APW Bydgoszcz*, #4729.
76. Council of Ministers meeting, January 24, 1886.
77. Speech by Gossler, February 24, 1886, *Abgeordnetenhaus*.
78. Jerzy Pabisz, "Wyniki wyborów do Parlamentu Związku Północnoniemieckiego i Parlamentu Rzeszy Niemieckiej na terenie Śląsku w latach 1867-1918," *Studia i Materiały z Dziejów Śląsku* (1966): 186-383.
79. Trzeciakowski, *Kulturkampf*, p. 44.
80. Speeches by Huene, January 12, 1880, and Franz, February 3, 1881, *Abgeordnetenhaus*.
81. Speech of February 5, 1885, *Ibid*.
82. Speech of February 11, 1875, *Ibid*.; Gossler took the position that this dialect was a low-class, undeveloped language which relied on German for its larger words; speech of February 6, 1884, *Ibid*.
83. See speech of December 7, 1880, *Ibid*.
84. Speech of February 7, 1881, *Ibid*.
85. Lech Trzeciakowski, "Polskie ugrupowania polityczne zaborze pruskiego wobec Niemiec, 1871-1918," *Dzieje Najnowsze* 4(1972): 30; idem, *Kulturkampf*, p. 217.
86. Speech of December 17, 1884, *Reichstag*.
87. Speech of February 3, 1881, *Abgeordnetenhaus*.
88. Speech of February 7, 1881, *Ibid*.
89. Bismarck/Scholz memorandum, February 17, 1886, *GPSA Berlin*, Rep. 84a, #4066.
90. Council of Ministers meeting, March 25, 1896, *Ibid*., #4088.
91. Decree of September 7, 1887, *Ibid*., Rep. 8 30:II, #2857.
92. Bismarck memorandum, "Die Unterrichtssprache in den Volksschulen der Provinzen Posen und Westpreussen," June 20, 1887, *Ibid*., Rep. 84a, #4067.
93. Order of December 19, 1887, *Ibid*., Rep. 8 30:II, #2857.
94. Council of Ministers meeting, December 1, 1881, quoted by Trzeciakowski, *Kulturkampf*, p. 158.
95. *Akten zur preussischen Kirchenpolitik 1885-1914*, ed. E. Gatz, (Mainz, 1977), p. xxvi; Heckel, p. 538.
96. Wendt, p. 34.
97. Bismarck to Gossler, March 3, 1886, *Gesammelte Werke*, VIc:313.
98. Trzeciakowski, *Kulturkampf*, pp. 169ff.; *Kirchenpolitik*, p. xxviii.
99. Schlözer to Bismarck, June 6, 1886, in *Kirchenpolitik*, p. 20; Heckel, p. 541; Arthur von Brauer, *Im Dienste Bismarcks*, ed. H. Rogge (Berlin, 1936), p. 201.
100. Gossler to Bismarck, June 5, 1886, in *Kirchenpolitik*, p. 105.
101. Gossler to Poznanian *Oberpräsident* Günther, February 8, 1886, *AP Poznań* XXIV D IIIa 70, vol. 2; Dettmer, p. 90.

102. Bismarck to Gossler, April 25, 1887, *PA Bonn*, Preussen 4:1.

103. Zedlitz to Gossler, October 6, 1886, in *Kirchenpolitik*, p. 31, cf. p. xxxviii.

104. Gossler to Zedlitz, April 9, 1887, *AP Poznań* XXIV D I 30; *Kirchenpolitik*, p. 24.

105. Quoted by Rantzau in memorandum to German Foreign Office, December 26, 1889, in *Kirchenpolitik*, p. 105.

106. Order by Dinder, quoted in *Germania*, December 2, 1887, *PA Bonn* Preussen 8:2.

107. Dinder to Zedlitz, January 26, 1888, *Ibid.*, Preussen 4:1.

108. Gossler to Bismarck, December 10, 1887, *Ibid.*, Preussen 8:2.

109. *Kuryer Poznański*, January 1, 1888,; collection of press commentary, December 1887, *Ibid.*

110. Bismarck to Schlözer, May 27, 1888, *Ibid.*

111. Order of October 11, 1888, *GPSA Berlin, Rep. B 30:II,* #2857.

112. Bismarck to Gossler, April 25, 1887, *PA Bonn*, Preussen 4:1.

113. *Kirchenpolitik*, pp. 80ff.

114. Report from Bromberg, November 23, 1881, *GPSA Berlin, Rep. 84a,* #5964.

115. Speech of February 25, 1886, *Abgeordnetenhaus*.

116. Council of Ministers meeting, February 7, 1886.

117. Memorandum, January 27, 1886, quoted by Hermann Oncken, "Preussen und Polen im 19. Jahrhundert," in *Deutschland und Polen*, ed. A. Brackmann (Munich, 1933), p. 231.

118. Puttkamer order, February 11, 1886, *AP Poznań* XII A 4, vol. 1.

119. Council of Ministers meeting, May 8, 1886.

120. Mai, p. 161; Żnin *Landrat* to Zedlitz, April 8, 1889, *GPSA Berlin* Rep. B 30, #110; Szubin *Landrat* to Zedlitz, February 2, 1888, *Ibid.*, Rep. B 30:I #589.

121. Council of Ministers meeting, February 7, 1886; Gossler to Zedlitz, April 8, 1886, *Ibid.*, #659.

122. Council of Ministers meetings, January 24 and February 21, 1886, *Ibid.*, Rep. 84a, #4066-7.

123. Speech of January 29, 1886, *Abgeordnetenhaus*; cf. letter of April 25, 1887, *PA Bonn*, Preussen 4:1.

124. Speech of January 28, 1886, *Abgeordnetenhaus*.

125. *Gesammelte Werke*, IX:205.

126. Bismarck to Schlözer, *PA Bonn*, Preussen 2:1, January 31, 1886.

127. *Ibid.*

128. Speech of January 29, 1886, *Abgeordnetenhaus*; *Gesammelte Werke*, IX:262.

129. *Politische Reden*, XIII:272ff.

130. Council of Ministers meeting, January 10, 1886.

131. Korth, pp. 31f.

132. Quoted in report from Poznań, May 10, 1893, *GPSA Berlin*, Rep. 84a, #5964.

133. Speech of May 7, 1887, *Abgeordnetenhaus*.

134. Bismarck to Gossler, June 20, 1887, *GPSA Berlin*, Rep. 84a, #4067.
135. *Bismarcks Erbe* (Berlin, 1915), p. 151.
136. p. 135; see also Rothfels, p. 90; Feldman, pp. 355f.
137. Herzfeld, II:74.

Chapter IV: Polish National Solidarity under Attack

Polish spokesmen reacted initially with surprise and dismay to the flurry of measures directed against them by Bismarck. During previous decades, Polish parliamentarians had settled into an increasingly formal pattern of protest and opposition. Aside from occasional rhetorical excesses, they no longer saw themselves as a revolutionary factor; in spite of Bismarck's constant focus on pan-Polish plots, he probably did not see them as such a factor either. Polish gentry representatives were aware that the government no longer paid much attention to them; they were also aware that their way of life and their position in Prussian-Polish society would continue regardless. Part of their surprise at this "signal for a war of extermination" was because it came "just at a time when we are everywhere on the side of order."[1] As veterans of the *Kulturkampf*, they were used to being at odds with the government, but they were unprepared for anything like the Settlement Law. Since most of them were noble estate owners, it was this particular aspect of the anti-Polish offensive, representing an assault on their economic as well as political existence, which virtually monopolized their attention during the following years.

Some Polish spokesmen tried to strike a pose of confidence and defiance. One professed to be flattered by Bismarck's attack, which implied that "we are feared, that one sees in us a viable principle, that the most powerful men of this century are struggling against us with their most powerful weapons."[2] Another was more defiant still:

> "If the great statesman himself did not anticipate that sooner or later the Polish question would be on the agenda (of international politics), why would there be occasion to persecute a political and moral corpse with a hatred that only proves that it is alive? It is the hatred of this great man that demonstrates that we are living and will continue to live. . . . Despite this hatred, we are not going to capitulate; more than ever we are going to be a

people united as brothers. Victory will be ours; dishonor, if not disgrace, will be yours!"[3]

But from the beginning such assertions were mixed with expressions of pessimism and despair, and the latter soon came to predominate. Wierzbiński (in the course of the speech just cited) conceded that, "in view of (Bismarck's) wrath, we are far from having any illusions; we know very well that a natural force, with which we are unable to fight with equal weapons, is opposing us."[4] Stablewski, while challenging the government that it was "not in a position to destroy us," acknowledged at the same time its ability to do everything short of that: "You can inflict much harm upon us; you can have your pleasure by martyring a living organism; you can cripple generations spiritually, ruin them materially."[5] Without waiting to see how effective the Settlement Law would actually be, many Poles seemed to feel that they were overmatched. *Kuryer Poznański* spoke of the "dreadful deeds" of the Settlement Commission, "rapidly removing the estates of our large landowners" from Polish possession.[6] Czarliński began his remarks during the annual discussion of the Commission's activities with the assurance that he did not want "to spoil (the Landtag's) pleasure over the growing success of this reprehensible law, (but) to inspire the children (of Landtag members) with the necessity of atonement for the crimes of their fathers."[7]

Such expressions of pessimism and defeatism were justified less by the actual results of Bismarck's measures than by the sometimes embarrassing failure of the counter-measures of the Polish leadership. Not only did these fail to deter the government from doing more or less as it pleased with its Poles, they also drew the attention of some Poles to the inadequacies of the traditional noble political elite. The only response to the expulsions (aside from the censure motion) was the establishment of committees to aid the expellees. This aid was concentrated on the minority which was unable to return to Russia or Austria for political reasons (*i.e.*, intellectuals and political activists), but little was done for the mass of farm workers, guilty at most of draft evasion, toward which the Prussian-Polish leadership seemed to feel no special obligation.[8] The chief response to the Settlement Law, which threatened the leadership much more directly, was the "Land Bank (*Bank Ziemski*)" of 1886. This Land Bank was patterned after the Galician "Rescue Bank (*Bank Ratunku*)," established by the nobility there less for national reasons than to help insolvent estate owners hold onto their land by providing management help and refinancing. *Nowa Reforma*, a liberal Galician newspaper, warned Poznanians against taking the Rescue Bank as their model; the result would be just another credit institution for incompetent estate owners instead of a real counterpart to the Settlement Commission. A true counter-measure would have to compete with Germans at forced sales and parcel estates out to Polish settlers.⁹ But the organizers of the Poznanian bank apparently did not think they could manage such a project on their own; they felt dependent upon Galician help and were persuaded also to accept Galician conditions. For example, parcelling was to be kept strictly in the background and employed only if the owner himself requested it; the primary goal of the Land Bank was to help current owners hold onto their estates intact.¹⁰ The Land Bank was even partially controlled by a Cracow "Committee for the Poznanian Bank" and from the beginning appeared to be devoted more to the economic interests of the landowners than to the national interest.¹¹

The Land Bank was proclaimed in November 1886, with a starting capital of 50,000 Marks but with the intention of raising an additional 3 million Marks by selling shares throughout Poland. At first this figure did not seem unrealistic; despite the depressed economic situation, newspaper editors as well as Bank spokesmen were confident that Galicians and other Poles the world over would provide the necessary support.¹² To their disappointment, however, after a year of fund-raising the bank managed to sell only 298 shares at 1000 Marks each, producing only 10% of the anticipated capital. Most disappointing was the weak response from Poles outside Germany: only 51 shares were bought by Galicians and 27 in Congress Poland during the first year. Prussian Poles complained about being let down by their Polish brethren; newspapers in Galicia and Congress Poland responded by speaking "in a very unfriendly manner" about the Land Bank project, warning Prussian Poles that "if they could not help themselves, (others) were not going to help them either, for this would not do any good."¹³

For a couple of years the Land Bank continued to aim for its 3 million Marks and the Polish press was confident that it would be successful. But by 1888 it could no longer hide its disappointment with the slow start; as *Kuryer Poznański* conceded, the Land Bank has not been able to begin operations "with success," *i.e.*, it had not been able to keep a single Polish estate from going into the hands of the Settlement Commission.¹⁴ Regular reports on the bank's progress disappeared from the press and Prussian officials (who from the beginning had watched it very carefully) limited their reports to the single sentence: "The Polish Land Bank has not been able to begin operations due to a shortage of funds."¹⁵ Even newspapers friendly to the Polish leadership began to speculate that the Land Bank would fold without ever getting started. *Gazeta Toruńska* suggested that the bank's noble directors were "good people but bad musicians" and urged that its management be placed in "more practical and experienced hands."[16] Finally, in July 1888, the bank lowered its capital goal to 1.2 million Marks (in order to get itself registered) and its previous director (Żółtowski) was replaced by Teodor Kalkstein.[17]

Kalkstein, though a noble estate owner himself, was a vocal critic of the bank's previous leadership and an advocate of parcelling along *Rentengut* lines. In an 1887 essay, "Our Situation and the German Colonization Law of 26 April 1886," he argued that Bismarck's offensive did not require intensified efforts "to save large-estate ownership." After all, many Polish estates were in serious difficulty long before 1886 due to "frivolity, disorder, divisions among heirs, shortage of credit and capital, high interest rates, foreign competition, low tariffs, etc.," all of which had little to do with the Settlement Law. "The question of the existence of large land ownership is not at all a financial question of the large-estate owners but a social question." In the interest of social peace as well as national economy, it was necessary to "reduce the social significance of large landownership and latifundian economy and raise peasant ownership and economy to a higher economic and social position. In a word, a different division of the land among the social classes is the postulate of the times." It was in the interest even of the nobility to "support and accelerate the realization of this organic process by spontaneously creating medium-sized peasant farms or agricultural settlements upon which the lower classes of our society can find a foothold." The development of a stronger middle-class peasantry, for Kalkstein the backbone of all strong, nationally-conscious societies, would be of great benefit to the national cause as well.[18]

Upon taking over the Land Bank, Kalkstein ignored Galician wishes and turned it more towards parcelling. In May 1889 it was able to buy its first estate and the first subdivision took place at the end of that year.[19] Ironically, the Land Bank remained in precarious financial condition until the *Rentengut* laws of 1890-1 rescued it in effect (see below, p. 128). By the end of 1890, it had purchased about 4000 ha. of land (60% of it from Germans) and settled about 250 families. About 100 of these had full-sized farms, the rest smaller worker plots.[20] This still seemed little in comparison with the state's efforts in the opposite direction. The Settlement Commission had bought about 50,000 ha. by that time (90% from Poles), though only about 25% of this had been settled.[21] Already apparent as a factor in the Poles' favor was the great "land hunger" of the small peasants, tenants, and farm workers in Poznania and West Prussia, who jumped at parcels of almost any size. This made it unnecessay for the Poles to offer the financial and other incentives which the Settlement Commission required to attract Germans from outside the province.

Alongside efforts to fight the Settlement Commission on its own terms with the Land Bank and other parcelling agencies, Polish leaders considered various ways of using their position in the Prussian and German parliaments to oppose Bismarck's policies. The memory of the successful effort in response to the expulsions was still fresh; perhaps something could be done to amend the colonization, school, and other anti-Polish measures of 1886-7. The dominant clerical element in the *Koło Polskie* continued to stress bi-national confessional interests and preferred to work closely with the German Center Party. The two parties had a similar social program and common hostility toward liberalism, materialism, and socialism.[22] The several priests in the *Koło* delegation were not yet convinced that the *Kulturkampf* was over and responded to Bismarck's newest measures as anti-Catholic rather than anti-Polish as such. Stablewski described even the Settlement Commission as a Protestantizing rather than Germanizing agency.[23] *Kuryer Poznański* also followed this line, attacking the Commission's introduction of additional Protestants into Poznania, charging that the removal of Polish from the school curriculum would have a Protestantizing effect, and appearing generally more apprehensive about the religious than the national consequences of the new policies.[24] Its "political program" for 1888, a curious combination of clerical and agrarian concerns directed at all "Catholic" representatives, listed four top priorities, omitting anything specifically Polish: make the state safe for the Church, restore Church control of education, solve the "social question," and raise agricultural tariffs.[25]

Theoretically, of course, the Center Party was not the only German political force with which the Poles might work. In the midst of the agricultural depression, some Poles began to consider fellow German agrarians as possible allies. Others considered an appeal to the Germans of Poznania and West Prussia on the basis of provincial loyalties and resentment against the price these provinces were paying for Bismarck's effort to get at the Poles, *e.g.*, exclusion from provincial and local self-government rights and the proliferation of counties and county bureaucracies which imposed additional expenses on the country's poorest regions.[26] But such regional loyalties scarcely existed in the face of the overriding national differences and German agrarians were usually members of the *Kartell* parties which were Bismarck's strongest supporters. German liberalism remained another possibility, except that the clerical and agrarian coloration of the *Koło* made German liberal support increasingly unlikely. The Social Democrats gratuitously supported most Polish demands, including even the restoration of an independent Poland, but this was of no practical significance, and in any case the *Koło* was as anti-socialist as any German party. Thus the majority vote on the Reichstag censure motion was essentially an exception; there was no permanent constellation of German parties that could effectively protect the Poles from the measures of Bismarck and his government. The Center remained the only source of significant support elsewhere in Germany.

The Center-Polish alliance found expression in election alliances for the 1887 Reichstag campaign. In at least two districts where Poles were in the minority (Stuhm/Sztum-Marienwerder and Flotow/Złotów-Schlochau/Człuchów), they nominated German Catholics to run on their ticket to demonstrate their confessional as well as national character.[27] In districts where the *Koło* did not put up candidates (or in run-off elections), Poles were asked to support the Center candidate.[28] But the 1887 election turned out badly for both Center and Poles. Each seemed to feel that it had given the partner more than it received in return and the partnership began to suffer. *Germania* and the Polish press engaged in mutual recrimination, each claiming that the other side put national before confessional loyalties after all. Bismarck's inclusion of Catholics among the new settlers served to defuse Center opposition to the Settlement Law. The appointment of Dinder also had its effect; as Polish suspicion of their German archbishop became more vocal, it was easier for German Catholics to accept Bismarck's contention that Polish Catholicism was merely a servant of Polish nationalism. Finally, however Polish clericals chose to see it, the *Kulturkampf* was in fact over and German Catholics were free to indulge their national feelings along with their countrymen. As a result, after 1887 the Poles seemed to get less unequivocal support from the Center than at any time since the Empire was founded.

Ultimately, the most promising means of opposing Bismarck's designs upon the Poles was the increased mobilization of the Polish masses. Aside from a minority of Organic Work enthusiasts, this had been largely neglected previously by the Polish political leadership. Signs of mass politicization after 1871 (cited above) were more often inadvertent outgrowths of the *Kulturkampf* rather than the result of the efforts of gentry leaders. Such indications continued after 1886, motivated especially by the new language and school policies, and the tone became still more militant. There was ample evidence that measures directed supposedly at nobles and clergy were alienating other Poles as well. Poles who were prevented from learning to read and write their language or using it to deal with state officials or acquiring homesteads created by the Settlement Commission fell easily into a common front with their upper classes against the government. As Stablewski put it, "through such laws you bring the rights of nationality to the full consciousness of the whole nation, simultaneously with this consciousness, however, feelings which must fill the hearts of the whole population with bitterness."[29] A colleague put this more bluntly: "Your measures are going to have a good side for us too; the whole Polish nation, nobles *and* peasants, . . . will finally come to a full consciousness of belonging together."[30] Kantak drew attention to the extension of the national movement to previously aloof regions (*e.g.*, Upper Silesia, Kashubia, even Masuria) as a result of Bismarck's policies: "It is the pressure which we (all) feel that awakens the consciousness of opposition and which fans the flame of life even there where it was already threatening to go out."[31] Kashubia, for example, was an especially poor, over-populated region with few Polish nobles but with many residents who were forced to work as migrant farm workers; it epitomized Polish "land hunger" and thus also resentment of being excluded from the Settlement Commission's homesteads. The otherwise pessimistic prognosis of *Kuryer Poznański* for 1888 saw some reason for hope in that "those who slept until now are awaking; those who were indifferent are beginning to understand the sinfulness of such indifference."[32]

These statements by Polish spokesmen were not merely wishful thinking; they seem to correspond to reality and to other evidence of growing national militancy and political awareness after 1886. For example, four new Polish newspapers began operation in that year alone; one of these, *Gazeta Olsztyńska*, provided the first evidence of a Polish movement in East Prussia. Violations of press laws by Polish journalists continued at a high level and several editors spent as much time in jail as out.[33] Government reports on the public mood in the Polish regencies provide similar evidence. At first some of these suggested the response that Bismarck wanted to read; an 1886 report from Danzig claimed that "the Polish laws have so far not called forth any visible excitement within the mass of the Polish population; (only) the leaders are naturally exasperated and give expression to this mood by their conduct."[34] Others were closer to the mark, however: "It could hardly be doubted that the latest Landtag debates and the proposed measures . . . are going to result in a still tighter unification of Polish elements."[35] In May 1886 this reporter detected a "deep ill-feeling and a tendency to stand up even more decisively for (Polish) national interests." There was evidence "even among the lower classes of the Polish population, among peasants and workers . . . (of) a lively and excited national feeling and even an exasperated mood."[36] "An intensification of national differences in the province" was also discernible and, especially among the educated classes, "the division between Germans and Poles has become even sharper."[37] These official reports have a certain credibility if only because they relate the response which Bismarck least desired and anticipated.

This heightened popular resentment found some expression in a series of well-attended public rallies protesting the removal of Polish from the school curriculum. Each county in Poznania had at least one of these and some towns staged several in succession; Gossler counted almost 100 altogether.³⁸ They were particularly pleasing to the *Koło* leadership, for they were usually organized by local nobles and clergy and seemed to reaffirm National Solidarity. And while led by nobles, an encouraging proportion of peasants and townspeople were included among the activists.³⁹ The most common response of these rallies was to organize Polish instruction on a private basis. A few such classes did go into operation but were then stopped by a Zedlitz decree.⁴⁰ But the clergy continued to urge from the pulpit that the Polish family take it upon itself to teach its children what they needed to know about their language.⁴¹

The assemblies failed in the end to produce effective counter-measures to Bismarck's policies; in this sense, like the Land Bank, parliamentary tactics, and other aspects of the noble-clerical response, they were unsuccessful as a resistance strategy. Compounding this lack of success was the surprisingly weak resistance of many Polish estate owners to the temptations of the Settlement Commission. No sooner had the Settlement Law been passed than scores of Polish nobles, including members of some very prominent families, offered properties for sale. As an official in Bromberg noted, many Polish nobles were not "at all averse to selling to the state."⁴² Among the sales which received the most attention and caused the most concern in the Polish press was one by former Herrenhaus member Józef Mielżyński of a quite large (c. 4000 ha.) estate for 2.2 million Marks.⁴³ Józef Czarnecki sold an estate of similar size, setting off "considerable excitement" among his countrymen.⁴⁴ Mieczysław Łyskowski, a partner in one of the few Polish-controlled banks in Germany, sold an 800-ha. estate in Mogilno County in January 1887.⁴⁵ Bogdan Hutten-Czapski, one of the few Polish nobles to hold an influential position in German government circles, did the same with an estate in Brodnica/Strasburg County, getting what the press called a "fabulously high price" for it.⁴⁶ In September 1887 Julian Czarliński, also a former parliamentarian, sold his home estate in Kościerzyna/Berent County.⁴⁷ A Reichstag deputy, Ludwik Graeve, also sold his estate and was obliged to resign his seat in the aftermath.⁴⁸

This high level of sales to the Settlement Commission, combined with the slow start of the Land Bank, caused some loss of confidence in the traditional noble leadership. Hostile observers had a field day dealing with these two subjects; a pro-government paper in Warsaw ridiculed the "intellectual poverty and weakness" of Prussian-Polish nobles, the way "the greatest Polish patriots are giving up their estates with pleasure at the sight of the Prussian Marks," and suggested that the Polish national cause in Germany was "irretrievably lost."[49] Even Polish papers began to wonder aloud whether the Poles would be able to hold out much longer. As *Gazeta Toruńska* (usually a firm supporter of the noble establishment), put it in 1886: "Prince Bismarck knew what he was saying when he asserted in the Landtag that the Poles themselves would ask that they be bought out. And they want to found Land Banks!"[50] *Koło* spokesmen insisted on the distinction between themselves and those nobles who sold their estates: "We cannot absolve of serious guilt such Poles who frivolously and flippantly offer their paternal inheritance for settlement."[51] *Gazeta Toruńska* was concerned to make this same distinction and lessen the unfavorable impact on Polish political leaders; it criticized the land sales precisely because they "were bringing our representatives into an odd and ever more difficult situation and finally they will not dare to lift their eyes, much less seize the floor in the name of this people."[52] Despite these efforts, however, many Poles tended to associate the Commission's customers with the traditional political leadership as parts of one and the same noble class. As a Prussian official observed, "the constantly decreasing number of Polish estate owners" and the "more and more declining prestige of the Polish nobility" were linked together, causing some Poles to look to other means of opposing Bismarck's offensive, perhaps by "strengthening (economic) organizations, (and) especially through the improvement of the Polish artisan class."[53]

These developments helped set the stage for the appearance of unprecedented opposition to the traditional noble leadership from within the Polish camp. The most vocal spokesman for this movement was Roman Szymański, editor/publisher of the newspaper *Orędownik* in Poznań.[54] Szymański had been agitating among and mobilizing the townspeople of Poznania since about 1870. As a Positivist, he felt that more emphasis should be put on economic development and education and less on political maneuvering and empty posturing by the noble leadership. He was critical of the lingering tendency of *Koło* leaders to engage in unnecessary nationalist rhetoric, which was of no help in dealing with more immediate problems. "Let us leave the restoration of a future Poland to God, whereas today we went only to secure for ourselves our national existence in the frontiers of the Prussian state under the rule of the Prussian monarchs."[55] Szymański tended toward an ethnic understanding of "Prussian Poland," while the *Koło* leadership continued to think in terms of the frontiers of 1771, which omitted many Polish-speaking Prussians (in Upper Silesia and Masuria). "In Silesia . . . the Polish spirit is awakening and is undeniably growing; . . . in West

Prussia it has already grown. . . . Even in Ermland the Polish people are awakening."⁵⁶ "Agitation ought to be conducted in two directions: in depth and in breadth; . . . in depth in the Duchy and in West Prussia, in breadth in Ermland and in Upper Silesia, . . . the whole Polish people, however and wherever it lives under Prussian domination."⁵⁷ Szymański's efforts to create a separate Polish-bourgeois political identity were criticized harshly from the start by the defenders of National Solidarity. His specifically middle-class rally in 1872 to protest Bismarck's differentiation between Polish leaders and people was opposed by *Dziennik Poznański*; his 1879 "Association of Polish Voters in Poznań" was branded "illegal" by the *Koło* leadership.⁵⁸

For the most part, Szymański still did not contest *Koło* authority from the time *Orędownik* ("The Advocate") was founded in 1872 (with the support of Maximilian Jackowski and other nobles in the Organic Work movement) until the late-1880s. Throughout the *Kulturkampf* period, he supported the idea of National Solidarity and the unity of Catholic faith and Polish nation. His first resonse to the Settlement Law was that "the salvation of the landed property must have our complete attention. Everything else with which the national spirit has occupied itself until now must be put to the side and remain *in suspenso* until the storm is past."⁵⁹ He was mainly concerned to move in alongside the traditional leadership, not dislodge it entirely. As late as 1887, he cautioned his supporters against thinking that they could take over by themselves in the way that the middle classes in many other parts of Europe were doing. "Our middle classes will need the help, advice, and direction of the upper classes for a long time yet."⁶⁰ "The middle class in Prussian Poland is too weakly developed, too poorly situated materially, for it to be able to step in for the educated upper classes under present conditions. . . . In the middle class there is little bourgeois self-reliance, in places virtually none at all."⁶¹ "Our middle classes are not going to reach the point so quickly where they can take the election organizations upon their own shoulders."⁶²

But at about this same time, Szymański's attitude began to change. While the *Koło* leadership seemed unable to cope with the situation created by Bismarck's measures, it continued to exclude the Polish townspeople from a political role. The nobility and Church remained in firm control of the *Koło*, which was the sole political organization of Germany's Polish population. In fact, it would be described more accurately as the political organization of the Polish nobility in Germany, with strong support from the Catholic hierarchy. It always reflected the conservative, clerical, and agrarian interests and attitudes of this group; it existed, not wherever Poles live (for example, not in Upper Silesia), but only where Polish nobles lived. By the 1880s it seemed increasingly anachronistic in terms of its ideology of National Solidarity and its essentially authoritarian structure, still little affected by universal suffrage, industrialization, liberal-clerical conflict, and the various frictions arising from the era of "mass-man" and the Long Depression. It consisted of an election committee in each county where nationally conscious Poles lived, supervised by provincial election committees in Poznania and West Prussia. These committees consisted mainly of nobles and clergy; in 1888, of some 250 county committee members in Poznania, only 10 were peasants and perhaps again as many came from the urban lower-middle classes.[63] At election time the county committee would propose a nominee to run on the *Koło* ticket, normally an estate owner or a clergyman; a popular assembly would be summoned, the man presented as a "good Catholic and a good Pole," approved by acclamation, and ratified by the provincial board. Frequently a retiring representative chose his own successor and had him acclaimed by the assembly, which seldom questioned guidance by the "older brothers."[64] While peasants and burghers might have token seats on county committees, they were not normally nominated for parliamentary seats or appointed to the provincial committees. At the time of Bismarck's offensive in 1886, 13 of 16 Polish Reichstag deputies were noble estate owners and a 14th was a noble clergyman,[65] a predominance which even the German Conservative Party could not match. This system may have suited a time when most Prussian Poles were either disfranchised or relatively apolitical, but Bismarck's *Kulturkampf* (and his universal suffrage) had changed this; growing numbers of Poles, especially townsmen, were politically as well as nationally conscious. And they logically became less passive toward their own leaders as they did so toward the policies of the Prussian and German governments.

The turning point for Szymański came with the 1887 Reichstag elections. The number of Polish seats was reduced from 16 to 13, which raised expectations that the *Koło* structure (*e.g.*, the provincial election committees) would be broadened to include some middle-class and peasant members. Szymański demanded "absolutely, besides nobles and clergy, at least two representatives of the urban 'intelligentsia.'"[66] Instead, the Poznanian committee reemerged in 1888 in its traditional composition: five estate owners, two priests, the editor of *Dziennik Poznański*, and Poznania's leading industrialist (Stefan Cegielski of the Cegielski Works in Poznań.)[67] Szymański's attacks became stronger now and he began to question the fitness of the nobility as a class for its national leadership role. In December 1888 he resigned his token seat on the Poznań city election committee and called for organized opposition to the *Koło* establishment. He charged that "counter-measures such as the noble 'Land Bank,' and the effectiveness and policies of Polish representatives, no longer evoke trust; the leadership of the nobility and clergy, which until now have passed for the natural protectors of the middle and lower classes, turns out to be fruitless."[68] He also began to move away from the sacrosanct National Solidarity concept, concluding that the *Koło* "represented merely the interests of the aristocracy and large landed property but not those of the Polish bourgeoisie and artisan class." Due to the ineffective performance of the noble leadership in the face of Bismarck's offensive and the sale of so many estates to the Settlement Commission, he felt that it had "lost the right to fight for the interests of the whole Polish nationality," that it no longer possessed "sufficient understanding," and should be replaced "preferably by Polish bourgeois."[69] He even suggested the possibility of a separate Polish middle-class party to compete with the *Koło*, but he took no steps in this direction at this time.[70]

For the time being, Szymański's opposition movement did not meet with much success. His attempt in Wąbrzeźno/Briesen to oppose a *Koło* nominee in a Landtag by-election came to nothing; he was simply voted down by the assembly in favor of the *Koło*'s choice.[71] His urban middle-class supporters remained a small minority in a still largely agrarian province and failed to find support among other segments of Prussian-Polish society. Another problem was the absence of a clear program which might suggest alternatives to the policies of *Koło* leaders. Szymański's positions were reflective mainly of middle-class economic interests, including a "Buy Polish" campaign aimed at his followers' German and Jewish competition. In his efforts to establish a position distinct from that of the *Koło*, he opposed even those policies which were popular or marked by some success, e.g., the rallies in opposition to Prussian school policy. "Only a society which feels itself to be strong can annoy the government, demonstrate against it; we Poles under Prussian rule are not such a society."[72] In other words, he suggested that the Poles respond to the government's offensive against them by being more accommodating, which was hardly a popular position while Bismarck was still increasing the pressure.

Thus, in spite of their dissatisfaction with the leadership of nobles and clergy, most Poles were not yet inclined to turn to the *Orędownik* faction as a replacement. Virtually all the other Polish newspapers came to the defense of the *Koło* leadership against Szymański's attacks. The only exception was *Postęp*, a second organ of the urban population founded in 1886 by Stanisław Knapowski. Otherwise, all the principal papers (*Dziennik Poznański, Kuryer Poznański, Gazeta Toruńska,* and *Goniec*

Wielkopolski) began to polemicize "in the most lively manner against the introduction of such tendencies, which rest upon 'purely democratic' foundations, into the national-Polish party."[73] *Kuryer Poznański* was clerical-conservative in German terms while the other three papers cited above were more or less national-liberal, except that in the Polish context there was no longer much of a difference between these two standpoints. If the press is to be taken as any reflection of the overall balance of political forces in Prussian Poland, this was a very conservative region indeed. Except for Szymański's small movement (perhaps a Polish counterpart to the German Progressives), Prussian-Polish opinion and politics were thoroughly dominated by Polish equivalents of the German *Kartell* parties. Socialism and secular liberalism were virtually nonexistent; there was no need, of course, for a Catholic party while the *Koło* remained at least as clerical as the German Center Party.

In spite of this negative response, Szymański persevered in his opposition through the 1890 Reichstag campaign. He branded the Poznanian election committee an "agent of the nobles' policies" and urged his supporters to withhold their financial contributions and abstain from attendance at its public functions. This was the last straw for supporters of the *Koło* establishment, who denounced him as "sinful and un-Polish" and accused him of trying to "split the Poles into two camps." Prussian officials monitoring these developments became increasingly interested in this "remarkable discrepancy" between Polish factions, but they also observed correctly that Szymański's campaign "does not seem to have fallen upon fertile ground; . . . not one single voice has been raised in favor of *Orędownik*" at public campaign rallies.[74] The 1890 elections turned out better for the Poles, who regained the three seats lost in 1887; Szymański seemed to have little effect on this outcome and his opposition became somewhat less vocal afterwards. While this brief revolt should be kept in proper perspective, it did nevertheless have its impact on a traditional political elite used to unanimity and subservience. Though this was not the first case of political differences within the Polish camp (cf. pp. 27ff.), it was the first one with social overtones. Earlier disputes had concerned mainly questions of tactics or positions on specific issues, carried out between members of the one "establishment." Szymański and his followers, however, saw themselves as the vanguard of a growing, previously slighted urban (to some extent also rural) middle class in opposition to an establishment representing essentially the nobility and Catholic hierarchy but not doing a very good job for Poles in general. Moreover, important economic and social trends seemed to presage a renewal of this challenge sooner or later in the future.

This new restiveness of the townspeople in Prussian Poland was based as much on the rapid growth of the urban population itself as on the weak response of *Koło* leaders to Bismarck's offensive. While it found political expression only in the late 1880s, the growth of the urban element in terms of numbers, organizations, and self-confidence had been evident for some time already. One factor in this growth was the "opening up" of eastern towns after 1867 (the abolition of remaining guild privileges and fees that had been charged to those wanting to start a business). This made it easier for Poles to move into ocucpations which had previously been largely the preserve of Germans and Jews. Between 1871 and 1895, the number of towns in Poznania with German-Jewish majorities was cut in half.[75] The fact that many traditional artisanal occupations were becoming less profitable in the wake of industrialization encouraged their abandonment by Germans and (especially) Jews, who (as noted previously) were leaving the Polish provinces in large numbers in favor of the more developed German West or other countries. Poles did not so much "push the Germans out" (as German nationalists claimed) as simply fill the vacancies they found, beginning with those occupations requiring least in the way of capital and training and working up from there. In a sense, the occupations taken up by the emerging Polish middle class were determined by the departing Germans and Jews.[76] A Landtag report described the situation in a presumably typical Poznanian town, Zaniemyśl/Santomischel: the percentage of basic tradesmen (bakers, butchers, millers, cobblers, tailors, carpenters, masons, and blacksmiths) who were Polish jumped from 22% in 1885 to 55% twenty years later.[77] In the quarter-century between 1882 and 1907, the proportion of Poznanian "industrialists" (mainly artisans) who were Polish rose from 48% to 63% and the increase in the "trade" category (consisting mainly of small merchants) was even more notable: from 28% to 49%.[78]

Parallel to this growth of the Polish merchant and artisan classes (and perhaps contributing to it) was the continued strong development of economic self-help organizations serving and supported by them. These were part of the general effort by Poles during the Age of Positivism to improve national strength through economic and educational development. But while most of the institutions of Organic Work (*e.g.*, the peasant organizations and various cultural societies) were devised and led by members of the nobility, the artisan and merchant organizations were largely the creation of the urban middle class itself (with help, to be sure, from the clergy). The success enjoyed by these organizations doubtless contributed much to middle-class pride and self-confidence and thus led indirectly to demands for a larger political role in Polish society.

The first of the artisan-oriented organizations to have more than a short life-span dates from 1860: the "Industrial Society (*Towarzystwo Przemysłowe*)" under the chairmanship of Cegielski. In the following year a subsidiary "Credit Society for the Industrialists of the City of Poznań (*Towarzystwo Pożyczkowe dla Przemysłowców Miasta Poznania*)" was established, the first of the credit cooperatives or "people's banks," mutual savings and loan associations whose purpose was to pool the capital of the entire membership in order to make business loans to members who could make use of them. The number of such credit co-ops reached 23 in Poznania by 1870, with several more in West Prussia. They were organized at first along the lines suggested by Hermann Schulze-Delitzsch and associated with the German co-op movement. In 1871, however, 19 Polish organizations broke away and organized themselves separately as the "Union of Polish Co-operative Societies (*Związek Polskich Spółek Zarobkowych*)" under the direction of the priest Augustyn Szamarzewski.[79] The separate Polish association was allegedly formed to facilitate the flow of funds between co-ops, keep joint records, publish information centrally, and sponsor new branches; while nationalist motives were not cited, they can be surmised, especially since the step was taken shortly after the contested inclusion of Poznania and West Prussia in the new German Empire.

The number of Polish credit co-ops reached 86 by 1879, after which there followed a levelling off of activity during the 1880s; some of the weaker units (including all those attempted in Upper Silesia) failed. By 1887 there remained only 73, but in terms of financial strength and membership the movement continued to grow even during these years:

	1873	1890
membership	6,660	26,553
deposits	2.6 million Marks	12.5 million Marks.[80]

They expanded to serve other than artisan needs; indeed, non-artisans (mainly peasants) constituted 63% of the membership by 1890.[81] In 1886, in order to provide complete banking services for member co-ops (but also to be free of reliance upon German banks, which might be subject to government pressure as part of Bismarck's new policy), the "Co-op Union" established its own bank, the "Union Bank" (*Bank Związku*). In sharp contrast to the noble Land Bank of the same year, the Union Bank began with a modest amount of capital but grew rapidly during the following years until it held deposits of almost 2.5 million Marks in 1900.[82] Some Polish co-ops did not join this union at first, but a new Prussian co-op law in 1889 imposed tighter regulations and compelled all those not belonging to central associations to undergo audits by state (German) accountants, which served to push the remaining Polish co-ops into the single association.[83]

These organizations were not characterized at first by any particular class attitudes. Under National Solidarity it did not matter much whether a priest, physician, artisan or noble was in charge of a particular co-op. They often went out of their way to get the participation of local nobles and were frequently willing to offer the chairmanship as a reward to one who would provide his name and a large deposit. Until 1889, however, the principle of unlimited liability applied to individual members of credit co-ops, which caused the wealthier estate owners to remain wary of involvement. The 1889 law permitted limited liability arrangements and thus encouraged such participation. Even then, the participation of wealthy nobles did not always turn out well. Many of them served simultaneously as heads of several such organizations. Where they did become full members they seldom contributed much in the way of deposits, since they were unlikely to need aid on the scale on which the co-ops operated.[84] Moreover they were often imperious in their dealings with other members and there were numerous cases of conflict between noble leaders and the membership of "people's banks."[85] More often, therefore, the chairmanship was in the hands of a priest or a member of the educated professional class. Clergy were quite welcome and useful as co-op leaders. The Church itself was not able to identify too closely with Polish economic organizations, nor could it put its own funds in the credit co-ops. But there was nothing to stop individual priests from contributing personal savings and participating in co-op activities, and many of them did so. This clerical involvement was clearly related to the *Kulturkampf* (cf. p. 26) but it was also part of the new policy of social action under Pope Leo XIII. Some spokesmen for the emerging middle classes(notably Szymański) expressed concern about the prominent clerical role in supposedly middle class organizations, particularly in view of the Church's strong support of the *Koło* leadership; more often, however, clerical help was acknowledged to be indispensable in those smaller towns where the Polish middle class was just beginning to get on its feet.

Attempts by Szymański and others to exploit poltically the success of the credit co-op movement and get their support for an anti-noble campaign were not successful. It was co-op policy to abstain from politics, from the Polish national movement as well as from inner-Polish quarrels. They made no political contributions and frowned on simultaneous membership in more militant nationalist organizations. They were doubtless aware of the suspicious attitude of Prussian officialdom and feared that any identification with the national cause might provoke a crackdown that would undermine their principal mission: to strengthen the Polish middle class economically. As it was, some Prussian officials questioned the "non-political" activities of some co-ops, *e.g.*, their sponsorship of lectures on Polish history and culture. Such departures from specifically co-op objectives took place usually in organizations led by nobles or priests, whereas artisan leaders showed a preference for practical, occupational topics.[86] While these organizations did not serve directly as the economic and organizational foundation for the middle class's bid for political leadership, they were nonetheless of long-term political significance. They contributed to a stronger resistance by Polish society to the Prussian government by helping the development of a strong middle class, something Polish society had traditionally lacked. They provided the opportunity for many artisans and merchants to acquire their first experience in the management of a social enterprise. And, as suggested above, they symbolized and contributed to the growing self-confidence of the middle class and thus assured the continued development of the assertiveness first expressed by Szymański. Along with Bismarck's measures, this likelihood of renewed opposition by the urban population contributed to the phenomenon to be examined next: the growth of "loyalism" among many members of the political establishment in Prussian Poland.

Loyalism, in the passive sense of renouncing serious efforts to restore an independent Poland or otherwise overturn the 1815/1871 arrangement, was largely taken for granted by Polish leaders in all three partitioning empires by 1886. Aside from occasional rhetorical lapses, their programs were typically limited to efforts to preserve Polish national substance within the existing political framework. As an active policy, however, loyalism meant more: cooperation with the conservative governments of the partitioning empires in pursuit of political and economic interests common to Polish and non-Polish conservatives alike. This latter kind of loyalism was practiced after 1867 with considerable success in Austrian Poland under the leadership of Agenor Gołuchowski. For obvious reasons it was less tempting to Poles living in the Russia of Alexander III, but even here there were some *"ugodowcy* (compromisers)", (*e.g.*, entrepreneurs and magnates who saw economic benefits for themselves and perhaps for Poles generally from such an approach), whose ideas were expressed by the St. Petersburg newspaper *Kraj*.[87] In Prussian Poland, where conditions were somewhere between Galicia and Congress Poland, Polish conservatives might also have been willing to give up their increasingly formal opposition posture and ally with their peers in the German Conservative Party in support of order, religion, and higher grain prices.[88] Falk's dismissal and replacement by the conservative Eulenburg in 1879 awakened some first hopes for improvement: "Bitterly disappointed (with the liberals) we turn now to the conservatives at the helm."[89] But Eulenburg quickly dashed such hopes. For the most part, such latent inclinations were frustrated by the *Kulturkampf* and Bismarck's consistent refusal to make the slightest concession in their direction. During the 1870s, only a few Poles of any prominence associated themselves with the Prussian government, and these were apolitical or at least aloof from the Polish national movement, e.g, Hutten-Czapski and several members of the Radziwiłł family.[90] Antoni Radziwiłł, adjutant general in the Prussian army, and his family ran one of the most influential salons in Berlin, attended by most top politicians (with the notable exception of Bismarck).[91] Other Polish representatives might declare their loyalty to Prussia or Germany or to the King-Emperor personally, but pride essentially kept them from offering unequivocal declarations of loyalty under all circumstances. They refused in the last analysis to accept their position in Germany as natural and "organic," insisting that it was contractual, based upon the rights and guarantees of 1815.

This situation began to change slowly in the 1880s. In 1881, government losses in the elections of that year put the Poles in a position to provide or deny it a Reichstag majority. A group of *Koło* members, led by Witold Skarżyński, thought that this might be a good time to try some bargaining with the government.[92] Kantak rejected this proposal as beneath Polish dignity, but during the following years Polish parliamentarians began to vote for selected government measures which might benefit Poles economically.[93] They also began to participate more actively in parliamentary committees dealing with matters of interest to them. In the Prussian upper house (Herrenhaus) especially, Polish members began to feel more or less at home with their German peers and provocative statements were generally avoided in favor of professions of innocence and devotion to common conservative values. As the *Kulturkampf* wound down, the Church and its press also began to gravitate toward a loyalist position. This was reflected in the more sad than defiant tone adopted by clerical representatives: "It is a historical puzzle why such a war of destruction has been inaugurated against us precisely in the last decade. . . . One sought supposedly to bring the two peoples closer together and (instead) makes the gap between them greater with each day."[94] While conceding that the Polish people felt "a great ill-temper and bitterness down to the hut of the lowest wage laborer," Stablewski emphasized that they expressed their dissatisfaction only within legal limits; virtually no one thought any longer of "conspiracies and revolutions."⁹⁵ He suggested that Bismarck ought to try the Austrian approach to the Polish problem; "in all of Poland the gratitude and joy over this is unanimous. . . . May one learn from Austria how to win over peoples."⁹⁶ For his part, however, Bismarck never accepted Galicia as a model. He argued that (Polish) Galicia was neither ethnically mixed nor that vital to Austria (which in fact had occasionally considered exchanging it for more Danubian lands), thus she could afford to experiment with Polish autonomy. "The old Prussian provinces, however, are not divided from Poznania and West Prussia by any natural frontiers and the renunciation of them would not be feasible."⁹⁷

In 1884, Skarżyński took his views to the public in an "open letter," provoking a controversy with the older nationalist leaders.⁹⁸ The latter, led by Kantak and Niegolewski and with *Goniec Wielkopolski* as their organ, insisted on a line of strict opposition and adherence to the demands of previous decades. When one of the loyalists, Cegielski, received the nomination for Poznań's Reichstag seat in 1884, the *Goniec* group supported an opposition candidacy by Niegolewski. After a couple of public meetings and a closely contested battle, Cegielski won out, but only on the day before the election did Niegolewski cease his criticism and reaffirm National Solidarity.⁹⁹ Landtag elections the following year led to the same division; this time Kantak came out against the nomination of Kantecki (editor of *Kuryer Poznański*). The nominating assembly was so rowdy that it was closed by Prussian police, after which the *Koło* appeased the nationalists by nominating Kantak after all.¹⁰⁰ But Niegolewski and Kantak each died within the year and the loyalists came to constitute a sizable minority within the *Koło* by the time Bismarck launched his offensive in 1886. The new measures did not seem calculated to encourage this trend, yet in fact they did so. By intimidating many Polish nobles, the government apparently persuaded them that loyalism was the only remaining hope for salvation from its apparent intent to liquidate them as a social as well as political factor. There seemed no longer any way of opposing these measures short of mobilizing the Polish masses, which might just as easily result in their radicalization and the loss of noble political control. The Settlement Law (which seemed very awesome at first), the ineffectiveness of Polish counter-measures, and the appearance of serious dissent within the Polish camp combined to move leading Poles closer to loyalism even in the absence of government concessions.

Józef Kościelski, a noble estate owner, gravitated from liberal nationalism in the 1860s to become the chief spokesman and symbol of loyalism in Prussian Poland in the 1880s.¹⁰¹ He was appointed to the Herrenhaus in 1881 and elected to the Reichstag (over the opposition of the

Kantak/Niegolewski faction) in 1884. His position is summed up in the following excerpt from a Reichstag speech:

> "Perhaps someday, . . . if the government does not switch to another, more just path, the . . . designation 'enemies of the state (*Reichsfeinde*)' will find its justified application. . . . The feeling of belonging together, which is demanded here from all non-Germanic citizens of the German Empire, must be offered material for nourishment. . . . Of course it is much easier to campaign constantly against the hostility toward the Empire of the non-German elements than simply to have it put to the test how long this alleged hostility toward the Empire could still exist with a little consideration for the most legitimate demands and claims."[102]

Polish representatives stressed increasingly their aversion to revolution and their distance from the Polish radical-nationalist tradition. Even Czarliński, though not himself one of the loyalists, noted that "there are enough rational Poles in Poznania, completely conscious of their duties to state and sovereign, who will suppress any forceful rebellion at once."[103] This sentiment found its strongest expression in another speech by Kościelski: "We want always to stand behind the government in everything it undertakes to preserve the threatened social order. . . . We feel no desire to go from the frying pan into the fire. Rather, I believe . . . that we . . . have every reason to work with you here on the external and internal development of the Empire."[104]

Polish loyalists tried, among other approaches, to establish a common front with German conservatives on the basis of their common aversion to socialism. Ferdynand Radziwiłł warned that it was high time for all the forces of order to bury their quarrels and join together in the struggle with socialism.[105] Stablewski included among his criticisms of the Settlement Law the argument that "for the spread of socialist teachings among the rural population you could not have found a more effective means than this bill."[106] Polish representatives seemed to be on solid ground here in view of the apparent immunity of their region to socialism. Long after the Social Democrats had become a major factor in German politics, they hardly existed in Poznania, in spite of their pro-Polish party program. In the 1887 elections, they receved only 226 votes in that province, most of these from Germans.[107] This was attributable perhaps to the lack of industry in Poznania but even in Upper Silesia, where the SPD concentrated more of its efforts, it was scarcely able to dent the virtual monopoly of the Center Party on the loyalty of the Polish population there.

Little came of these Polish overtures to German conservatives. Most of them felt little need for closer relations with such Poles. Moreover, other

Polish spokesmen continued to sound anything but loyalist, *e.g.*, Landtag leader Jażdżewski, who threatened that "dissatisfied subjects can also become enemies of their own state under certain circumstances."[108] And Polish published opinion for the most part did not reflect the loyalism of individual representatives in Berlin, which fact could not long be kept from Germans thanks to the Tiedemann-inspired translations of selected Polish press articles. Most German representatives assumed that Polish loyalists either had not had a genuine change of heart and were merely pursuing a new tactic or were generals without an army. Bismarck found great sport in challenging would-be loyalists to swear their unequivocal loyalty to Germany and their acceptance of the status quo; individual representatives would respond by declaring their loyalty to the King, the constitution, religion, etc., but could not bring themselves to take the last step of renouncing completely their hopes that Poland might again revive in some form or other. Even Kościelski conceded that "we do not want to give up the belief that we will once again rise to political life."[109]

Polish loyalists were encouraged less by the response of German conservatives than by the prospect that Bismarck, their chief persecutor, might be leaving office soon (with the death of his aged protector, Wilhelm I). This latter event occurred in March 1888 and provided a first opportunity for them to launch a major loyalist initiative. The new Emperor Friedrich had earlier held anti-Polish attitudes not unlike those of Bismarck. He refused to learn Polish, in spite of Bismarck's urgings, declaring, "No, I do not want to, I do not want to learn anything. I simply do not like them. I do not want to learn Polish, they must learn German." In spite of their soldierly qualities, "when (Poles) have taken off the uniform, they are the same old way again, and basically they are and will remain alien to us."[110] More recently, however, he had made a number of public statements which encouraged Polish leaders to hope for a change in policy. On a visit to Poznań he assured his audience that "we do not any longer have to fear the dangers of alien manners and alien nature in our state."[111] Upon taking office he added the reassurance that "every one of my subjects is equally close to my heart . . . (for) all have demonstrated equally their full devotion in the days of danger (*i.e.*, 1870-1)."[112] His English wife Victoria also visited Poznania and made a favorable impression on Polish nobles who turned out in force to greet her. They were prevented from appearing as a separate national group but the Empress sought them out nonetheless and had a friendly conversation (in French) with them.[113] The Polish press response to Friedrich's words was enthusiastic; they constituted a "favorable omen," reflected a "spirit of sublime magnanimity," and created hopes for the "suspension of the proceedings against our nationality."[113a] The perennial hopes of

Polish nobles of somehow driving a wedge between Bismarck and the Hohenzollerns seemed to come to life again. They began to imagine differences between Friedrich and his polonophobe ministers and expressed confidence that once he got well and put his own ideas into practice things would get better for the Poles.

Under loyalist prodding, the Polish parliamentary delegation decided to take the first step and sent a special declaration of loyalty to Friedrich. It was similar to those sent by many German groups, except that it referred to the "different language and ancestry" of their "sorely-tried region." A cabinet meeting was summoned hastily to decide what ought to be done about this, especially since the Emperor indicated his intention of accepting and responding to this declaration. Bismarck could not attend, but his ministers were unanimous in the conviction that it should not be answered and that Friedrich needed to be warned of the serious political significance of the outwardly harmless document. Gossler saw this as a "well-prepared coup," perhaps the "significant step on the part of Polish representatives" long forecast by the Polish press. The decision was made to confer with Bismarck and urge the Emperor either not to answer the declaration or to let the cabinet draw up his reply.[114] Bismarck supported the latter course and Friedrich went along; Puttkamer drew up a reply "so sharp the Poles will never forget it," which caused one Polish noble to complain that he "could scarcely catch his breath under the German pressure."[115] Bismarck's public response to the loyalist overture was that he had never doubted the loyalty of the Polish masses, was glad to have their leaders aboard now too, and looked forward to their pro-government votes in parliament.[116] Bismarck's deep-rooted distrust and dislike of the Polish nobility rendered him essentially immune to any loyalist gestures.[117] This episode in 1888 did not seriously dim loyalist hopes, however. They attributed the rebuff to the ministers rather than to the Emperor. They drew hope from the subsequent dismissal of Puttkamer, the elevation of several Polish nobles to the Herrenhaus, and persistent rumors of Bismarck's own imminent departure. When Friedrich died of throat cancer after a few months in office, the hopes placed in him were quickly transferred (with even less justification) to his son, Wilhelm II.

The loyalist initiative of 1888 was generally approved by Polish published opinion. Most of the press considered the declaration of loyalty to be consistent with Polish "dignity" and conducive to a "strengthening of the legal foundation upon which our representatives will continue to work."[118] But soon thereafter it (and the remaining non-loyalist representatives) began to urge caution upon the parliamentarians, warning them against rushing into loyalism without some reciprocation by the government. Kościelski came under growing personal criticism; he was reported to socialize primarily with Germans, to be pursuing his policy behind the back of *Koło* leaders, and accused of running roughshod over the traditional policies of the *Koło*. Several times during the 1886-1890 period he was reprimanded by the *Koło* itself for excessively loyalist statements.[119] *Gazeta Toruńska* charged that his attitude was "neither in harmony with the behavior of the *Koło Polskie* until now, nor does it enjoy the sympathy of the (population as a) whole."[120] As long as Bismarck was in office, it seemed unlikely that loyalism could be made palatable to most Poles. Here too Szymański was something of an exception; he and Kościelski had little in common, but they were both loyalists. Actually there were two distinct forms assumed by loyalism:[121] the conservative-monarchist accent on social order and legitimacy as represented by Kościelski, and the Positivist-bourgeois emphasis on social and economic progress free of sterile political maneuvring and futile opposition as represented by Szymański.

In the short run, Kościelski and the loyalists created in effect another fissure in the edifice of National Solidarity, similar to that of Szymański and his townspeople on the other side of the political spectrum. By 1889 a lack of coordination within the *Koło* delegation was apparent, as the loyalist-dominated Herrenhaus group began voting differently from the other delegations.[122] Despite a lack of reciprocity by the government, and without the general backing of the Polish people, Kościelski led a small but influential group of nobles and Church leaders toward a policy of understanding with the government at almost any cost. As a basically authoritarian politician, he was not particularly sensitive to public opinion. He also conceded in 1886 that "an understanding is not at all desired" by the government.[123] He apparently felt that he could change this by his own efforts and that the Polish masses would provide their usual blind support. Since this loyalist movement represented a split within the traditional political leadership group, it served to weaken the noble-clerical front just as it was coming under heavy new attacks from the government. But having failed to oppose effectively the Settlement Law by means of the Land Bank, having failed to find any relief from anti-Polish measures through parliamentary tactics, having been unable to channel the growing discontent of the Polish masses into effective countermeasures, and challenged now by a small but growing segment of the Polish middle class, many conservative and clerical leaders decided with Kościelski that they no longer had any alternative to loyalism. An event over which they had no control (Bismarck's dismissal in 1890) allowed them to pick up some additional support and give loyalism a more extensive audition during the Caprivi Era.

Notes

1. Speech by Stablewski, January 29, 1886, *Abgeordnetenhaus*.
2. Speech by Kościelski, April 15, 1886, *Herrenhaus*.
3. Speech by Wierzbiński, February 22, 1886, *Abgeordnetenhaus*.
4. *Ibid*.
5. Speech of January 2, 1888, *Ibid*.
6. January 1, 1888 *PA Bonn*, Preussen 4.
7. February 18, 1888, *Abgeordnetenhaus*.
8. Mai, pp. 57ff.
9. Report from Poznań, August 12, 1886, *GPSA Berlin*, Rep. 84a, #5964.
10. Szembek, p. 268.
11. Ludwig Bernhard, *Die Polenfrage*, 3rd edit., (Munich/Leipzig, 1920), p. 124.
12. *Ibid*.
13. Quotes taken from the report from Poznań, August 20, 1887, *GPSA Berlin*, Rep. 84a, #4067.
14. January 1, 1888, *PA Bonn*, Preussen 4.
15. Report from Poznań, May 28, 1888, *GPSA Berlin*, Rep. 84a, #5964.
16. July 1, 1888, *Ibid.*, Rep. B 30:I, #658.
17. *Gazeta Toruńska*, July 14, 1888, *Ibid*.
18. "Położenie nasza a ustawa o kolonizacji niemieckiej z dnia 26.IV 1886," in *Wielkopolska*, pp. 21ff.
19. *Gazeta Toruńska*, May 28 and October 31, 1889, *GPSA Berlin* Rep. B 30:I, #658.
20. Bernhard, p. 511.
21. Mai, p. 152; see also Witold Jakóbczyk, "The First Decade of the Settlement Commission's Activities," *Polish Review* 17(1972).
22. Pater, p. 304.
23. Speeches of January 29 and February 23, 1886, *Abgeordnetenhaus*.
24. January 1, 1888, *PA Bonn*, Preussen 4.
25. January 2, 1888, *Ibid*.
26. As pointed out by Jażdżewski, May 9, 1887, *Abgeordnetenhaus*.
27. *Gazeta Toruńska*, February 15, 1887, *GPSA Berlin*, Rep. B 30:I, #658.
28. *Pielgrzym*, February 19 and March 1, 1887, *Ibid*.
29. February 23, 1886, *Abgeordnetenhaus*.
30. Speech by Ostrowicz, February 22, 1886, *Ibid*.
31. April 1, 1886, *Ibid*.
32. January 1, 1888, *PA Bonn*, Preussen 4.
33. Mai, pp. 174ff.
34. Report of May 29, 1886, *GPSA Berlin*, Rep. 84a, #5957.
35. Report from Poznań, February 14, 1886, *Ibid.*, #5964.
36. Report from Poznań, May 10, 1886, *Ibid*.
37. Report from Poznań, March 3, 1887, *Ibid*.
38. Gossler to Zedlitz, May 29, 1888, in *Kirchenpolitik*, p. 67.
39. *Gazeta Toruńska*, July 1888, *GPSA Berlin*, Rep. B 30:I, #658.

Polish National Solidarity under Attack 117

40. See page 78 and Lech Trzeciakowski, *Polityka polskich klas posiadających w erze Capriviego* (Poznań, 1960), p. 34.
41. Report from Bromberg, August 19, 1888, *GPSA Berlin*, Rep. B 30:I, #553.
42. Report from Bromberg, December 30, 1886, *Ibid.*, Rep. 84a, #5964.
43. Report from Marienwerder, November 30, 1886, *Ibid.*, #5957.
44. Quote taken from report from Poznań, August 20, 1887, *Ibid.*, #5964.
45. *Gazeta Toruńska*, January 9, 1887, *Ibid.*, Rep. B 30:I, #658; the bank went out of business at the end of 1887.
46. *Orędownik*, January 9, 1887, *Ibid.*
47. *Gazeta Toruńska*, September 21, 1887, *Ibid.*; note: in my article, "The Development of Loyalism in Prussian Poland," *Slavonic and East European Review* 52 (1974):555, I incorrectly indentify the Łyskowski family member as Ignacy and the Czarliński member as Leon; my apologies to the families concerned and my thanks to Mr. Olgierd Czarliński of Oxford, England, for calling these errors to my attention.
48. *Orędownik*, June 18, 1890, *Ibid.*
49. *Dniewnik Warshavski*, August 2, 1887, translated from the Russian, *PA Bonn*, Preussen 4.
50. April 24, 1888, *Ibid.*
51. Speech by Ostrowicz, February 18, 188, *Abgeordnetenhaus.*
52. March 27, 1888, *GPSA Berlin*, Rep. B 30:I, #658.
53. Report from Poznań, December 10, 1887, *Ibid.*, Rep. 84a, #5964.
54. See Lech Trzeciakowski, "Roman Szymański," in *Wielkopolanie XIX wieku*, ed. W. Jakóbczyk (Poznań, 1969), II:341-361.
55. *Orędownik* in 1885, *Wielkopolska*, pp. 215f.
56. *Orędownik* in 1874, *Poznańskie, Pomorze, Warmia i Mazury*, p. 7.
57. *Orędownik* in 1875, *Wielkopolska*, p. 207.
58. Trzeciakowski, *Kulturkampf*, p. 228; Stanisław Karwowski, "Historya Dziennika Poznańskiego," in *Książka jubileuszowa Dziennika Poznańskiego 1859-1909* (Poznań, 1909), p. 54.
59. Quoted in Reinhard Höhn and Helmut Seydel, "Der Kampf um die Wiedergewinnung des deutschen Ostens—Erfahrungen der preussischen Ostsiedlung," in *Gestgabe für Heinrich Himmler* (Darmstadt, 1941), p. 79.
60. *Orędownik*, July 8, 1887, *PA Bonn*, Preussen 4.
61. *Orędownik*, September 21, 1887, *GPSA Berlin*, Rep. B 30:I, #658.
62. *Orędownik*, November 30, 1887, *Ibid.*
63. Trzeciakowski, *Polityka*, p. 20; see also Zdzisław Grot, "Koło Polskie w Berlinie," *Wiek XIX*, Kieniewicz Festschrift (1967), pp. 237-250.
64. Quotes taken from the report of such a proceeding in Konitz/Chojnice—Tuchel/Tuchola district, *Gazeta Toruńska*, February 2, 1887, *GPSA Berlin*, Rep. B 30:I, #658.
65. Hans Pfeiffer, *Der polnische Adel und die preussische Polenpolitik*, diss. Jena (Würzburg, 1939), pp. 96ff.
66. *Orędownik* in 1888, *Wielkopolska*, pp 228f.
67. Trzeciakowski, *Polityka*, p. 38.
68. *Orędownik*, February 17, 1888, *GPSA Berlin*, Rep. B 30:I, #659.

69. Quotes taken from report from Poznań, August 13, 1889, *Ibid.*, Rep. 84a, #5964.
70. Trzeciakowski, *Polityka*, p. 38; *Gazeta Toruńska*, August 29, 1888, GPSA Berlin, Rep. B 30:I, #658.
71. *Gazeta Toruńska*, August 20, 1888, *Ibid.*
72. *Orędownik*, February 28, 1888, *PA Bonn*, Preussen 8:2.
73. Quote taken from report from Poznań, August 13, 1889, GPSA Berlin, Rep. 84a, #5964.
74. Quotes taken from report from Poznań, February 28, 1890, *Ibid.*
75. Wegener, p. 142; see also Czesław Łuczak, *Położenie ekonomiczne rzemiosła wielkopolskiego w okresie zaborów* (Poznań, 1962).
76. Wegener, p. 154.
77. *Deutsche Kulturarbeit*, p. 126.
78. Jakóbczyk, *Studia*, III:18.
79. Franz Spandowski, *Genossenschaftliche Probleme in dem "Verband der Erwerbs- und Wirtschaftsgenossenschaften der Provinzen Posen und Westpreussen,"* diss. Freiburg (Posen, 1915), pp. 6ff., 12ff.; see also Rus Kusztelan, *Ks. Patron Augustyn Szamarzewski* (Poznań, 1918).
80. *Wielkopolska*, p. xxvii.
81. Spandowski, p. 10.
82. Władysław Tomaszewski, *Die Entwicklung der polonischen Erwerbs und Wirtschaftsgenossenschaften in den Provinzen Posen, Westpreussen, und Schlesien, 1861-1912* (Poznań, 1913), p. 15; see also Władysław Tomaszewski, *Bank Związku Spółek Zarobkowych (1886-1910)* (Poznań, 1911); Friedrich Swart, "Polnische Genossenschaftswesen in der Provinz Posen," in *Die Ostmark* (Leipzig, 1911), pp. 133ff.; Kazimierz Zimmermann, *"Bank Przemysłowców" in Posen* (Posen, 1907).
83. Spandowski, p. 14.
84. Szembek, p. 128.
85. Szymański celebrated the case of a noble chairman who was compelled to resign by an aroused membership when he tried to dictate his choices for the other top positions, *Orędownik*, December 28, 1886, GPSA Berlin, Rep. B 30:I, #659.
86. Paweł Spandowski, *Towarzystwa przemysłowe* (Posen, 1909), pp. 81, 89.
87. Laubert, p. 151.
88. In 1879 the *Koło* was still opposed to agricultural tariffs, (in spite of its members' economic interests) on grounds that it would tend to exacerbate the economic division of Poland; see speech by Niegolewski, July 12, 1879, *Reichstag*.
89. Speech by Łyskowski, December 1, 1879, *Abgeordnetenhaus*.
90. Bogdan Hutten-Czapski, *Sechzig Jahre Politik und Gesellschaft* (Berlin, 1936); Marie Radziwiłł, *Briefe vom deutschen Kaiserhof* (Berlin, 1936).
91. Nowakowski, pp. 263ff.
92. Trzeciakowski, *Kulturkampf*, p. 270.
93. Minutes of *Koło* caucus meeting, January 18, 1882, in Trzeciakowski, "Polskie ugrupowania polityczne," p. 28; see speech by Skarżyński supporting a

tax break for the sugar industry, June 4, 1883, *Reichstag*.
94. Speech by Stablewski, January 17, 1879, *Abgeordnetenhaus*.
95. February 6, 1884, *Ibid*.
96. December 3, 1880, and March 17, 1882, *Ibid*.
97. *Gedanken und Erinnerungen*, II:271f.
98. "List otwarty do Centralnego Wyborczego dla Wielkiego Księstwa Poznańskiego," (Poznań, 1884).
99. Karwowski, pp. 61f.; report from Poznań, November 8, 1884, *GPSA Berlin*, Rep. 84a, #5964.
100. Karwowski, p. 65.
101. Skarżyński's parliamentary career ended in 1884; see Adam Galos, "Józef Kościelski," in *Polski Słownik Biograficzny* (Wrocław, 1968), XIV/I:420-424; Alfred Kucner, "Polityka 'Koła Polskiego' w Berlinie w erze Kanclerza Capriviego," *Nauka i Sztuka* 3(1947):42-76.
102. March 11, 1885, *Reichstag*.
103. May 9, 1887, *Abgeordnetenhaus*.
104. January 28, 1888, *Reichstag*.
105. February 27, 1886, *Herrenhaus*.
106. February 23, 1886, *Abgeordnetenhaus*.
107. Hans-Ulrich Wehler, *Sozialdemokratie und Nationalstaat* (Würzburg, 1962), p. 110; see also Stanisław Kubiak, *Ruch socjalistyczny w Poznaniu, 1872-1890* (Poznań, 1961); Witold Jakóbczyk, "Z dziejów ruchu robotniczego w Poznaniu," *Studia Poznańskie* 9(1953):376-402.
108. February 9, 1887, *Abgeordnetenhaus*.
109. February 27, 1886, *Herrenhaus*.
110. Busch, I:554.
111. Quoted by Stablewski, January 29, 1886, *Abgeordnetenhaus*.
112. *Gazeta Toruńska*, March 17, 1888, *GPSA Berlin*, Rep. B 30:I, #658.
113. Ludwig Raschdau, *Unter Bismarck und Caprivi* (Berlin, 1939), p. 30.
113a. *Gazeta Toruńska*, March 17, 1888.
114. Council of Ministers meeting, May 16, 1888, *PA Bonn*, Preussen 4.
115. Quotes from *Dniewnik Warshawski*, February 20, 1889, *Ibid.*; Bismarck's comment in the margin of the translation of this article: "I deeply regret that!"
116. *Politische Briefe*, IV:229.
117. There were only a couple of exceptions to this rule during his career: Count Bniński of the Herrenhaus (cf. Bismarck speech of February 6, 1872, Herrenhaus) and Count Radoliński ("One of the few Polish nobles completely safe for Your Majesty and the Prussian State") (cf. *Gesammelte Werke*,XIV:983, Bismarck to Wilhelm I, December 30, 1887).
118. *Gazeta Toruńska*, August 1, 1888, *GPSA Berlin*, Rep. B 30:I, #658.
119. Kucner, pp. 48f.
120. March 29, 1888, *GPSA Berlin*, Rep. B 30:I, #658.
121. Rose, p. 53.
122. *Gazeta Toruńska*, May 2, 1889, *GPSA Berlin*, *Ibid*.
123. April 15, 1886, *Herrenhaus*.

Chapter V:
An Era of Reconciliation

Improved Prussian-Polish relations followed the appointment of Leo von Caprivi as German Chancellor and Prussian Minister-President in March 1890. This was not a direct consequence of the changeover in the sense that Caprivi entered office with the intention of revising Bismarck's Polish policies. But the Reinsurance Treaty with Russia was allowed to lapse a short time later, setting up a new diplomatic and strategic situation in the East. This in turn made the government more interested in the offers of cooperation by Polish loyalists. Caprivi agreed in effect with Bismarck that domestic Polish policies and relations with Russia were interwoven. While Bismarck justified a hard line toward Prussian Poles as a sign of his good intentions toward Russia, so Caprivi saw a more conciliatory policy toward them as a logical consequence of the break with Russia. For Polish loyalists it was a happy coincidence that just as they determined to get on the government's side in any case the diplomatic situation changed to the benefit of their cause.

Even before 1890, those German strategists who did not share Bismarck's confidence in the durability of the Russian alliance were increasingly concerned about the prospect of a two-front war with France and Russia. In their deliberations of ways to deal with such an eventuality, the Polish question played a central role. General Alfred von Waldersee, chief of the General Staff (1888-1891), was convinced that a showdown with Russia was inevitable sooner or later and willing even to consider a "preventive" war. He felt it would be necessary, when this clash came, to "strike up the melody, 'Poland is not yet Lost.'"[1] "A necessary result of our war (with Russia) will be the attempt to restore Poland; I truly do not overlook the disadvantages . . . but I am convinced that it is the only way to be rid of the Russians for good and, with a little skill, it is the most effective means of creating problems that Russian war strategy is not equal to."[2] Caprivi himself, while head of the Navy (1882-8), belonged to this group; he too was convinced that war with Russia was inevitable and was wont to predict each spring that "next year we shall have a war on two fronts."[3] Even Bismarck's record contains similar reflections. In 1870 he envisioned the annexation of additional Polish lands in the event of a successful war with Russia; "then we would have something in the North like Austria in the South; what Hungary is there Poland would have become for us."[4] Again in 1883: "Even a victorious war against Russia would result for us in the danger of new confusion in the Polish area; encouragement of Polish national ambitions would be a great misfortune for us, but still a smaller one compared to the defeat of Germany by Russia."[5] With the expiration of the Three Emperors League in 1887, as even Bismarck began to despair of keeping Russia in the fold indefinitely, the Polish aspect surfaced again. As he coached Wilhelm I prior to a meeting with Tsar Alexander III, "in case of war (with Russia), Austria will not be able to abstain from reviving the Polish question. We would regret this, but between the two evils, the proximity of the Poles or victorious Russian armies among us, the former would be less disturbing."[6] Italy's Premier Crispi recorded a similar comment at this time: "Poland is a source of weakness (for Russia) and Austria is popular in Poland. With some slight encouragement, the Poles could be made to rebel; . . . a state might be formed for some Austrian archduke to rule over."[7]

For Bismarck, this "playing of the Polish card" was always viewed as a last resort in case Russia insisted on being hostile; primarily he was determined to avoid such a situation. Even if it proved unavoidable, "setting up Poland all the way to the Daugava/Dvina and Dniepr would then lead to the creation of an alliance of the three empires against this kingdom" and a return to the situation at the time of the first partition.[8] But opponents like Waldersee and Caprivi seemed to view both war with Russia and the ressurrection of Poland much more nonchalantly. By 1888, Waldersee was engaged in speculation about the frontiers of such a Polish state, its customs relationship with Germany, and the port facilities it might enjoy.[9] It was only a small step from consideration of the role the Poles might play in a war with Russia to consideration of how this might relate to domestic Prussian Polish policy. Waldersee realized that by the late-1880s Germany had become so unpopular among Poles that she would be unable to "raise an armed force of 100 Poles," even against the traditional Russian enemy.[10] The implication was that if victory over Russia in a two-front war might depend upon Polish support, and if existing Polish policies discouraged such support, one might have to make some gestures and concessions to Prussian Poles. This necessary connection between domestic Polish policy and eastern strategic considerations may also explain the reluctance of Army leaders to respond with any enthusiasm to Bismarck's anti-Polish campaign. Of all the Prussian ministers, War Minister Bronsart seemed most

An Era of Reconciliation

reluctant to embark on a stepped-up nationality struggle in 1886 and introduced his quota of anti-Polish measures primarily to avoid further browbeating by nationalist bureaucrats like Tiedemann and Gossler. General Richard von Seeckt, commander of the Army in Poznania (and father of the Weimar Republic's Army chief), confided to Polish acquaintances that he thought Bismarck's new Polish policies were "harmful to Germany."[11] "I do not think that those who fought with such bravery (in the wars of unification) are traitors, nor are they bad subjects."[12] He urged a "fair accommodation" towards the Poles and was a friend of Archbishop Stablewski; his suggestions were usually ignored, however, and his "soft" position on the Polish question led eventually to his transfer from the province in 1897.[13] While Seeckt himself was apparently polonophile, other military leaders probably were not; but they were aware that the Polish provinces were the weakest point in Germany's defensive posture. Numerically superior Russian forces could concentrate along the Poznanian border less than 300 km. from Berlin. Further alienation of the Poles who lived along both sides of this border could only make the situation worse.

In addition to the impact of the new concern about Russia on Prussian Polish policy, there are indications that Caprivi was personally a lot less antagonistic than Bismarck toward the Poles. Unfortunately, he has left historians very little evidence from which to determine his thoughts on Polish matters. In response mainly to the constant bickering of his own predecessor during his tenure as chancellor, Caprivi (Bismarck: a man of "tender consideration and sublime gallantry beyond any doubt"[14]) determined not to cause the same problem for his successor. After he left office, he wrote no memoirs, burned virtually all of his private political papers, and generally abstained from making comments on political matters.[15] Most of his extant statements on Polish questions were made in front of audiences containing the Poles he wanted to win over or German nationalists he did not want to upset, and may therefore be less than candid. The evidence which is available suggests that Caprivi, like Bismarck, belonged to the general category of Prussian-state rather than German-ethnic nationalist; he was not bothered by the existence of alien nationalities in Germany as long as they were politically loyal.

In practice toward Prussian Poles, however, Caprivi seems to have conformed much more closely than Bismarck to this state-nationalist ideal. As he remarked in response to one of Gossler's many proposals for action against the Poles: "Despite all the large and small countermeasures, . . . the question remains: should we continue to look for petty, stop-gap measures or is it not (better) to examine whether we cannot make *Prussian* fellow-citizens out of the Poles?"[16] When Jażdżewski charged that Bismarck's policy toward the Poles had been "filled with hate," Caprivi did not contest this characterization. "But it does not apply to the present policy. We do not hate the Poles. We regard them as fellow-citizens—difficult fellow-citizens at times, sometimes also fellow-citizens who have gone astray from our point of view, but always our fellow-citizens with whom it will always be a pleasure to work together for the good of the state."[17] To be sure, there was sometimes a note of opportunism in Caprivi's approach: "The Poles siding with us . . . is always preferable to their siding against us," which meant letting them believe that they would get "further in the pursuit of their unrealizable goals with us than against us."[18] Certainly it is doubtful that major changes in Polish policy would have come about from Caprivi's personal convictions alone, because neither these convictions nor Caprivi's position in the government were sufficiently strong. It took the prospect of a two-front war and a number of opening moves by Polish loyalists to usher in an era of comparatively good feeling under Caprivi's chancellorship.

Caprivi lacked Bismarck's ability, even were he so disposed, to impose a radically different Polish policy on his government. He had to share power with other influential figures of the New Course, both holdovers and new appointees, who were closer to Bismarck's position. By March 1890, half of the Prussian ministers had been appointed by Wilhelm II; the rest of the pre-1888 officeholders left within a year. But the one who stayed longest was Culture Minister Gossler, whose ministry was the key one as far as domestic Polish policies were concerned. Gossler continued in the same vein as under Bismarck, devising ever more ambitious projects for combatting the Polish danger. His hard line stemmed partially from his own strong nationalism, but partially also from a skepticism about the new Polish amiability which was itself the result of a better understanding of local Polish affairs. He was aware of the pressures on the traditional noble leadership as a major factor behind the rise of Polish loyalism.

> "With the nobility it is all over—that is what the (Polish) papers say—the nobility cannot hold out, the nobility is selling its Polish property. . . . Other population groups are presented as the authorized heirs of the formerly powerful nobility. This is a quite conscious struggle of the third and fourth estates—with the nobility it will not last long, then it will be against the clergy."[19]

Gossler exaggerated the immediate threat to the traditional leadership, which still had the passive support of the great majority of Poles. But he was correct in his analysis of the longer-term direction in which Prussian-

An Era of Reconciliation

Polish society was moving. On one hand, the fact that the Polish nobility was under attack at home caused it to seek an understanding with the government; on the other, it made little sense to enter into agreements with a leadership group in the process of being displaced, one which might not be able to carry with it the Polish people as a whole.

In any case, Gossler continued to work on new anti-Polish measures. Unlike Bismarck, he recognized that the real struggle for a government bent upon Germanization was not with the moribund nobility but with the rising bourgeoisie. He proposed to supplement existing Polish policies with an economic attack on the middle classes, beginning with the professions. He wanted, for example, to suppress the increase of Polish physicians and pharmacists in the eastern provinces; when he sensed a lack of interest on Caprivi's part, he circulated his proposals to the other ministers as well. He recited all that he had been doing to quell the Polish threat: improving German schools, strengthening state control over Polish schools, transferring Polish teachers westward and replacing them with Germans, giving state scholarships exclusively to Germans, etc. Nonetheless, "the (Polish) patriotism pervading the bourgeois way of life has not ceased to work systematically and purposefully for the extension of its power." He produced statistics which showed a rapid rise in the number of Polish physicians; during the previous twenty years, Polish doctors increased from 21% to 40% of the total in Poznań Regency, from 25% to 36% in Bromberg, and from 8% to 18% in Marienwerder. He assumed that the Poles were making similar advances in the other professions. He proposed that the state counter this trend by supporting German professionals in the Polish areas, for example by directing all state business to them and offering direct subsidies to new doctors willing to settle in Poznania and West Prussia.[20] Caprivi responded with apparent annoyance to this initiative by Gossler, informing the cabinet that there were no funds available for "the financial support of German doctors," nor would there likely be any in the future.[21] Gossler turned next to new efforts to neutralize the political influence of the Polish clergy. He urged Caprivi to intervene with the Vatican to cut off outside (Galician) support for Upper Silesian priests who were resisting Archbishop Kopp's ban on the use of Polish.[22] He also demanded action against the "growing pan-Polish agitation existing in Upper Silesia, cleverly directed in secret and supported by (outside) funds."[23] But he was unsuccessful in these efforts and was dropped from office in March 1891.[24]

The appointment of Caprivi's personal choice, erstwhile Poznanian *Oberpräsident* Zedlitz, as Gossler's successor was the most significant ministerial change of the period as far as Prussian Poles were concerned.

Zedlitz had been Bismarck's viceroy in Poznania, including among his duties the chairmanship of the Settlement Commission, but he had also developed close personal ties to the leading Polish loyalists. He was a conservative, a supporter of a strong religious influence in public life, and close to agrarian interests, all qualities which he had in common with most Polish leaders. Ferdynand Radziwiłł described him as a man "whose benevolent and noble endeavors . . . deserve confidence and are finding the gratitude of all the members of the province."²⁵ In return, Zedlitz was favorably disposed toward the loyalists and expressed faith in their credibility. Speaking generally on another occasion, he suggested that "one must show confidence in people if one wants to educate them."²⁶ A report from his office in Poznań in 1890 noted that Caprivi had been well received by many Poles, who were increasingly inclined to participate in state affairs locally. "Through the collaboration of respected Poles in the state, provincial, and county administrations, the existing national differences will gradually disappear and in this way a thriving cooperation of both nationalities will be attained."²⁷ In response to the fears of Poznanian Germans that they might suffer from attempts to conciliate the Poles, Zedlitz was blunt: "Concerning the fear of Poles, I have always . . . found that in many respects the government and also our good countrymen themselves are seeing ghosts. We have to live together in this province and I find it is better that we get along together."²⁸ Zedlitz soon became the most visible representative of a changed approach to the Poles and the most promising phase of the "Era of Reconciliation (*Versöhnungsära*)" coincided with his single year as Culture Minister (1891-2).

For most Polish loyalists, however, the key man remained neither Caprivi nor Zedlitz but Emperor Wilhelm. After one of his frequent confrontations with Gossler, Stablewski fell back on the emperor-minister dichotomy characteristic of many loyalist statements:

> "The fresh breeze that blows from the heights of the throne also gives us hope that it will banish the bad atmosphere that the ambitions of 'diligent spirits' have spread. The broad view of the Monarch, who has so comprehended the needs of his people in the depths of the earth and in the workshops, and has so opened his royal heart to them, gives us too the hope that in the long run he will penetrate into the cottages of the Polish nation. . . . I have lost all hope that (Gossler) will permit justice to be granted to us; but fortunately there is still a higher authority in the Prussian State than that of a minister; . . . ministers are not everlasting and Minister Gossler too will go one day."²⁹

It is difficult to understand just what caused Polish loyalists to think that

Wilhelm might be on their side. There is no evidence that he was more favorably inclined toward them than most of his ministers; in his memoirs he does not even indicate an interest in the Polish question.[30] After March 1890 there may have been an assumption that Bismarck's adversary must be the Poles' friend, but more likely this focus on the Emperor reflected a traditional noble inclination to direct appeals to the throne. A few loyalist Poles were close to the court or otherwise had some influence in Berlin, but these were not political persons. A Radziwiłł princess wrote a volume of "letters from the German Imperial Court" without even mentioning the Polish question.[31] Hutten-Czapski was devoted more to Catholic Church than Polish-national interests and became influential only when his sponsor Hohenlohe became chancellor in 1894. Even then he admitted to "admiring the powerful statesman" Bismarck and also had great praise for the militantly anti-Polish Archbishop Kopp of Breslau.[32] These were the only Poles within striking distance of the Court and they were unlikely to exert any effective influence on Wilhelm to satisfy important Polish aspirations.

Tangible concessions to go along with the friendlier tone of the Caprivi government were slow in coming and relatively minor at first. In November-December 1890, the expulsion orders of 1885 were amended to permit again the importation of (mostly Polish) farm workers from Russia and Austria, at least on a seasonal basis. Agrarian organizations (such as the "Central Union of West Prussian Farmers") had urged such a course since 1885, but Bismarck continued to feel that nationalist considerations should come before agrarian interests.[33] Attempts since 1885 to keep alien workers out of Prussia had not been very successful; illegal border crossings were "still taking place to a large extent" and the problems stemming from this sizable force of floating workers in some frontier counties remained.[34] Local officials, often close to agrarian interests themselves, were apparently doing little to stop the crossings or prosecute estate owners for encouraging them. Even then the province of East Prussia alone reported some 6000 vacant farm worker positions at the time Caprivi took over and (over Gossler's objections) the policy change was made.[35] The new orders were for a three-year period (made permanent in 1894) and contained various provisions to keep the workers from staying too long, *e.g.*, they had to return home for at least 2½ months each year.[36] Interior Minister Herrfurth assured the Landtag that they would be permitted only "to the extent that is necessary for agriculture . . . and without raising national-political objections." In response to the negative reaction of German nationalists, he argued that unless the state wanted to compel German farm workers to remain in the East or persuade the agrarians to pay better wages, there was little alternative to the use of alien labor.³⁷

The admission of seasonal farm workers who happened to be mostly Poles was clearly not a concession to the Poles primarily. German agrarians were the major consideration, though Polish estate owners doubtless benefited too. It did not elicit much favorable comment from Polish representatives, loyalist or not. Officials in southern West Prussia, the region most adversely affected by the 1885 expulsions, noted that "the level of political satisfaction" was not raised especially by this "concession," which the Polish press characterized as "quite inadequate."³⁸ Czarliński expressed some appreciation but predicted that unless the workers were allowed to stay and set up homes and be free of anti-Polish discrimination, they would have no desire to come and the labor shortage would remain.³⁹ *Dziennik Poznański* even tried to get interested Russian-Polish workers to boycott seasonal job offers until they could stay permanently.⁴⁰ To no avail, however; by 1914 the number of Polish seasonal farm workers in Germany was approximately 300,000.⁴¹

A second "concession" to the Poles was contained in the *Rentengut* laws of 1890 and 1891, the first of these permitting institutions and private persons to sell land parcels for time payments and the second creating a state *Rentenbank* to help finance such projects.⁴² The significant fact about these laws was that no mention was made of nationality and thus Poles were able to participate and obtain homesteads in much the same way that Germans exclusively could do under the Settlement Law of 1886. Again there was no stated intention to please the Poles, who were scarcely aware that they had been granted a favor. Polish spokesmen hardly bothered to take a position on these bills while they were under consideration in the Landtag. Perhaps they were misled by the government's presentation of the *Rentengut* laws as extensions of the social aspect of the Settlement Law.⁴³ But in fact they benefited considerably from the new measures; the General Commission in Bromberg, in charge of their implementation in the Polish provinces, soon began to compete with the Settlement Commission. The exclusion from the *Rentengut* laws of Poznania and West Prussia (where the Settlement Commission operated) was apparently not considered, or rejected by the National Liberals.⁴⁴ Among the institutions which derived immediate and substantial benefit was the Land Bank. It was still hard-pressed for funds in 1891, but was now able to draw on ample credit from the *Rentenbank* for its parcelling projects. Of course, Polish parcelling institutions had to meet certain conditions, *e.g.*, keep their plots above a minimum size and include a certain percentage of Germans among their settlers. The Land Bank agreed to these conditions until 1896, when it was established financially and able to continue its efforts without state help; it then ended its relationship with the *Rentenbank*.[45]

An obviously unforeseen consequence of the *Rentengut* laws was that the General Commission, working often with Polish parcelling agencies, began to outdistance the Settlement Commission in terms of the number of families settled. Aside from working with Polish as well as German settlers, it also offered a variety of smaller plots, aiming mainly at the farm workers and tenants already present in the region. According to the director of the Bromberg General Commission, not only did the Prussian Constitution not permit discrimination on the basis of nationality but there were even reasons for giving preference to Poles. "The character traits of the Pole (mobility, frugality, land hunger) . . . make the Polish population especially well-suited for the filling of *Rentengüter*."[46] "If it is possible, through the mediation of state agencies and provision of state credit, for these social classes to establish a secure existence, providing them with a sufficient livelihood, hopefully the realization of the benevolent support of the state . . . will make them unavailable to the temptations of the Polish party leaders."[47] To be sure, most of the land subdivided for Poles with the help of the General Commission had been purchased from Poles to begin with, but the significance of this activity becomes clear when the 2,781 parcels created under the General Commission 1891-4 (62% of which went to Poles), is compared to the approximately 1000 parcels set up by the Settlement Commission during the same period.[48] Polish settlement activity supported by the General Commission reached a peak in 1893, when the government stepped in. Prussian Minister-President Eulenburg acknowledged that "under the laws there is the possibility of encouraging the settlement of farmers without respect to nationality," but he wanted to know how many Poles were involved and whether the Polish national movement was exploiting the situation.[49] After 1895, such activity declined, due partially to tighter restrictions by the government, partially to the ability of Polish parcelling organizations to go it alone.[50] But by this time the damage had been done and, while neither the government nor Polish leaders referred normally to the *Rentengut* laws as a concession, they were a significant aspect of the Era of Reconciliation.

A third concession, also outwardly minor but of considerable long-term importance, was the government's permission to the Union of Polish Cooperatives to audit the accounts of member organizations. By implication this also authorized the Union to supervise and be responsible for its own affairs relatively free of official interference. In return, it agreed to drop the word "Polish" from its title and drop any national restrictions for membership. According to the 1880 cooperative law, all co-ops were required to belong to central organizations, but it took a two-year struggle with the Prussian bureaucracy before the Polish Union was recognized as such.[51] In the eyes of Prussian officials, who were convinced that Polish economic organizations were involved in the national movement, this was a major concession. But it failed to have much impact on Polish opinion, though Prof. Buzek cites it as the most important of the Caprivi Era concessions.[52]

More notable concessions were made under Culture Minister Zedlitz, who controlled the school and religious affairs traditionally of greatest concern to Poles. Any hopes of significantly improving Prussian-Polish relations, and permitting Polish loyalists to sell their policy to the Polish people generally, depended upon concessions in these areas. Zedlitz began his stint in Berlin with the intention of making some changes in Prussian school policy, not only to appease the Poles but to improve the religious instruction which he considered so important. He was concerned that Polish children were not getting enough out of their Polish-language classes because they no longer received formal training in their mother tongue. Soon after taking office, he reversed Gossler's policy forbidding public school teachers to engage in after-hours, privately supported instruction in Polish. An April 1891 decree permitted the use of both public school teachers and buildings for such instruction programs and thus essentially permitted the classes themselves. He also ordered local officials to make sure that, where sizable numbers of Polish children were being taught religion in German and having trouble learning, they should be provided instruction in Polish.[53]

There remained the problem of provincial officials who maintained their Bismarckian or nationalist attitudes in spite of ministerial changes in Berlin. Tiedemann remained head of Bromberg Regency and Gossler turned up again as *Oberpräsident* of West Prussia. Such officials were typically overenthusiastic in their execution of anti-Polish measures and grudging in their implementation of such infrequent relaxations as Zedlitz proposed. Tiedemann attempted at first to ignore the private instruction ruling, then interpreted it to mean very little change. His compliance was brought about only by an additional order from Zedlitz, pointing out that he "was not happy to see that (you) have considered yourself authorized to execute my decree of April 11th in a manner contrary to its contents."[54] Later that year, when it became known that local officials were preventing German-speaking pupils from participating in the Polish classes, Zedlitz again interceded, ordering his officials to leave it up to the parents to decide whether their children participated. As far as he was concerned, if German parents considered it useful for their children to know Polish, this should not be the state's concern.[55]

Polish representatives took note of this concession but did not express any particular gratitude. For one thing, Zedlitz was primarily concerned about the efficacy of religious instruction; his decree therefore applied only to overwhelmingly Polish school districts in Poznania where religion was still taught in Polish. For another, the support of these classes meant a considerable financial burden for many smaller communities, not all of which were able to take advantage of the decree. No sooner had Zedlitz announced the private instruction concession than Jażdżewski argued that the state, having formally recognized the need for Polish children to study their language, ought to reintroduce it into the regular curriculum. Zedlitz was left between Poles who were still dissatisfied and aroused German nationalists, causing him to complain that, after his "indication of quite considerable good faith," he had only been presented with new Polish demands which German opinion made it impossible to meet.[56]

The most noteworthy concession of the Caprivi Era came in November 1891 with the appointment of the prominent loyalist and *Koło* spokesman Florian Stablewski as Archbishop of Poznań-Gniezno/Gnesen. Dinder had died 18 months earlier; his tenure had been generally disappointing from the standpoint of German nationalist objectives and perhaps some members of the government did not feel that they were giving up very much. As the *Posener Zeitung* noted, "What good did it do for Bismarck to select the German Dinder as prince of the Church in Poznania? His priests saw in him only an alien, a shepherd forced upon them by the government; they prepared every possible difficulty for him and followed his directions only reluctantly."[57] Caprivi also questioned whether a loyalist Pole would not be just as effective as Dinder had been.[58] In addition, there was a simultaneous archiepiscopal vacancy in Strassburg and the Vatican apparently wanted the German government to choose between having its way there and in Poznania. The Poles may have received this concession only because their chair was considered less crucial than the Alsatian one.[59]

While Gossler was Culture Minister, it seemed that the government, the Vatican, and cathedral canons would never be able to agree. The Pope insisted that his willingness to overrule the right of canons to nominate candidates in 1886 was an exception and that he was unwilling to impose a German candidate a second time.[60] Gossler, on the other hand, held out for a German, even if the vacancy should last for many years. "The fact that the Poles in the Reichstag have voted for the army bill (cf. p. 140) cannot be reason enough to let them have their way in this situation; this would mean sacrificing German interests in the province."[61] But with Zedlitz' arrival the several sides gradually came together. Stablewski's name appeared only toward the end of the search process; it may have resulted from a request Caprivi made of Kościelski: "You can appreciate how you could favorably influence the compromise policy begun by yourself and your friends, which has impressed the government favorably, . . . if you would suggest to me candidates of Polish origin who would be guaranteed good Prussians."[62] Stablewski had, to be sure, a long record of vocal opposition to the government, especially during the *Kulturkampf*. But he had since mellowed, especially since Bismarck's dismissal, and now was among the most unequivocally loyalist of Polish representatives. As he assured the Landtag prior to his nomination in 1891: "As a result of what we have heard from the heights of the throne, that all subjects are to be handled with equal love and equal justice, . . . we want to protect and support this state in everything that concerns its existence, the integrity of its borders, its power position and development." His only qualification was that "we want to remain Poles in the Prussian State."[63] In September, in the course of a major address to the annual Catholic Congress held that year in Thorn/Toruń, he went still further. He urged all "westerners" and Christians to unite against the eastern menace (Russia) and against the threat of internal social upheaval. In his concern for the well-being of the Church and the survival of western civilization, the Polish question was scarcely touched upon.[64] This address was probably a crucial factor in Caprivi's approval of his appointment as Archbishop the following month. The government insisted in return that he appoint a German assistant and that Archbishop Kopp (whose appointment to that position had been purchased with the reopening of the Pelplin Seminary in West Prussia) be elevated now to Cardinal.[65] At the time of his appointment, Stablewski further assured the government that "I have already had the chance repeatedly to spell out openly and clearly my ideas of my own obligations toward the state; not with a view to external pressures but from internal moral motivation, I feel obligated to the faithful support of the government in activities which have the goal of strengthening the state and the good of all its subjects."[66]

Stablewski's appointment had a very strong impact on Polish opinion. True, some editorial comment was concerned about the possibility that he might have paid too high a price, perhaps by promising to keep the Church out of Polish national affairs or encouraging a war with Russia. This concern was fed by Wilhelm's speech upon Stablewski's installation in January 1892: "As far as it lies within your office, I expect you to succeed in reconciling the differences which have no place among children of one country."[67] In his first annual pastoral letter (*Hirtenbrief*), Stablewski spoke confidently of the future and of the "generous heart of our most gracious royal lord . . . (who has indicated) that his heart encompasses all subjects of his Empire regardless of nationality" and urged Poles to make this feeling mutual.[68] While some Poles, having achievd the nomination of one of their own as Archbishop, were disappointed with the meagre fall-out for nationalist purposes, Germans tended to be pleasantly surprised. The *Posener Zeitung* remarked after a few years that "in fact, one cannot be any more loyal than the Poznanian Archbishop has become since the day he took office."[69] Stablewski lined the Poznanian Church up firmly behind loyalist initiatives and eventually supplanted Kościelski as the most visible symbol of Prussian-Polish loyalism.

That the Caprivi government did not make more substantial concessions or respond more enthusiastically to Polish loyalist overtures was due to a number of factors: German nationalist opinion, Bismarckian holdovers, preoccupation with other matters, and traditional distrust of the Polish nobles. As Caprivi told his cabinet, "one can be pleased about (the Poles') approach but we still need evidence that their words can be trusted, for the past does not offer any guarantee for this."[70] He addressed the Poles themselves in the same vein: "We have heard this message, this milder tone—but complete belief has still been absent here and there. If you continue along the path of reconciliation you will make it possible for the government and the Germans in Poznania as well to follow you."[71] While unable to offer new concessions at this time, he clearly sought to encourage the loyalists by holding out to them the prospect of concessions if they persevered. In the meantime, a loyalist paper described his words on this occasion as "the first time that Polish representatives have heard words of peace and good will from the mouth . . . of a Prussian Minister-President."[72]

Actually, it was not so much doubt as to the sincerity of the Polish loyalists but questions about the extent of support for them among the Polish population at large which caused their offers of alliance to be treated with reserve. Outspoken loyalists remained a minority even in the parliamentary delegations. Following the 1890 elections to the Reichstag, perhaps half of that delegation could be termed loyalist. In the Prussian lower house, however, which dealt most often with Polish matters, there were only three outspoken loyalists (Stablewski, Cegielski, Czartoryski); the delegation as a whole remained under the control of relatively hard-line nationalists like Jażdżewski and Czarliński. Only the comparatively insignificant Herrenhaus faction, where most of the 13 Polish peers had made their peace with the government well before 1890, could be considered a loyalist stronghold.[73] Among the Polish press, only *Kuryer Poznański* gave its unequivocal support to the loyalist concept. In an 1890 editorial entitled "A Program for the not-too-distant

Future," published the day after Bismarck's dismissal, it urged Prussian Poles to become full citizens and participate fully in public affairs as the best means of receiving equal treatment by the new government. "Polish representatives to legislative bodies ought to proceed not by means of abstention and protest but by mutual work with the Germans for the general good of the country, for the preservation and defense of the throne against elements which would like to weaken it."[74] But most of the Polish press reaction to the *Kuryer* statement was negative and that paper was compelled to reaffirm its Polish patriotism subsequently.[75] *Dziennik Poznański* termed *Kuryer's* program a "political absurdity" and reminded the *Koło* representatives that their primary duty was to defend Polish interests and not be misled by "nebulous daydreams or vague promises.... Everything that has taken place in our public affairs since the resignation of Prince Bismarck seems to confirm that a change in the direction and the spirit of (Polish) policies is not to be expected; the necessity for these policies is merely presented in a somewhat milder form."[76]

Despite this negative response at first, Polish published opinion seemed to undergo a fairly rapid transformation during the following year, which may or may not reflect a similar trend among the Polish people generally. Local officials noted that "a shift has taken place in the position of the Polish press, with the exception of the very extreme and radical organs; generally the word has been issued by the leading papers not to proceed aggressively against the state government."[77] The term "extreme" refers here to *Goniec Wielkopolski*, organ of the chauvinistic intelligentsia, which grew if anything in anti-Prussian vehemence during the Caprivi Era. The term "radical" refers to *Orędownik* and *Postęp*, organs of the urban middle classes, which criticized the loyalist initiatives not because they were loyalist *per se* but because they were under the direction of the traditional noble leadership. Even then, Szymański's chief complaint was that *Koło* leaders were not very convincing loyalists, that they were not sufficiently sincere or credible in their loyalism. Otherwise, by early 1891 most of the Prussian-Polish political "establishment" seemed to be willing to give loyalism a try. Cardinal Ledóchowski, following a meeting with Kościelski and Stablewski, was reported to be "full of praise and appreciation for His Majesty the King and his ministers" and was sure that an era of peace had begun in Prussia.[78] Though the concessions to date had been quite minor, and there was little else but Caprivi's "milder tone" (and Gossler's dismissal) to go by, *Dziennik Poznański* declared that "after Prince Bismarck resigned and the new German government declared that it would consider all justified wishes, the opposition of the Poles on all issues had to cease."⁷⁹ A couple of months later, following Zedlitz' decree permitting private instruction in Polish, this paper seemed completely converted to loyalism:

> "A word of quite ambivalent meaning from the mouth of the Emperor concerning his intention to exercise justice toward all subjects without discrimination as to nationality or religion, a position far from the hostility and persecution . . . in the higher spheres of (his) government, has sufficed to do away with all the hostile bitterness which twenty years of hard and reckless persecution had produced and allowed to collect in all segments of our population."

Stablewski read this passage to the Landtag in order to convince German representatives and ministers that Prussian Poles were indeed lining up behind the loyalists. He claimed that *Dziennik*'s views were representative of the "whole public opinion among us; in Poznania, the two chief papers, *Dziennik Poznański* and *Kuryer Poznański*, are the expression of public opinion and in fact govern it."⁸⁰

Kościelski meanwhile stepped up his efforts to sell loyalism to the government, through personal contacts as well as parliamentary speeches. In talks with German conservatives he tried to convince them that younger Polish nobles had given up the idea of ever having Poznania and West Prussia included in a restored Poland.⁸¹ Caprivi in return held discussions with him regarding the situation in the Polish provinces.⁸² Few Germans proclaimed their loyalty to the Prussian State and its King as often or as enthusiastically as did Kościelski. In a June 1891 speech, which attracted much attention among Germans and Poles alike, he described himself as a "Prussian of Polish nationality" and called for a joint effort by German and Polish conservatives against the revolutionary menace within and the Russian menace without. He argued that monarchist principles ought to take precedence over nationalist ones, that for Poles and Germans alike loyalty to state and monarch ought to come before nationality.

> "All party considerations, even national rivalries, are pushed into the background today by the social question. . . . I do not think it should matter whether a Prussian prays to God in German or Polish, whether he toasts his king in Polish or German. . . . Today there are only two parties: the state-supporting party of order and the state-destroying party of revolution."

Poles, he maintained, belonged overwhelmingly to the former party; the New Era had permitted them to express their "constant and sympathetic interest in the health and welfare of the Empire . . . and (the desire), according to our strength, to cooperate in its internal development."[83] In place of the previous "cool, indifferent, and disapproving" attitude, Poles were now saying, "here we are, let us contribute faithfully and honestly to the development of the Empire; we do not want to be an obstruction . . . but rather a positive factor."[84] Of course, "we will never become Germans simply because God has created us as Poles. . . . Not the existence of the Poles in the East is a weakness but the effort to Germanize them." It was in the state's interest to maintain a "non-German but faithful and loyal population" on its eastern frontier.[85]

Koło leaders in the Prussian lower house refused still to be swayed by the new situation. Following Kościelski's speech of June 12, 1891, he was summoned before a caucus of the Landtag delegations, dominated by Jażdżewski and Czarliński, and personally censured. A resolution was passed (though not made public) declaring that his statement had been "uttered without the authorization of the Koło and was incompatible with the views and principles of the Koło."[86] In response, Kuryer carried a series of harsh attacks on Jażdżewski, reportedly authored by his fellow priest Stablewski; attempts were made to dislodge him as faction leader if he would not get into line. Jażdżewski acknowledged that "we no longer feel the previous resentment so strongly," but at the same time spoke ominously of the growing dissatisfaction of the Polish masses and questioned the long-term ability of "peaceful forces" to contain it.[87] Czarliński insisted that rescission of the Settlement Law should be a prerequisite of loyalism; "One cannot speak of a reconciliation between the nationalities as long as this unjust law exists."[88] Only the appointment of Stablewski as Archbishop caused this opposition in the Landtag delegation to die down temporarily and led to a fairly unified loyalist stance by the Koło by the end of 1891.

Concerning the Settlement Law, this was one part of Bismarck's legacy which Caprivi consistently refused to alter.[89] Polish loyalists could only rationalize that progress was still to be made on other fronts and that the Settlement Law had turned out to be less awesome than anticipated and was not being pushed quite as energetically under Caprivi. There was actually some justification for the latter view, for the Settlement Commission went through a period of doldrums in the early 1890s. It remained unsure of itself in terms of organization and basic policies. With Zedlitz' appointment as Culture Minister, his place as *Oberpräsident* of Poznania and heir-apparent to the chairmanship of the Settlement Commission went to Hugo von Wilamowitz-Moellendorff. But Wilamowitz had always maintained good relations with local Polish nobles[90] and had opposed the Settlement Law from the start. Zedlitz suggested that the job of chairman go to the Agriculture Minister Heyden, who considered it too much of a burden and declined. It was finally given to a middle-echelon executive secretary (*Rat*), Wittenberg, minus its near-cabinet status and prestige.⁹¹ Whether or not this was a factor, the Commission's buying activity declined from 8,527 ha. in 1891 to 6,262 ha. in 1894.⁹² Prof. Buzek, a contemporary, suggested even that the Caprivi government had "given up the extermination battle in the economic sphere," without actually withdrawing the 1886 law.⁹³ But this was not the result of any conscious change of policy; the Settlement Commission continued to expend a great deal of effort but for various reasons the results diminished. It was hinderd by the gradual exhaustion of financially weak Polish estates for sale, the prohibition against buying from Germans prior to 1892, growing Polish competition, the disappointing progress of some western settlers in spite of the financial support it provided, and finally the exhaustion of its original funding. It still bought up much more land than the various Polish agencies during the Caprivi Era (31,620 ha. *vs. c.* 8,000 ha.), but because it created larger farms, it wound up settling only 925 families during this period, fewer than the Poles who concentrated on smaller, worker-peasant plots.⁹⁴

The problems facing the Settlement Commission forced a reconsideration of the question of buying from Germans. Heyden argued that such purchases were necessary if the Commission were to continue its settlement activity at all, since the number of available Polish estates had shrunk to the point where there was no longer any selection possible. He also felt that existing restrictions merely gave Polish estate owners an unfair advantage and guaranteed them a good price in case liquidation was necessary. For different reasons, Trade Minister Berlepsch agreed; he wanted to focus on the social-political task of replacing inefficient nobles of either nationality with middle-class farmers. Miquel, now Finance Minister, feared on the other hand that a relaxation would turn the Commission into an agency to aid bankrupt German estate owners; Caprivi, without stating a firm opinion in cabinet, apparently agreed.⁹⁵ But the new Minister-President Eulenburg finally gave the Commission permission to purchase occasionally from Germans, and to overrun its budget as well, in 1892.⁹⁶ Eventually, the Commission required an additional financial injection in 1898 to function at the desired level, by which time it was buying primarily from Germans.

Despite the continued existence of the Settlement Commission, the period after Stablewski's appointment saw the heyday of reconciliation in Prussian Poland. Kościelski wrote Caprivi suggesting that a few school concessions would suffice to make of Prussian Poland a *"treue Wacht an der Weichsel."*⁹⁷ During a visit to Poznań by Empress

Friedrich, "both nationalities competed to show homage to the illustrious guest," according to official reports.[98] Stablewski had high praise for the new Culture Minister:

> "Gossler . . . judged our conditions based on the clippings from Polish newspapers which were put in front of him. Then came Count Zedlitz, who saw things with his own eyes and recognized quite correctly that only through decades of judicious work could the differences be alleviated. . . . Just ask around—everywhere you will hear what he has done for the province and its peace."[99]

Dziennik was now convinced that "the position of the Prussian government toward the Poles has changed visibly since the resignation of Prince Bismarck," though (like most loyalists) it still attributed the change to the "noble sentiments and powerful initiatives of the Monarch" rather than to Caprivi and Zedlitz.[100] Radziwiłł prefaced his contribution to the annual discussion of the Settlement Commission with the remark: "Nothing is further from my mind than the intention of bringing any kind of political criticism into this discussion."[101] Government officials noted an "improved mood" among the Poles, including their willingness for the first time to celebrate the Emperor's birthday, whereas local Germans showed signs of a "profound disquiet."[102]

The government also seemed pleased with the results of its softer policy toward its Poles, especially the impact on Russian Poland. A West Prussian *Landrat* visiting Warsaw reported that "the entire Polish population would greet the Germans as liberators and saviours" in the event of a Russian-German war.[103] Russian Foreign Minister Giers complained to Ambassador Schweinitz that (in the latter's words) "the Poles are convinced that Emperor Wilhelm will restore their empire; there is nothing great and beautiful that they do not expect from his great intelligence and courage."[104] To confirm these sentiments, Caprivi sent Hutten-Czapski on an intelligence mission to Russian Poland; Hutten's report was very optimistic. As he recalled later, "the resignation of Bismarck, the school concessions by Caprivi in Poznania, and finally the appointment of Stablewski as Archbishop had brought about a real change of mood." Stablewski's appointment had made an even stronger impression there than in Poznania, so much so that the Russians were censoring news about him and other Prussian-Polish developments. Hutten was certain that Russian Poles could be made to participate actively on Germany's side in the event of a war with Russia, provided that the present course were continued.[105] Wilhelm too was aware of the strategic pay-off of Caprivi's approach to the Poles. As he declared in July 1892:

An Era of Reconciliation

"I have my good reasons for being polonophile. . . . The *entire* Polish national feeling is concentrated on me, each meeting begins with a glass being emptied to me. The hope of liberation from the Russian yoke fills them completely and in a war with Russia all Poland would stand in revolution on my side with the express intention of having themselves annexed by me."[106]

When Eulenburg tried to suggest that the Poles might be pursuing national aims of their own, Wilhelm replied, "no, they have given that up. The educated element . . . wants to come under Prussia. . . . (In any case), for the time being I view the matter simply from a military standpoint. . . . For the time being *I* am the goal and we want to take note of that."[107] This rather hyperbolic analysis was based roughly on official sources but also on the report of an American correspondent and a Prussian officer under disguise, both of whom confirmed what the other sources had to say about the prevailing sentiment in Russian Poland.[108] Indeed, in 1893 the German Consul in Warsaw even received a letter from a group of Polish nobles pleading for liberation by Germany from the Russian yoke.[109]

In March 1892, while such amicable feelings were at their peak and seemed capable of further development,[110] Caprivi and Zedlitz were caught overreaching themselves in their efforts to increase religious influence in the public schools and win Center support for their government. Emperor Wilhelm withdrew his support from, and thus helped bring down, the Zedlitz school bill. This in turn caused, exactly two years after Bismarck's dismissal, the fall of Zedlitz, and Caprivi also in his role as Prussian Minister-President.[111] Caprivi's position as head of the Prussian government was taken by Botho zu Eulenburg, a cousin to Phillip and to the former Interior Minister; Zedlitz' position was taken by Robert Bosse. Caprivi remained German Chancellor and Prussian Foreign Minister; the "Caprivi Era" therefore continued for another 2½ years. But these changes were of considerable importance for Polish policy, which was mainly a Prussian-state rather than a German-national matter. And both Eulenburg and Bosse were considerably more nationalistic and less inclined toward appeasement of the Poles than their predecessors. As Holstein foresaw upon hearing of the changes: "One good thing about the selection: the coquetting with the Poles will probably cease."[112]

While Eulenburg did not appear to have particularly strong feelings about Polish matters, Bosse went out of his way to dampen any expectations of further concessions in school affairs. Soon after taking office, he paid a visit to Poznania and pronounced himself satisfied with school conditions as they were. "I consider it out of the question that the state school administration should offer its hand in order to call into question again the happy results of a long and respectable cultural project for the benefit of Polish-national whims."[113] He began to restrict the applicability of Zedlitz' private-instruction decree, suggesting that German pupils should not be allowed to attend if there was danger of Polonization or if their other school work might suffer.[114] In January 1893 he further tightened restrictions on attendance at these classes: it was to be limited to pupils who had reached the third grade and had a good knowledge of German already; classes were to consume no more than two hours weekly; they were to be limited to the study of reading and writing, and not include literature or related subjects; Germans could participate only in separate classes; and officials were to protect Polish pupils from being coerced into attendance.[115] These restrictions provided local officials with all the encouragement they needed to inhibit the private instruction program in many areas. Bosse ruled out the idea that the state might again take over this task: "We remain unshakably firm with the system we have." For good measure he also denied the very existence of an "era of reconciliation;" while some Polish leaders had "submitted to political circumstances, . . . look at the Polish press: a wild agitation against everything German."[116]

Yet the Era of Reconciliation did not come to an end immediately in 1892. For one thing, the strategic justification remained in spite of the personal attitudes of Eulenburg and Bosse. For another, a new justification appeared in the form of the crucial role the *Koło Polskie* might play in the struggle for several key Reichstag bills in the 1893-4 period. In 1890 already, following the *Kartell's* loss of its majority that year, some loyalists thought their Reichstag votes might serve as a lever to gain concessions. There was some talk of a Conservative-Center coalition at this time, which would fall short of a majority unless the 16 *Koło* votes were included. The *Kreuzzeitung* suggested such a coalition of forces "favoring a stable German state" in July 1890.[117] Some historians suggest that parliamentary considerations were behind Caprivi's milder approach to the Poles from the beginning.[118] But there is little evidence of a direct attempt by Caprivi to win Polish leaders for such a coalition, or any other. Rather, the *Koło* began to support his bills on its own and apparently to his surprise. When the Poles voted for the 1890 army bill, Caprivi reacted almost suspiciously, asking whether Bismarck's measures had made them so tractable or if they "consider the present government to be so weak that they believe they can offer it something that they did not offer to the previous government."[119] The *Koło* also voted for the navy bill of 1891-2 and Kościelski, aware of the importance of naval matters to

An Era of Reconciliation

Emperor Wilhelm, even served as floor manager for it. He received a friendly note from Wilhelm, and a diplomat in Berlin described him as the "Emperor's new friend."[120] Germans derided him however as "admiralski" and anti-loyalist Poles christened him "Admiral of Lake Gopło (a lake in Poznania)." But the fundamental weakness of such a strategy was that Poles could be a vital element in a Reichstag coalition but the government retained its dependable majority in the Prussian Landtag, where most anti-Polish laws had originated and where their repeal would have to take place. And with Caprivi's ouster, interest in the Conservative-Center coalition, which was strongly opposed by Wilhelm, waned. Between the replacement of Zedlitz and Caprivi in Prussia and the army bill of 1893, when the Koło regained its leverage in a vital Reichstag controversy, 15 months passed. During this period the spirit of reconciliation stagnated, opposition to it formed on the part of both German and Polish nationalists, and it became less a matter of conviction than a somewhat cynical *quid pro quo* arrangement.

Notes

1. Waldersee to Rechenberg, German Consul in Warsaw, November 16, 1887, in Alfred von Waldersee, *Briefwechsel,* ed. H.O. Meisner (Stuttgart, 1928), I:112; see also Karl-Ernst Jeismann, *Das Problem des Präventivkriegs im europäischen Staatensystems* (Freiburg, 1957).
2. Waldersee to Yorck, November 17, 1887, in H.O. Meisner, "Briefwechsel zwischen Chef des General-Stabes Waldersee und Militär-Attaché Yorck von Wartenburg, 1885-1894," *Historisch-politisches Archiv zur Deutschen Geschichte des 19. und 20. Jahrhunderts* 1(1930):152.
3. Alfred von Tirpitz, *My Memoirs* (New York, 1919), I:37; see also Rudolf Stadelmann, "Der Neue Kurs in Deutschland," *Geschichte in Wissenschaft und Unterricht* 4(1953):541.
4. Busch, I:303.
5. Bismarch to Wilhelm I, November 16, 1883, *Die Grosse Politik der Europäischen Kabinette, 1871-1914* (Berlin, 1922), III:303.
6. November 10, 1887, *Ibid.*
7. Francesco Crispi, *Memoirs* (London, 1912), II:213; see also Bismarck to Bronsart, December 30, 1887, *Gesammelte Werke* VIc: 378; Chlodwig zu Hohenlohe-Schillingsfürst, *Denkwürdigkeiten* (Stuttgart, 1907), II:461.
8. Hohenlohe, II:343.
9. Waldersee to Yorck, May 18, 1888, Meisner, p. 164.
10. Alfred von Waldersee, *Denkwürdigkeiten* (Stuttgart, 1925), I:303.
11. Hutten-Czapski, p. 191.
12. Quoted by Czarliński, March 1, 1892, *Abgeordnetenhaus.*
13. Hans von Seeckt, *Aus meinem Leben* (Leipzig, 1941), p. 17.
14. *Gesammelte Werke,* VIII:707.

15. Heinrich Otto Meisner, "Reichskanzler Caprivi," *Zeitschrift für die Gesamte Staatswissenschaft* 111(1953):739; the "Caprivi Papers" listed in the bibliography under *GPSA Berlin* consist of an envelope with a few personal letters and citations; some letters to a professor-friend constitute virtually the sum of published post-1894 statements by Caprivi; see Max Schneidewin, "Briefe des toten Reichskanzlers von Caprivi," *Deutsche Revue* 47(1922):136-47, 247-58.

16. Marginal comment on Gossler memorandum of October 16, 1890, *PA Bonn*, Preussen 4.

17. Speeches of May 2, 1891, *Abgeordnetenhaus*.

18. Caprivi memorandum of November 18, 1893, *PA Bonn*, Preussen 8:2.

19. Speech of March 12, 1890, *Abgeordnetenhaus*.

20. Gossler memorandum of October 16, 1890, *PA Bonn*, Preussen 4.

21. Council of Ministers meeting, October 24, 1890, *Ibid*.

22. Gossler memorandum of November 4, 1890, *Ibid*.

23. Gossler memorandum of February 18, 1891, *Ibid*.

24. John Röhl, *Germany without Bismarck* (Cambridge, 1967), p. 77.

25. Speech of April 26, 1890, *Herrenhaus*.

26. Otto zu Stolberg-Wernigerode, *Die Unentschiedene Generation* (Munich, 1968), p. 266.

27. Report from Poznań, July 19, 1890, *GPSA Berlin*, Rep. 84a, #5964.

28. Quoted by Schroeder, March 3, 1894, *Abgeordnetenhaus*.

29. Speech of March 12, 1890, *ibid*.

30. Wilhelm II, *Ereignisse und Gestalten, 1878–1915* (Leipzig, 1922); *Kaiserreden*, ed. O. Klaussmann (Leipzig, 1902).

31. Radziwiłł, *passim*.

32. Hutten-Czapski, pp. 157, 256; see also Fritz Hartung, "Graf von Hutten-Czapski," *Historische Zeitschrift* 153(1936):548-59.

33. Johannes Nichtweiss, *Ausländische Saisonarbeiter in der Landwirtschaft der östlichen und mittleren Gebiete des Deutschen Reiches* (East Berlin, 1959), pp. 33ff.; see also Juliusz Trziński, *Russisch-polnische und galizische Wanderarbeiter im Grossherzogtum Posen* (Stuttgart, 1906).

34. Speech by Gossler, March 12, 1890, *Abgeordnetenhaus*.

35. Sering, p. 8.

36. Puhle, p. 256.

37. Speech of January 28, 1891, *Abgeordnetenhaus*.

38. Report from Marienwerder, March 18, 1891, *GPSA Berlin*, Rep. 84a, #5967.

39. Speech of March 16, 1891, *Abgeordnetenhaus*.

40. Report from Poznań, February 21, 1891, *GPSA Berlin*, Rep. 84a, #5964.

41. Puhle, p. 256; Adam Galos and Kazimierz Wajda, "Migrations in the Polish western Territories annexed by Prussia, 1815-1914," in *Employment-seeking Emigrations of the Poles worldwide*, ed. C. Bobińska & A. Pilch (Cracow, 1975), p. 73.

42. Document #165, April 25, 1890, and document 233, April 2, 1891, *Abgeordnetenhaus: Anlagen*.

43. Speech by Lucius, May 3, 1890, *Abgeordnetenhaus;* see also Paul Waldhecker, "Ansiedlungskommission und General-Kommission," *Jahrbuch für Gesetzgebung, Verwaltung und Volkswirtschaft im Deutschen Reich* 21(1897):202–227.
44. Sering, p. 201.
45. Bernhard, p. 154.
46. Höhn/Seydel, p. 107.
47. Beutner to Wilamowitz, March 1, 1893, *AP Poznań*, XVI C 40-1.
48. Szembek, p. 235.
49. Eulenburg to Wilamowitz, January 2, 1893, *Ibid.*
50. Swart, p. 145; E. Stumpfe, *Polenfrage und Ansiedlungskommission* (Berlin, 1902), p. 4.
51. Bernhard, p. 139.
52. P. 221.
53. Zedlitz decree of April 11, 1891, *GPSA Berlin* Rep. B 30:II #2526.
54. Zedlitz to Tiedemann, May 5, 1891, *Ibid.*
55. Zedlitz memorandum of October 2, 1891, *Ibid.*
56. Speeches of May 8, 1891, *Abgeordnetenhaus.*
57. Leonhard Müller, *Die nationalpolnische Presse, Katholizismus und der katholische Klerus, 1896–9* (Breslau, 1931), p. 10.
58. Speech of November 27, 1891, *Reichstag.*
59. Trzeciakowski, *Polityka*, p. 101.
60. Rampolla to Schlözer, July 12, 1890, *Kirchenpolitik*, p. 128.
61. Gossler to Caprivi, July 29, 1890, *Ibid.*, p. 135.
62. Caprivi to Kościelski, September 15, 1891, Kucner, p. 67.
63. Speech of May 4, 1981, *Abgeordnetenhaus.*
64. Full text in Roman Komierowski, *Koło polskie w Berlinie, 1875–1900* (Poznań, 1905), pp. 216ff.
65. Caprivi to Schlözer, October 18, 1891, *Kirchenpolitik*, p. 146.
66. *Ibid.*; see also Adam Galos, "Tragizm Ugody," *Przegląd Zachodni* 21(1975):236; Harry Rosenthal, "The Election of Archbishop Stablewski," *Slavic Review* 28(1969):265–275.
67. *Kaiserreden*, p. 67.
68. January 18, 1892, *AP Poznań* XXIV D III a 59.
69. Müller, p. 10.
70. Council of Ministers meeting, April 12, 1891, *GPSA Berlin*, Rep. 84a, #40891.
71. Speech of May 2, 1891, *Abgeordnetenhaus.*
72. *Kraj* (St. Petersburg), May 21, 1891, *PA Bonn*, Preussen 4.
73. Trzeciakowski, *Politkya*, pp. 62, 77.
74. March 19, 1890, quoted by Trzeciakowski, "Polskie upgrupowania," p. 31.
75. Report from Poznań, February 16, 1890, *GPSA Berlin*, Rep. 84a, #5967.

76. June 13, 1890, *PA Bonn* Preussen 4.
77. Report from Poznań, March 29, 1890, *GPSA Berlin*, Rep. 84a, #5967.
78. Schlözer to Caprivi, March 11, 1891, *Kirchenpolitik*, p. 142.
79. March 21, 1891, *PA Bonn*, Preussen 4.
80. Quoted by Stablewski, May 4, 1891, *Abgeordnetenhaus*.
81. Erhard von Wedel, *Zwischen Kaiser und Kanzler* (Leipzig, 1943), pp. 108ff.
82. Kucner, P. 65.
83. Speech of June 12, 1891, *Herrenhaus*.
84. Speech of December 2, 1892, *Reichstag*.
85. Speech of March 21, 1893, *Herrenhaus*.
86. Caucus meeting, June 18, 1891, *Biblioteka Kórnicka*, Rep. 1454-8.
87. Speech of May 2, 1891, *Abgeordnetenhaus*.
88. *Ibid.*
89. Spech of May 2, 1891, *Ibid.*
90. See speech of January 22, 1878, *Ibid.*
91. Council of Ministers meeting, February 23, 1891, *GPSA Berlin*, Rep. 84a, #4089.
92. *Deutsche Kulturarbeit*, p. 24.
93. Buzek, p. 144.
94. Bernhard, p. 511; Perdelwitz, p. 85.
95. Council of Ministers meetings, May 28 and July 3, 1891, *GPSA Berlin*, Rep. 84a, #4089.
96. *Ibid.*, meeting of August 13, 1892.
97. Quoted in Trzeciakowski, *Polityka*, p. 80.
98. Report from Poznań, December 2, 1891, *GPSA Berlin*, Rep. 84a, #5957.
99. Maximilian Harden, "Erzbischof Stablewski über die Polenfrage," *Die Zukunft*, January 10, 1892, p. 6.
100. March 9, 1892, *PA Bonn*, Preussen 4.
101. Speech of March 28, 1892, *Herrenhaus*.
102. Report from Bromberg, March 4, 1892, *GPSA Berlin*, Rep. 84a, #5957.
103. Report of January 5, 1892, *PA Bonn*, I.A. Russland 83, #2, vol. 2.
104. Report of February 20, 1892, *Ibid.*, Europa Generalia, #79, vol. 2; Caprivi's marginal comment: "Thanks! Very flattering;" Consul Rechenberg's report from Warsaw, March 11, 1892, also indicated that Wilhelm was the object of "lively sympathy," *Ibid.*
105. Hutten-Czapski, pp. 167, 172f.
106. Conversation of July 11, 1892, John Röhl, "A Document of 1892 on Germany, Prussia, and Poland," *Historical Journal* 7(1964):143-9.
107. *Ibid.*
108. See Poultney Bigelow, *Prussian Memories* (New York, 1915), pp. 102ff.
109. Rechenberg to Caprivi, November 27, 1893, *PA Bonn*, Europe Generalia, #79.

An Era of Reconciliation

110. According to Raschdau, p. 208, Caprivi intended to do so.
111. Röhl, *Germany*, p. 84.
112. Norman Rich, *Friedrich von Holstein* (Cambridge, 1965), I:385.
113. Memorandum of August 31, 1892, *PA Bonn*, Preussen 8.
114. Memorandum of December 1, 1892, *GPSA Berlin*, Rep. B 30:II, #2526.
115. Memorandum of January 14, 1893, *Ibid.*
116. Speech of February 13, 1893, *Abgeordnetenhaus*.
117. Harry Rosenthal, "Germans and Poles in 1890: Possibilities for a New Course," *East European Quarterly* 5(1971):306.
118. Pfeiffer, p. 64; Laubert, p. 138.
119. Speech of May 2, 1891, *Abgeordnetenhaus*.
120. Trzeciakowski, "Polskie ugrupowania," p. 33; Komierowski, p. 237; Kucner, pp. 65ff.

Chapter VI:
The Populist Revolt and the Failure of Loyalism

The major problem underlying the "Era of Reconciliation" was that it did not result primarily from a genuine change of heart on the part of either Polish nobles or their government. Rather, both sides were more or less conscripted into the closer relationship by fear of outside forces. As noted previously, an important motive behind the Caprivi policy was fear of war with Russia. Similarly, fear of the effect of Bismarck's measures and of their own restive middle classes were key factors in the growth of Polish loyalism. The result was a rather makeshift partnership. In the absence of underlying conviction on either side, the Era of Reconciliation depended upon a steady stream of tangible results in order that it could be justified in the face of a generally hostile public opinion. By 1892-3 it became clear that the Caprivi government was between two chairs, unwilling to make the concessions that might solidify loyalist feeling among the Poles while doing just enough to evoke a strong reaction from German nationalists.

In the forefront of this nationalist reaction to Caprivi's Polish policy was the National Liberal Reichstag representative from Bremerhaven-Kehdingen, Otto von Bismarck. Even after his fall, Bismarck continued to exercise considerable influence over German public opinion. At first it looked like he might use this influence to ease Caprivi's task. He had, after all, been an early booster, suggesting in 1886 that Caprivi "ought to receive an important position in the Army (War Minister or Chief of the General Staff)."[1] When the latter job went to Waldersee instead, Bismarck attributed this to Wilhelm II's weakness for courtiers as opposed to independent-minded men like Caprivi and himself.[2] Even when it turned out in 1890 that Caprivi was to have his own job, Bismarck pronounced himself "exceptionally satisfied with this choice" and claimed that it was he who "had proposed this personality to the Emperor."[3] But before long, after the change in German foreign policy and the consequent new approach to the Poles, Bismarck began to criticize his successor.

At first, Bismarck limited his criticism to the foreign policy area and avoided attacking Caprivi personally. His attitude toward anything which suggested a resurrected Poland had not changed; even with Russia no longer an ally, he still preferred her to an independent Poland as a neighbor. He feared that the "New Course" would lead to war with Russia; Germany, if she did not want to see an independent Poland, "would have to take the Poles, of which we already have enough, more than is desirable for us, from Russia."[4] But by late-1891, with the appointment of Archbishop Stablewski, his long-time parliamentary foe, Bismarck's attacks began to grow in intensity. He also began to disapprove of Caprivi personally: not only was his name of Slavic derivation but he had cut down some of the large trees surrounding the Chancellor's residence in order to gain more sunlight, which for Bismarck reflected a Slavic rather than Germanic outlook.[5] He interpreted the "present fluctuation in the policy of the government toward the Poles" as an attempt to win the dubious loyalty of the Poles at the high price of Russian hostility.[6] As for the domestic impact, "it has repeatedly been the misfortune of Prussian (Polish) policy that it can sow but is unable to wait for the time of harvest. . . . Trust in the care and protection of the Prussian government (on the part of eastern Germans) is badly shaken."[7] The fact that Stablewski had become an outspoken loyalist and "spoken better with respect to the German nation than a Pole otherwise does" could not obscure the fact that (for Bismarck) the obvious basis of the Era of Reconciliation was a common German-Polish front against Russia.[8] He felt that concern about war with Russia was causing the Caprivi government to lose sight of the danger which Polish nationalism presented for Germany.

> "The struggle with Polonism, which is everywhere political and pan-Polish, cannot be let out of sight. . . . The filling of the Gniezno Archbishop's chair with a well-known sponsor of the pan-Polish idea was a weakness and a mistake of foreign as well as domestic policy. Nothing more fatal to our foreign policy could be done than going along with a Prussian Polish policy which has similarities to the Austrian."[9]

Similarly the following month: "A Pole was made Archbishop and he was given a position which, in the interest of German policy, would have belonged to a German Catholic. . . . The policy toward the Poles in Poznania has weakened the trust that our government formerly enjoyed in Russia and has lessened our influence as well."[10] He began to despair finally that "everything that we have toiled to construct in Germany's interest in the eastern border region is slowly crumbling again."[11]

Of course, Bismarck did not trust the Polish loyalists at all and warned

The Populist Revolt and the Failure of Loyalism

Caprivi against taking Kościelski and Stablewski at their word:

"I know that tone! That is only for the beginning, to appease the Emperor and the government. Ledóchowski also did that very cleverly for a while; but my successor did not have to imitate me precisely there where I committed a mistake. . . . No responsible person believes that they are not speculating today on the restoration of the Polish empire."[12]

Caprivi's concessions constituted for him a dangerous "encouragement of Polish wishes. . . . Polish covetousness has been encouraged recently and that is a serious experiment, especially since there lies in the Polish question a European question of war and peace."[13] On only one occasion did he seem to waver somewhat in his categorical distrust of Polish loyalism; when the Poles joined with the *Kartell* parties to assure passage of the 1893 Army bill (see below, p. 157) he wondered at the "German patriotism of the Polish nobles. . . . They have become ministerial today, which has not been the case for a century." Even then he remained convinced that they would not be "ministerial in the long run, at least not those who are the carriers of the Polish national movement, the Polish nobility and the Polish clergy; that is surely . . . more than doubtful."[14]

Bismarck's criticism of the New Course in Polish policy reinforced and perhaps inspired a similar reaction from other segments of German society. German opposition to the concessions of the Caprivi Era was most vocal in the nationally-mixed areas of the Prussian East. There is little evidence that Germans and Poles in Poznania and West Prussia participated in any "era of reconciliation" at the provincial or local levels. The motives of the Caprivi government weighed little compared to the increased state attention and funds which Poznanian Germans had enjoyed since 1886. Conservative Polish nobles made some effort during the Caprivi Era to bridge the gap separating them from their German counterparts and neighbors. One example was a bi-national "Provincial Society for the Combatting of Social-Democratic Tendencies" in 1891. This joined Polish loyalists (Kościelski, Cegielski, Komierowski) with German officials and parliamentarians (Wilamowitz, Heinrich von Tiedemann, and the provincial police chief) in what proved to be a very short-lived undertaking.[15] A more promising basis for this kind of conservative cooperation across national lines was the growing agrarian dissatisfaction, except that this implied opposition to precisely the government toward which the Poles wanted to demonstrate their loyalty. For the most part, German representatives from Poznania and West Prussia continued to be the most outspoken opponents of Caprivi's Polish policy. Heinrich von Tiedemann saw Zedlitz' approval of private instruction in Polish as "well-suited to call forth objections and fears among the Germans of Poznania."[16] These representatives were overwhelmingly from the *Kartell* parties and clearly more at home with the Bismarckian approach.

After a few years in office, Caprivi acquired many other opponents for reasons unrelated to the Polish question. They used his Polish policies, however, as part of their open opposition and behind-the-scenes intrigue against him. His alleged softness on the Polish question was often just a pretext to attack him by rivals who were not really interested in the Polish question *per se*. Waldersee, for example, an earlier advocate of a Polish policy based on strategic considerations, turned sharply against Caprivi's policy after his own fall from grace in 1891. By 1893 he consorted with Bismarck and criticized Caprivi's naïvete in taking seriously Polish "windbags" (Kościelski and his friends), who "relate wonderful things about what the noble Polish nation would accomplish; and German simpletons crawl into the trap. In my opinion, no one in Russian Poland will move a finger if war breaks out; instead they will wait and see which way things go."[17] The Pan-German League, founded in 1891 as part of the general growth of nationalist and imperialist sentiment during these years, also made room in its program for attacks on Caprivi's Polish policy. At first it was concerned almost exclusively with colonial matters; (it arose in response to Caprivi's lack of interest in imperialism, as evidenced by his Zanzibar-for-Helgoland treaty with Britain). It quickly acquired a sizable membership, only to go into decline by 1893. Then, under the prodding of Alfred Hugenberg, it began to turn its attention more to nationalist concerns at home, among which the Polish question assumed an important place. Hugenberg warned that "a large number of substitute leaders, more active and more dangerous, are appearing among the newly-arisen Polish urban middle classes, in place of the . . . large landowners that we have taken from them." He demanded stronger Germanization meausures which would make use of the state's economic and cultural weapons to attack the entire spectrum of Polish society, not merely the nobility.[18]

This opposition to Caprivi's Polish policy soon became an important factor impeding further progress toward reconciliation. The strategic rationale behind reconciliation remained, supplemented now by the need for Polish support of key government measures in the Reichstag. But adverse nationalist opinion, declining support from the Emperor, and loss of control over Prussian state affairs halted whatever impetus toward reconciliation had developed since 1890. Even the most committed Polish loyalists had to acknowledge that powerful segments of German public opinion were not behind the government's modest reconciliation effort. Simultaneously, the government became aware that Polish public opinion was not very supportive of loyalism either, and this led eventually to the end of the Era of Reconciliation. Sometime during the 1892-3 period, the number and significance of government concessions and friendly gestures toward the Poles ceased to be sufficient to maintain support for loyalism by large segments of the Prussian-Polish population. Public opinion in Poznania and West Prussia, as measured by newspaper editorials and public speeches, began to turn against loyalism again. The leading loyalists themselves remained fairly committed to their policy; some felt there was no longer any alternative to it. They ignored early indications that reconciliation was not making very satisfactory progress and began to engage in wishful thinking. But they began to lose the popular support without which loyalism could not work.

As it became evident that Prussian officials fell into two categories, those like Caprivi who might be sympathetic but who now lacked the means to determine state policy and those like Bosse who were not interested in reconciliation, the loyalists increasingly fell back on Emperor Wilhelm as their sole remaining hope. They often exceeded the most conservative of Germans in giving vent to their monarchist sentiments and proclaiming their devotion to the person of the Emperor. Though in fact Wilhelm did not play much of a role in the concessions of the Caprivi Era, the loyalist press attributed every small change in the Poles' favor to his personal intervention. *Kuryer Poznański* responded to the appointment of Stablewski in the following fashion: "Poles everywhere are filled with gratitude for the crown and assembled in solid ranks around the person of the exalted Monarch. . . . The whole society (is) united . . . in the sincere and infallible conviction that it must adhere faithfully and constantly to the standard of the just Monarch."[19] This paper attributed the German-nationalist reaction against concessions to the Poles to Bismarck's anger in learning that the Poles were more loyal to their king than he, that they wished to serve Wilhelm and not himself.[20] When Eulenburg expressed his continued support for the Settlement Law, *Dziennik Poznański* rationalized that such support was temporary and Polish loyalists might still change his mind.[21] Attacks by Poznanian-German representatives were interpreted as "agitation against their king," who had supposedly recognized the "loyalty and special national position" of Prussian Poles.[22] When a local school official declared that Polish would not again have a position in the regular curriculum, the loyalist press demanded his dismissal on grounds that he could not possibly be in accord with official policy. When Bosse confirmed this position, *Kuryer* suggested that he had merely been given some wrong information or had not meant what he said.[23] When he continued to make his hostility clear beyond any doubt, loyalists were left only with the hope that Wilhelm would intercede: "Prussian ministers change! A wink suffices, and they step back into obscurity. . . . An Imperial *sic volo* and Bosse will go the same way that Falk and Gossler went before him."[24] As long as Wilhelm did not speak out publicly against the Poles (or Caprivi's policy toward them), one might still believe that it was just a matter of time until the obstructionist ministers and lower officials were removed. But for most uncommitted observers, it seemed increasingly clear that the Polish loyalists were trying to hold fast to an untenable position.

Some loyalists tried to blame this adverse German opinion on the remaining non-loyalist Poles. They felt that if they could quiet such opposition voices in their own community, German distrust and opposition to a relaxed Polish policy would die down. In Stablewski's opinion, "since the government is now also filled with the best intentions, . . . good things would be forthcoming if it were not for the screamers in the press and the parliaments."[25] But most Poles offered their support to loyalism only tentatively and skeptically in the first place. Before long they became impatient and even less likely to remain quiet in order that the *Koło* might maintain the façade of a Polish society united in loyalism. *Gazeta Toruńska* warned that "the continuation of the previous system is making the position of (the loyalists) in their own society impossible. . . . A people to whom the necessary conditions of existence are denied . . . must inevitably save itself by going over to the opposition, but this excludes a reconciliation."[26] Jażdżewski also warned the government that "it cannot go on like this any longer. We are in an extremely bad position with respect to our voters when we come home and tell the people: the government does not want . . . to accommodate the people in the least."[27] When Eulenburg reaffirmed his support for the Settlement Law, *Gazeta Toruńska* concluded: "He has taken such a hostile position against us that it would appear that the government wants us to understand clearly that it does not think much of our intentions and does not believe in a policy of reconciliation."[28]

The middle-class opposition press, *Orędownik* and *Postęp*, continued its attacks on the *Koło* leadership throughout the Caprivi Era. Szymański had some difficulty faulting the Establishment for its loyalism, since he had argued for a similar approach himself since the 1870s. He had always urged it as an alternative to the policies of sterile opposition and protest which the *Koło* had traditionally followed, but now his adversaries had moved over to a position not that different from his own. For some time after Caprivi's arrival, Szymański adopted a wait-and-see attitude, expressing gratitude to Wilhelm for the new ministers and for his promise to treat all subjects equally. That the *Koło* establishment had come around to a position long advocated by himself was just another indication that he and his urban following deserved a greater voice in Prussian-Polish affairs. Along with most of the Prussian-Polish press, *Orędownik* issued a laudatory declaration on the Emperor's birthday for several years after 1890.[29] In 1892, it was still Szymański's position that "loyalty is today an indispensable condition for the calm social and national development of Polish society under Prussian rule."[30] It was of primary importance, however, who pursued this loyalist course: credible life-long loyalists like himself or opportunistic nobles and clergy who had done an abrupt about-face after many years of futile opposition. He contended that loyalism had to appear sincere and be based on broad popular support if it was to overcome German suspicions and thus be successful. "(Our) opposition stems from the fact that the nobility alone directs policies; yesterday's policy was to wail and bluster, today's is loyal, . . . and Polish lands are being lost without end."[31] Szymański wanted Poles to practice loyalism more matter-of-factly, quietly acknowledging their acceptance of Prussian rule while avoiding the obsequious declarations, embarrassing to Poles and unconvincing to Germans, to which Kościelski was given. In addition, he saw no reason to tie Polish loyalism to pan-Polish support in case of a war with Russia. His concept of loyalism did not call for an arrangement on the international level between Germany and the Polish "nation," just a willingness on the part of those Poles living inside Germany to accept their place there. Loyalism, in other words, was a strictly domestic question; Szymański seemed quite unconcerned about the restoration of a Polish state, especially if it would take a war to do so.

But this distinction between the loyalism of the middle-class Positivists and that advocated by the *Koło* during the Caprivi Era became increasingly difficult to maintain. Though Szymański was reluctant to abandon his idea of loyalism, his movement required more daylight between his position and that of the *Koło* leadership. In March 1893, he finally decided to break with loyalism, concluding that the government had decided on its own to stop dealing with the Poles.[32] This change of heart may have been motivated by genuine disappointment with the lack of significant concessions. More likely, however, it stemmed from the desire to enlist the growing number of Polish anti-loyalists in his own continuing struggle with the *Koło* leadership. Even then, his anti-loyalist statements remained much less vehement than those to be found in other Polish papers. *Goniec Wielkopolski*, for example, took the position that "no Pole can call himself a Prussian" without becoming, "like Kościelski, a renegade who is destroying the honor of the Polish people in every way."³³ But *Goniec* and the others represented sub-groups of the nobility essentially; they attacked loyalism as a misguided policy without calling into question the legitimacy of the traditional leadership itself or appealing to class enmity. Thus they were treated relatively lightly, almost patronizingly, by *Koło* leaders, whereas Szymański's attacks on loyalism were part of the older, generalized attack on National Solidarity under noble leadership and consequently drew a more energetic response.

Szymański's political challenge to the *Koło* organization resumed in January 1892. He presented himself increasingly as the head of a "People's Party" in opposition to the loyalist "Court Party" which dominated the *Koło Polskie*. His followers came to be called "Populists *(ludowcy)*" (though they had little in common with either the Russian revolutionaries or the Galician agrarian democrats of the same name). The occasion was a by-election to fill Stablewski's place in the Landtag. The Populists were opposed to the *Koło*'s choice, Żółtowski, a loyalist and head of the estate owner's organization; they urged instead the nomination of Piotr Wawrzyniak, a conservative loyalist and priest, to be sure, but also head of the Co-op Union and thus a symbol of middle-class self-reliance. The main thing for the Populists was to establish a precedent for challenging the hand-picked nominees of local election committees. This Landtag district was composed of three counties (Września/Wreschen, Środa/Schroda, and Śrem/Schrimm), each with its own election committee; Wawrzyniak emerged victorious over Żółtowski in all three and his ratification by the Provincial Elections Committee seemed assured. But he then declined the nomination, claiming inability to get away from his co-op responsibilities but apparently under some *Koło* pressure as well. This allowed the provincial committee to nominate Żółtowski, runner-up in two of the counties (and one of its own).³⁴ The Populists raged, called a series of protest assemblies, and demanded the opportunity to choose another candidate democratically, but as long as they were unwilling to break with the *Koło* altogether, there was little they could do. In the end, most of them fell into line behind the official candidate, who won the election.³⁵

During the following year, as support for loyalism began to waver, attention began to focus on the "Great Army Bill" of 1893. At first, the *Koło Polskie* spoke against the bill, citing the depressed economic conditions and the increased tax burden which the enlarged army would entail.³⁶ But then the reduction of the term of service from three years to two, designed to lessen resistance to it among Germans, made it possible for the Poles to support it as well. Kościelski was able to persuade a bare plurality of his colleagues (7:5, with 4 abstaining or absent, in a caucus of the Reichstag delegation) to continue their support of the government.³⁷

Among the Polish press, *Kuryer* was willing to go along with the decision of the *Koło* representatives; *Dziennik* agreed but only after warning them that, in the absence of major concessions, "the extreme limit" of support for the government had been reached.[38] Polish support was not sufficient to give the Army bill a majority, however; after its defeat in May 1893, Caprivi dissolved the Reichstag and called for new elections. The resulting campaign led to an intensified struggle in the Polish provinces between the loyalist *Koło* and the Populists (and other anti-loyalists) in the course of which Polish National Solidarity was virtually sundered.

Szymański's assault began with the demand for the removal of all Polish representatives who had favored the Army bill in caucus.[39] His strategy was to nominate rival candidates in selected county assemblies and, "as soon as you are not in a position to bring your own candidate through, limit yourselves to raising protests and breaking up the assemblies. For the salvation of the Polish nation!"[40] This was seldom difficult to do since Prussian police monitored each Polish poltical meeting with orders to close it if it got at all boisterous. In Bromberg the *Koło* organization proposed a loyalist estate owner and the Populists nominated the lawyer Moczyński. An uproar ensued and the meeting was terminated by police before a vote could be taken. A second meeting was called with the Populists in the majority; Moczyński was voted the nomination but the Provincial Elections Committee refused to ratify this. Finally, the *Koło* proposed Czarliński (a noble estate owner but also an outspoken opponent of the loyalist line) as a compromise candidate and he received the nomination at a third voter assembly.[41]

But Bromberg, with its large German majority, seemed to be an unlikely victory for the Poles regardless of whom they nominated. More important was the concurrent struggle in Poznań, where nomination by the *Koło* was tantamount to election. At the voter assembly here, Szymański introduced a motion critical of the *Koło*'s policies; when committee leaders refused to put it to a vote the meeting was broken up without having agreed on a candidate for the Reichstag. The following week the city committee made a second attempt to get its choice (Cegielski) endorsed by the voters, but this meeting was also broken up by the dissidents. The Populists tried to gain a majority for Jażdżewski, acknowledging that they would get further with a dissident membr of the Establishment (as in Bromberg) than by trying to run a member of their own middle-class movement. But the *Koło* organization in Poznań decided to forego a third assembly and simply forewarded Cegielski's name to the provincial body for ratification. A petition signed by 136 voters was included as sufficient evidence that he had public support and that another public meeting was unnecessary.[42] Szymański concluded from this that "today only open revolt against the Elections Committee can save us" and warned that the Populists would be forced to put up a rival Polish candidate.[43]

Anti-loyalists within the party organization (e.g., Jażdżewski) were unwilling to break completely with National Solidarity by running against Cegielski, so Szymański himself decided to run. In spite of the strong groundswell of anti-loyalist opinion, however, only a small part of these Poles was willing to line up with the Populists. *Goniec,* the most outspokenly anti-loyalist of all papers, refused to have anything to do with the Populist secession.[44] Szymański's own statement directed at Niegolewski nine years earlier was now thrown back at him: "Breaking solidarity and the attempt to set oneself up as a candidate are national crimes."[45] Even *Postęp,* while echoing Szymański's line on most issues, refused to support him because of his past adherence to loyalism.[46] In the election for the Reighstag seat from Poznań, Szymański finished far behind his rival, 1,869 to 9,413. His only satisfaction came from forcing the *Koło* into a run-off with the German Progressives before it could claim the seat. He asserted that his rebellion had "pumped new life into the people and, we hope, the higher echelons too;" the size of his protest voted demonstrated that "the previous unanimity within the Poznań citizenry has disappeared."[47]

The Populist insurrection was not limited to Bromberg and Poznań; similar disruptive actions took place in Inowrocław/Hohensalza, Wągrowiec/Wongrowitz, and Środa.[47a] But for the most part Populist strength was limited to the larger cities. In most rural counties, loyalist candidates were reaffirmed without much of a struggle. Szymański's rebellion had no adverse effects on Polish electoral fortunes overall; the 1893 Reichstag election was the best to date for the *Koło Polskie.* It won 12 of Poznania's 15 seats, a record 6 seats in West Prussia, and managed even to win the predominately German-Catholic Allenstein/Olsztyń-Rössel/Reszel district in East Prussia for the first (and last) time. By softening their attitude toward the German and Prussian states, Poles were able to pick up unprecedented support from supporters of German opposition parties, e.g., Center supporters in Allenstein-Rössel who supported the *Koło* in the run-off. In other cases, especially Bromberg, where Czarliński won with the help of Progressive support in the run-off, it was rather opposition (to the Army bill) which attracted German support for a Polish candidate.[48]

German parties in support of the Army bill also registered major gains in the 1893 elections; Caprivi was now able to count on 182 of the 199 votes he needed for passage. This meant that the 19 Polish seats would make the difference. But despite their earlier vote, and the continued adherence of the *Koło* leadership to loyalism, the obvious displeasure with this policy which had surfaced during the recent campaign made a second vote for the Army bill quite doubtful.[49] But the Poles remained the only uncommitted party of sufficient strength to provide the government with its majority on this crucial bill. It was more or less compelled therefore to produce additional concessions and keep the Era of Reconciliation going for a little longer.

Caprivi devised a number of gestures designed to reinforce the loyalist stance of the Poles. Word was leaked that Emperor Wilhelm had met with Ledóchowski during a visit to Rome and invited him to Berlin. *Kuryer* reported that Wilhelm had actually apologized for the Cardinal's bad treatment and forced abdication at Bismarck's hands: "Please forget the past; I knew nothing of the sad events as they happened."[50] During the recent election campaign Wilhelm had also paid a visit to Poznań and visited publicly with Polish as well as German supporters of his Army bill.[51] Caprivi then threw his support behind a request by War Minister Kaltenborn that the Army be permitted to determine for itself the ethnic make-up of units in Polish areas, free from the restrictions imposed in 1886. He wanted to be able to station more Polish recruits in Poznania and West Prussia in order to "promote *esprit de corps* and remedy the shortage of Polish-speaking non-commissioned officers." Wilhelm obliged with an order authorizing the commander of the 5th Army Corps in Poznań to use his own discretion in stationing Polish troops there.[52] This change had little real effect since the Army's own guidelines were quite strict: no more than 5% of any unit could be Polish and these Poles had to be politically reliable and fluent in German.[53] In the short run, however, this measure evoked some mild satisfaction from the Polish press at a crucial time.

Caprivi's ability to offer more substantial concessions, especially in the key school and language areas, was severely restricted because he no longer controlled Prussian state affairs. When he first suggested to Bosse that he reinstate Polish in the Poznanian schools, the minister refused, describing such a concession as "a retreat along the entire front" and an insult of sorts to the Germans of Poznania.[54] As a Prussian minister with a firm *Kartell* majority, Bosse was unsympathetic to Caprivi's need to get a Reichstag majority by appeasing Catholics and Poles. He considered it foolish to alienate German nationalists, upon whom the government would always depend, in order to placate the Poles, with whose opposition it had always lived and would doubtless continue to do so. Caprivi wrote privately to loyalist leaders anyway, admitting past injustices, trying to reinforce their loyalist feelings, and hinting broadly that Polish would indeed find its way back into the curriculum before long.[55] Once again, these government gestures and Polish hopes that more substantial concessions would yet be forthcoming sufficed. The loyalists were able to summon a thin majority for the Army bill in caucus and then prevail upon the rest of their colleagues to go along in the interest of party solidarity. All but one of them (Czarliński) voted for the Army bill (July 15, 1893), providing it with its margin of victory.[56]

From the time of the Reichstag elections of 1893 until the second vote on the Army bill, the attention of Polish political life was riveted on the parliamentarians in Berlin. It was generally assumed that they would be able to exploit their position to gain some kind of major concession. As *Dziennik* pointed out, on its merits alone the Army bill was almost without support among the Polish people. A vote for it could only be considered as a means to an end: concessions on important national issues. If Poles were going to shoulder new burdens to pay for German defense, "the recognition of our national rights in the school-language areas, the change from the system of denationalization, is the only concession that we consider appropriate."[57] Loyalist leaders did nothing to dispell such expectations and Polish public opinion seemed to hold its breath after the passage of the Army bill to see how the government would respond. After several days it was announced that Kościelski had received the following telegram from the Emperor: "I thank you and your countrymen for your loyalty to me and my house; let it be an example to all. For your devoted labor, I bestow upon you the 'Order of the Crown, Second Class.' "[58] The reaction by the anti-loyalists, and the bulk of Polish opinion, is not difficult to imagine. In the words of *Gazeta Toruńska*: "The government, and through it the Emperor, know very well that bestowing an order upon Kościelski without granting ameliorations due the Poles simply abandons this representative to verbal attacks and would render impossible any further activity in the direction of compromise."[59]

The Populists were not long in living up to this prediction. They called for an "emergency" session of Poznań voters, out of which grew the demand for a special meeting of the city elections committee. The chairman of that committee, Dobrowolski (editor of *Dziennik Poznański*), mindful of the ease with which Cegielski had survived Szymański's recent challenge at the polls, called a meeting to reaffirm his committee and the *Koło*'s policies. But he found himself confronted by about 800 predominately hostile townspeople; a resolution censuring the *Koło* for its support of the Army bill passed easily, whereupon the committee resigned.[60] A meeting was then called to elect a new committee and this time over 1000 persons showed up. Such a head count (by Prussian police observers) was very high by contemporary standards and suggests the increased interest in politics among the Poznań townspeople. *Orędownik* and *Postęp* called for a new committee consisting of "new forces who have greater contact with the middle classes and with the Polish people, forces who respect the will of the voters and thus would gain trust and respect for themselves."[61] But Dobrowolski and his committee announced that they had withdrawn their resignations; the meeting turned disorderly, even violent, and was closed by police before it could transact its business.[62] The *Koło* organization called a third meeting, this time charging admission in an effort to hold down the number of supposedly insolvent Populists. According to police reports, the two sides were represented in roughly equal numbers, but the meeting was conducted by Dobrowolski, who determined the outcome of all (voice) votes in favor of the loyalists. There were charges of fraud in the Populist press but, as expected, the Provincial Elections Committee confirmed the loyalist-dominated committee for Poznań.[63] In the meantime, however, the Poznań Populists took the unprecedented step of establishing a rival elections committee for their city and *Kuryer* feared that "through the formation of this committee the feud in the Polish camp has become chronic."[64] In Bromberg, the elections committee called a meeting to express support for Czarliński's lone hold-out against the Army bill. Here it was the loyalists who caused the disruption, but a second assembly left the anti-loyalist faction in control of the *Koło* organization in this second-largest Poznanian city.[65]

The establishment of a rival Populist elections committee in Poznań and the anti-loyalist takeover in Bromberg helped remove the last restraints upon the loyalists. Leading the way in a very heated counterattack was Archbishop Stablewski, *Kuryer Poznański*, and the Church organization in general. Aside from his other dissenting opinions, Szymański had also developed the politically dangerous habit of criticizing the Church for its identification with loyalism and its intervention in secular political affairs. He suggested that it was serving as a prop for the declining nobility; he also questioned the political trustworthiness of the many clerics active in middle-class economic organizations (which he looked to as bastions of his own brand of petty-bourgeois political consciousness rather than clerical loyalism). *Orędownik* frequently carried reports that younger clerics sympathized with the Populists but were being suppressed by the loyalist hierarchy.[66] Even more seriously, Szymański began to criticize Archbishop Stablewski personally. He suggested that he owed his high office to a willingness to compromise Polish interests on school and language issues, that he had become a representative of Prussian-state rather than Polish-national interests.[67] By the time of the Army bill debates of 1893, Szymański and other anti-loyalists had come to the same conclusion as German nationalists earlier: it made little difference whether a German like Dinder or a Pole like Stablewski occupied the Archbishop's chair. But since the *Kulturkampf* the identification of Polish nationalism with the Catholic Church and clergy had become an article of political faith for virtually all Poles. Especially in the countryside, the clergy retained a sacrosanct position in worldly as well as spiritual matters.

Stablewski did not hesitate to use all the resources of his position and organization to combat critics of loyalism, especially the Populist upstarts. During the Army bill controversy, he wrote to anti-loyalist priests like Jażdżewski (who was, of course, his subordinate now), urging a vote for the bill.[68] *Kuryer* announced that Ledóchowski, and presumably the Pope too, supported the loyalist position on the Army bill.[69] The Church employed "all available means of power" against the Populists (in the words of a government monitor of Polish affairs). It circulated anti-Populist form letters for clerics to sign and read in their sermons; the faithful were also urged to refrain from reading the Populist press. Stablewski also warned against reading these newspapers and prohibited his priests from attending Populist assemblies. Cegielski did his part by banning the distribution of *Orędownik* and *Postęp* at his Poznań factory.[70]

In response to Szymański's allegations that the clergy was internally divided on the loyalism issue, an assembly of Poznanian clergy was summoned to Gniezno in September 1893 to reaffirm its support for the policy of its Archbishop. A resolution warned that, "should there be someone among the clergy of our archdiocese who would forget his calling and his priestly oath and share in the sinful attacks by the (Populist) press against the Archbishop, then the whole clergy will certainly look upon this priest as an errant brother." The chairman of this assembly was more direct: "If such a degenerate priest should be found, . . . the clergy will reject him as a rotten and poisonous growth." *Orędownik* was described in this resolution as "lacking in all Catholic feeling; although it is written in Polish it is no Polish paper and wants instead to poison the community with the poison that it has collected from the streets of Poznań."[71] The Poznań city clergy convened at the same time and described *Orędownik* and *Postęp* as "sinful, immeasurably harmful, threatening in their consequences, and even opposed to the principles of our Holy Faith." They were guilty of sowing distrust of the wealthy among workers and artisans, dividing the community, disrupting legal political assemblies, opposing the *Koło* in elections, publicly criticizing respected leaders, and claiming to speak for the people, whereas "in fact, *all* classes of our community have the same interest in the well-being of our working and trading classes."⁷² A non-fraternization policy was imposed on the Poznanian clergy, extending also to their participation in Populist-dominated economic organizations. For example, the "Society of Polish-Catholic Artisans," an outgrowth of *Rerum Novarum*, with Church financial backing, was chaired by Szymański but had a priest (Stychel) as its "patron." Stychel now gave the Society the choice of doing without him or Szymański; when it opted for the former alternative, he declared an end to all Church support.⁷³ Stychel was then installed as head of a rival "Union of Catholic Worker Societies," though this organization attracted mainly rural people unaffected by Populist agitation.⁷⁴

Another major group mobilized (like the clergy) against the Populists was the peasantry, specifically the peasant organizations under the guidance of "Patron" Maximilian Jackowski. Jackowski was a clerical-conservative and loyalist, only too happy to lead his peasants against the "yellow journalists" of Poznań.⁷⁵ Unlike the urban economic organizations, the peasant societies were not usually the result of peasant initiative or expressions of a desire for political self-reliance. Those individual societies existing in 1873 had been taken over and coordinated by the "Central Economic Society" (the organization of estate owners), which appointed Jackowski as their Patron. The purpose of his position was to ensure unity of policy between the peasants and the estate owners. Since 1873, the number of peasant organizations had grown rapidly, totalling 154 by 1889.⁷⁶ Like the credit co-ops, they insisted that "religious and political matters do not belong to the associations' competence and may not be discussed at the meetings."⁷⁷ But their strong adherence to National Solidarity, whether voluntary or manipulated by the noble directors, implied a political standpoint in favor of the *Koło*. As Jackowski put it, "the societies cast the seed of mutual understanding. . . . They produce conservative material which is the protective bulwark against socialism in the social organism."⁷⁸ For Jackowski and other loyalists, "socialism" was stretched to include the Populists rather than the negligible Marxist presence in Poznania. Taking their cue from their patron, many peasant organizations began to circulate petitions expressing their "contempt and indignation" toward the Populists, accusing them of "socialist and anarchist desires," and declaring it the "duty of every peasant society member to do what is possible to exterminate such excrescences as *Orędownik* and *Postęp*."⁷⁹ Yet another aspect of the loyalist counter-attack against the supposedly socialistic Populists was the pamphlet, "Ein Wort zu ernster Stunde an die deutschen Mitbürger von einem polnischem Bürger," published by *Kuryer*. Its main purpose was to reassure the government and German opinion of the broad support for loyalism among the Poles: "The only representative fundamentally opposed to the new course of the Prussian government (Czarliński) . . . has been elected in Bromberg, possibly through the decisive assistance of socialists."[80] It lambasted *Orędownik* also, a paper which "has always held up to its readers the agitation and procedures of the socialists as a model." Szymański was described here as "limited, short-sighted, mendacious, driven by megalomania," and bound to wind up as a "socialist of the most common type." Most seriously, he had confused "those quite calm souls who adhere thoroughly to the loyal policy of reconciliation."[81]

Partially in response to this loyalist offensive, partially in preparation for the upcoming Landtag elections, Poznań's Populists took the final step in their secession from the *Koło* and constituted themselves the "National People's Party (*Narodowa Partia Ludowa*)" in September-October 1893. Major elements in the Populists' informal platform included: a., the willingness to perform one's duty as a Prussian/German citizen as long as one's nationality was respected, b., a focus on the economic strengthening of Polish society, c., increased popular participation in the decisions of the *Koło*, d., identification with Catholicism but subordination of religion to national interests, e., strict opposition to socialism, f., an appeal to all Polish-speaking Prussians, including Upper Silesians and Masurians.[83] While still not a very large movement, the People's Party also contained a number of internal divisions. For example, some (like Szymański) held lingering loyalist views from earlier times and were loath to give up this viewpoint simply because the *Koło* and Church had expropriated it. But anti-loyalism became the prevailing viewpoint among the urban middle classes and a central feature of the new party. There were also differences concerning the Church and religion in general. Szymański remained at odds with the Church and its Archbishop, whom he accused of being the "source of the present unrest and dissatisfaction . . . within the community" and out to hinder free expression in worldly matters.[84] He produced a Galician priest and peasant leader Stanisław Stojałowski who agreed to support the Populists publicly and lamented that "even (in Galicia) only a small part of my colleagues stand on the side of the people . . . since all sorts of things prevent them from coming out in public with their views."[85] Other Populists were strongly clerical in outlook, however, and very concerned to win the approval of the clergy. While the Church was stepping up its attack on the Populists, some 600 of them met to reaffirm the Catholic nature of their movement. They declared their loyalty to Stablewski as spiritual leader and denied any association with Social Democracy.[86]

The Populists were also divided by the issue of anti-Semitism. Knapowski represented the anti-Semitic wing of the movement. He favored the exclusion of Jews from the economic associations; he tried to organize anti-Semitism politically, both as part of the People's Party and in league with German anti-Semitic organizations. He drew an estimated 500 persons to an anti-Semitic rally in March 1894, where he warned of "growing Jewish power" and "the exploitation of Poles by Jews."[87] Szymański, on the other hand, argued that "we must keep away from anti-Semitic agitation, for we have no grounds for it."[88] Populists were similarly divided on the related question of use of the boycott weapon, popular with many Polish tradesmen as a means of encouraging Poles to patronize them rather than their German and Jewish competition. Knapowski favored it; his attacks on the nobility included the charge that they bought from Jews rather than from their own countrymen.[89] Szymański opposed the boycott tactic; in many towns, Germans and Jews still constituted a majority of the population and an even larger majority of the purchasing power. To alienate them would only slow Polish economic progress.[90]

Despite these differences, the common desire to see increased urban participation in political affairs and to impress their notion of political consciousness upon the Polish national movement sufficed as foundations of the People's Party. Its first opportunity to compete with the Koło came with the Landtag elections of October-November 1893. The Koło leaders largely defused the loyalism issue, however, by proposing Jażdżewski as one of their three choices in Poznań. He agreed to one last appeal to the Emperor, to be followed by the return to a strict opposition stance. He also avoided harsh attacks on the Populists and refused to endorse the more categorical Church-sponsored denunciations.[91] The People's Party, as an outgrowth of the dissident Poznań elections committee, remained limited to that city. Powerful dissident movements appeared in other towns as well, bearing the Populist label, but these remained inside the Koło structure. Such Populist candidates were successful in voter assemblies in Inowrocław, Mogilno, and Środa.[92] In Bromberg, where Populists controlled the elections committee, they nominated one of their own. In Jarocin/Jarotschin they managed at least to cause enough of an uproar to prevent a vote on the Koło's choice, obliging the Provincial Elections Committee once again to anoint a nominee who had not been ratified by a voters assembly.[93] The loyalist provincial committee ratified the successful Populist candidates, loyalist or not.[94] But in Poznań the schism remained unresolved and two Polish parties competed with each other. Their actual relative strength was distorted by the three-class voting system. Neither Polish party made it to the run-off; the Koło came in third with 55 "electors" out of 263 possible and the Populists trailed with only 9 electors.[95] In the run-off the two parties again were at odds;

the Populists urged a vote for the kindred German Progressives (who won) while the *Koło* urged a vote for the German Conservatives in preference to the "Jewish candidate" of the Progressives.[96]

In spite of the Populist defeat, Szymański professed to be encouraged. He announced again that the "political principles of the 'Court Party' and the People's Party are far apart" and made it clear that his secession would continue.[97] Government observers were clearly impressed by the growth and dynamism of the Populist movement.[98] The inner-Polish feud even disrupted Kościuszko Day ceremonies in March 1894; *Orędownik* refused to publish a proclamation signed by Jackowski and other loyalists and Jackowski resigned from the Kościuszko Day committee rather than serve with Szymański and other Populists.[99]

In the meantime, attention in Berlin shifted to a new object of parliamentary struggle in the Reichstag: a series of trade treaties which Caprivi had negotiated with various European countries, designed to open up new markets for German industry at a time when it was struggling through another trough of the Long Depression. Germany agreed in return to lower its agricultural tariffs against the products of these mostly agrarian countries.[100] Several of these treaties (the most important of which was with Austria-Hungary) had passed already and evoked vehement agrarian protests. Some German agrarians in Poznania were even incensed enough to vote Polish rather than support a German party which favored the trade treaties.[101] Two treaties (with Romania and Russia) remained to be approved and it appeared that once again the government would be able to put together a majority for them only with Polish support.

Polish loyalists now faced an additional dilemma. Thus far they had proceeded under the assumption that support for the government and cooperation with German conservatives, with whom they shared social attitudes and economic interests, were two aspects of the one policy of loyalism. But opposition to the trade treaties was concentrated in the ranks of the German Conservative Party. Moreover, the *Koło Polskie* represented one of the most agrarian regions of the Empire; its members were drawn almost exclusively from the ranks of large-estate owners. It had reluctantly come out in favor of the treaty with Austria-Hungary in December 1891, but only 8 members had actually cast votes for it.[102] Some loyalists expressed the opinion that, since most Poles were engaged in agriculture, the *Koło* ought to reflect the wishes of the agrarians as an integral part of its national policy.[103] *Kuryer* argued that it was time "to do something for agriculture" after so much favoring of "liberals and industrialists" and took a position against the Russian trade treaty, though it was no doubt heavily favored by Russian-Polish nobles.[104] When the

Bund der Landwirte was founded as the chief vehicle of the new agrarian discontent in 1893, Polish agrarians were on hand and some even joined.[105] The *Koło*'s chief spokesman on farm questions acknowledged the proximity of the *BdL* to Polish economic interests: "In the main we are pursuing the same goal; our agricultural program is basically theirs, our ultimate goal is the protection and welfare of agriculture."[106] The *Koło* refused to support the *BdL* officially, however, recognizing that its chief aim was to topple the Caprivi government which Poles had every reason still to support.[107] Eventually, repelled by its growing nationalism and attacks on Polish "renegades" who were supporting the government, Poles declined to participate in this organization to any extent.[108] They opted in effect for a loyalism directed at the government rather than one emphasizing joint conservative-agrarian interests and directed at German parties and interest groups.

As might be surmised, the loyalist policy of the *Koło* during the Caprivi Era caused its relations with German opposition parties to cool considerably. In particular, its support for the Army bill alienated many members of the Progressive Party, which seemed to grow more nationalistic during the period. When Bosse declared in the Landtag that Germans and not Poles were on the defensive in the eastern provinces, he was rewarded with applause from the left side of the house.[109] With Windthorst's death in 1891, the Center came under the leadership of Huene and Ballestrem (Silesian magnate and industrialist respectively), who were more conservative and also more nationalistic than their predecessor.[110] The Center Party press complained increasingly of Polish attempts to invade its domain in Upper Silesia. Polish loyalists denied any such intent; Stablewski declared in 1892 that "it seems inappropriate and unjustified to pull Silesia into the sphere of the political activity and aspirations of those Poles united with Prussia after 1772. The legal-political position of the Poles in Poznania is a different one from that of a Silesian. . . . In Silesia the people lack any historical tradition."[111] After 1893 even, when support of the Army bill by Huene and Ballestrem led to their fall from leadership, the old close ties between Center and Poles were not restored. Instead, loyalist leaders seemed more concerned to replace their previous relationship with German opposition parties with ties to German conservatives, an effort which would be largely negated by their vote for the trade treaties.

Thus, aside from anti-loyalist agitation on the home front, several important considerations stood against Polish support for the Romanian and Russian trade treaties. If Caprivi hoped to get Polish Reichstag support he had to deliver on his promise to return the Polish language to the elementary school curriculum in Poznania. In his efforts to overcome the opposition of Bosse and Eulenburg, he was supported by *Oberpräsident* Wilamowitz, who (like his predecessor Zedlitz) was an advocate of a conciliatory approach to the Poles. His most effective point with the government in Berlin was that Stablewski threatened to have the Church take over the job of teaching Polish if the state would not do so.[112] Stablewski's own increasingly insistent submissions were also influential. He demanded that Polish be re-introduced into the curriculum in some form or other; "The religious interest would be taken care of and the state would have the instruction in its own hands."[113] Otherwise, as he confided to Kościelski in October 1893:

> "If they do not issue a pertinent order (returning Polish to the curriculum) now, at the beginning of the semester, and want to delay it until later, we will not be able to hold out here. . . . If it cannot be coaxed from them now, it will be necessary to roll up our flags in the face of the indignation arising out of continuous (unfulfilled) expectations."[114]

Apparently the possibility that Stablewski himself might abandon loyalism and provoke a confrontation, which even Bosse agreed was "of such great political consequence . . . and so undesirable," caused him finally to drop his opposition and agree to the introduction of a minimal amount of Polish into the curriculum. In return, however, he insisted that Caprivi acknowledge the "limited and final nature" of this concession and agree simultaneously to take steps to further improve German schools in Poznania and reaffirm the government's adherence "unswervingly to the idea of educating Polish youth to become German citizens." Bosse's face-saving explanation for this change of mind was that the private classes permitted by Zedlitz had been exploited "far beyond the scope of the decree of 1891." They had helped turn Polish schoolteachers into "tools of Polish agitation" and had become "far more harmful than regular school instruction in Polish reading and writing, kept within moderate limits, would be."[115] Actually, the private classes did not flourish that well, which is why Polish leaders were so insistent that Polish be brought back into the regular curriculum. Early reports spoke of almost 500 such classes organized in Poznania, but by the 1892-3 school year, Poles were complaining about the high cost of such efforts and many classes were reported to have failed.[116]

To secure the support of the Prussian cabinet, Caprivi stressed that the traditional Polish leadership, due to its loyalist policy and various other reasons, was just then under heavy attack from within. This made it possible for the government to gain valuable parliamentary support from the *Koło* at a relatively small cost. In fact, it was "in the interest of the government to intensify this division (among the Poles); what we can utilize for our foreign policy and what we can exploit domestically for pro-government purposes is the aristocratic segment of the Poles. . . . To retain (this support) is worth a few hours of Polish instruction each week . . . and the granting of such a limited Polish language program will not hinder the progress of the German nationality."[117]

These arguments prevailed and Polish was permitted back into the curriculum effective February 1894. Even with this concession, the Polish position on the Romanian trade treaty remained uncertain until the very end. Only on the day of the vote itself (December 13, 1893) did the *Koło* announce its support; the measure carried 189:165, with 15 Polish representatives providing once again the margin of victory.[118]

Although this was the one time during the Caprivi Era that the government directly met a demand of the Polish leadership, it had little impact on the growing anti-loyalist sentiment in the Polish provinces. For one thing, as formulated by Bosse the new measure was extremely limited in scope. It applied only to schools in Poznania where religion was taught in Polish; attendance was voluntary and instruction was for only two hours weekly for a maximum of two years. Private classes were simultaneously prohibited. Though Bosse asked that his new policy be carried out "in a loyal manner, avoiding petty and exasperating individual measures," local officials retained a good deal of say over which pupils could attend the classes and when they had acquired enough Polish to benefit from their religious instruction.[119] Some Poles wondered even if they were not losing more than they gained by this concession.[120] Stablewski expressed his dissatisfaction with the two-year limit in a letter to Caprivi.[121] *Dziennik* also concentrated on the shortcomings of this measure, calling it "nothing at all. . . . For our part, we are not satisfied with this trifle. . . . They are handling us like Cinderella, not like citizens."[122] Only *Kuryer* tried to present Bosse's measure as a real concession: "When someone gives something without being forced to do so, that is a concession."[123]

No sooner did the government announce its concession than it turned to the task of protecting itself from the anticipated German-nationalist backlash. Conservatives raged about Caprivi's "purchase" of Polish votes for his trade treaties; the *Kreuzzeitung* denounced his Polish policy as "one of the most disastrous errors of this statesman, an error so serious it will be immensely difficult to rectify."[124] The cabinet actually hoped that this change of policy would not become "too public;" it would be implemented quietly and discussed publicly only if the Landtag raised the issue.[125] When the question did come up there, Bosse tried to trivialize the concession, focusing instead on the drawbacks of the private classes he had done away with. He insisted that "this is not a departure from our position thus far on the Polish language issue . . . and I can vouch for (the fact that) . . . more extensive demands will not be able to count upon us for implementation."[126] Jażdżewski responded that he knew "absolutely nothing at all about concessions on the part of the government."[127] *Dziennik* also came to the conclusion now that there had been "no particular successes . . . despite the so-called New Course; . . . neither an improvement nor a change has occurred."[128] Hutten-Czapski noted at this time that "for several months already the Polish public has felt itself deeply disappointed in the hopes it had tied to the 'New Course' after it became apparent that no fundamental concessions were to be expected from the government."[129]

When the last of the trade treaties, the Russian, came up for a vote, even Kościelski conceded that he had not made up his mind to support it. Polish agrarian organizations came out firmly against it.[130] But Caprivi was able to form a majority for it without relying on the *Koło* this time and it passed 200:146.[131] Fifteen Poles again voted with the government, but only after announcing that they were doing so for the last time unless a major concession was forthcoming. Thus the qualified return of Polish to the public schools marked the end rather than a continuation of the Era of Reconciliation.

By this time, support for loyalism even within the conservative *Koło* leadership was clearly waning. The support of trade treaties which ran counter to their economic interests was evidently the last straw for many Polish estate owners. As these Polish agrarians became disenchanted, the loyalist front broke down. The end came when Kościelski agreed to line up the Poles for yet another Caprivi measure: a new naval bill. But the *Koło* caucus voted overwhelmingly to abstain on this issue and Kościelski, having lost his credibility in government eyes as a spokesman for his faction, felt compelled to resign his seat on March 10, 1894.[132]

This meant a by-election and another contest between the Populists and the *Koło*. In Mogilno the Populists were able to nominate one of their own. In Inowrocław one meeting was broken up by police before a decision could be made; a second one was attended by a crowd of 1500-2000 persons (in a town of only 10,000 population), illustrating once again the mushrooming involvement of Polish townspeople in political affairs. Here, and in the third county of this district (Strzelno/Strelno), a majority was eventually found for Wawrzyniak, who thus seemed assured of the nomination once again.[133] Again he declined it, but this time the Provincial Elections Committee chose a physician close to the Populists (Krzymiński) to replace him. He won election handily and vowed to represent policies diametrically opposed to Kościelski's.[134]

Thus, as a result of Populist attacks, mixed feelings on the part of agrarians, and disillusionment on the part of moderate nationalists, loyalism ceased to be the policy of the *Koło* in March 1894. Simultaneously, the Prussian government, under pressure of its own from nationalist and agrarian sources, decided to abandon its policy of reconciliation and make no further concessions to the Poles. A Polish fair was held at Lwów/L'viv in September 1894, attended by a large contingent of Poznanians, who apparently wanted to reaffirm their Polish patriotism in the wake of their unsuccessful effort to come to an understanding with the Caprivi government. Kusztelan, head of the Union Bank and chairman of the *Koło* election committee in Poznań, described Prussian Poland as a "land of tears and misfortune, where we are robbed of our native language and ordered to pray in a foreign tongue. . . . (But) we assure you that we will not give up; we are and will remain a Polish land. Whoever eats the bread of this Polish land must sooner or late become Polish."[135] Kościelski maintained after his resignation that loyalism was still not finished, that his resignation was intended in fact to save it.[136] Thus he received the most attention at Lwów when he chided the partitioning powers which thought that "by drawing certain colored lines on the body of a nation they are able to dismember and destroy it. But the whole has remained in existence, one blood and one heart that beats and feels the same. The parts of the whole organism, conscious of belonging together, support each other and learn from each other."[137] He pointed specifically to the growth of the Polish national movement in previously passive regions and boasted that "we were the first to summon our younger brothers in Upper Silesia to the national task."[138]

Kościelski later sought to disavow the implications of these remarks, allowing that "I did in fact emphasize in one of the speeches . . . the solidarity of the whole Polish nation, without respect to political frontiers, but I meant primarily *ethnographic* solidarity." He reaffirmed his "loyal adherence to the dynasty and happy participation in the tasks of the state" and expressed the hope that the Era of Reconciliation might continue.[139] Stablewski too sought to minimize his fellow loyalist's remarks:

> "We still see ourselves as Prussian subjects; we have recognized the existing political situation without reservation. What will be in 200 or 300 years, we do not know, and no one can stop us from picturing this distant future as we please. But this image of the future will never keep us from the happy and complete fulfillment of our citizenship duties."[140]

But the government, having decided already to close the door on further cooperation in any case, seized upon the Lwów statements to declare that the Poles had ended their policy of cooperation. The German nationalist press cited these speeches as confirmation of its suspicion that Polish loyalists had not been sincere in the first place. Actually, the Caprivi policy had worked quite well as far as the conservative Polish nobility was concerned; as Szymański pointed out, they had become loyal and therefore harmless and seriously compromised in the eyes of Polish public opinion. The government's intentions had been foiled mainly by the unexpected emergence of a more numerous, economically more vigorous, and ultimately more formidable foe in the form of the Polish middle classes. "There will not be any more trouble from the nobility; instead an even greater and at any rate more complex difficulty for the state government is probably going to arise from the people themselves."[141]

Since Polish loyalists had always put their faith in the person of the Emperor, so now it was some apparently off-the-cuff remarks by Wilhelm during a visit to Thorn which were interpreted by them as the official sign that the Era of Reconciliation was over. As suggested earlier, Wilhelm apparently did not have very pronounced views of his own on the Polish question. It is likely that during this visit to West Prussia, *Oberpräsident* Gossler managed to put in a bad word for the Poles and the result was a characteristically rash utterance by the Emperor. As he addressed the crowd of Germans and Poles who greeted him in Thorn: "It has come to my attention that the Polish residents here are not conducting themselves as one must hope and wish. Let them know that they can only count upon my sympathy and grace to the same extent as the Germans if they act without reservation as Prussian subjects."[142] Upon leaving later that day, he added: "I want that which I said today at noon to be generally understood; I was not just talking through my hat. I can also be very unpleasant and will be so if necessary."[143] These remarks suggested among other things a difference of opinion between Emperor and Chancellor on the Polish question and this was added to the growing list of differences which isolated Caprivi and opened him up to attack. He submitted his resignation the following month and the way was open for what both Germans and Poles expected to be a return to a Bismarckian approach to Prussian-Polish relations.

Notes

1. December 13, 1886, *Gesammelte Werke* VIII:

2. December 5, 1889, *Ibid.*:
3. *Ibid.*, VII:695.
4. Interview with *Novoje Wremja*, July 22, 1890, *Neue Tischgespräche und Interviews*, ed. H.v. Poschinger, 2nd edit. (Leipzig, 1895), I:354.
5. *Gedanken und Erinnerungen*, III:117f.
6. Talk with members of Ratzeburg Kreistag, November 30, 1891, *Gesammelte Werke*, IX:177; see also Bismarck's articles for the *Hamburger Nachrichten* in Hermann Hofmann, *Fürst Bismarck, 1890-8* (Stuttgart, 1913-4), I:397, II:2.
7. *Hamburger Nachrichten*, January 13, 1892.
8. Interview with Moritz Benedikt, editor of *Neue Freie Presse* (Vienna), June 23, 1892, *Gesammelte Werke* IX:217.
9. Interview with Hans Kleser, May 31, 1892, *Ibid.*, IX:205.
10. Benedikt interview, *Ibid.*, IX:217.
11. Speech at Jena, July 31, 1892, *Ibid.*, XIII:142.
12. Interview with Maximilian Harden, October 29, 1892, *Ibid.*, IX:265.
13. Speech to National Liberal Reichstag delegation, April 20, 1894, *Politische Reden*, XIII:247f.
14. Speech in Braunschweig, July 21, 1893, *Ibid.*, XIII:210.
15. *Wielkopolska*, p. 223; Trzeciakowski, *Polityka*, p. 95.
16. Speech of May 2, 1891, *Abgeordnetenhaus*.
17. Waldersee, *Denkwürdigkeiten*, II:228.
18. Alfred Hugenberg, quoting from his 1894 article, "Der preussische Staat als Kolonisator," in *Streiflichter aus Vergangenheit und Gegenwart*, 2nd edit. (Berlin, 1927), p. 302; Mildred Wertheimer, *The Pan-German League, 1890-1914*, Columbia diss. (New York, 1924), p. 43.
19. January 27, 1892; *note*: except where noted, citations of Polish newspapers are based on official translations, "Zusammenstellungen über die polnische Tagesliteratur," *PA Bonn*, Preussen 4:2; this is a comprehensive weekly survey of political articles in the domestic and foreign Polish press, beginning in January 1892 and replacing the more random samplings begun by Tiedemann a decade earlier.
20. October 25, 1892.
21. March 11, 1892.
22. *Dziennik Poznański*, September 29, 1893.
23. January 16, 1893.
24. *Kuryer Poznański*, August 1, 1893.
25. Quoted by Harden, p. 7.
26. June 25, 1892.
27. Speech of February 12, 1893, *Abgeordnetenhaus*.
28. March 15, 1893.
29. January 27, 1892.
30. *Orędownik*, April 1, 1892.
31. *Ibid.*;, January 24, 1892.
32. *Ibid.*, March 6, 1893.
33. April 15, 1893.
34. Minutes of county voter assemblies, *Biblioteka Raczyńskich*, #869 (Śrem),

pp. 6-10, #870 (Środa), p. 9, #871 (Września); Wawrzyniak letter of resignation, #869, p. 11.

35. *Orędownik*, February 1 and February 22, 1892; *Kuryer Poznański*, March 28, 1892; editor's remark, March 21, 1892, *GPSA Berlin*, Rep. B 30:I, #661.
36. Speech by Komierowski, December 10, 1892, *Reichstag*.
37. Speech by Komierowski, May 5, 1893, *Ibid.*; Trzeciakowski, *Polityka*, p. 68.
38. May 10, 1893.
39. *Orędownik*, Mary 19, 1893.
40. *Ibid.*, May 21, 1893.
41. *Kuryer Poznański*, May 16, 1893; minutes of voter assemblies of May 19 and May 24, 1893, *Biblioteka Raczyńskich*, #883; pp. 11ff.; Trzeciakowski, *Polityka*, p. 122.
42. *Biblioteka Raczyńskich*, #854, pp. 6ff.; *Kuryer Proznański*, May 20, May 27, and May 31, 1893.
43. *Orędownik*, May 25, 1893.
44. May 24, 1893.
45. *Kuryer Poznański*, June 17, 1893.
46. June 10, 1893.
47. *Orędownik*, June 9 and June 17, 1893; Karwowski, p. 77; Trzeciakowski, *Polityka*, p. 123.
47a. Minutes of voter assembly in Wągrowiec, May 28, 1893, *Biblioteka Raczyńskich*, #III; *Orędownik*, May 31, 1893.
48. *Orędownik*, June 28, 1893.
49. Letters of Kościelski and Stablewski to Caprivi warned of the difficulties standing in the way of a second favorable vote by the *Koło*; Trzeciakowski, *Polityka*, p. 69.
50. Marschall to Caprivi, April 28, 1893, PA Bonn, Polen I.A.B.g 14; *Kuryer Poznański*, April 29, 1893; J. Alden Nichols, *Germany after Bismarck* (New York, 1968), p. 251.
51. Trzeciakowski, *Polityka*, p. 69.
52. Kaltenborn memorandum, March 20, 1893, *GPSA Berlin*, Rep. 84a., #4067; Council of Ministers meeting, May 16, 1893, *PA Bonn*, Preussen 4.
53. Council of Ministers meeting, February 27, 1894, *Ibid.*
54. Bosse to Caprivi, May 22, 1893; Caprivi to Bosse, May 24, 1893; Bosse to Caprivi, May 30, 1893, *Ibid.*, Preussen 8:2.
55. Trzeciakowski, *Polityka*, p. 71; Wilhelm von Massow, *Polennot im deutschen Osten*, 2nd edit. (Berlin, 1907), p. 73.
56. Trzeciakowski, *Polityka*, p. 71.
57. July 15, 1893.
58. *Kuryer Poznański*, July 21, 1893.
59. July 19, 1893.
60. *Postęp*, July 21, 1893.
61. July 29, 1893.
62. *Dziennik Poznański*, July 30, 1893; *Orędownik*, July 30, 1893.
63. Minutes of voter assembly, August 16, 1893, *Biblioteka Raczyńskich* #854;

police report, August 16, 1893, *PA Bonn*, Preussen 4:2; *Kuryer Poznański*, September 15, 1893.

64. August 22, 1893; *Orędownik*, August 20, 1893.

65. *Dziennik Poznański*, August 4, 1893; *Orędownik*, August 15, 1893; Trzeciakowski, *Polityka*, p. 127.

66. April 12 and August 22, 1893.

67. *Orędownik*, October 17 and October 26, 1892; May 19, 1893.

68. Galos, p. 241.

69. May 18, 1893.

70. Quote from editor of Polish press survey, September 1893, *PA Bonn*, Preussen 4:2; *Orędownik*, August 2 and August 17, 1893; *Kuryer Poznański*, August 8, 1893.

71. *Kuryer Poznański*, September 8, 1893.

72. *Ibid.*

73. *Orędownik*, August 9, 1893.

74. Fritz Vosberg, "Polnische Organisationen," *Ostland* 1 (1912):229.

75. Witold Jakóbczyk, *Patron Jackowski* (Poznań, 1938), p. 262.

76. *Ibid.*, pp. 117ff.; see also Stanisław Borowski, *Rozwarstwienie wsi wielkopolskiej w latach 1807-1914* (Poznań, 1962).

77. Szembek, p. 384.

78. *Wielkopolska*, p. xlix.

79. *Dziennik Poznański*, September 6, 1893, quoting one example of this genre, drawn up by the peasant association's patron (a priest) and vice-patron (an estate owner). More than a score of such petitions were circulated and published by the loyalist press in September 1893.

80. p. 17.

81. *Ibid.*, pp. 17ff.

82. *Orędownik*, October 31, 1893.

83. Editor's remarks, September 1893, *PA Bonn*, Preussen 4:2.

84. *Orędownik*, September 7, 1893; September 10, 1893.

85. *Ibid.*, September 1, 1893.

86. Police report, September 14, 1893, *PA Bonn*, Preussen 4:2.

87. *Orędownik*, March 6, 1894.

88. *Ibid.*, August 22, 1892; the *Koło* too was confronted with the anti-Semitic issue at this time. Cegielski wanted it to adopt an anti-Semitic program, arguing that "the Jewish question is a social one, for society is being oppressed by the Jews. From the social standpoint we are against Jews, though politically we cannot lend our hand to the removal of Jewish rights. We cannot join with the anti-Semites, though it is also difficult to declare ourselves against them. Jews are enemies of the Poles too." But he failed to attract support from other members and the issue died in caucus; *Biblioteka Kórnicka*, May 24, 1893, Rep. 1454-8.

89. Jakóbczyk, *Jackowski*, p. 260.

90. *Orędownik*, December 16, 1892.

91. *Ibid.*, October 3, 1893.

92. *Ibid.*, October 10, 1893; police report, October 25, 1893, *PA Bonn*, Preussen 4:2, #661.

93. Orędownik, October 18, 1893.
94. Kuryer Poznałnski, October 22, 1893.
95. Dziennik Poznański, November 4, 1893.
96. Kuryer Poznański, November 4, 1893; Orędownik, November 9, 1893.
97. Ibid., November 4, 1893.
98. Report from Poznań, March 1894, PA Bonn, Preussen 4:2.
99. Kuryer Poznański, March 9, 1894, which for its part questioned whether such celebrations were in keeping with loyalist attitudes.
100. See Walther Lotz, Die Handelspolitik des Deutschen Reiches unter Graf Caprivi und Fürst Hohenlohe, 1890-1900 (Leipzig, 1901).
101. Report by Landrat in Lissa/Leszno, AP Poznań, XVI A 107.
102. Sarah Tirrell, German Agrarian Politics after Bismarck's Fall (New York, 1951), pp. 123ff.
103. Komierowski, p. 231; Wielkopolska, p. xxxviii.
104. April 25, 1893.
105. Report from Poznań, May 27, 1893, GPSA Berlin, Rep. 84a, #5964; Puhle, pp. 35ff.
106. Speech by Dziembowski, December 12, 1893, Reichstag.
107. Minutes of caucus meeting, May 24, 1893, Biblioteka Kórnicka, Rep. 1454-8; Tirrell, p. 179; Harry Rosenthal, "Nation or Class: the Bund der Landwirte and the Poles," Australian Journal of Politics and History 19(1973):200.
108. Tirrell, pp. 188f.; see also Hanne-Lore Land, Die Konservativen und die preussische Polenpolitik, 1886-1912 (Berlin, 1963).
109. Speech of February 13, 1894, Abgeordnetenhaus.
110. Ronald Ross, Beleaguered Tower (South Bend, 1976), pp. 68ff.; John Zeender, The German Center Party, 1890-1906 (Philadelphia, 1976), p. 34.
111. Quoted by Laubert, p. 152.
112. Wilamowitz memorandum, September 27, 1893, GPSA Berlin, Rep. 84a, #4067.
113. Stablewski to Bosse, January 13, 1893, Kirchenpolitik, p. 157; Korth, p. 50.
114. Quoted by Kucner, p. 69.
115. Bosse to Caprivi, November 14, 1893, PA Bonn, Preussen 8:2.
116. Reports from Poznań, February 24 and August 27, 1892; report from Bromberg, March 4, 1892, GPSA Berlin, Rep. 84a, #5964.
117. Caprivi memorandum, November 18, 1893, PA Bonn, Rep. B 30:II, #2526.
118. Tirrell, pp. 240ff.; Puhle, p. 228.
119. Bosse decree, April 16, 1894, GPSA Berlin, Rep. B 30:II, #2526.
120. Report from Poznań, May 22, 1894, Ibid., Rep. 84a, #5964.
121. Harry Rosenthal, "Poles, Prussians, and Elementary Education in 19th Century Posen," Canadian-American Slavic Studies 7(1973):216.
122. March 4, 1894.
123. Quoted by the editor of the Polish press survey, May 1894, PA Bonn, Preussen 4:2.

124. February 14, 1894, quoted by Rosenthal, "National or Class," p. 203; Tirrell, p. 265.
125. Council of Ministers meeting, February 27, 1894, GPSA Berlin, Rep. 84a, #4067.
126. Speech of March 1, 1894, Abgeordnetenhaus.
127. Speech of March 5, 1894, Ibid.
128. January 5 and February 15, 1894.
129. p. 317.
130. Editor's remark, February 1894, PA Bonn, Preussen 4:2.
131. Tirrell, p. 293; Puhle, p. 229.
132. Trzeciakowski, Polityka, p. 133.
133. Minutes of voter assemblies, Strzelno, April 15, 1894, and Mogilno, April 28, 1894, Biblioteka Raczyńskich, #889, #891; police reports, April 16 and April 30, 1894, GPSA Berlin, Rep. B 30:I, #590; Dziennik Poznański, April 17 and May 1, 1894.
134. Orędownik, May 24, 1894.
135. September 16, 1894, quoted in Deutsche Ostmark, ed. Alldeutscher Verband (Berlin, 1894), p. 63.
136. Czas, March 20, 1894.
137. Deutsche Ostmark, p. 38.
138. Quoted by Cardinal von Widdern, Polnische Eroberungszüge im heutigen Deutschland und die deutsche Abwehr (Lissa, 1913), p. 5.
139. Letter to Neue Freie Presse, September 25, 1894, PA Bonn, Preussen 4.
140. Speech of September 26, 1894, quoted by Lotte Kaminski, Auseinandersetzungen um die polnische Frage zur Zeit der Reichskanzlerschaft des Fürsten zu Hohenlohe-Schillingsfürst, diss. Hamburg, (Hamburg, 1938), p. 38.
141. Orędownik, January 21, 1894.
142. Quoted by Otto Hoetzsch, "Nationalitätenkampf und Nationalitätenpolitik in der Ostmark," Deutsche Ostmark, p 613.
143. Tagebuch Wilhelms II (1888-1902), ed. E. Schröder (Breslau, 1903), p. 182.

Chapter VII:
Prussian Polish Policy at the Crossroads: the Hohenlohe Era

Caprivi was succeeded as chancellor in 1894 by Chlodwig zu Hohenlohe-Schillingsfürst, who thus inherited the task of imposing some consistency on Prussian Polish policy after the zig-zag course of the previous decade. Hohenlohe was not especially well suited to the achievement of this goal. He does not appear to have had very pronounced views of his own on this matter and his position in cabinet vis-à-vis the Emperor and other powerful ministers was even weaker than Caprivi's. As a career diplomat, he indicated some feeling for the strategic concerns of the Caprivi Era:

> "It does not seem advisable to me for our assimilation methods to go clearly beyond the methods which Russia uses... The sympathy which the German state may still enjoy today, though in strongly diminished amount, in some levels of the population of the Kingdom of Poland, through the contrast with Russia, is under certain circumstances a favorable political factor for us and in my opinion should not be given up by us without necessity."[1]

But he showed no particular inclination to shape his own domestic Polish policies to such considerations. He did assure the Landtag that "a state which has taken foreign nationalities into itself has the obligation also to respect the mother tongue of the foreign nationalities."[2] This might suggest an approach similar to Caprivi's, except that Hohenlohe was hardly adamant about this principle in practice and in an even less favorable position than Caprivi to impose personal views on "his" government. According to his long-time associate Hutten-Czapski, he had a general aversion to nationality issues, a legacy perhaps of his tenure as governor in Alsace-Lorraine. He was aware that something was amiss in the eastern provinces, that "conditions there were becoming increasingly intolerable," but he was not inclined to devote any special personal attention to their solution. The Polish question "always remained something peripheral for him, though precisely here a more prudent leadership was necessary."[3]

In fact, several subordinate ministers (Vice-chancellor and Finance Minister Miquel, Culture Minister Bosse, and Imperial Treasury Secretary Posadowsky, in particular) had more to say about the evolution of Prussian Polish policy during the key period after 1894. As with Bismarck and Caprivi, we will look first at the statements of principle and intent by these men before turning to the actual (and frequently contrasting) policies that developed during the Hohenlohe Era. Such a survey of the public statements of the 1894-1900 period does not indicate much change from the past. As under Bismarck and Caprivi, Prussian leaders continued to deny any desire to Germanize Prussian Poles in the sense of getting them to adopt German as their mother tongue. Miquel conceded that "we would not be able to Germanize the Poles in the foreseeable future even if we wanted to do so."[4] Posadowsky, Silesian-born but with a home estate in Poznania, where he had also held *Landrat* positions since the 1870s, had long been considered a moderate on the Polish question. He criticized the 1885 expulsions and advocated the extension of provincial self-government to Poznania. He too described any attempt to Germanize Prussian Poles as "futile and, according to my knowledge of the situation, foolish also."[5] Even Bosse, who usually took the hardest line against the Poles, claimed publicly to be "very satisfied when the Polish children speak Polish at home with their parents and learn German at school; that is what we want."[6] He described the state's "ultimate goal" as little more than a kind of bi-lingualism, "leading the subjects of Polish language—primarily by acquainting them with the German language—out of their social and economic isolation over to their German fellow-citizens." In the meantime, however, they were "to be protected emphatically from any influence which makes a reconciliation with the existing political situation impossible."[7]

This suggests one of the major incongruities of Prussian Polish policy, one which only grew worse after 1894. Prussian ministers regularly declared their desire to retain the loyalty of the majority of Poles and their willingness to treat them the same as German-speaking subjects. "Far be it from the Prussian Government to conduct a political struggle against the Poles, who are its subjects like the subjects of German language. . . . We will always measure the Polish citizens of Prussia by the same standard as the citizens of German language."[8] At the same time, however, they upheld the need for discriminatory laws to deal with the recalcitrant minority. Hohenlohe was convinced that "a kind of

Polishness, a kind of national propaganda, is being cultivated which stands in conscious opposition to the Prussian State. . . . To oppose this with all available means is a requirement of political wisdom. . . . (One must) prevent the spread of illusions which can only end finally in bitter disappointment in the face of the facts."⁹ Or Bosse: "We must oppose with complete determination all agitation and aspirations of a national-Polish tendency. . . . (These have) grown startlingly . . . (and) are aimed directly at the existence and against the interests of our fatherland. . . . We have to have hold of the Poles, not they of us."¹⁰

In other words, the existence of a Polish national movement, however small or moderate, became the justification for anti-Polish laws which affected the entire population. "The behavior of a *part* of the Polish population," said Posadowsky, "has provided the decisive grounds" for the anti-Polish laws. And he established virtually insurmountable conditions for getting these revoked:

> "On the day when the Polish population in its entirety convinces the Prussian Government that it considers itself *inseparably* tied to the Prussian Monarchy, as soon as no kind of utterance occurs any longer in the press or in public assemblies which persuades us that the *opposite* hope predominates in many Polish hearts . . . (and) the *whole* of the Polish population sees its entire future only in the development of Prussia and Germany."¹¹

Hohenlohe took the same position: "The Polish subjects must learn to feel thoroughly like Prussian citizens. . . . This goal has not been achieved yet."¹² "The anti-German tendencies which are still cultivated within the Polish population (must) disappear completely, . . . (then) any anti-Polish attitude on the German side will stop by itself."¹³

This was not the only argument used to justify anti-Polish measures. At other times they were presented as part of a necessary effort to protect the German minority in Polish regions. Posadowsky felt the state had an obligation to help such Germans preserve their "economic and political position, which is absolutely necessary for the good of the Prussian State."¹⁴ For Bosse it was a matter of "holding onto the outpost against aggressive Polish nationalism in the eastern marches."¹⁵ Miquel expressed this attitude even more simply: "We are on the defensive; you (Poles) are on the attack."¹⁶ In retrospect it may be difficult to understand why Europe's most powerful state should fear the relatively small (6% of the Empire's total) Polish population within its frontiers. But this feeling of being on the defensive, doubtless fed by the growing assertiveness of the Polish national movement, adverse demographic trends, and the ineffectiveness of previous state efforts to alter such trends, was apparently quite sincere. There were also fewer references to the supra-national origin and ideals of the Prussian State after 1894, even in the form of lip service as under Bismarck and Caprivi. For Bosse, Prussia was simply "a German state—not a federal state, which is put together out of individual German, Polish, Danish elements or nationalities; rather we are a German national state."[17] This speech by Bosse on February 27, 1896, (other excerpts from which are quoted above) was the most hostile speech the Poles had heard since Bismarck and helped to destroy the remaining loyalist illusions. Szymański described it as an intentional, "carefully phrased message to the leaders of our 'Court Party.'"[18] It seemed clear, as the Hohenlohe government turned to the task of establishing a more consistent Polish policy for the long haul, that it was not going to move any longer in a conciliatory direction in any case.

Before turning to the development of government Polish policy, one must take note of an important new dimension to Prussian-Polish relations after 1894: the appearance of an influential non-governmental pressure group which advocated a harsher nationalistic policy toward Prussian Poles. This was the *Deutscher Ostmarkenverein* (German Eastern Marches Association), as it came to be called officially in 1899; its members were commonly referred to as "Hakatists," from the initials of the three co-founders: Adolf Hansemann, a member of the Berlin banking family, Hermann Kennemann, and Heinrich von Tiedemann, the latter two among the largest German landowners in Poznania. This organization appeared in the wake of pilgrimages by Germans from Poznania and West Prussia to Varzin, Bismarck's summer residence in Pomerania, in 1894. Bismarck was then the most prominent critic of Caprivi's Polish policy and a few words from him were considered a good way to launch a new anti-Polish organization. Actually, Bismarck's remarks to these "pilgrims" indicated primarily that he had lost touch with the changed nature of the Polish nationalist movement and thus with the real concerns of his audience. He dwelt mainly on his o. 1 favorite themes: Polish national character or lack of same, the dangers inherent in a resurrected Polish state, the lessons of Polish history, etc. He maintained that Polish peasants and workers were basically good Prussians and that the only trouble for the state came from nobles and clergy. He even remarked that he was not sure a Polish middle class really existed as yet. Of course his audience, consisting mainly of Junkers and burghers, was quite aware that the problems they were facing were a function increasingly of the Polish urban population rather than the nobles and clergy. The question of a restored Poland and similar traditional issues of Prussian-Polish controversy had become quite secondary to them. Bismarck was essentially used here as a figurehead or status symbol by the sponsors of the new movement. They were willing to overlook the details of his talks, playing up the generally anti-Polish tenor of his remarks and his vague assurance that "with you, gentlemen, I feel myself in agreement."[19]

The *Ostmarkenverein* grew out of a combination of German nationalism, agrarian opposition to Caprivi, and middle-class sensitivity to Polish economic and demographic gains. Its program was essentially the same as the Polish program of the Pan-German League (with which it also shared much of its membership):

— Instruction of all children in German
— State subsidies for Germans and their institutions in Polish areas
— Germanization of all place-names
— Restriction of Polish recruits to German areas
— Curtailment of the use of alien seasonal labor
— Exclusion of Poles from *Rentengüter*
— Extension of Settlement Commission operations to Upper Silesia and Masuria[20]

While supporting the Settlement Law of 1886, it stressed the primary importance of the economic struggle in eastern towns.[21] Bismarck became a charter member of the *Ostmarkenverein*, perhaps because he saw it as another weapon against Caprivi. Since most of its early members were large landowners (60% of the Poznanians and West Prussians at the 1894 organizational meeting were Junkers), he may well have considered it primarily an arm of the agrarian protest movement. The anti-Polish feelings of some of the pilgrims to Varzin seemed indeed to stem mainly from the *Koło*'s vote for Caprivi's trade treaties.[22] But it is highly unlikely that Bismarck sympathized with the *Ostmarkenverein*'s Polish program. He never showed much interest in the "economic struggle" between Germans and Poles and it was not his style to have the state call on the help of such volunteers in dealing politically with the Poles.

The creation of the *Ostmarkenverein*, the first important German organization with specifically anti-Polish thrust, was symptomatic of (and a further contribution to) the division of the Prussian East into two hostile national camps. The Poles responded sharply to the new organization; Jażdżewski warned, "do not unnecessarily, through new combat organizations, carry displeasure and unrest into our sufficiently tested populace."[23] It became a very prominent topic in the Polish press; one paper began to publish the names of members, calling on its readers to shun them.[24] On the whole, Germans in the Polish regions were reluctant to become associated with the *Ostmarkenverein*. Only about 3500 Germans in Poznania (*i.e.*, c .5% of the total) were members in 1895.²⁵ Most Prussian officials either denounced it or at least made a point of their non-membership in it. According to a pole of *Landräte*, the "better classes" were not anxious to join, either because they saw no reason to alienate their Polish workers and customers or for social-status reasons.²⁶ A report from provincial headquarters in Poznań was very critical of the *Ostmarkenverein*, charging that it had "contributed definitely to the intensification of national differences and also done serious harm to Germans in many cases," dividing them as well as contributing to Polish solidarity.²⁷ *Oberpräsident* Wilamowitz also took an aloof position:

> "Efforts of German organizations or societies to support the state government in its efforts of German colonization and the strengthening and enlargement of the German element generally will have to receive full recognition and encouragement; they must be careful, however, not to make the neighborly economic and social relationships between the two nationalities still harsher and more difficult than they already are."²⁸

Among the ministers in Berlin, only Interior Minister Köller expressed publicly any sympathy for the *Ostmarkenverein*; he argued that it was more pro-German than anti-Polish, that it was not unlike many Polish organizations, and that "every German who lives in the eastern marches must promote German nationality there." But he was compelled to retract this support the following day and did not retain his ministerial post for long in any case.²⁹

The *Ostmarkenverein* soon lost most of its agrarian character and ceased to draw most of its membership from the eastern marches. By the turn of the century, teachers and officials constituted the largest segment of the organization, followed by businessmen, with Junkers only a small factor.³⁰ Among its 26,000 members in 1902 (vs. only 22,000 for the older Pan-German League) were prominent intellectuals and political figures (including Treitschke, Erdmannsdörffer, Lamprecht, Schmoller, Haeckel, and Weber), many of whom were not really all that chauvinistic, but only about 15% of the members lived in Poznania, and half of these were employed there by the state as teachers or civil servants.³¹ The actual significance and influence of the *Ostmarkenverein* in Berlin remain difficult to determine. Schieder describes it as an "extended arm" of the government,³² which overlooks its origin as an opposition pressure group. Hutten-Czapski saw it as the "driving force behind the German Polish policies . . . (through) the supervisory role over the government which it increasingly arrogated to itself."³³ It cannot be denied that it achieved some influence at the national level, behind the scenes at least; Hakatists were employed as state secretaries in both the Justice (Hugenberg) and Interior (Schwerin) ministries, both of which were heavily involved with Polish matters.[34] On the other hand, at least until 1898, the government did not acknowledge it as an ally and there is little evidence of a direct Hakatist influence in the choice of policies under Hohenlohe.

While no attempt was made to reverse Caprivi's policies or return to Bismarckian norms immediately after 1894, there began behind the scenes a comprehensive reconsideration of Prussian Polish policy, the results of which emerged in 1897-8. There was an overriding desire at this time to have done with the long, zig-zag course of frequently changing policies toward the Poles. An 1896 Crown Council described Poznania as "almost in a state of revolution" and declared its nationality problem to be "of the highest priority and one of the fundamental tasks of the state government."[35] Hohenlohe expressed the opinion that "a firm and consistent position, while avoiding unnecessary severity, toward all Polish separatist efforts appearing within the state area can only be described as urgently required."[36] It was generally acknowledged that a crossroads of sorts had been reached; if the government did not choose to continue Caprivi's conciliatory policy, then a more purposeful and consistent anti-Polish policy seemed to be the only alternative. Given the growing strength and dissatisfaction of the Polish national movement and its envelopment of ever larger areas of Polish society in Prussia, the relatively passive and inconsistent policies of the past were no longer considered sufficient. A somewhat revised, though far from innovative, policy emerged by 1898 and remained in place with minor alterations until World War I. The Hohenlohe chancellorship, often passed over quickly in accounts of Prussian-Polish relations, is important for this reason; while the clashes of the Bülow Era were more spectacular, they stemmed logically from policies established in 1897-8.

In 1895 Interior Minister Köller called on Wilamowitz to pull together the current state of Prussian Polish policy, the various laws and official attitudes which comprised an increasingly confused and contradictory position. Wilamowitz replied with a lengthy resumé of past measures and current options of which he was aware, acknowledging that the government in the past "through repeated wavering in this policy . . . has held up the assimilation of the population of the eastern marches."[37] This report was placed before the cabinet with a large number of suggestions for changes in Polish policy. There was a delay when Köller left office in 1895, but his successor Recke took it up in 1896. He asked his fellow ministers to supplement it with any ideas they might have and this became the basis for a series of extended discussions of the Polish problem lasting from October 1896 to June 1897.[38]

The introduction which Wilamowitz appended to this 1895 report epitomizes the ambivalence of Prussian Polish policy at this time. On the one hand, he took it for granted that "in principle the subjects of his majesty the King, whether they be of German or foreign descent or language, are to be treated completely equally; . . . (on the other hand), we are concerned only to determine in which cases and to what extent exceptions to this policy are necessary." He recognized the government's dilemma in the wake of previous policies:

> "Through concessions in the language sphere or the granting of more extensive special political rights according to the Galician model, . . . the opposite was achieved, the 'state in the state' was formed, the endeavors directed at the restoration of a Polish state were supported and considerably strengthened. But the opposite (policy), the ruthless fight against and forcible suppression of everything Polish, will not make the Poles into Germans; . . . an exclusively hostile posture toward the mass of the Polish population, organized and self-contained as it already is, will cause it to be welded together even more tightly, removed even more from any German influence, and filled even more with hate and bitterness against everything German."[39]

Wilamowitz' own suggestions betrayed no coherent plan of action; they generally reflected this equivocal, on-the-one-hand-this analysis of the basic problem. He was unwilling to abandon previous, ineffective anti-Polish measures but he could not suggest significant new measures which might be more effective in dealing with a Polish population that was nationally aroused, economically vigorous, and well organized.

> "On the one hand, all of those arrangements which are necessary and designed to prevent a further growth and strengthening of the Polish population, . . . to integrate this alien population with the German element, and make it accessible to German influence, must be maintained and . . . carried through steadfastly; on the other hand, however, the loyal subjects of Polish language must be allowed to enjoy completely the benefits of a just and well-disposed administration without demanding from them the denial of their nationality . . . and be able to acquire the same rights and advantages which the political and social system provides for loyal German subjects through the fulfillment of the same conditions."[40]

The Settlement Law of 1886 retained a prominent place in the battery of measures aimed at the Polish problem and received much of the attention during this 1896-7 review. All agreed that it had turned out to be quite a disappointment; after eight years in operation it was subject to growing criticism by nationalists and derision by opponents. A particularly trenchant critique by Hans Delbrück, influential editor of the *Preussische Jahrbücher,* appeared in 1894. He calculated that the 853 German farmers which the Settlement Commission had managed to get started through 1893 had cost the Prussian State about 12,000 Marks each. At the current rate Germans were being settled, it would be a century before the German population of Poznania and West Prussia could be raised by even 100,000 persons. The Poles, of course, added this many to their own population every few years through natural increase alone. As Jażdżewski asked, "What does the government expect to achieve with this futile number of its charges (the number of settlers stood at 1842 when he spoke) in view of the statistically demonstrable increase of the Poles?"[41] Delbrück argued that such factors as the higher Polish birth rate, continuing German emigration westward, intermarriage (which he thought led more often to Polish than German offspring), and a generally higher level of national consciousness among Poles were all likely to frustrate the government's efforts to Germanize by means of settlement or population policies. "It is clear," he concluded, "that the whole project is worthless with respect to the nationality question in our eastern regions."[42] He urged the state instead to continue with Caprivi's policy of trying to make the Poles into good citizens, which they had been during the wars of unification and were apparently again under loyalist leadership since 1890. "But even the best attitude cannot last in the long run in the face of this kind of treatment, and in any case a fundamental requirement is that in the future any irritation of those classes of the Polish population which one believes can be trusted be avoided."[43] As for the allegedly threatened Germans in the Polish regions, they would be better off to learn Polish in order to compete better economically and they would gain in national consciousness and self-reliance if they were not able to rely on the state for support.[44]

More disturbing even than Delbrück's critique were Bismarck's remarks to the pilgrims at Varzin in 1894. They amounted to a denial of responsibility for what was commonly viewed as his own creation. He claimed now that the settlement project did not reflect his views as much as those of his National Liberal allies at the time.

> "It was not my program that the Settlement Commission should concentrate primarily upon the settlement of small farmers of *German* nationality; Polish peasants are not dangerous and it is not decisive whether the workers are Polish or German. The main thing was for the large (Polish

estates) to become domain, under lessees over which the state would have lasting influence. The requirement to buy and colonize quickly originated with another party involved, but not with me. I was not able to supervise these measures, only suggest them."[45]

The following week he even seemed to endorse the non-discriminatory approach of the General Commission; he expressed satisfaction that "by way of *Rentengüter* a way has been found to establish peacefully and gradually, if not a German population then at least a population loyal to Germany."[46]

The problems of the Settlement Commission continued to mount after 1894. On top of those cited above, there was a rapid rise in the price of land in the Polish provinces, something quite unforeseen by the drafters of the law in 1886. The price per hectare rose from 571 Marks in 1895 to 1383 Marks in 1906. The price of land as a multiple of the annual tax increased almost as much, from 64 to 125, during the same period.[47] As a result, the Commission's operating capital was devalued and the Prussian taxpayer was faced with the prospect of pumping more and more money into the fund just to keep it operating at its unimpressive current level.

In 1896, the Prussian cabinet discussed whether the settlement project was even worth continuing. Miquel, though instrumental in passing the law in 1886, was especially skeptical of the value of investing additional money in it. When the cabinet began its detailed examination of the Polish question in late-1896, he concluded that the Commission's efforts to date did not "represent a decisive success, guaranteed for the long run, for the numerical relationship, or even for a shift in the property relationship, between the German and Polish populations." He listed a number of problems undermining its effectiveness:

1. "A not inconsiderable part of the estates purchased by the Settlement Commission has been bought from Germans."
2. Polish estate owners, at which the 1886 law was aimed, were becoming less of a problem than Polish peasants; Polish holdings in the peasant category continued to outnumber German by a 13:8 ratio in Poznania, with no sign of a change in the latter's favor.
3. The General Commission had cancelled out much of the Settlement Commission's efforts (see above, p. 128).
4. Many more Poles than Germans were "hungry" for homesteads, allowing Polish land developers to demand higher prices from their clients and operate more profitably than the Commission.[48]

Miquel declined to suggest an end to the project; it would have to be continued now just to avoid falling further behind. Previously he had urged the Commission to stick to truly mixed areas and "not invest deep inside solidly Polish areas."[49] He now proposed a quite radical change of course for the Commission, including its merger with the General Commission under the latter body's philosophy. "In place of the tendency of the law of 1886 to give the impression of directly suppressing the Poles, one should put a general policy of encouraging settlements in the eastern provinces."[50]

This sugestions did not find the support of Hohenlohe or his cabinet, but it is an example of the progressive loss of confidence in the Settlement Law since the time that Bismarck suggested he could buy up the entire Polish nobility with 100 million Marks. Hohenlohe opposed any effort to disguise the nationalist aims of the project by merging it with the *Rentengut* idea. Wilamowitz also doubted that the Commission could afford to "limit its activity in the foreseeable future; rather it will have to extend it still further and more freely." He suggested that it be given additional money and a freer hand to keep some estates intact in case suitable homesteaders were not available.[51] Bosse claimed that the problem was precisely that "political considerations have been much less decisive than economic" since the Commission ceased to be run by the Poznanian *Oberpräsident* in 1891. He feared that any de-emphasis of the settlement project "would be understood as a turning-away from a determined national policy, when such a policy is more necessary than ever after the experiences of the last five years."[52] Posadowsky, while acknolwedging that the project had had little political impact thus far, felt that it was necessary, not any longer to Germanize the Polish provinces but merely to maintain the existing national balance.[53] But all agreed that some changes were necessary to eliminate the problems which Miquel had delineated and which had so frustrated the Settlement Commission during its first decade.

The easiest of these problems to deal with was the competition of the General Commission. For a time, this agency continued to resist efforts to get it to fall into line with the government's stance on the Polish question. When Agriculture Minister Hammerstein urged that it not settle Poles in areas where the Settlement Commission operated, its director maintained that "the *Rentengut* Law . . . pursues solely an economic, not a political aim; therefore the nationality of the sale is not a consideration *per se*." He cited the 1867/1871 Constitution: "Every citizen has the right to buy real estate of any kind at any place within the Confederation." In fact, he admitted a General Commission policy to raise the proportion of Polish clients closer to their 60% share of the general population in its area of operations.[54] Publicly the government acknowledged that there was no legal way to avoid giving Poles access to homesteads created under the *Rentengut* laws; Hammerstein conceded in 1896 that it was "a general law of the land under which the German and Polish nationalities have been treated equally and will continue to be so treated in the future."[55] But later that year he was able to persuade the two commissions to coordinate their affairs. At the same time, the General Commission stopped creating plots of less than 3 ha. (which affected Poles disproportionately) and the Polish Land Bank ended its relationship with the Commission rather than accept new conditions for the increased settlement of Germans.[56] By 1897 the General Commission ceased to be a factor in the "land battle" in the Polish provinces. But it had already created only slightly fewer homesteads than the Settlement Commission: 1792 (vs. 2342) between 1891 and 1896, 48% of which had gone to Poles.[57]

A second problem cited by Miquel proved more difficult to resolve: the high percentage of Commission funds going to purchase land from German estate owners. Eulenburg had opened the door slightly in 1893; in 1894 the cabinet permitted the Commission "to buy a few German estates . . . in a special case."[58] But in 1895 already it bought more land from Germans than from Poles and the nationalist justification for the project threatened to disappear from view. In 1896 the government became alarmed at this trend and ordered the Commission "to slow down the purchase of estates generally, and especially to buy German estates only in very exceptional cases where pressing grounds . . . are present."[59]

It was not only that buying German estates to create German farms had no apparent national impact; Bosse feared also that "the departure of German estate owners, who personify the superiority of the German race for the Polish peasants, is under some conditions a loss which is not compensated for by the establishment of German peasant villages, which are economically weak because of the heavy burden of payments and debts."[60] Hohenlohe also desired that "the purchase of estates from Germans not become the rule. . . . It would be politically incorrect to facilitate the departure of the (German estate owners) especially from these provinces."[61] Miquel argued for the "fundamental exclusion of the purchase of estates from Germans," but the Commission itself sought instead an end to any distinction between German and Polish estates.[62] Hohenlohe decided finally to relax most of the remaining restrictions:

> "Since the cases mount up where German owners who cannot hold out parcel their estates among Polish settlers, I would have no misgivings about extending the limits within which purchases from Germans have been

allowed to take place thus far, *e.g.*, where they are necessary for the suitable rounding-off of an existing settlement complex or for the creation of compact settlement areas."[63]

With this the last inhibitions disappeared and the Commission bought an ever larger majority of its land from Germans in the following years. It seemed no longer to have a choice if it wished to continue functioning, for Polish estates were increasingly scarce on the market and were usually picked off first by Polish parcelling agencies. In some years after 1900, the ratio of German to Polish land purchased by the Commission was more than 8:1. Czarliński quite accurately described the Commission by this time as "an institute for the maintenance of bankrupt large German landowners."[64]

A third problem cited by Miquel, the Polish peasant, went unresolved also, mainly because it was not addressed by the 1886 law. Polish nobles continued to lose their estates faster than they acquired new ones; by 1900 Polish estate ownership had declined by an additional 68,000 ha. since 1886.[65] But, as Hohenlohe noted, "the depossession of Polish estate owners is in fact no longer of such decisive importance as earlier, since they have lost considerable political influence and given up the leadership role in the national struggle to other elements."[66] The Polish peasantry, on the other hand, continued to add considerably to its share of land, resulting in a net gain for the Poles as a whole and effectively frustrating the Settlement Law. The government decided in 1897 that the purchase of land from Polish peasants might be undertaken more systematically.[67] But the Germans continued to lose the battle for peasant holdings; in 1900, Interior Minister Rheinbaben, citing figures for several counties in western Poznania where 1300 German peasants had sold over 10,000 ha. to Polish counterparts in the previous several years, expressed the fear that the unsubsidized German peasantry might soon disappear altogether from many parts of that province.[68]

The fourth problem besetting the Settlement Commission (as seen by Miquel) was the shortage of suitable German applicants (with the necessary down-payment) who were willing to move to Poznania or West Prussia. The Commission had bought up a good deal of land by 1896-7 but only about half of it had been settled. In its desire to create middle-class German farmers, it was forced to recruit from a limited class of Germans who were not willing to move eastward in sufficient numbers, thus slowing up the project.[69] The average delay between purchase of an estate and settlement by German farmers was three years and in some cases this process took six years. Thus the number of actual settlers continued to seem quite small compared to the state's financial outlay.⁷⁰ Hohenlohe thought it might be advisable for the Commission to lower the financial (and social) standards it applied to potential settlers and permit smaller farmers to apply.⁷¹ Bosse also wanted to "make use of the economically weak German population from the better working classes through the establishment of leaseholds." The Commission might also be encouraged to recruit less from western Germany and more from the Ostelbian provinces, "which are less demanding and can get used to the conditions in the eastern provinces more easily."⁷² War Minister Heinrich von Gossler suggested that veterans would be ideal settlers and should be given special treatment and financial support. The Emperor liked this last idea for defense reasons and also because it reminded him of the Roman practice of settling border regions with soldiers.⁷³ Others feared that it would be a mistake to burden the project with settlers who would have to be more heavily subsidized, though the government agreed in 1898 to experiment with the settlement of a hundred such veterans.⁷⁴

Posadowsky returned to some of Bismarck's ideas: selling some estates intact to Germans or leaving them under German managers. He was willing to offer below-market interest rates or subsidies to attract "efficient German owners who could offer sufficient down-payment. . . . able, moneyed German owners and thereby leaders for the neighboring German population."⁷⁵ Such a shift in emphasis was rejected, however, because such estates invariably employed a Polish labor force (though the cabinet agreed that "in special cases an estate could be sold intact or divided into [larger] parts.")⁷⁶ Attempts (*e.g.*, by Bosse) to revive the idea of smaller worker-peasant plots met with a negative response; as Posadowsky noted, estate owners wanted just plain workers, not farmer-workers.⁷⁷ Hohenlohe speculated that there might be a way to get German farm workers to come east, "assuming that the consideration of profitability is not viewed as the decisive factor."⁷⁸ Nothing further was done about this, but it was unlikely that anything could be done about the central role of Polish farm workers under existing economic conditions. Wilamowitz described them as "useful and necessary for the functioning of agriculture; even if one wanted to, they could not be supplanted by the much more demanding German workers. Even less could the (seasonal) Russian-Polish workers . . . be replaced by German workers."⁷⁹ And a Settlement Commission official acknowledged that "the workers of the West, used to a higher standard of living, cannot compete with the less demanding Poles. They would refuse to move into the run-down cottages and work in the ranks with Poles for German landowners."⁸⁰ Even Bosse's suggestion that at least the Settlement Commission itself be prevented from employing Polish workers on estates it had purchased (and was operating on an interim basis) proved unfeasible.⁸¹

This reliance on a Polish farm-labor force made it very difficult to register any gains in the national balance. Posadowsky warned that "if the immigration (of seasonal workers, some of which invariably found ways to stay on) continued for another ten years as hitherto, all the recently proposed measures will not help at all. Economic interest must be subordinate to the preservation of nationality."[82] But where Prussian Polish policy ran up against the interests of the agrarians, the latter tended to win out. The government resolved to limit the immigration of aliens to the extent that the interests of agriculture permitted and make greater efforts to see that they left on time each year, but they could not be dispensed with altogether.

In sum, aside from suppressing the competition of the General Commission, little was done during the Hohenlohe years (or thereafter) to deal with the problems plaguing the settlement project. The policies of the Settlement Commission were changed in a number of minor ways after 1897. Its chairmanship returned to the Poznanian *Oberpräsident*; it tried to settle its lands more quickly and focus on more limited areas, *e.g.*, where Reichstag elections were typically close between Germans and Poles. But the only substantial step taken was to increase its operating capital by another 100 million Marks in 1898.[84] But due to the rapid rise in land prices, this helped no more than the other half-measures. Miquel suggested that it might be necessary to start selling off royal domain all over Prussia to raise the money to buy land in the Polish provinces. By 1900, the Commission no longer distinguished between German and Polish, noble and peasant land; even German peasant land was bought up for fear that it might go to the Poles.[85] It bought up whatever land was available in the two provinces, parcelling it if settlers were available, holding onto it or creating leaseholds if they were not. Posadowsky, while expressing hope that the various cosmetic measures would suffice to solve the Commission's problems, recognized that they might not, in which case "one will have to resort to more drastic exceptional measures."[86]

Such "drastic exceptional measures" were in fact introduced under Chancellor Bernhard von Bülow (1900-1909), culminating in the Expropriation Law of 1908, but even these failed to turn the Settlement Law of 1886 into a success. The final figures on Prussian state settlement activity between 1886 and 1918 certainly indicate a major effort. The Settlement Commission eventually purchased 466,750 ha. of land, amounting to some 8½% of all the land in the two provinces in which it operated.[87] Socially, the parcelling activity by Germans and Poles together had a considerable impact; the number of large estates (500 ha. or more) declined by 24% while the number of farms in the 5-100 ha.

range increased by 32%.⁸⁸ The Settlement Commission spent some 734 million Marks and established 21,886 homesteads for German farmers. An additional 57,481 ha. were purchased under the *Rentengut* laws to create 5858 more homesteads, a majority of which also went to Germans.⁸⁹ If one assumes that these homesteads supported typically large farm families, the total number of Germans involved may have reached 150,000, about 3% of the population of the two provinces.⁹⁰ On the other hand, 71.5% of this land was owned previously by Germans anyway; in addition, 26.5% of the settlers lived in Poznania or West Prussia already and thus added nothing to the national balance there.⁹¹ While the amount of land held by Poles in the form of large estates dropped, the amount of such land held by Germans dropped even more sharply; a 67,000 ha. edge of estate-land ownership in 1886 declined to 19,000 ha. by 1908. Altogether, the Poles lost about 195,000 ha. to Germans or the state between 1861 and 1886; during the first ten years of the Settlement Commission, they lost an additional 50,000 ha. But during the crucial 1896-1914 period they turned this trend around completely and registered a gain of 181,437 ha.⁹² This figure serves better than any amount of words as a comment on the effectiveness of the Settlement Law of 1886.

The other major area of Prussian-Polish conflict, school policy, saw few major changes during the Hohenlohe Era. Bosse remained at his post from Zedlitz' ouster until 1899, imposing a certain continuity. He did introduce minor additional measures designed to make the public schools more clearly instruments of the government's Germanization policy. For example, teachers who did an especially good job of teaching German to their Polish pupils were rewarded with special bonuses.⁹³ He attempted also to prevent separate associations of Polish teachers and to keep the Catholic Teachers Association from meeting in Poznania, though these efforts were not supported by Hohenlohe.⁹⁴ More noteworthy was the increasingly nationalistic tone of his public remarks after Caprivi's departure. He was usually the most aggressive and unyielding of the ministers involved with Polish affairs and opposed anything which smacked of conciliation:

> "Every attempt which has ever been made to accommodate the Poles through broad concessions has failed to find the right understanding among the Poles themselves. . . . It is necessary to strengthen the threatened German position more than previously in order to awaken the safe feeling in the German element and all who honestly want to stand on its side that the state government stands behind them with firm will and its entire strength. . . . For the achievement of that which is recognized, after all, as necessary for national reasons, no sacrifice seems too large and thus the

ultimate means for its execution should be provided in full measure."[95]

In response to continued Polish complaints about his school policies, he insisted in 1895 that conditions in Poznania would have to change radically before he would consider "extending the very cautious handling of the provision of Polish language instruction. . . . We live in a German country and the children whom the Prussian and German elementary schools have to train should be brought up as Germans and Prussians."[96] In fact, such classes as had been created in 1894 tended to disappear from time to time from this or that individual school with no official explanation.[97] Bosse and other officials made it increasingly clear that the major job of the public schools in Polish areas was to teach German to Polish children. According to the 1895 report by Wilamowitz,

> "The Prussian State recognizes only a *German* school, which in the formerly Polish territories has the difficult task of instilling a knowledge of the German language in children even when they hear or speak no word of German at home. . . . Only the mastery of this language can actually provide the means of making full use of the legal equality of all subjects of the united and entirely *German* state Prussia. . . . (Furthermore), the difference of language is one of the main obstacles to the assimilation of the Polish with the German population of the state and a principal means of preserving the Poles in an isolated, alien, if not hostile position against the German State. Therefore it is an imperative command of political wisdom to work with all means toward the learning of the German language on the part of Polish subjects."[98]

Bosse reiterated in 1896 that the schools were German and their most important goal the complete mastery of German, the official language. He frequently expressed his lack of concern for the job done by the schools teaching Polish: "It is much more important for a child, for a Prussian child in any case, to learn to obey than to know Polish fluently."[99]

Wilamowitz recognized two major obstacles to the successful fulfillment of the schools' principal mission. First was the problem of getting the right kind of teachers. Polish teachers were still hired in Prussia but sent as a matter of course to purely German areas to work. But, "since religious instruction for children of Polish native language is still given largely in Polish, elementary school teachers must for the most part be in command of this language and thus the school administration is forced to use Poles as teachers even when they are not entirely suited to the linguistic and political tasks of the school."[100] The Church showed no signs of bending in its insistence that all pupils receive religious instruction in their native language and there were not very many politically reliable German-Catholic teachers who knew Polish. The second obstacle was the "great poverty of the school districts" in the Polish regions. The state had spent a great deal of money here, especially since 1886, but this was "mainly for the construction of Protestant and German schools."[101] As a result, by 1895 there were 55 students per Protestant teacher but 84 per Catholic teacher; some districts had a ratio as high as 200:1.[102] Thus, as Wilamowitz recognized, "it is precisely the Catholic schools visited by Polish children which are still overfilled (200 pupils per teacher) and equipped with dilapidated, defective, and inadequate school buildings. Instruction in general and especially the successful learning of the German language suffers from this most noticeably."[103]

To deal with this situation, a number of steps emerged from the major discussion of Polish policy in 1896-7. More money (20 million Marks to start with and 2 million more annually) was allocated for the schools in Polish regions; this time, as opposed to 1886, it was to be used to bring Catholic schools up to par. The teacher-student ratio was to be lowered so that Polish children could be given more individualized instruction in German. Grants were provided for German teachers-in-training who were willing to study enough Polish to work in Poznanian schools, though Bosse was quick to add the warning that "this course must be limited to the most elementary subjects, *i.e*, basic grammar and a couple hundred words of vocabulary; . . . a further extension would be dangerous."[104] Teachers who were especially successful in teaching German received higher rewards, which were intended to "strengthen simultaneously in the teacher the feeling of dependence on the state and arm them against the temptations of Polish agitation."[105] State-subsidized nursery schools were established to introduce Polish children to German before actual schooling began. Finally, another effort was made to enforce attendance by adolescents at trade schools after they had finished their formal schooling.[106]

Another subject of discussion in 1896-7 was the use of the Polish language in public. Some ministers favored steps to inhibit its use, among other things in order to undermine the rapidly expanding Polish organizations. Wilamowitz saw no way to prohibit these directly: "Since these organizations normally operate strictly within legal limits and the economic and humanitarian aims pursued by them deserve state favor, state officials must limit themselves for the time being to the strict supervision of all Polish organizations and meetings."[107] Unfortunately, the Prussian civil service (having excluded Poles in the past) did not have enough such monitors who were fluent in Polish. This suggested to Wilamowitz the possibility of a "legal requirement . . . which would authorize officials under circumstances to demand the exclusive use of the German language" in order that they might carry out their supervisory duty. "If one could raise this demand generally, exclusive Polish organizations would be hit most emphatically."[108] But he advised against such a course for the time being, unless "the national-Polish party switches to a more rigorous agitation and presents the state government with greater difficulties." In any case, Prussian courts had already forbidden the closing of public meetings simply because police monitors could not understand the language being used (cf. above, p. 24).[109]

When this subject came up in January 1897, Recke suggested that the government try again to restrict the use of Polish in public, beginning with regions where relatively few Poles lived. If this provoked a new court case and the decision again went against the government, other measures could be considered.[110] It was not long thereafter that complaints began to roll in, especially from Upper Silesia and West Prussia. In the latter case, *Oberpräsident* Gossler considered virtually every Polish meeting political; he watched them very closely and closed many of them. Official replies to such complaints by Poles (and by the Center Party in Upper Silesia) were at best disingenuous. Recke told the Landtag that it was not state policy to close Polish meetings unless a dialect of some kind were used.[111] His counterpart on the Imperial level, Boetticher, replied a couple of months later that "*we* do not close meetings; we just order German spoken and then the *Poles* close them."[112] But before the year was out, the courts decided again that the Poles were entitled to use their language in public meetings. Simultaneous efforts in 1897 to pass a new assembly law which would achieve the government's end in this way met defeat (205:209) in the Landtag.[113]

The government was thus limited to various petty, bureaucratic, even ludicrous measures against the public use of Polish. Examples include the requirement that government censors be given German translations of all Polish plays before they could be performed.[114] Justice Minister Schönstedt accused Poles of only pretending not to understand German in court in order to avail themselves of their right to an interpreter.[115] Army bands were ordered not to play Polish songs.[116] Emperor Wilhelm changed the Poznanian provincial colors in 1896 from the Polish red-white to the Prussian black-white; (however, the latter happened to be the traditional Polish mourning colors, thus their display could be interpreted variously).[117] Recke declared in 1899 that only the German spelling of place-names would henceforth be legal, *e.g.*, effective in getting mail delivered.[118] Some Poles were pressured by zealous officials to spell their names in such a way that they would appear German and registration of the Polish forms of first names was discouraged.[119] While the right of assembly by Prussian citizens was reaffirmed, organizations with foreign membership like the Falcons (Sokół) and the Congress of Polish Doctors were forbidden to hold their conventions in Prussia.[120] A list of this kind of chicanery could run on endlessly and seems in any case to have grown rapidly during the Hohenlohe Era.

Prussian policy toward the Catholic Church in Poznania also remained essentially unchanged after 1894. Wilamowitz urged a continued effort to separate Catholicism from Polish nationalism, avoiding the impression that the state was against the Church or its belief *per se*. He suggested that more attention be paid to the needs of German Catholics in Polish regions and to the rise of German clerics in the Poznanian hierarchy:

> "Through the visible equalization of Germans with Poles in the Church, (one could) overcome the existing prejudices, ease the existence of German Catholics in and their immigration to the Polish regions, and loosen up the solid phalanx of Polish-Catholic clergy through the penetration of the German language and German priests of genuine German sentiment."[121]

There was little to be done about the existing, predominately Polish clergy, but "the cooperation of the Archbishop should be gained to see that the clergy occupies itself less with politics than with its spiritual calling and that those clergy who exhibit an anti-German posture or who are active in the interests of Polish particularism at least be held back from new positions or other advantages."[122] He claimed some success in getting Stablewski to reprimand or transfer outspokenly anti-government or anti-loyalist priests.[123] In general, Stablewski remained a valuable asset to the government and his complaints rated an Imperial reply. When Bosse accused him of naivete and weakness, Hohenlohe and Miquel came quickly to his defense as an "honorable man."[124]

At the same time, however, the government did not hesitate to exploit Stablewski's loyalism. It seized every opportunity, every case of Polish nationalism on the part of individual clergy, to make new demands of him. Working through him, Bosse sought (with little success) to stop priests from accepting nomination to Reichstag seats or otherwise being active politically.[125] He also sought to keep female orders from teaching or similar duties, charging that they were full of "fanatic Poles who proselyte even among the sick they care for."[126] The Church's policy of using the native language wherever possible to service its members provided an opening for other government demands: "According to its own principles the Church cannot refuse to use the German language for its members of German native language even in formerly Polish territories."¹²⁷ About 7% of the Catholics in Poznania were German; in particular there was a significant German-Catholic minority among the clients of the Settlement Commission.¹²⁸ The government demanded repeatedly that Stablewski pay more attention to the needs of his newly-arrived German-speaking followers, mainly by hiring German priests for them.¹²⁹ For Wilamowitz, this was "the point at which we must begin, first to prevent Catholic Germans from being Polonized, further to achieve entry and, ulimately at least, equality for the German language in the Church congregations of this province." When Stablewski complained about school and church policies, officials frequently responded by bringing up the question of how he was caring for German Catholics.¹³⁰ It was difficult for Stablewski to refuse to meet whatever demands the government made in this respect, even when it opened him up to accusations by Populists that he was "Germanizing through the Church."¹³¹

The bureaucracy in Polish regions was virtually all-German by this time; no Poles had been hired at higher levels since 1886. Wilamowitz urged that Poles "by no means be excluded from state positions; . . . rather all jobs must be accessible to them just as to German subjects, only not in the formerly Polish territories." In Polish-speaking areas officials should be German, "exclusively in the higher positions and as much as possible in the lower ones. . . . The employment of officials . . . provides a highly desirable opportunity to strengthen the German element in all parts of the province, especially in the towns."¹³² In 1896-7 the cabinet considered whether to try to extend this exclusion of Poles to the lower levels of the civil service. Hohenlohe was among those in favor of such a blanket exclusion; he saw "a very important means of Germanization . . . in the most consistent possible implementation of the principle to use only German officials in all spheres of the civil service in Polish areas and to transplant the Polish elements of the civil service to purely German regions."¹³³ But the ministers in charge of the courts, railroads, postal service, etc., argued that they could not do without Polish employees in the lower ranks. Schönstedt asserted that Poles were needed for such positions as court recorder, jail guards, and translators, and some knowledge of Polish was necessary even for higher positions. The cabinet decided that Poles would not be posted to the eastern provinces unless absolutely necessary but that a total ban on them was not practicable.¹³⁴

As for the Army, there was of course no question of doing entirely without Poles. Wilamowitz recognized that "the term of military service provides a continuation of training and education for the male youth" in the German language. Under Hohenlohe, Polish recruits were encouraged to improve their German through special classes and Polish-speaking chaplains were carefully watched for any sign of "Polish tendencies."[135] As the result of a minor concession under Caprivi (cf. above, p. 157), up to 10% of the troops stationed in the Fifth Army Corps (hqs. Poznań) could be Polish. The cabinet resolved to diminish this percentage, but again without insisting on the total exclusion of Poles.[136]

The problem was no longer the purging of Poles from the civil service but how to attract competent German officials to serve in the Polish areas in their place. It was conceded by top officials in Berlin (and by Poznanians such as Wilamowitz) that the Polish regions were not considered by German civil servants to be a very desirable place to live and work. They especially disliked the smaller, predominately Polish *Kreisstädte* and usually took the first opportunity to transfer out. The 1886 proliferation of counties (cf. above, p. 82) turned out to be counter-productive in the sense that a lot of *Landräte* and their subordinates found themselves in quite small market towns hardly suited to the role of administrative center and without suitable housing. But, as Wilamowitz argued, precisely Poznania "ought not to serve . . . to take up inferior officials; on the contrary, the most diligent and capable belong in this difficult and exposed outpost, so altogether important for the good of the state."[137] Hohenlohe proposed therefore that steps be taken to make life more pleasant for German officials in nationally-mixed areas; his cabinet resolved to find new methods to get the best officials, rotate them less often, and give them special bonuses or perquisites.[138]

The most significant change in the area of general administration was the new emphasis on the nationalist role of Prussian state officials. They tended after 1894 to abandon the last pretense of supra-national objectivity and became instead the instruments of a Germanization policy directed at a part of the citizens they were theoretically serving. Existing policy called for "officials, especially teachers, to abstain from participation in national-Polish endeavors and demonstrations of any kind. In particular, the participation in organizations which . . . make themselves useful to national-Polish endeavors will not be tolerated."[139] In 1898 Miquel drew up a directive calling on all Prussian officials in Polish areas to do much more than this: to work actively off-duty as well as on in a German-nationalist sense. "Through their total, including non-official and social behavior," they were to "strengthen German national and Prussian state consciousness, *e.g.*, by becoming active in unofficial German patriotic organizations, clubs, and as volunteers." To be sure, he also cautioned that "any aggressive activity against the Polish-speaking population is to be avoided and the participation of willing elements is everywhere to be kept open to them. . . . A conciliatory spirit directed at the eventual filing away of existing frictions must guide the activities of officials and teachers."[140] Nonetheless, this represented a clear theoretical break with the past for the Prussian state bureaucracy. Hohenlohe realized this and sought to have the words "German national" left out of Miquel's statement, arguing that "only Prussian state feeling is to be demanded." He also wanted such aggressively nationalist organizations as the *Ostmarkenverein* excluded from the list which officials ought to join. But he failed to get his way here; Miquel's original wording was retained and Prussian officials were now to be servants of both Prussian-state and German-national ideals.[141] Subsequent guidelines ordered them to speak only German at home, keep their children out of Polish religious situations, and "in all election campaigns in which Polish and German nationality are opposed . . . profess (their) German sentiments frankly and unambiguously."[142]

Two other major new policies which emerged from the deliberations of 1896-7 called for the expenditures of large amounts of tax money: one for the direct subsidization of Germans in Polish areas, the other to concentrate state investments there in order quickly to raise the standard of material culture. The first of these programs took the form of a *Dispositionsfonds* (best translated in the vernacular as "slush fund") to be turned over to the *Oberpräsidenten* of Poznania, West Prussia, and Silesia (though neighboring areas of East Prussia, Pomerania, and even Westphalia also got a share). Its goal was to "carry through suitable measures for the encouragement and solidification of the German nationality" in the Polish provinces.[143] It began with 400 thousand Marks (350 thousand of which was new and the rest taken from similar programs which had not worked well in the past); half of this money was to go to German organizations (among which the *Ostmarkenverein* was specifically mentioned as a suitable conduit), the remainder directly to individuals.[144] The ministers were all in favor of this program and had no difficulty devising worthy recipients. Bosse advocated "special material advantages from state funds for native German clergy who work in the German interest at difficult posts in Poznania and West Prussia; also support and recognition to loyal Polish clerics in order to bind them."[145] He also urged special support for the Lutheran Church: "Whatever is done for the strengthening of the resistance of the Lutheran Church in the eastern border provinces serves the interest of the state."[146] Recke felt the same way about state support for German artisans, and businessmen and organizations (*e.g.*, the *Ostmarkenverein*) which supposedly contributed to German solidarity.[147] Miquel added his concern for German lawyers, doctors, and pharmacists. Posadowsky went even further, suggesting that the state "bring as many German people as possible into Poznania, e.g., doctors, pharmacists, artisans, lawyers, and diligent clergy, and support them if they cannot survive in the diaspora."[148] Altogether, the following categories were approved by the cabinet in July 1897:

—subsidies for Lutheran churches and clergy
—awards and fellowships for pro-German Catholic clergy
—subsidies for German professional persons, artisans, and merchants allegedly hurt by Polish boycotts
—German pre-schools, trade schools, and libraries
—bonuses for state officials
—construction of new schools to relieve congestion
—rewards for teachers who showed especially good results in the teaching of German
—stipends for Germans willing to learn Polish
—new health centers and sanitation facilities.[149]

The list of possible recipients was almost endless and before long there were far more worthy projects than funds. Bosse suggested a doubling of the Fund to 800 thousand Marks, but Miquel had to apply the financial brake.[150] But the brake was soon released again; by 1914 over 25 million Marks had been spent through this Fund, about 20% of this amount taking the form of bonuses for officials.[151]

The second new spending program went under the name *Hebungspolitik*, being an effort to "lift" Poznania and neighboring areas economically and culturally and make them sufficiently attractive so that Germans would want to stay or even immigrate there. Simultaneously, the Poles might be reminded that life in an advanced country like Germany had its advantages as well. In 1895 Wilamowitz painted the following picture of his home province:

> "Not only the economic but also the entire social conditions of this province appear to the rest of the state as very unpleasant. . . . Everywhere one encounters the most exaggerated notions of the unpleasantness and disadvantages to which the Germans are subject through living together with Poles, from whom the government supposedly provides no protection."[152]

He urged that "everthing possible must be done to raise economic conditions and neighborly peace." He was confident that, if times are good, "if it is a matter of competition in intelligence, perseverence, industriousness, and wealth, the German is far superior to the Pole." But if times are bad, "the Pole is in the advantage to a certain extent through his less demanding nature."[153] Bosse concurred, noting that the "building of the Bromberg Canal in 1773 and the Eastern Railway in 1853 have done more to strengthen the German nationality in the eastern marches than all the regulations and decrees."[154]

The city of Poznań was the recipient of many of the results of *Hebungspolitik*. The government launched a crash program to make this a more attractive and hygienic place and to make this center of the Prussian-Polish national movement a center for the display of the benefits of German material culture as well. When Poznań's Mayor Witting complained that his city's fortification ring was hindering development, Miquel and Posadowsky agreed to have it removed, with the state picking up most of the cost.[155] State funds were also poured into various cultural projects in order to "make life in Poznań agreeable."[156] This meant a sudden wealth of impressive new buildings which are still prominent in the Poznań of today: the university (then royal academy), "Kaiser-Wilhelm-Library," theater, museum, etc. Needless to say, in the granting of contracts to build these things, German artisans and businesses received preference.[157] Other state projects included the regulation of the Warta/Warthe River and the building of a port in Poznań.[158] Poznania also received special consideration in railroad construction and before long this lightly populated province had one of the densest track networks in Germany.[159] Posadowsky urged that similar efforts be undertaken in the smaller provincial towns as well, "in order to make life agreeable for educated Germans who still have no *Heimatgefühl* (feeling of belonging there). . . . One ought not shy away from spending considerable funds for these purposes."[160]

Hebungspolitik reflected a new realization that by 1900 the focus of the nationality struggle had shifted from the land and settlement projects to the cities and small towns. Posadowsky stressed that "the main difficulty of the Polish question today lies in the conditions in the towns, where the quite intransigent Polish middle class has taken over political leadership and trade and industry. Many partially German towns face the danger of complete Polonization."[161] Germans managed to hold their own in Poznania's overall population after 1900 (about 38%), but the Poles continued to grow more rapidly in the towns, in spite of the *Dispositionsfonds* and *Hebungspolitik*. The German share of Poznania's urban population fell from 55% in 1895 to 51% in 1910.[162] And much of the German figure consisted of civilian and military employees of the state; about 15% of the Germans in Poznania lived off government.[163] One is tempted to conclude, considering the impact of the Settlement

Law of 1886 and *Hebungspolitik* in 1898, that as soon as the government decided that a problem needed its help, things began to go downhill for the German cause.

In any case, by 1898 the state government under Hohenlohe was clearly committed to a slightly modernized version of Bismarck's later policy toward the Poles. It had by no means resolved the contradictions and problems inherent in that policy, however. It was not willing to break completely with the supra-national Prussian tradition and declare forthrightly its Germanizing intent. Indeed, despite many appearances to the contrary, it may not in fact have had such a conscious goal. But to Prussian Poles its policy could only appear as a concerted, quasi-legal attack on their nationality, demanding from them the most strenuous resistance short of outright rebellion. For the government the theory-practice dichotomy led to a hesitant, incoherent, annoyingly but ineffectively repressive policy against the Poles. The Poles responded with a much more single-minded (and thus more effective) course of thought and action, away from loyalism and toward what came to be known as "National Democracy."

Notes

1. Memorandum, January 12, 1897, *PA Bonn*, Preussen 4.
2. Speech of May 2, 1897, *Herrenhaus*.
3. Hutten-Czapski, pp. 318f.
4. Speech of March 29, 1898, *Reichstag*.
5. Speech of March 23, 1898, *Ibid.*; Martin Schmidt, *Graf Posadowsky*, diss. Halle (Halle, 1935), pp. 1-8.
6. Speech of April 28, 1897, *Abgeordnetenhaus*.
7. Memorandum, January 12, 1897, *PA Bonn*, Preussen 4.
8. Posadowsky speech, March 23, 1898, *Reichstag*.
9. Speech of January 20, 1898, *Abgeordnetenhaus*.
10. Speech of February 27, 1896, *Ibid.*
11. Speech of March 28, 1898, *Reichstag*.
12. Speech of February 5, 1897, *Ibid.*
13. Speech of January 20, 1898, *Abgeordnetenhaus*.
14. Speech of March 23, 1898, *Reichstag*.
15. Speech of February 27, 1896, *Abgeordnetenhaus*.
16. Speech of March 29, 1898, *Reichstag*.
17. Speech of February 27, 1896, *Abgeordnetenhaus*.
18. *Orędownik*, March 1, 1896.
19. *Politische Reden*, XL:274ff.
20. Kaminski, p. 21; *Deutsche Ostmark*, p. 43.

21. Richard Tims, *Germanizing Prussian Poland*, 2nd edit. (New York, 1966), pp. 47, 58.
22. Adam Galos, Felix-Heinrich Gentzen, & Witold Jakóbczyk, *Die Hakatisten* (East Berlin, 1966), pp. 34ff, 44.
23. Speech of Feburuary 16, 1895, *Abgeordnetenhaus*.
24. *Dziennik Poznański*, January 8, 1895.
25. Tims, p. 44; Korth, p. 55.
26. Summary of reports from Bromberg Regency, *GPSA Berlin*, Rep. B:30, #679.
27. Report from Poznań, November 30, 1895, *Ibid.*, Rep. 84a, #5965.
28. Memorandum, November 28, 1895, *PA Bonn*, Preussen 4; One example of this, a Zabern-like incident, occurred in 1896: a drunken German official and *Ostmarkenverein* member accosted a crowd of Poles waiting peacefully to greet Archbishop Stablewski and began berating them. A skirmish resulted, a half-dozen Poles were arrested, but they were then acquitted by an all-German jury which blamed the incident on the official. Cf. editor's summary,November 1896, *PA Bonn*, Preussen 4:2.
29. Speeches of February 15-6, 1895, *Abgeordnetenhaus*.
30. Wegener, p. 202; *Wielkopolska*, p. xviii; *Hakatisten*, p. 77.
31. Tims, p. 45; Wegener, p. 202.
32. Schieder, p. 35.
33. Hutten-Czapski, p. 318.
34. Broszat, p. 121.
35. Korth, p. 56.
36. Memorandum of January 6, 1897, *PA Bonn*, Preussen 4.
37. Wilamowitz to Köller, November 23, 1895, *Ibid.*
38. Recke memorandum of October 2, 1896, *Ibid.*
39. Wilamowitz memorandum, November 23, 1895, *Ibid.*
40. *Ibid.*
41. Speech of March 12, 1895, *Abgeordnetenhaus*.
42. Hans Delbrück, *Die Polenfrage* (Berlin, 1894), pp. 6ff.
43. *Ibid.*, p. 26.
44. *Ibid.*, pp. 33ff.; Max Weber read the same results but came to another conclusion; in his 1895 *Antrittsrede* at Freiburg Univ., he urged the state not to give up but to try harder, buying up even more land and closing the eastern frontier. Cf. Max Weber, "Der Nationalstaat und die Volkswirtschaftspolitik," in *Gesammelte Politische Schriften*, 3rd edit., ed. J. Winckelmann (Tübingen, 1971), p. 10.
45. Speech to Poznanian Germans, September 16, 1894, *Politische Reden*, XI:274ff.
46. Speech to Germans from West Prussia, September 23, 1894, *Ibid.*, pp. 291ff.
47. *Deutsche Kulturarbeit*, p. 24; Erich Zechlin, "Die Polenfrage in Preussen einschliesslich der Tätigkeit der Ansiedlungskommission," *Ostland* 1(1912): appendix; Laubert, p. 132.
48. Memorandum of November 30, 1896, *PA Bonn*, Preussen 4.

49. Memorandum of June 26, 1894, *GPSA Berlin*, Rep. 84a, #4090.
50. Memorandum of November 30, 1896, *PA Bonn*, Preussen 4.
51. Memorandum of November 23, 1895, *Ibid.*
52. Memorandum of December 29, 1986, *Ibid.*
53. Council of Ministers meeting, July 22, 1897, *Ibid.*
54. Hammerstein to Wilamowitz, May 4, 1895, *AP Poznań* XVI C, 40-1; General Commission to Wilamowitz, January 2 and November 7, 1895, *PA Bonn*, Preussen 4.
55. Speech of March 16, 1896, *Abgeordnetenhaus*.
56. Hammerstein memorandum of December 11, 1896, *PA Bonn*, Preussen 4; Szembek, p. 237; *Orędownik*, October 15, 1897.
57. Höhn/Seydel, p. 108.
58. Council of Ministers meeting, June 29, 1894, *GPSA Berlin*, Rep. 84a, #4090.
59. *Ibid.*, February 1, 1896.
60. memorandum of December 29, 1896, *PA Bonn*, Preussen 4.
61. Memorandum of February 6, 1897, *Ibid.*
62. Council of Ministers meeting, July 22, 1897; Settlement Commission memorandum, December 28, 1896, *Ibid.*
63. Memorandum of February 6, 1897, *Ibid.*
64. Speech of December 15, 1897, *Reichstag.*
65. Szembek, p. 306.
66. Memorandum of February 6, 1897, *PA Bonn*, Preussen 4.
67. Council of Ministers meeting, July 22, 1897, *Ibid.*
68. *Ibid.*, June 13, 1900.
69. Comments by Sachs, *Ibid.*, February 2, 1898.
70. By 1896 about 6000 Germans had been settled at a cost of 70 million Marks according to Mizerski, March 27, 1897, *Abgeordnetenhaus.*
71. Memorandum of December 11, 1896, *PA Bonn*, Preussen 4.
72. Memorandum of December 29, 1896, *Ibid.*
73. Gossler memorandum of December 5, 1896; Crown Council meeting, October 14, 1897, *Ibid.*
74. Council of Ministers meetings, July 22, 1897, and February 2, 1898, *Ibid.*
75. *Ibid.*
76. *Ibid.*
77. *Ibid.*
78. Memorandum of February 6, 1897, *Ibid.*
79. Memorandum of November 23, 1895, *Ibid.*
80. Comments by Sachs, Council of Ministers meeting, February 2, 1898, *Ibid.*
81. *Ibid.*, July 22, 1897.
82. *Ibid.*
83. Hohenlohe memorandum, January 21, 1897; Recke order, March 10, 1898, *Ibid.*
84. Council of Ministers meeting, December 10, 1897, *Ibid.*

85. *Ibid.*, June 13 and October 9, 1900.
86. *Ibid.*
87. Enno Meyer, "Die Polen im preussischen Staat von 1815 bis 1914," in *Deutschland und Polen*, ed. H. Fechner (Würzburg, 1964), p. 67.
88. Borowski, pp. 273ff.
89. Karl-Rolf Schultz-Klinken, "Preussische und deutsche Ostsiedlungspolitik von 1886 bis 1945," *Zeitschrift für Agrargeschichte und Agrarsoziologie* 21(1973):203.
90. Laubert, p. 134.
91. Jakóbczyk, *Studia*, III:8; Meyer, p. 67; *Polen und Deutschland*, ed. Göttinger Arbeitskreis (Göttingen, 1949), p. 36.
92. Jakóbczyk, *Studia*, III:8; Schultz-Klinken, p. 203; Bernhard, p. 569.
93. Bosse memorandum of December 10, 1894, *GPSA Berlin*, Rep. B 30:II, #2882.
94. Council of Ministers meetings, October 5 and November 6, 1896, *PA Bonn*, Preussen 4.
95. Memorandum of January 12, 1897, *Ibid.*
96. Speech of February 22, 1895, *Abgeordnetenhaus*.
97. *Dziennik Poznański*, September 29, 1895.
98. Memorandum of November 23, 1895, *PA Bonn*, Preussen 4.
99. Crown Council meeting, October 7, 1896, cited by Korth, p. 56; speech of January 29, 1897, *Abgeordnetenhaus*.
100. Memorandum of November 23, 1895, *PA Bonn*, Preussen 4.
101. *Ibid.*
102. Jakóbczyk, *Studia*, III:12.
103. Memorandum of November 23, 1895, *PA Bonn*, Preussen 4.
104. Memorandum of January 12, 1897, *Ibid.*
105. *Ibid.*
106. *Ibid.*; Council of Ministers meeting, July 22, 1897, *Ibid.*
107. Memorandum of November 23, 1895, *Ibid.*
108. *Ibid.*; cf. "Die Ueberwachung polnischer Versammlungen," *GPSA Berlin*, Rep. B 30:I, #698.
109. *Ibid.*; Hans-Jürgen Wichardt, "Die Polenpolitik Preussens und die Vereins- u. Versammlungs-Freiheit in der Rechtsprechung des Kgl. Preussischen Oberverwaltungsgerichts." *Zeitschrift für Ostforschung* 27 (1978):70.
110. Memorandum of January 23, 1897, *PA Bonn*, Preussen 4.
111. Speech of January 29, 1897, *Abgeordnetenhaus*.
112. Speech of March 29, 1897, *Reichstag*.
113. Report from Poznań, December 4, 1897; *GPSA Berlin*, Rep. 84a, #5964; Broszat, p. 125; editor's comment, August 1897, *PA Bonn*, Preussen 4.
114. Speech by Rzepnikowski, February 21, 1895, *Abgeordnetenhaus*.
115. Speech by Czarliński, December 15, 1895, *Reichstag*.
116. Speech by Motty, January 20, 1897, *Abgeordnetenhaus*.
117. *Kuryer Poznański*, November 12, 1896.
118. Decree of August 2, 1899, *PA Bonn*, Preussen 4.

119. Speech by Krzymiński, March 29, 1897; Guttzeit, pp. 247ff.
120. Council of Ministers meetings, June 23, 1897, and July 2, 1898, *PA Bonn*, Preussen 4.
121. Memorandum of November 23, 1895, *Ibid.*
122. *Ibid.*
123. Wilamowitz report of September 8, 1897, *GPSA Berlin*, Rep. B 30:II, #2471.
124. Council of Ministers meeting, June 10, 1896, *PA Bonn*, Preussen 4.
125. Bosse to Gossler, October 10, 1896, *Ibid.*
126. Speech of April 28, 1897, *Abgeordnetenhaus*; male orders were already banned from Polish areas.
127. Wilamowitz memorandum of November 23, 1895, *PA Bonn*, Preussen 4.
128. Waldemar Mitscherlich, "Irrtümer über das wirtschaftliche Vordringen der Polen," *Jahrbuch für Gesetzgebung, Verwaltung und Volkwirtschafts im Deutschen Reich* 35,4(1911):56.
129. Wittenberg to Stablewski, November 1, 1893, *GPSA Berlin*, Rep. 84a, #4090.
130. Hammerstein memorandum of April 5, 1899; Council of Ministers meeting, April 8, 1899, *PA Bonn*, Preussen 4.
131. *Orędownik*, January 5, 1896.
132. Memorandum of November 23, 1895, *PA Bonn*, Preussen 4.
133. Memorandum of January 6, 1897, *Ibid.*
134. Council of Ministers meeting, October 12, 1896, and February 9, 1897; Recke memorandum of January 23, 1897; Thielen memorandum of December 31, 1896, *Ibid.*
135. Gossler memorandum of December 5, 1896, *Ibid.*
136. Council of Ministers meeting, July 22, 1897, *Ibid.*
137. Memorandum of November 23, 1895, *Ibid.*
138. Hohenlohe memorandum of January 6, 1897; Council of Ministers meeting, July 22, 1897, *Ibid.*
139. Recke memorandum of January 23, 1897, *Ibid.*
140. Memorandum of March 14, 1898, *Ibid.*
141. Council of Ministers meetings, March 12 and 19, 1898; *Ibid.* Korth, p. 55.
142. Report from Danzig, October 5, 1898, *GPSA Berlin*, Rep. B 30:II, #2876.
143. Council of Ministers meeting, July 4, 1898, *PA Bonn*, Preussen 4.
144. Council of Ministers meetings, July 22 and September 16, 1897; Crown Council meeting, October 14, 1897, *Ibid.*
145. Memorandum of January 12, 1897, *Ibid.*
146. *Ibid.*
147. Memorandum of January 23, 1897, *Ibid.*
148. Council of Ministers meeting, July 22, 1897, *Ibid.*
149. *Ibid.*; Wilamowitz to Tiedemann, March 23, 1898, *GPSA Berlin*, Rep. B 30, #860; Bosse memorandum of July 4, 1898, *PA Bonn*, Preussen 4.
150. Council of Ministers meetings, November 28 and December 5, 1898, *Ibid.*
151. Lech Trzeciakowski, *Walka o Polskość miast Poznańskiego na przełomie*

XIX i XX wieku (Poznań, 1964), p. 49; Grześ, p. 269; Guttzeit, p. 104.
  152. Memorandum of November 23, 1895, *PA Bonn,* Preussen 4.
  153. *Ibid.*
  154. Memorandum of January 12, 1897, *Ibid.*
  155. Council of Ministers meetings, February 2, 1898, and June 13, August 27, and October 9, 1900. *Ibid.*
  156. Council of Ministers meeting, March 19, 1898, *Ibid.*
  157. *Ibid.,* June 13, 1900.
  158. *Ibid.*
  159. *Wielkopolska,* p. xix.
  160. Council of Ministers meeting, June 13, 1900, *PA Bonn, Preussen 4.*
  161. *Ibid.,* July 22, 1897.
  162. Laubert, pp. 123f.; Perdelwitz, p. 92; Trzeciakowski, *Walka,* p. 217.
  163. Broszat, p. 129.

Chapter VIII:
The Triumph of Nationalist Enmity

Prussian Poles were sufficiently disillusioned with the "Era of Reconciliation" by October 1894 so that they greeted the news of Caprivi's dismissal with equanimity. They acknowledged Caprivi's good intentions; *Dziennik* conceded that, "as for relations here, the administration of Count Caprivi has left behind a nice memory."[1] When Caprivi died in 1899, this same newspaper eulogized him as "a national politician, like all of his opponents, only he was a better one, for he had a noble conception of his national position." It recalled "the last Christian politician of the most recent period" as a man of "somewhat more humane views of our conditions and needs and of personal courtesy also."[2] In the immediate wake of his dismissal, however, it seemed clear that rougher times were on the horizon. *Dziennik* declared that henceforth Poles would fulfill their obligations to the state only to the extent that it gave them equality and protection for their "national rights," including those rights stemming from "international treaties."[3]

The prevailing tone of Polish editorials and parliamentary speeches became increasingly belligerent after 1894. Czarliński's 1895 remarks were typical of the new attitude: "We are no longer willing to keep holding our heads down quietly so that you can conveniently beat around on them when you feel like it. . . . I have seen a lot of Pole-eaters already . . . but I have not yet seen a single one who had also digested even one Pole."[4] Most Poles boycotted opening ceremonies at the Poznań Fair in 1895 when their language was excluded from use. When the one-hundredth anniversary of the final partition of Poland rolled around, *Orędownik* entitled its thoughts on the subject, "100 Years of Servitude and Misfortune."[5] Jażdżewski concluded that "the incitement in the national area has recently become so great and crude that peaceful coexistence between members of the two nationalities is almost impossible."[6] After a particularly hostile speech by Bosse in 1896, *Dziennik* publicly abandoned "the illusion that we will ever be able to move our German fellow-citizens or the government. . . . Resurrection will take place only out of your own strength, out of yourselves."[7]

During the following years *Dziennik* itself became more moderate, probably the result of a clerical-conservative editor (Lebiński) and Kościelski's appointment to its editorial board in 1896.[8] Its 1897 declaration that, "even in our dreams it does not occur to us to separate from this state"[9] did not seem to reflect the prevailing mood in Polish society after 1894. *Dziennik* gradually adopted *Kuryer's* clerical and loyalist positions and readership; and the latter paper ceased publication in 1905. Thus loyalism did not disappear entirely with the end of the Caprivi Era. Archbishop Stablewski still saw no alternative to a continuation of that policy. The Church-controlled press continued to publish panegyrics on the Emperor's birthday and in 1896 Stablewski ordered all church services to include a reference to the twenty-fifth anniversary of the founding of the German Empire.[10] He and Kościelski were among Polish leaders who emerged from a gala dinner given by Emperor Wilhelm in 1896 "exceedingly pleased by the grace of the ruling couple."[11] *Kuryer* continued to urge support for defense measures, e.g., the 1896 naval bill: "In politics as in one's private life, only he who fulfills all his own duties can make demands. . . . Our enemies want us to be pushed completely into rigid opposition."[12] Stablewski attempted (in vain) to win over nonloyalist priests, including Jażdżewski and Wawrzyniak, by arranging Papal distinctions for them.[13] The remaining loyalists continued to hope for a turn-around in German public opinion. *Kuryer* described the Reichstag's (inconsequential) disapproval of the Prussian Settlement Commission in 1896 as a "joyful and festive moment; . . . the German nation has damned the anti-Polish agitation; . . . (it) has not lost its feeling for right and justice."[14]

But as Hohenlohe's revised policies emerged in 1896-7, even these loyalist hold-outs began to concede the futility of their cause. *Kuryer* acknowledged that "Bismarckians" in the government had apparently won out over those sharing the views of Caprivi and Zedlitz.[15] Hutten-Czapski saw the triumph of a policy "undesirable for the whole Monarchy" and tried to reaffirm a quickly disappearing ideal: "The political foundation of our state is not the national principle but the state principle. We can have only one position: . . . the royal Prussian."[16] A more or less "official" declaration by the last of the Polish loyalists that they too considered the Era of Reconciliation gone for good came upon the heels of another hard-line speech by Bosse in February 1897. Komierowski alleged "a total passivity or even disregard for (Polish) rights on the part of the responsible state ministers," leading to "a condition of bitterness . . . (that) can hardly make allowance for any state interest."[17] *Kuryer* accepted the grounds for this declaration, expressing the hope that with the loyalism issue out of the way National Solidarity might be restored.

Poles ceased any longer to consider support for government defense bills. When the Landtag sought to pay tribute to the deceased Bismarck in 1899, the Polish fraction demonstratively walked out.[18] Only Stablewski refused to change his tune; he remained a loyalist, even amidst the additional provocations of the Bülow Era, until his death in 1906.

Hopes that the disappearance of loyalism as a major issue between Poles would bring the Populists and the *Koło* establishment together failed to materialize. The feud within the Polish camp continued little changed after 1894. An effort to rejoin the rival elections committees in Poznań in October 1894 drew some 1200 persons. Apparently most of them supported the Populists, for Knapowski was made chairman and simply gavelled through. Populist nominees and resolutions until the uproar from the other side caused the police to close the meeting. Populists claimed now to have inherited a legitimate, united city committee, but the *Koło* refused to recognize it and continued its support of the former committee headed by Kusztelan.[19] In Poznań municipal elections, which followed shortly thereafter, the Populists came in third behind the German Progressives and the *Koło*; the latter received more than three times as many votes as Szymański's movement. This was a considerable disappointment, especially since Poznań was the chief Populist stronghold.[20] Prior to the Landtag elections of December 1894, Populist opposition in the voter assemblies seemed weaker and they did not put up a candidate of their own.[21] A Populist convention in 1895 attracted only 300 members, mostly artisans, suggesting that without the issue of loyalism much of the interest in Szymański's movement was beginning to fade.[22] But Populist dissent did not cease, nor did it disappear as a separate movement.

Polish political attention seemed to shift from the parliamentary scene in Berlin back to the provinces after 1894. There was increased emphasis on local economic and cultural organizations in the wake of loyalism's failure. Symbolic of this shift in priorities was Wawrzyniak's resignation of his Landtag seat in order to concentrate on what he felt to be the more important work of his co-op organizations.[23] The economic struggle for land and for the development of the urban population came to be viewed as decisive by both the Poles and the Hohenlohe government. This may help explain why the make-up of the *Koło* delegations did not change as much as one might expect after the involvement of so many representatives in the failure of loyalism. Nobles continued to dominate the delegations, but what they did was now considered less important. They were less able to make policy on their own without regard for Polish public opinion. Leaders of the self-help organizations (*e.g.*, Wawrzyniak, Kusztelan, Żółtowski, and Jackowski) became just as visible and influential as the *Koło* members.[24]

Polish self-help organizations experienced continued rapid growth after 1894, especially with the renewed economic upswing in 1896. Taking the credit co-ops as representative:[25]

	co-ops	members	deposits
1895	93	32,282	16.8 million Mk.
1900	126	53,505	37.8 million Mk.
1910	265	125,108	204.6 million Mk.

In 1897 the main Prussian co-op bank (*Preussische Kasse*) agreed to open up a credit line to the Polish co-ops. There were some strings attached: it would deal only with individual organizations (not with the Union) and these individual co-ops had to admit Germans and use German as a second language. But the prospect of ample credit, which the burgeoning Polish middle classes could put to good use, was sufficiently lucrative to cause most Polish co-ops to accept these terms. This connection also strengthened the confidence of wealthier Poles in the reliability of the Polish co-ops and thus encouraged their deposits. After 1900, due most likely to political pressure, the *Preussische Kasse* began to cut back on the amount of credit it was willing to extend, but by then the Polish co-ops were able to get along without this help and soon established an equally good relationship with the (private) Berlin *Effektenbank* instead.[26]

Parcelling co-ops and parcelling banks, specializing in the creation of peasant homesteads through the subdivision of larger properties, constituted a newly prominent type of Polish self-help organization. Some of these were affiliates of the Land Bank, which continued to try wherever possible to keep estates intact, though it sometimes sold off parts of an estate in order to erase debts and save the rest. By 1905 it could claim to have kept some 25,000 ha. of Polish land from possibly falling into German hands. There were also smaller peasant parcelling co-ops, whose membership usually consisted of seasonal laborers hungry for a farm of their own. By 1910 there were 19 such organizations with deposits of 12 million Marks, which by then had handled some 30,000 ha. of land. Most active were the parcelling banks (*e.g.,* the *Bank Parcellacyjny* and the *Towarzystwo Włościan Parcellacyjny;*) parcelling was their sole business; they aimed for a quick turnover and colonized quickly.[27] Altogether, these Polish parcelling organizations outdistanced the Settlement Commission (see above, p. 191). They settled some 35,000 families on about 150,000 ha. of land while the state settled about 25,000 German families on about 124,000 ha.[28]

The other Polish organizations also continued their growth after 1894.

The Triumph of Nationalist Enmity

By 1911, 373 Polish peasant associations contained some 15,000 members, equivalent to 36% of the independent Polish farmers in Poznania. Related peasant organizations (producer or consumer co-ops of the "*Rolnik*" type) had an additional 6000 members. The Union of Industrial Societies (founded in 1895) had 2500 members in 40 branches by 1906.[29] An estimated 25% of the Poles in Poznania belonged to at least one such organization.[30] Much of the growth was in areas where the Polish national movement was less well established; 103 of the 127 organizations in West Prussia dated from after 1900 and the first permanent credit co-op in Upper Silesia dated only from 1895.[31] The development of the Polish urban and rural middle classes, partially reflected in the growth of these economic organizations, continued to affect the inner-Polish balance of political power and influence. They were increasingly confident of their ability to compete with Germans and to prosper even in the face of growing official hostility. They were correspondingly less interested in haggling for minor concessions in Berlin and their attitude toward the government hardened. Their self-reliance and assertiveness contrasted increasingly with the traditional attitudes and tactics of the Church and noble estate-owners.

The government was, of course, aware of the growth of the network of Polish economic organizations; this was a major concern during the 1896-7 deliberations on Polish policy. Some ministers proposed tighter state control over Polish co-ops by taking back their rights to audit their own records. Others sought ways to prevent them from consumating the financial connection with the *Preussische Kasse*. They charged that the non-political activities of Polish co-ops and their non-discrimination against Germans were only a façade, that they were in fact working with Polish parcelling agencies to frustrate the Settlement Law of 1886.[32] Bosse felt that "the *Preussische Kasse* must, in the state interest, make use of its authority to say 'no' to all undertakings whose goals are directed against the existing political order. That the Union Bank is such an organization, fighting against the aims of the state, can . . . scarcely be doubted."[33] Only Miquel spoke up for the Polish co-ops:

> "Definite assurance was given that Germans would be excluded neither principally nor factually from co-ops associated with the Union Bank; in fact a large number of these co-ops . . . include a not insignificant number of German members and association publications appear in German and Polish. . . . One must be careful not to resort to measures whose internal justification is questionable, which hit the Poles even where they are not proceeding aggressively against German nationality, and which can be interpreted with some justification as unwarranted economic discrimination against Polish subjects."[34]

Underlying Miquel's position was doubtless the liberal's dislike of state interference in co-op affairs generally. As long as the funds of the *Preussische Kasse* went only to those co-ops which admitted Germans and used their language, he saw no reason for state action. His position apparently carried the day, for the Council of Ministers resolved in June 1897 to do nothing about the relationship between the *Preussische Kasse* and the Polish co-ops as long as the latter remained non-political and nationally non-exclusive.[35]

Szymański and his Populists continued to be frustrated in their efforts to enlist these "bourgeois" organizations in their own political cause. Wawrzyniak ordered his credit co-ops to stay out of politics; Patron Jackowski and the peasant associations remained downright hostile. In the latter's opinion, "only in the peasant organizations is the true 'people's movement,'" in contrast to the "perverse striving" of Szymański's urbanites.[36] The Populists were also unable, in spite of the discrediting of loyalism, to improve their own position in Polish society and politics. This was due partially to the quick-footedness of many former loyalists, who quickly abandoned loyalism and returned to a more acceptable nationalist position. In addition, many anti-loyalists had no other reasons to sympathize with the middle-class Populist movement. Once loyalism ceased to be the issue, many previous opponents of the *Koło* returned to the fold. There was little change in *Koło* leadership as a result of loyalism's demise; essentially the same men (aside from Kościelski) remained in the election committees and the parliamentary delegations. The loyalist Radziwiłł became head of the *Koło* fraction in December 1894, but the prominent anti-loyalist Czarliński was made vice-chairman in an apparent unity gesture. The Populists remained outsiders, still limited more or less to the small (albeit rapidly growing) Polish urban population. Populism in Prussian Poland remained a movement of artisans and small merchants, with some peasants and workers and a few intellectuals maintaining a somewhat "platonic" relationship to it.[37] But among the Polish electorate as a whole they remained a small minority. Szymański conceded in 1898 that the "People's Party" remained limited pretty much to Poznań and its suburbs. "In the province there are a few centers which have a more or less extensive organization. In other places only the seeds of an organization appear, and there are many counties which . . . possess none at all."[38]

The Populist "program" (as pieced together from several programmatic statements of the 1895-8 period) remained less than comprehensive and tied to lower-middle-class interests. Populists urged recognition of the established facts of 1867 and 1871 but opposed those loyalists who were inclined "to pursue politics on their own in Berlin, behind the backs of the people." They approved of the shift of the focus of the national effort from Berlin to the economic battle in the provinces. They desired a "more effective defense of the national existence than previously," especially in areas where the *Koło* was inactive. Polish strategy should be based on the assumption that Prussia would not change her policies and that the national struggle would continue. They continued to demand that the middle classes be led into political life and sought to awaken in them the necessary consciousness and abilities to carry out more important citizenship duties. They demanded to see "representatives of all classes" in leading positions, with economic success counting as much as academic background when nominations were made for parliamentary seats. Szymański continued to question the nobility's fitness to lead: "One cannot count on the nobility any more; Poland exists only in the people and in the middle classes. . . . The people must protect itself from the downright demoralizing influence of the nobility . . . (which) constitutes a genuine danger for the further political development and education of the Polish people." The people, he felt, must lead themselves, "skillfully or unskillfully, in any case, however, independently." Populists also opposed economic liberalism and big business and urged protective legislation for artisans.[39]

The political program of the *Koło*, by contrast, could be summarized as a desire that Prussian Poles be given those rights enjoyed by Poles in Austrian Galicia. As *Dziennik* editorialized, "Who could take it badly, in view of the honest justice and consideration which the Galician Poles (living in quite similar political conditions) enjoy, if the Prussian Poles drew comparisons?"[40] Polish parliamentarians frequently cited evidence of Austrian satisfaction with their Polish subjects. Emperor Francis Joseph allegedly declared that his Poles "provided the proof that consideration for their national characteristics and respect for historical traditions will only strengthen the bond between the state and its constituent territories."[41] But as the Populists pointed out, Galician loyalists had not waited until their backs were against the wall, until the government was actively suppressing them, before offering to make a deal. They had won their concessions at a time when the Austrian government was shaken by military defeat. Galician loyalism was also very conservative; it depended upon a restricted franchise and found itself in trouble after 1906 when the Ukrainians of eastern Galicia received the vote.[42]

As suggested above, the Poznanian Populists were to some extent stymied after 1894; they seemed condemned to minority status for the foreseeable future. It took the appearance of a new movement, National Democracy, to produce a more substantial transformation of Prussian-Polish politics. To some extent, the historian's interest in the Poznanian

"People's Party" is determined by its role as precursor of the more prominent National Democratic movement. After a century of oscillation between loyalism and rebellion, or trying to assume various awkward positions between these poles, National Democracy arose during the post-1894 era and became the most influential political-ideological force in Poland by the time a new state appeared in 1918.

The history of Polish National Democracy dates from the 1880s. It emerged from the discontent of many younger educated Poles with loyalism and apolitical Positivism. A secret *Liga Polska* was established by five emigrés (led by Zygmunt Miłkowski) in Switzerland in 1887. It urged a radical-nationalist if not exactly insurrectionary stance and a resurrected, federalized Poland in the frontiers of 1772 (with some additions from ethnic Poland as well). It established a "national treasury" at Rapperswil, much of the interest from which was to go for the support of clandestine activities inside Poland. Its early impact was limited mainly to Russian Poland; attempts to get established in Galicia foundered on personal frictions and there was virtually no *Liga* activity in Prussian Poland. Its major organ inside Poland was *Głos*, established in Warsaw in 1886 under Jan Popławski and preaching a combination of nationalism, populism, and socialism. *Głos* demanded land reform, the subordination of noble-class to national interests, continued stress on education and Organic Work, and measures against capitalist exploitation. Its concept of Poland tended to be more ethnic-Piast than historical-Jagiellonian, considering Upper Silesia and access to the Baltic more vital than the Ukraine. Also associated with the *Liga* was "Zet," a student organization led by Zygmunt Balicki, which also tried to combine socialism and nationalism.[43]

In the 1890s, this movement was decisively affected by the rise of Roman Dmowski as its strongest personality inside Poland. He moved to take direction of the *Liga* from the emigrés and precipitated a split between the socialist and conservative-nationalist elements within the movement. When the organization changed its name in 1893 to *Liga Narodowa*, with Dmowski in charge, the result was essentially a new organization altogether. At first it retained a large socialist/populist element; it allied with the PPS (see below, p. 224) in joint demonstrations in 1894 but then the two groups grew apart. These 1894 demonstrations led to a crackdown by Russian authorities, with mass arrests and the closing of *Głos*. Dmowski and Popławski left Russian Poland for Lwów, which became the new headquarters. *Przegląd Wszechpolski* was acquired in 1895 as the new press organ.[44]

In 1897, the "National-Democratic Party" was launched in Russian Poland, essentially a front for the *Liga*, an attempt to appeal to those who preferred a party with a stated program rather than an underground conspiracy. The *Liga* itself remained small, its membership drawn mainly from the professional class. A coherent program developed only slowly; Balicki, head of the revived youth auxiliary, *Związek Młodzieży Polskiej*, continued to urge an opening to the left. Popławski was a romantic nationalist who scorned the lower-middle classes ("the least intelligent class in any society") and felt closest to Austria, though even Germany was preferable to Russia.[45] But the views of Dmowski gradually won out and dominated the National Democratic "platform" of 1897, which stressed the following points:

A. "National egoism," a phrase of Treitschke's via Balicki,[46] was the first element. This denoted an uncompromising struggle for Polish national interests without special regard for moral consistency or the interests of other nations. Altruism, humanitarianism, and international morality were illusions, according to Dmowski; National Democrats favored universal suffrage in Prussian Poland (because they benefited from it) but opposed it in Galicia (where Ukrainians would benefit at the expense of Poles). Dmowski made considerable display of his hard-nosed realism, embracing Machiavelli and Social Darwinism, expressing his admiration for British imperialism and Japanese military aggression, and urging Poles to stop denouncing Bismarck and start imitating him.[47] According to *Przegląd Wszechpolski*, "every state's policy, be it the Prussian, be it the Polish, is covetous in relation to other nations; it must strive constantly to conquer new territories or win back lost ones."[48]

B. National Democrats, like the Poznanian Populists, defined Poland more in ethnic than historical terms, favoring the Piast form of the Middle Ages (and today) to the large Jagiellonian state of the early-modern period with its eastward extension into Lithuanian/White Russian/Ukrainian regions. This meant a new emphasis on Polish-speaking regions which had not belonged to the Commonwealth (*e.g.*, Upper Silesia and Masuria) or had relatively "unawakened" Polish populations (*e.g.*, Kashubia and Ermland). Even areas without significant Polish populations but considered strategically desirable (*e.g.*, Danzig, Königsberg, and the bulk of Silesia) were coveted. The *Liga* also urged special efforts to organize for national purposes the hundreds of thousands of Poles living in Berlin or the Ruhr. This predominately bourgeois movement clearly preferred the relatively prosperous and developed Prussian areas (Poznania with its large population of self-reliant peasants and growing middle class, West Prussia with its access to the sea, and Upper Silesia with its industrial concentrations) to the backward, semi-feudal society of the old Polish East.

C. As a logical consequence of this concept of the Polish nation,

Dmowski viewed Germany rather than Russia as the major obstacle to Polish aspirations. Indeed, despite the contentious past, he urged a Polish alliance with Russia to save the advanced western areas from Germanization. There was also Austria, of course, but he considered her too weak to matter in the coming struggle between Germany and Russia.[49] Another reason for focusing on Germany was that Russia and Austria could do without their Polish possessions if necessary; Congress Poland and Galicia were peripheral to the main substance of those empires and did not contain significant numbers of Russians/Germans. Germany, argued Dmowski, had to take a hard line against the Poles, especially as they began to reach out for Upper Silesia, Danzig, and even East Prussia. Moreover, virtually all of Prussian Poland was ethnically mixed to some degree; in fact, the portion of Germany that Dmowski wanted for his Polish state contained more Germans than Poles. A German state would never willingly give these lands up; it would always seek instead to complete their Germanization. Dmowski tried to look at the Polish problem from the perspective of the Prussian government: "The Polish element in Prussia is now stronger in every respect than it was thirty or even fifty years ago.... Through concessions to Polish nationality it cannot secure for itself possession of its eastern provinces, for ... that would not delay the natural striving of our national policy, namely the unification of all formerly Polish territories."[50] The escalation of the national struggle after 1894 was logical for Dmowski; he expected this trend to continue. It was not a matter of any particular government or chancellor, but a basic geopolitical necessity: "One cannot give in to the illusion that German public opinion will protest against Prussian arbitrariness and lack of consideration.... We cannot reckon with a basic change in the political conditions of the German people.... We must conduct a life-and-death struggle, in which the stronger side is not choosy about the means used, not only with Prussia but also with all of Germany, not with individual parties but with the entire German society."[51] Thus he considered a harsh Prussian Polish policy to be required by German reason-of-state. If things were simply permitted to drift, the Poles would emerge victorious, if only for demographic reasons. "German policy is defensive, although it makes use of aggressive means.... We are happy to ascertain the defensive character of German policy, all the more since ... he who is on the defensive normally loses."[52]

National Democrats aimed at a broader cross-section of Polish society than did Szymański's Populists. Though predominately urban middle-class, their membership rolls contained significant numbers of younger nobles, clergy, peasants, and workers.[53] Their program resembled that of the Poznanian Populists in many respects, but it took a broader, longer-term, more geopolitical view of things. Both groups rejected loyalist-type initives aimed at an amelioration of Prussian Polish policies. Some Poznanian Populists (though notably not Szymański) came also to share Dmowski's view of the German-Russian problem; Kulerski's *Gazeta Grudziązka*, emerging as the Populist voice in West Prussia, admitted that "we warmly desire that it should come to an understanding between the Polish and the Russian nations," for the latter were fellow Slavs and better than the Germans.[54] Both movements opposed socialism; both were at least covertly, often openly, anti-Semitic. Dmowski resisted the economic and cultural influence of Jews in Poland and expressed fears of racial contamination. He wanted Jews to be isolated, boycotted, and ultimately pressured into emigration.[55] Both groups opposed the traditional political monopoly exercised by the nobility and clergy. They favored Organic Work to mobilize the masses, except that the National Democrats understood this to be more an educational and propaganda tool, a means to an end rather than the end itself. It did not, for example, imply the abandonment of revolutionary activity.

In spite of these similarities, National Democracy was slow to establish itself in Prussian Poland. When it did so, it did not build at first upon the Populist foundation. The beginnings of National Democracy in Prussian Poland are associated mainly with Bernard Chrzanowski, a Poznań lawyer who (together with Władysław Rabski and other young professionals) established the weekly *Przegląd Poznański* in 1894. This younger intelligentsia, which called itself "Young Poland" and modeled itself after the Young Czechs, was the core of the movement in Poznania.[56] Their program resembled Dmowski's views; it was anti-loyalist, positivistic, opposed to undue clerical influence, and convinced that Prussian Polish policies were popular with most Germans and unlikely to improve in the future: "Merciless struggle against the Polish element is an inflexible principle of Prussian policy."[57] They were persuaded that Germany sought ethnic homogeneity in her Polish provinces; neither Polish cooperation or Polish opposition in Berlin was likely to have much effect. The only appropriate stance for Prussian Poles was "wartime law internally, solidarity externally, military severity, and a flaming 'a tooth for a tooth.'"[58] They urged a policy of "struggle, not compromise, . . . (and) the creation of a political party based on the intelligentsia; our landed gentry . . . weakens each year; . . . one cannot, of course, trust the direction of our national concerns to the clergy; the Populist Party does not comprise in its program the interests of the whole society."[59]

Though this "Young Poland" group shared many positions and interests with Szymański's Populists (they did join to block the nomination of loyalists and to have *Koło* caucus meetings made public), they refused at first to form a real alliance. Essentially, Chrzanowski found the lower-middle-class Populists unsophisticated and narrow-minded. In his opinion, Szymański himself was "the only intelligent, thinking person in the Poznanian branch of the People's Party." He described the Populists on the whole as low-brow, demagogic, and tending to treat "each rebellious assembly, each symptom of partisanship," as a sign of "bourgeois maturity and independence."[60] Populists, on the other hand, preferred grass-roots efforts in the provinces and were distrustful of the nationalist phrase-mongering and grand pronouncements on world politics in which the intelligentsia indulged. They were also suspicious of the radical, semi-conspiratorial side of National Democracy.[61]

Przegląd Poznański was unable to survive as the organ of the Poznanian intelligentsia alone and had to cease publication after only a couple of years. Its supporters apparently began to realize the need for some sort of mass base, such as the Populists had developed in the larger towns, and began to change their attitude toward them. The Populists, an increasingly frustrated minority themselves, were also interested in finding new associates and the two groups moved closer together. While still attacking the class egotism of the Populists, Przegląd Poznański acknowledged also that "this movement has the future on its side; it will spread out over the entire Prussian partition from Upper Silesia to Ermland, and with its weight will push all of our coteries to the floor."[62] The "coteries" (defined as those prominent individuals, without program or organization, who were used to the blind allegiance of unsophisticated voters) were more clever, to be sure, and were still able to emerge victorious over Populist challengers most of the time, but it was only a matter of time until the latter prevailed, assuming that they found the right leadership.[63] Rabski suggested that the Young Poland intelligentsia and the Populists were actually two aspects of the same "democratic" movement, the former sophisticated but numerically small, the latter more numerous and pragmatic but lacking the proper organization and leadership.[64] By 1897 other members of this group credited the Poznanian Populists with having involved a broader cross-section of society in politics, weaning Poles away from loyalism, and had words of praise for Szymański personally.[65]

Shortly before the 1898 Reichstag elections, Chrzanowski published an open letter in Orędownik suggesting a merger. He expressed his sympathy with the Populists as against their Koło opponents:

> "I associate myself with them publicly. . . . The landed nobility, which has been on top until now, . . . is leaning toward its demise. (On the other hand,) the Polish peasant is purchasing land, . . . the worker and artisan . .

. are working their way up among the competitors of other races; . . . all feel a more and more lively love for their language and land and are gathering themselves together for the common defense. But they also want what they desire to be respected and for their opinions to find consideration. . . . Naturally these are people without discrete manners, raw in their appearance, but who would deny their warm Polish sentiments? Only such a broad, democratic movement, such as has enlivened the Czechs, . . . can protect us from destruction."

While conceding a natural inclination to prefer a fellow lawyer (Motty, the *Koło* candidate) over the Populist cobbler Andrzejewski, Chrzanowski announced that he would in fact support the latter.[66]

Buoyed by this new support from the intelligentsia, the Poznanian Populists resumed their attack on the *Koło* establishment. "Almost everywhere stand at the head (of institutions) untouchable big-shots, representatives of the clergy, of the nobility, or people who belong to their social class. . . . Everywhere we find nominally elected (in fact, however, life-long functioning) directors, supervisors, etc."[67] The conflict between Szymański and Archbishop Stablewski became especially sharp; the former asserted that the "ecclesiastical interests of the spiritual authorities and the national interests of Polish society as a whole diverge."[68] He spoke frequently of the danger of the Church becoming, at least inadvertently, a Germanizing agency as a result of Stablewski's continued loyalism. The Church, for its part, continued to rail against the Populists and to urge its members not to read the Populist press.[69]

An important new source of divisiveness within the Polish camp was the question of Polish relations with the different German parties. The *Koło*, with the blessings of the Church, continued to look primarily to the Center Party. But this relationship was no longer the same, due partially to frictions arising in Upper Silesia. Individual Poles were beginning to challenge the Center's previous political monopoly on the representation of Upper Silesian Catholics. The government drew frequent attention to Polish efforts here, blaming them on the purposeful extension of pan-Polish agitation from Poznania or Galicia.[70] Bosse warned in 1897 that

"the Polish question has long since ceased to constitute a local quandary peculiar to the province of Poznania. The Polish movement has not only increased in strength within its original seat, it is also expanding geographically into areas in which it was unknown until recently. There is already a Polish question in some counties of Pomerania, in Berlin, in the western provinces, not to speak of Silesia."[71]

Bosse saw the most dangerous aspect of the Polish problem to be its spread into strictly German areas; he was ready now to override agricultural interests and cut off the flow of seasonal workers from Russia and Galicia. He foresaw "a considerable and growing surplus Polish working population" and was content to keep it in the predominately Polish regions; the state would have to concentrate on saving the mixed areas and give up its efforts to Germanize overwhelmingly Polish districts.[72] Actually, Poznanian Poles were not especially involved or interested in Upper Silesia.[73] And, as Jażdżewski noted:

> "When one enslaves a people in every way intellectually, discriminates against and insults its holiest values—then one does not need to import agitation from outside, then agitation appears by itself among the people as a natural necessity, . . . and then the feelings of the population against such unworthy treatment and degradation justifiably mushroom. . . . If the royal state government does not finally open its eyes . . . to this strange monstrosity, . . . a mistaken and morbid method of government, . . . then may it bear the responsibility itself for the consequences of its misrule."[74]

In any case, Huene himself was successfully challenged by a Pole for the right to represent the Center in the Pless/Pszczyna-Rybnik district in 1895. A "Polish-Catholic" candidate (Szmula) ran against the Center's chosen candidate in Oppeln/Opole and won in 1898.[75] Neither of these Poles was associated with the *Koło*; they represented rather an effort by Upper Silesian Poles to gain a greater role for themselves within the Center Party framework. The first '*Koło*" candidate to win in Upper Silesia was the National Democrat Wojciech Korfanty in 1903; in that year the *Koło* also collected 47% of the vote in Pszczyna-Rybnik and 33% in Lubliniec/Lublinitz. The major breakthrough came in 1907, when it won five of Upper Silesia's twelve seats, though it fell back to four seats in 1912 in the face of the equally rapid growth (and bi-national appeal) of the German Social Democratic Party in the industrial districts.[76]

Meanwhile, the Center continued to support the Polish position on school, language, and Church questions.[77] Election pacts between the two parties also continued to function in districts like Lissa/Leszno-Fraustadt/Wschowa and Meseritz/Międzyrzecz-Bomst/Babimost, where neither party had much of a chance by itself, or in the Ruhr, where the Poles regularly voted Center.[78] But the Center's own ambivalent relationship to the Hohenlohe government and the evident growth of friction in Upper Silesia caused some Poles to wonder how close the relationship should be. The Populists and the intelligentsia argued that if one must ally with a German party, the Progressives were a more attractive choice. The Progressive Landtag representative from Poznań (Jaeckel) distinguished himself in Polish eyes at this time by condemning government Polish policies and blaming them for exacerbating relations between Germans and Poles in Poznania. "The entire harsh policy against the Poles seems to me to be in the interest of the Junkers and agrarians. . . . I feel sorry for those who can only prove their national feeling through disrespect for the human rights of the members of another nationality." He claimed to speak for more Poznanian Germans than did the *Ostmarkenverein:* "By far the greater part of the Germans stands behind me. . . . Germans from the bourgeois classes, . . . not Junkers, social climbers, etc."[79] It is difficult to determine the accuracy of this last point; certainly most of the other German representatives from Poznania belonged to the "Kartell" parties. But Jaeckel's position was reaffirmed at a meeting of the Progressive Party in Poznań and followed up editorially by the *Posener Zeitung.*[80]

Poles responded with pleasure to this voice from the "other Germany;" Jażdżewski urged his countrymen to "appreciate his manly performance and thank him for it."[81] Some suggested that, "where the danger appears that a Hakatist could be elected, Poles must vote in their national interest for a Centrist or Progressive in the first round already."[82] Both Szymański and Kulerski declared themselves ready to support a Progressive over a Polish conservative, if necessary.[83] At the least, Populists felt that this consideration was an argument for candidates who might reasonably attract Progressive support, (*e.g.,* Czarliński, who had won a Reichstag seat from Bromberg with Progressive help in 1893) rather than clericals and agrarians. But the Poznanian elections committee, allegedly fearing the adverse effect of such a policy on Polish morale and voter discipline, opposed any deal with the Progressives.[84] In West Prussia, the provincial committee did alter the traditional *Koło* policy of not putting up candidates in hopeless districts or where the Center candidate was likely to win; Kulerski urged a candidacy in every possible district, if only to keep track of the progress of the national movement, and had himself put up as a candidate in two eastern-Pomeranian districts.[85]

In spite of the disappointments of the Caprivi Era, there were also still some Poles who saw German agrarians and Conservatives as possible partners. According to Witold Skarżyński, "our alliance with the Catholic Center fraction in all matters concerning the Church is wholly natural and rational. . . . Our parliamentary cooperation with the German agrarian party, represented in the *Bund der Landwirte,* in almost all economic matters would be similarly rational and in the national interest."[86] Several Polish representatives continued to function mainly as spokesmen for agrarian interests, defending the large sugar-beet growers or resisting efforts to tax them more heavily.[87] But most Poles refused to work with the German agrarian movement because of its strong nationalist orientation. For example, the *Bund der Landwirte's Deutsche Tageszeitung* argued in 1895 that "one must wipe out and exterminate everything that is not German and is opposed to German nationality," causing *Dziennik* to conclude that "there is no room in the *Bund der Landwirte* for Polish farmers."[87]

There remained the Social Democrats, of course, who also generally supported Polish national grievances. An "Association of Polish Socialists" was established as a subdivision of the SPD in 1890, but with headquarters in Berlin rather than Poznania; its paper, *Gazeta Robotnicza*, was also published in the German capital. Polish socialists moved in 1893 to establish a separate "Polish Socialist Party in the Prussian Partition" (PPS) demanding Polish candidates for predominately Polish districts, but this organization too was viewed largely as an adjunct to the SPD.[88] But the SPD itself was not a factor in the Landtag, where most of the Polish issues rose, nor was it yet a major factor in Reichstag elections in Polish areas. Polish spokesmen often boasted of the apparent Polish immunity to socialism and were determined to keep things that way, ignoring offers of support by the SPD. Even in 1912, when the SPD received 35% of the vote nation-wide, it drew only 4% in Poznania and 12% in heavily industrial Upper Silesia.[89]

Aside from the question of Polish relations with various German parties, the major point of contention between Populists and the *Koło* organization remained the issue of middle-class participation in political leadership. At a meeting of the West Prussian elections committee (which merged with the Poznanian body in 1903 to create a single *Koło* organization for all of Germany), Kulerski echoed Szymański's long-standing complaint: "It is not proper that only nobles and priests . . . sit on the Committee. . . . Members of all classes, nobles, burgher, peasant, artisan, workers must be represented on it." He proposed that the current committee of six be expanded to permit this, but the current leaders, Czarliński and Wolszlegier (noble and priest respectively), refused to budge. According to the former, "there are among the lower classes men who are of course suited to campaign work in the county committees but do not possess sufficient wealth, time, and intelligence to take part in the meetings and debates of the central (provincial) Elections Committee." The Committee decided to stay at its current size but promised that, "at the next election, members of all classes would be voted in where possible."[90]

Populists were not much more successful in Poznania. Here too, they demanded that the Committee be expanded to include "members of all classes" and that parliamentary representatives be made more accountable to their constituents. Both proposals were rejected by Chairman Żółtowski as impractical or forming the basis for future conflict. Three openings on the seven-member board had to be filled; two of these went to nobles associated with the *Koło* establishment (Brzeski and Swiencicki) and the third to a noble physician (Chłapowski). The latter was at least acceptable to the Populists by virtue of his role in economic organizations and opposition to loyalism. Meanwhile, the Populist Grossman, a merchant from Inowrocław, missed election by only a few votes, which indicated to a government monitor that "the circle of supporters of the Populist idea obviously continues to expand." Two alternate positions went to the physician Krysiewicz and the estate-owner Skarżyński, associated with "Young Poland" and, while not Populists themselves, "well known to sympathize with the *Orędownik* group and able to accept its demagogic tone."[91]

The contest moved next to the level of the popular assemblies in early 1898. At an assembly called by the *Koło* in Poznań, at least half the audience consisted of Populists, among whom Chrzanowski and his friends were now included. The clergy, on the other hand, was entirely absent, the result perhaps of Stablewski's efforts to keep them out of politics. The major issue was the Poles' position on the upcoming German naval bill. Jażdżewski had already rejected the idea of Polish support for this measure: "The present incomprehensible posture of the Prussian government has brought about a bad mood, to put it mildly, which absolutely prevents" an affirmative vote even for defense bills. He reminded the government of its "extremely weak, faint-hearted" response to Polish loyalism under Caprivi and again condemned the "complete shortsightedness of the Prussian government, which supposedly wants to 'collect' (*sammeln*) but which scatters instead."[92] Other Polish delegates, however, were apparently at least weighing the possibility of voting for the bill in the hope of a concession or two. At the Poznań voters assembly, Dziembowski refused to rule out an affirmative vote, arguing that the issue was not so simple, that such assemblies could not understand the complex business of the Reichstag deputies. But a resolution in opposition to the naval bill passed virtually unanimously. Poznań's representative, Cegielski, also considering a vote for the bill, refused an invitation to appear before this assembly and, in the wake of this resolution, declined to be a candidate for reelection from Poznań. The leader of the Reichstag fraction, Radziwiłł, also refused to be bound by it.

Szymański responded to this apparent arrogance on the part of the *Koło* representatives by renewing his demand for fresh faces in its line-up. He urged that "at least half new people be brought in," not just members of the intelligentsia but those "who have not seen a university but who possess healthy Polish thinking."[94] In his opinion, most of the current candidates fell into three categories: "1., waistrels who ruin their inheritances day and night, 2., crafty card-players who spend day and night at the gambling tables, and 3., people who are seeking a new livelihood in the Landtag, after they have wasted someone else's fortune and do not know how to work for themselves." He railed especially against Cegielski and Dziembowski, "leaders of the compromise party," who were likely to continue in Kościelski's footsteps.[95] The *Koło* was unable to persuade Cegielski to reconsider and accept its nomination; he ran instead in a quieter rural district. After rejecting Chrzanowski because of his new closeness to the Populists, the organization announced its support of Mieczysław Motty for the Reichstag seat from Poznań. Motty was then chairman of the Landtag fraction, a lawyer, founder of a bank, organizer of an industrial association, and (according to *Dziennik*) was "never counted among the compromisers."[96] The unsuccessful Populist candidate was Andrzejewski, a wealthy tailor and Union Bank official who promised to ignore "high politics" and concentrate on the economic problems of the Polish masses. For Szymański, this outcome was just another indication of the *Koło*'s social exclusiveness, its rejection of successful bourgeois while supporting (in other districts) nobles who had sold their estates to the Settlement Commission.[97] The rejection of Chrzanowski only helped push the intelligentsia into a closer alliance with the Populists in the up-coming election.

Elsewhere in 1898, all the *Koło* incumbents were renominated. Dziembowski was renominated by the Provincial Committee despite being turned down by two of the three county committees in his district.[98] The West Prussian Provincial Committee also overruled county committees to nominate the priest Neubauer. Aside from the lawyer Motty and the physician Krzymiński, the successful *Koło* candidates remained exclusively noble or clerical. Once again, the complaints of the Populists and nationalist intelligentsia seemed to have little impact. Szymański did not hide his disappointment at seeing the same old faces, "patrons of the court or compromise party, . . . people who have been bad adventurers in a policy which has gone completely bankrupt." He refused to support Motty: "The People's Party cannot vote for Mr. Motty, because it would thereby give up its honor. . . . The nomination of the candidate Motty is a provocation of the People's Party to fight! Good, you want struggle, you will have it!"[99] Instead, the Populists again ran their own candidate Andrzejewski in Poznań; elsewhere, where there was not time to mount opposition candidacies, Populists were urged to boycott the election.

This time the two Polish candidates ran one-two in Poznań. A run-off was necessary but the result was still quite close: Motty received 8734 votes to 7999 for Andrzejewski, much of the latter's vote presumably coming from German Progressive voters.[100]

This close race in Poznań led to renewed efforts by the *Koło* to close the inner-Polish rift by means of a mass assembly. As their price, the Populists demanded parity on the city committee and the chairmanship of that body for Chłapowski. *Dziennik* rejected these demands as excessive and again castigated the "secessionists" for their narrow class selfishness and "spiritual decadence."[101] But at the assembly the Populists clearly had the upper hand; all of their proposals were accepted by a majority and all the "establishment" motions were defeated. Czarliński was picked to be the next Landtag candidate from Poznań; he, Chrzanowski, and Pluciński joined Chłapowski on the city committee. *Orędownik*'s trimphant headline read: "Defeat and Destruction of the Court Party in Poznań."[102] *Kuryer* described the outcome as "the abdication in favor of the Populists of all elements which have thus far stood at the head of society."[103] *Goniec* was also happy with this outcome and claimed that its followers among the intelligentsia had tipped the scales in favor of the Populists:

> "The healthy principles of the Populist movement . . . have been disdained in a way harmful to our public good. . . . The middle and popular classes, rejecting compromise and things foreign, . . . form everywhere . . . not only the predominant but also the most patriotic part of our society. . . . The victory of the People's Party is therefore a victory of the national idea."

This journal confessed that in the past it had often condemned the Populists as rowdy and divisive, but "today the transition era has reached its end. We possess now a genuinely popular, simultaneously however legal, authority."[104]

Actually, this was an illusion. It soon turned out that conservatives were unwilling to accept the verdict of October 5, 1898, and withheld their support from the new committee.[105] And the Landtag campaign which followed shortly saw little diminution of the struggle between the *Koło* and Populists, with the latter showing increased support outside Poznań. At the Poznań-East assembly, voters went for the Populist Szuman even after *Kuryer* declared (in Stablewski's name) that "no Pole or Catholic can vote for him."[106] Populists were also in control in Inowrocław: Grossman received a majority for the Landtag nomination. Once again the Provincial Committee refused to ratify this (backing other candidates instead), leading *Gazeta Toruńska* to denounce this "blind partisanship and uncompromising hatred of a handful of reactionaries against the representatives of the middle and lower classes."[107] Szymański saw the threat of "a new rupture of solidarity. . . . The People's Party ought to be convinced now that . . . one cannot work together with the nobility."[108] The list of *Koło* candidates for the Landtag remained as noble-dominated as that for the Reichstag and this remained the situation for some time to come as well.[109] But Szymański declined now to continue his secession any longer: "No party can make this into a permanent method of combat. . . . Secession has constituted an obstacle for many knowledgeable citizens, so that they remained aloof from the Populist movement and even shunned it."[110] Perhaps he was also frustrated by the tendency of the intelligentsia to step into the openings created as a result of Populist pressure. The Populists had been able to block loyalist nobles from parliamentary seats, but they lacked suitable candidates of their own to take these places. As Szymański complained, "the nobility is becoming impoverished too quickly and the other clases are developing politically too slowly."[111] As a result, the main beneficiaries were Chłapowski, Chrzanowski, Krzymiński, etc., not the Populists themselves.[112]

The Landtag elections of October 1898 went badly for the Poles; they lost 4 of their 17 seats in the Prussian lower house. The Populists blamed the *Koło*'s reactionary candidates for the first-time-ever loss of Gniezno-Witkowo; *Kuryer* blamed the failure to win the Poznań city seat on the Populist-dominated city elections committee.[113] Szymański indicated that the new joint committee in Poznań was merely a marriage of convenience, that the "discord between the followers of the People's Party and the partisans of compromise in Poznań is so big that it will not be ironed out by anything."[114] He moved still closer to the *Liga Narodowa* sympathizers until the Populist and National Democratic movements effectively merged.[115] (Beginning with Chrzanowski in 1898, most of the "Young Poland" intelligentsia now joined the *Liga* formally.) In 1901, the Populists supported Chrzanowski against the *Koło* candidate in his successful campaign for the Reichstag seat from Poznań, making him the first National Democrat in that body.[116] In 1903 the six-member executive committee of the People's Party included two National Democrats. National Democrats also added two more Reichstag seats this year, Kulerski in West Prussia and Korfanty in Upper Silesia.[117] In 1906 the Populists and Poznanian National Democrats effectively merged when they set up a joint publishing company, *Nowa Drukarnia Polska*, to issue both *Orędownik* and the new National Democratic organ, *Kuryer Poznański* (the earlier, Church-affiliated paper of the same name having ceased publication the previous year.) The National Democrat Marian Seyda functioned as editor of both papers, taking over *Orędownik* from the aged Szymański (who died in 1908). Henceforth this paper differed from *Kuryer* only in its specific appeal to the urban lower-middle classes; the two papers shared the same National Democratic program. A formal constitution of the "National-Democratic Association" in Prussian Poland followed in 1909; Chrzanowski was chairman of this organization but other leaders had Populist backgrounds. Its membership was about 40% artisan and merchant, 20% intelligentsia, and the rest farmers, workers, etc. By 1912, 7 of the 18 Polish Reichstag members were either members of or closely associated with National Democracy and, as is generally known, this movement absorbed the *Koło* itself and emerged as the largest party in post-World War I Poland.[118]

As the new century dawned, it was evident that the corner had been turned with respect to the survival of Polish nationality in Prussia. Its national movement and organization were increasingly "modern," based on broad popular support by an educated and nationally-conscious citizenry. Poznania, traditionally somewhat apolitical and conservative, became the most adamantly nationalistic part of Poland by 1900, no longer reflecting the view of a complacent nobility and passive peasantry but the values of a confident and growing urban population. The growth of the number of Polish newspapers from 9 in 1877 to 35 in 1898 is only one indication of both the higher educational level and the growing political awareness of Prussian Poles. The combined circulation of these papers equalled 10% of the entire Prussian-Polish population by 1900.[119] In fact, the advances in economic, social, and cultural areas made by Poles under Prussian rule threatened to alienate them from other Poles; the resulting discrepancy promised to create serious problems should Poland get together again. Far from creating any feeling of obligation to Prussia/Germany, however, these advances led rather to heightened national pride and hence dissatisfaction with the situation of Poles in Germany.

Miquel, following a visit to Poznania in 1900, bore witness to these developments in remarks to the Prussian cabinet. They are sufficiently interesting and revealing to cite at some length:

> "The development and preservation of the German nationality in the province must be viewed as seriously endangered. . . . The Poles are everywhere soaring and the Germans are not able to offer sufficient opposition to them. . . . (In western counties), the German peasants are virtually melting away and the small-peasant land is going over more and more into

Polish hands. . . . In the cities, . . . Polish artisans possess the upper hand; German artisans are gradually moving away. . . . A kind of war situation exists between Germans and Poles in Poznania."[120]

He returned to this subject a few months later with an even more pessimistic assessment:

"The Polish people has completely transformed itself internally and steadily developed its good intellectual and political characteristics (namely its patriotism) while removing its weaknesses, like the lack of a bourgeois ethos and a tendency to suppress the peasantry; in particular, a healthy middle class has been produced. We are confronted by a different Polish nation than before. . . . For the Germans it is a matter now of a struggle for life or death against this united and determined nation. . . . Our task must be to strengthen the German nationality so that through its prosperity and progress the Poles will be forced to abandon their expansion into Germany. The difficulty of this task is not to be underestimated, especially since we currently have to fight with rather inadequate material, given the inferior character of the Germans in the East, to whom the Poles are just as superior in economic frugality and self-sufficiency as through their enthusiastic agitation and willingness to sacrifice."[121]

Other Prussian ministers also described Prussian Poles (and thus the prospects of the German-Polish struggle) in terms that would have pleased any Polish nationalist. The new Culture Minister, Konrad von Studt, agreed that "the Poles generally distinguish themselves from the Germans through fertility, perseverance, their self-sufficient nature, and a willingness to make national sacrifices."[122] Justice Minister Schönstedt concluded that, after several decades of trying to teach Poles German, it was now time to teach Poznanian Germans some Polish "so that the Germans might become more competitive in many fields."[123]

There were still two ways for the government to proceed from this juncture. It could recognize the situation as it was and adapt to it, accepting the permanence of the Polish presence in several eastern provinces. This would entail serious efforts to win the allegiance of Prussian Poles before they become hopelessly alienated from the Prussian-German state-idea. Or they could stick to the current course and hope that additional, more extreme measures might turn things around finally or at least prevent further harm to the German position. In short, the latter course was adopted under Bülow after 1900. He, Studt, and the new Interior Minister Rheinbaben were even less well-disposed toward the Poles than their sufficiently nationalistic predecessors. In fact, Bülow's aggressively anti-Polish sentiments put the others quite in the shade. He had been among those in the Foreign Office contemplating a two-front war with Russia and France in the 1880s; whereas the others saw the advisability of trying to win the Poles over to Germany's side, Bülow saw such a conflict as the opportunity for Germany to rid herself of her Polish population altogether: "We should seize the opportunity afforded us by war to drive the Poles *en masse* from our Polish provinces."[124] His memoirs suggest the following context for dealing with the Polish problem:

> "Bellicose, economically clever peoples of superior culture will generally reach farther with the arm of their political power than with the rule of their national culture, thus acquiring the task of having the national conquest follow upon the political. . . . No consideration for Polish nationality can stop us from seeing to the preservation and strengthening of German nationality in the formerly Polish areas. . . . It is German duty and German right to maintain and, if possible, increase our national position in the Prussian East."[125]

As might be expected from such opinions, the level of national bitterness and conflict in the Prussian East reached new heights under Bülow. The "more drastic exceptional measures" which Posadowsky had forecast earlier (in the event of the failure of current policies) were introduced. They brought about a situation of almost constant conflict between Germans and Poles, along economic, cultural, social, as well as political lines. Another 150 million Marks were added to the Settlement Commission's budget in 1902, followed by 150 million more in 1908 and 100 million more in 1913.[126] In 1904 the government forbade its civil servants to belong to Polish self-help organizations. Also in this year it tried to halt Polish parcelling efforts by interfering with their right to build houses on lands they wished to subdivide, but this was partially circumvented by the courts.[127] The most serious new step taken by Bülow was the decision to end the teaching of religion in Polish, a step long debated but never before risked. This led first to a scandal of sorts in Września: pupils unwilling to recite their catechism in German were subjected to corporal punishment, leading in turn to violent clashes between their parents and the German teachers. This unrest culminated in 1906 in school "strikes" throughout Poznania as parents kept their children out of school for several months rather than have them taught religion in German.[128]

In 1908, Polish organizations were compelled to use German as their official language in counties which were at least 40% German. The Expropriation Law of that same year permitted the state to confiscate (with compensation) Polish estates. This law marked the nadir of German-

Polish relations prior to World War I and did severe damage to the German image abroad. In fact, it provoked so much negative publicity, inside and outside Germany, that it was scarcely implemented. Only four Polish estates, comprising 1650 ha. altogether, were acquired under this law, and these were bought (in 1912) at above-market prices.[129]

Thus the period after 1900 saw a continued downward trend in relations between the government and the Polish population of Prussia. Cabinet ministers gradually refrained from speaking during the recurring "Poland debates;" Poles boycotted discussions of such issues as the Settlement Commission rather than engage in further pointless argument. When ministers did speak, it was with greater hostility than ever before, without even Bismarck's pretense of concern for the Polish common people. Interior Minister Recke's tone is fairly representative: "I warn you, . . . pull yourselves back within those limits into which you have been directed. Otherwise you can easily discover to your disadvantage that it is dangerous to play with fire."[130]

Thus also, the Caprivi Era remained the last attempt by a German government, however faint-hearted, to win the allegiance of Prussian-Poles. It was also the last time that a significant portion of the Polish population indicated a willingness to accept the existing political situation and its own place in Germany. Instead of the government seizing the loyalist movement as an opportunity to come to terms with these Poles on terms that no reasonable German could gainsay, precisely these moderate Poles were undermined and discredited and their places gradually taken by intransigent nationalists. Even Kościelski, chief representative of loyalism under Caprivi, reappeared in 1905 as founder and head of *Straż* (The Guard), a reactionary, philo-Sarmatian, nationalist organization with a membership at its peak of some 16,000.[131] After 1900 the ideas of National Democracy moved steadily to the fore (somewhat paralleling the much less thorough spread of the ideas of the *Ostmarkenverein* among Poznanian Germans; in fact, some observers referred to the National Democrats as "Polish Hakatists"). The two nationalities associated themselves increasingly with mutually exclusive visions of Prussian Poland's future and the potential for a lasting reconciliation evaporated.

It remains an open question whether this development would have occurred amidst another policy by the Prussian government. The situation in Galicia certainly indicates that such enmity was not preordained by the dynamics of Polish nationalism itself. By any measure Prussian Polish policy after 1871 failed; it did not succeed in increasing the German presence in the Polish provinces, nor did it render those Germans already there less vulnerable to hostile Polish surroundings. Poles continued to grow in numbers and in the level of their national culture, meanwhile developing politically in precisely that direction that the government least wanted to see, but for which it bears much of the responsibility. Which only goes to prove the aptness of Metternich's axiom: "If one cannot kill an enemy, one should also not beat him with a belt."

Notes

1. *Dziennik Poznański*, October 27, 1894.
2. *Ibid.*, February 8, 1899; *Dziennik's* 50th anniversary work of 1907 contains this additional assessment: "One cannot hide a certain sympathy for Count Caprivi, for of all the statemen who have influenced our fortunes during recent years, he proved to be a just man, governed by noble opinions;" (Karwowski, p. 77).
3. *Ibid.*, January 28, 1894.
4. Speech of February 4, 1895, *Abgeordnetenhaus*.
5. *Orędownik*, October 24, 1895.
6. Speech of January 21, 1896, *Abgeordnetenhaus*.
7. *Dziennik Poznański*, March 19, 1896.
8. *Orędownik*, March 25, 1897. Kościelski himself was no longer quite so loyalist, however; he was quite pleased when Heinrich von Tiedemann described him publicly as "the most dangerous opponent of German nationality who has ever lived," (Berthold Wiegand, *Die Anti-deutsche Propaganda der Polen (1890-1914)*, Danzig, 1940, p. 8).
9. *Dziennik Poznański*, November 30, 1897; cf. Wiegand, p. 23.
10. *Kuryer Poznański*, January 22, 1896.
11. *Ibid.*, September 11, 1896.
12. *Ibid.*, March 17, 1896.
13. Wilamowitz to Bosse, April 7, 1896, in *Kirchenpolitik*, p. 161.
14. *Kuryer Poznałnski*, July 3, 1896.
15. *Ibid.*, November 7, 1896.
16. Speech of May 25, 1897, *Herrenhaus*.
17. Speech of February 5, 1897, *Reichstag*.
18. January 21, 1899, *Abgeordnetenhaus*.
19. Police report, October 27, 1894, *PA Bonn*, Preussen 4:2; *Dziennik Poznański*, November 8, 1894.
20. *Orędownik*, November 24, 1894.
21. *Ibid.*, December 6, 1894.
22. Editor's note, April 18, 1895, *PA Bonn*, Preussen 4:2.
23. Jakóbczyk, "Ks. Piotr Wawrzyniak," in *Wielkopolanie XIX wieku*, ed. W. Jakóbczyk, Poznań, 1959, II:365-381.
24. Bernhard (pp. 139, 218) defines the most prominent men in Poznania after 1894 as those who played a major role in the economic organizations alongside

their political positions; traditional notables, who remained aloof from the "economic struggle," found themselves with diminished influence.

25. Tomaszewski, P. 31; Bernhard, p. 416; Wegener, pp. 175ff.
26. Bernhard, pp. 237ff., 273ff.; Wegener, pp. 177f.; *Wielkopolska*, p. xxvii.
27. Szembek, pp. 287ff., 297; Bernhard, p. 522; Tomaszewski, p. 21.
28. Jakóbczyk, *Studia*, III:14.
29. *Ibid.*, II:94f.
30. Kulczycki, p. 31.
31. Tomaszewski, p. 25; Oppen, p. 200.
32. Hammerstein memorandum, December 11, 1896, *PA Bonn*, Preussen 4; Bernhard, pp. 229ff.
33. Memorandum of January 6, 1897, *PA Bonn*, Preussen 4.
34. Memorandum of November 30, 1896, *Ibid.*; according to Miquel, 75% of the Polish co-ops had at least one German member; 30% of them used both languages officially.
35. Council of Ministers meeting, June 21, 1897; Crown Council meeting, october 14, 1897, *Ibid.*
36. Jakóbczyk, *Jackowski*, p. 274; Bernhard, pp. 254f.
37. See the analysis by Isa Moszczeńska, written to explain Poznanian matters to the readers of *Kuryer Lwówski*: "Aside from the nobility and clergy, there is a not numerous urban intelligentsia in the Prussian region. It forms no party and is not formed under a common flag. . . . Partly it shoves itself under the wings of the nobility and clergy, partly it sympathizes rather platonically with the Populist movement." In her opinion, the Poznanian nobility was "intellectually fallen and retarded, economically ruined, greatly diminished by the Settlement Commission, (and discredited) by its loyalist policies. . . . The only healthy, vital element which is not derailed is the Poznanian people, also the safest in national terms; called to political life by the constitution of the German Empire, brought to (national) consciousness by the nobility, trained for struggle by the clergy in the *Kulturkampf.*" (*Orędownik*, July 22, 1897)
38. *Ibid.*, September 24, 1898; Jerzy Marczewski, *Narodowa Demokracja w Poznańskiem, 1900-1914*, Warsaw, 1967, p. 80.
39. *Orędownik*, May 21, 1895, June 7-9, 1895, March 9, 1897, September 24, 1898; *Postęp*, October 16, 1898; Report of a People's Party meeting, October 31, 1897, *PA Bonn*, Preussen 4:2.
40. *Dziennik Poznański*, October ;8, 1895;.
41. Speech by Motty, February 5, 1896, *Abgeordnetenhaus*; Prime Minister Taaffe was also quoted to the effect that "the Poles are today the only element in Austria which represents the demands of general policy and not those of a certain party or nationality (*Ibid.*, February 27, 1896).
42. Rose, pp. 55ff.
43. Wilhelm Feldman, *Geschichte der politischen Ideen in Polen seit dessen Teilungen (1795-1914)*, Munich, 1917, p. 326; see also Peter Brock, "Polish Nationalism," in *Nationalism in Eastern Europe*, ed. P. Sugar and I. Lederer, Seattle, 1969, pp. 310-372; Władsław Pobóg-Malinowski, *Narodowa Demokracja, 1887-1918*, Warsaw, 1933; Lorraine Toporowski, "The Origins of the National

Democratic Party, 1886-1903," Columbia diss., 1973.
44. Marczewski, pp. 89ff.; Toporowski, pp. 217ff., 256, 280; Feldman, p. 344; Henryk Wereszycki, *Historia polityczna Polski w dobie popowstaniowej, 1864-1918,* Warsaw, 1948, p. 147.
45. Marczewski, p. 92; Toporowski, pp. 261ff.; Rose. p. 75; Feldman, pp. 3444, 349; Wereszycki, p. 237.
46. Zygmunt Balicki, *Egoizm narodowy wobec etyki,* Lwów, 1902.
47. Rose, pp. 75, 81; Roman Dmowski, *Myśli nowoczesnego Polaka,* Lwów, 1902
48. January, 1899, cited in *PA Bonn,* Preussen 4:2.
49. Roman Dmowski, *La question polonaise,* Paris, 1909, p. 22; see also Kurt-Georg Hausmann, 'Dmowskis Stellung zu Deutschland vor dem 1. Weltkrieg," *Zeitschrift für Ostforschung* 13(1954): 56-91.
50. *Przegląd Wszechpolski,* January, 1899, cited in *PA Bonn,* Preussen 4:2; Dmowski, *Question,* p. 43.
51. *Ibid.* (PW)
52.*Ibid.*
53. *Wielkopolska,* p. xliii.
54. November 26, 1896; similar views expressed by *Gazeta Toruńska,* October 7, 1896.
55. Brock, p. 345; Rose, p. 74; *Wielkopolska,* p. xliii.
56. Jakóbczyk, "Chrzanowski," in *Wielkopolanie XIX wieku,* II:471; Wereszycki, p. 236; Marczewski, p. 84; Jakóbczyk, *Studia,* III:186.
57. *Przegląd Poznański,* February 16 and March 18, 1896.
58. *Ibid.,* April 5, 1896.
59. Piotr Stroma, *Program "Przeglądu Poznańskiego",* Poznań, 1896, in *Wielkopolska,* p. 232.
60. *Przegląd Poznański,* November 4, 1894, March 29, 1896.
61. Trzeciakowski, 'Szymański," pp. 358ff.
62. *Przegląd Poznański,* February 23, 1896.
63. *Ibid.,* March 1, 1896.
64. *Ibid.,* May 31, 1896.
65. "The editor of *Orędownik,* Dr. Szymański, is one of the most successful Polish publicists. One may not share the views of *Orędownik,* one may and must contend with them, but one can always learn a lot from them." (*Dziennik Berliński,* July 28, 1897; cf. Wereszycki, p. 237).
66. *Orędownik,*May 15, 1898;' Marczewski, p. 86.
67. *Orędownik,* July 22, 1897.
68. *Ibid.,* September 17, 1897.
69. *Ibid.,* March 1, 1896, September 29, 1898; editor's remark, October 13, 1897, *PA Bonn,* Preussen 4:2.
70. Recke memoranda, January 2, 1897 and February 2, 1897, *PA Bonn,* Preuseen 4; Laubert, p. 145.
71. Memorandum, January 12, 1897, *PA Bonn,* Preussen 4; by 1905 there were about 25,000 Poles in Greater Berlin and about 200,000 in the Ruhr district, cf. Christoph Klessmann, *Polnische Bergarbeiter im Ruhrgebiet, 1870-1945* (Göt-

tingen, 1978), p. 261; Laubert, p. 147.

72. Memorandum, December 29, 1896, Ibid.
73. See above, p. 123, and Motty's denial of complicity, January 9, 1897, Abgeordnetenhaus.
74. Speech of March 30, 1897, Reichstag.
75. Dziennik Poznański, October 29, 1895; Pabisz, pp. 213f.
76. Ibid.
77. Germania (January 16, 1897) warned Germans that they could not complain of the treatment of their co-nationals in Bohemia, Hungary, and Russia as long as they were treating Prussian Poles the same way, a point also made by Lieber in the Reichstag (December 16, 1897).
78. Gazeta Toruńska, July 14, 1895; Koło "delegates meeting," June 2, 1898, Poznań, PA Bonn, Preussen 4:2.
79. Speech of January 10, 1897, Abgeordnetenhaus.
80. Dziennik Poznański, March 13, 1897. In response, Recke exerted pressure upon the Posener Zeitung to halt its criticism of government Polish policies, finally halting all state advertising in it. (memorandum of January 28, 1899; Council of Ministers meeting, April 8, 1899, PA Bonn, Preussen 4). The sanctions were removed following a period of good behavior. (Council of Ministers meeting, January 13, 1900, Ibid),
81. Speech of January 31, 1897, Abgeordnetenhaus.
82. Poznanian provincial Elections Committee, November 29, 1897, affirmed by voters assembly in Poznań, January 12, 1898, PA Bonn, Preussen 4:2.
83. Orędownik, October 26, 1897; Gazeta Grudziązka, October 26, 1897.
84. See footnote 82.
85. Koło delegates meeting, Graudenz, June 2, 1898, Ibid.
86. From his "Nasza Sprawa," in Wielkopolska, p. 226.
87. Speech by Motty, January 23, 1895, Reichstag: Dziennik Poznański, October 29, 1895.
88. Hans-Ulrich Wehler, Sozialdemokratie und Nationalstaat, Würzburg, 1962, pp. 119ff.; Speech by Wurm, January 19, 1899, Reichstag.
89. Ibid., p. 155. During the 1890s, due in part to the growing influence of Rosa Luxemburg (a very anti-nationalist Polish socialist), the SPD became less willing to cater to Polish national sensitivities; its relationship with the Polish party was broken off once in 1901, renewed again after a five-year PPS effort at independence, and ended finally only in 1912. (Ibid., pp. 139, 155)
90. Meeting of November 7, 1897, PA Bonn, Preussen 4:2.
91. Poznanian provincial Elections Committee meeting, November 29, 1897, as reported by state official, PA Bonn, Preussen 4:2; Orędownik, November 26, 1897.
92. Speech of December 6, 1897, Reichstag.
93. Dziennik Poznański, January 21, 1898; Kuryer Poznański, February 1, 1898; eventually the Koło decided not to vote for the naval bill after all. (Orędownik, March 27, 1898.)
94. Orędownik, February 15, 1898.
95. Ibid., May 8, 1898.

The Triumph of Nationalist Enmity 237

96. *Dziennik Poznański*, April 9 and May 11, 1898.
97. *Orędownik*, May 8, 1898. *Kuryer*'s description of a Populist meeting certainly seemed to support Szymański's charge of class bias: "Polish people were not to be seen there; there were only elements from the middle and lower classes, . . . elements among which corruption most easily finds its way." (*Kuryer Poznański*, April 29, 1898)
98. *Orędownik*, June 4, 1898.
99. *Ibid.*
100. Trzeciakowski, "Szymański," p. 358.
101. *Dziennik Poznański*, September 28 and October 2, 1898.
102. *Orędownik*, October 6, 1898.
103. *Kuryer Poznański*, October 6, 1898.
104. *Goniec Wielkopolski*, October 7, 1898.
105. *Gazeta Toruńska*, October 5, 1898.
106. *Kuryer Poznański*, October 9, 1898.
107. October 12, 1898.
108. *Orędownik*, October 16, 1898.
109. Only in 1912 does one see a major change; only then did noble estate owners become a minority in the parliamentary delegations. By this time, Poznań was represented in the Reichstag by a union official; the Reichstag fraction also contained a factory worker, newspaper editor, 3 lawyers, 2 physicians, and 5 priests (alongside the 5 estate owners). But much of this apparent shift was due to the acquisition of 4 *Koło* seats in Upper Silesia, where a Polish nobility did not exist. (Zechlin, pp. 138, 151)
110. *Orędownik*, October 22, 1898.
111. *Ibid.*, October 27, 1898.
112. Editor's remark, October 31, 1898, *PA Bonn*, Preussen 4:2; report from Poznań, November 28, 1898, *GPSA Berlin*, Rep. 84a, #5965.
113. *Orędownik*, November 8, 1898; *Kuryer Poznański*, October 29, 1898.
114. *Orędownik*, November 1, 1898.
115. Wereszycki, p. 238; Marczewski, p. 106; Jakóbczyk, *Studia*, III: 186.
116. *Orędownik* in 1901, quoted in *Wielkopolska*, p. 233.
117. National Democratic deputies continued to function as members of the single *Koło* in Berlin; Jakóbczyk, *Studia*, III:187; Wereszycki, p. 238.
118. Jakóbczyk, *Studia*, III:187ff.; Wereszycki, p. 239; Zechlin, p. 151'.
119. Müller, p. 15; Kulczycki, p. 35.
120. Council of Ministers meeting, June 13, 1900, *PA Bonn*, Preussen 4.
121. *Ibid.*, October 9, 1900.
122. *Ibid.*, June 13, 1900.
123. *Ibid.*
124. When Bismarck came across this recommendation his response was hardly sympathetic: "Eccentric conjectures of this kind must not be set down on paper!" (Marginal comment on letter from Bülow to Holstein, December 10, 1887, in *The Holstein Papers*, ed. N. Rich and M. Fisher, Cambridge, 1961, III:237)
125. Bernhard von Bülow, *Deutsche Politik*, Berlin, 1916, pp. 255, 260, 278.

126. Jakóbczyk, *Studia*, III:8.
127. Bernhard, *Polenfrage*, p. 242; *Polenpolitik*, pp. 6ff.
128. Korth, pp. 82ff.; Laubert, p. 148; Perdelwitz, pp. 86ff.
129. Bernhard, *Polenpolitik*, p. 9; Laubert, p. 148; Perdelwitz, p. 94. By contrast, according to Bernhard some 155,000 ha. of German land was confiscated by the Polish state after 1918.
130. Speech of February 21, 1898, *Abgeordnetenhaus*.
131. Galos, "Kościelski," p. 421; Massow, p. 78; Bernhard, *Polenfrage*, p. 193. The Sarmatian tribe of the Alans was a ruling caste in the Slavic realm during the Roman Era; many Polish nobles claimed to trace their ancestry back to these Iranian nomads, which may also explain Bismarck's remark on several occasions that the Polish nobles and masses were even racially distinct.

Bibliography

A. Archival Sources

1. *Politisches Archiv des Auswärtigen Amtes* Bonn, Abt. A

   Europa Generalia 75: "Redakteur Miarka"
   Europa Generalia 79: "Die polnische Frage"
   Preussen 4: "Polnische Agitationen"
   Preussen 4:1: "Die Haltung der polnischen Klerus"
   Preussen 4:2: "Zusammenstellungen über die polnische Tagesliteratur
   Preussen 8:2: "Die Unterrichtssprache in den Schulen der Erzdiözese Posen"
   I.A.B.g (Polen) 14: "Die Stellung des Erzbischofs von Posen und Gnesen als Primas von Polen"
   I.A.B.g (Polen) 15: "Schriftwechsel mit den General-Consulaten zu Warschau"
   Russland 83:2: "Innere Zustände Polens"

2. *Geheimes Preussisches Staatsarchiv* Berlin-*Dahlem*

   Königlich Preussische Regierung Bromberg
   Rep. 830, #110: "Ausführung des Gesetzes vom 11. April 1887 über die Landgemeinde-Verfassung in den östlichen Provinzen der Monarchie"
   Rep. 830, #679: "Förderung des Deutschtums in den Ostmarken"
   Rep. 830, #680: "Die Verwendung des Dispositionsfonds"
   Rep. 830:I, #553: "Agitationen in Wahlangelegenheiten"
   Rep. 830:I, #583: "Die Statistik über Reichstagswahlen"
   Rep. 830:8, #589-90: "Die Wahlen für den deutschen Reichstag"
   Rep. 830:I, #656: "Immediat-Zeitungsberichte"
   Rep. 830:I, #658-9: "Mittheilungen aus polnischen Zeitungen"
   Rep. 830:I, #661: "Gesamtüberblicke über die polnische Tagesliteratur"
   Rep. 830:I, #690: "Die erneuerten Bestrebungen für die polnische Nationalität'
   Rep. 830:I, #694-7: "Die Agitation des Polenthums"
   Rep. 830:I, #698: "Die Ueberwachung polnischer Versammlungen"
   Rep. 830:II, #2471: "Die Thätigkeit der polnischen Agitation"
   Rep. 830:II, #2526: "Die Förderung des deutschen Schulwesens

insbesondere die Ertheilung des confessionellen Religionunterrichts in deutscher Sprache"
Rep. 830:II, #2857: "Die Förderung des deutschen Schulwesens"
Rep. 830:II, #2876: "Die deutsche Unterrichtssprache"
Rep. 830:II, #2882: "Die deutsche Sprachunterricht"
Justizministerium, Rep. 84a (formerly in Bundesarchiv *Koblenz*)
I. (Registratur-Verwaltung): "Die nationalpolnische Bewegung"
4066-7: "Gesetzgebung und Berwaltung in den Provinzen Posen, Westpreussen, und Oberschlesien"
4072: "Die Beförderung deutscher Ansiedlungen in den Provinzen Westpreussen und Posen"
4088-9: "Die Ansiedlungskommission"
4149: "Die nationalpolnische Bewegung"
5957-8: "Zeitungsberichte der Regierungen aus der Provinz Westpreussen"
5964-5: "Zeitungsberichte der Regierungen aus der Provinz Posen"

3. *Staatliches Archivlager Göttingen*

Königliches Oberpräsidium von Preussen, Rep. 2:II
1870: "Die Revision der Ansiedlungsgesetzgebung"
2852: "Die Behandlung der masurisch-polnischen Ueberläufer"
3152: "Die Revision der Volksschulen in Bezug auf den Unterricht in der deutschen Sprache"

4. *Archiwum Państwowe Miasta Poznania i Województwa Poznańskiego*

Oberpräsidium

XII A 4: "Die Theilung der Kreise in der Provinz Posen"
XII G 12: "Die Kreisteilung für die Provinz Posen"
SV A 51: "Die Organisation des 2. landschaftlichen Credit-Instituts"
XVI A 10a: "Die Beförderung des ländlichen Genossenschaftswesens"
XVI A 107: "Die Bewegung unter den Landwirthen bezw. die Entwicklung von Landwirtschaftskammern"
XVI A 3a: "Die Zerstückelung des ländlichen Grundeigentums"
XVI C 40-1: "Der Verkauf von Grundstücken als Rentengüter"
XXIV B 8 g: "Gesuche und Beschwerden in Angelegenheiten der evangelischen Kirche"
XXIV D I 30: "Die Wiederbesetzung des erzbischöflichen Stuhles in Gnesen und Posen"
XXIV D I 30: "Das Ableben des Erzbischofs Dinder"
XXIV D IIIa 59: "Die Rundschreiben und Hirtenbriefe der katholischen Bischöfe"
XXIV D IIIa 70/105: "Die Vorbildung und Anstellung der katholischen Geistlichen"
XXIV D IIIf 28: "Die Wiederbesetzung vakant gewordener Pfarrstellen"
Polizeipräsidium
4877: "Die polnische Tagespresse"

Bibliography

5. *Wojewódzkie Archiwum Pańtwowe w Bydgoszczy*

   Królewska Regierung

   I 879, 629, 1215: Ausweisungen
   4729: "Geistliche, Kirchen-, und Schuleangelegenheiten"

6. *Biblioteka Raczyńskich (Poznań)*

   784: "Akta polskiego centralnego Komitetu Wyborczego"
   854: "Akta prowincyonalnego Komitetu Wyborczego w W.K. Poznania"
   855-893: records of Poznanian county election committees

7. *Biblioteka Kórnicka PAN*

   1454-8: Protokoły posiedzeń Koła Polskiego w sejmie pruskim

B. Published Sources

Akten zur preussischen Kirchenpolitik in den Bistümern Genesen-Posen, Kulm, und Ermland, 1885-1914, ed. E. Gatz, Veröffentlichungen der Kommission für Zeitgeschichte, Reihe A, Band 21, Mainz: Grünewald, 1977, 283 pp.

Also Sprach Bismarck, ed. H. v. Poschinger, Vienna: Konegen, 1910, 4 vols.

Die Aussprachen des Fürsten Bismarck, 1848-1894, ed. H. v. Poschinger, 2nd edit., Stuttgart: Deutsche Verlags-Anstalt, 1895, 2 vols.

Bausteine zur Bismarck-Pyramide, ed. H. v. Poschinger, Berlin: Stilke, 1904, 236 pp.

Bismarck, Otto von, *Die gesammelten Werke*, 3rd edit., Berlin: Stolberg, 1924-32, 15 vols.

Bismarck-Jahrbuch, ed. H. Kohl, Berlin: Härling, 1894-.

Bismarck als Erzieher, ed. P. Dehn, Munich: Lehmann, 1903, 584 pp.

Bismarck über Zeitgenossen—Zeitgenossen über Bismarck, ed. H.-J. Schoeps, Frankfurt/Main: Ullstein, 1972, 418 pp.

Bismarck-Portefeuille, ed. H. v. Poschinger, Stuttgart: Deutsche Verlags-Anstalt, 1898, 2 vols.

Deutsche Parteiprogramme seit 1861, ed. W. Treue, Quellensammlung zur Kulturgeschichte, vol. 3, Göttingen: Musterschmidt, 4th edit., 1968.

Deutsch Ostmark, Aktenstücke und Beiträge zur Polenfrage, ed. Alldeutscher Verband, Berlin: Priber, 1894, 112 pp.

Fürst Bismarck nach seiner Entlassung, ed. J. Penzler, Leipzig: Walther Fiedler, 1897, 7 vols.

Fürst Bismarck und die Diplomaten, 1852-1890, ed. H. v. Poschinger, Hamburg: Richter, 1900, 460 pp.

Fürst Bismarck und die Parliamentarier, ed. H. v. Poschinger, 2nd edit., Breslau: Trewendt, 1894, 3 vols.

Die Grosse Politik der europäischen Kabinette, 1871-1914, Berlin: Deutsche Verlagsgesellschaft für Politik und Geschichte, 1922.

The Holstein Papers, ed. N. Rich & M. Fisher, Cambridge: University

Press, 1957-61, 4 vols.
Jugendgeschichte des Fürsten Bismarck (bis 1851), ed. J. Penzler, Berlin: Trewendt, 1907, 2 vols.
Miquel, Johannes von, *Reden*, ed. Schultze & Thimme, Halle: Waisenhaus, 1913, 4 vols.
MdR—Biographisches Handbuch der Reichstage, ed. M. Schwartz, Hanover: Verlag für Literatur und Zeitgeschehen, 1965, 832 pp.
(Bismarck) *Neue Tischgespräche und Interviews*, ed. H. v. Poschinger, 2nd edit., Leipzig: Deutsche Verlags-Anstalt, 1895, 2 vols.
Neues Bismarck-Jahrbuch, Vienna: Konegen, 1911-.
Die politischen Berichte des Fürsten Bismarck aus Petersburg und Paris (1859-62), ed. L. Raschdau, Berlin: Reimar Hobbing, 1920, 2 vols.
Politische Briefe Bismarcks aus den Jahren 1849-1889, 3rd edit., Berlin: Steinitz, 1889, 4 vols.
Polenspiegel, Umtriebe der Polen nach ihrer eigenen Presse, ed. Ostmarkenverein, Berlin: Puttkamer & Mühlbrecht, 1908, 340 pp.
Die politischen Reden des Fürsten Bismarck, ed. H. Kohl, Stuttgart: Cotta, 1892-5, 14 vols.
Graf Posadowsky als Finanz-, Sozial-, und Handelspolitiker, ed. H. Ehrenberg, Leipzig: Weber, 1911, 4 vols.
Poznańskie, Pomorze, Warmia, i Mazury w latach 1864-1914, ed. Jakóbczyk & Wiśniewski, Warsaw: Państwowe Zakłady Wydawnictw Szkolnych, 1960, 34 pp.
Preussen im Bundestag, ed. H. v. Poschinger, Leipzig: Heizel, 1882-4, 4 vols.
Statistik des Deutschen Reiches, Die Volkszählung im Deutschen Reich, vols. 150-1, Berlin: Puttkamer & Mühlbrecht, 1903.
Statistisches Jahrbuch für das Deutsche Reich, ed. Kaiserliches Statistisches Amt, Berlin: Puttkamer & Mühlbrecht, 1880-.
Stenographische Berichte über die Verhandlungen des Landtages, Haus der Abgeordneten, Berlin: W. Moeser, 1867-1900.
Stenographische Berichte über die Verhandlungen des Landtages, Herrenhaus, Berlin: Reichsdruckerei, 1867-1900.
Stenographische Berichte über die Verhandlu..gen des Reichstages, Berlin: Norddeutsche Buchdruckerei, 1867-1900.
Die Vorgeschichte des Kulturkampfes, ed. A. Constabel, East Berlin: Rütten & Loening, 1956, 366 pp.
Wielkopolska (1851-1914), Wybór źródeł, ed. W. Jakóbczyk, Wrocław: Zakład im. Ossolińskich, 1954, 332.
Wilhelm II, *Kaiserreden*, ed. O. Klaussmann, Leipzig: Weber, 1902, 437 pp.
Zwanzig Jahre deutscher Kulturarbeit, 1886-1906, ed. Haus der Abgeordneten, Berlin: W. Moeser, 1907, 308 pp.

C. Memoirs, Diaries, and Letters

Herbert von Bismarck. Aus seiner politischen Privatkorrespondenz, ed. W. Bussmann, Deutsche Geschichtsquellen des 19. und 20. Jahrhunderts, vol.

44, Göttingen: Vandenhoek & Ruprecht, 1964, 598 pp.

Bismarck, Otto von, *Gedanken und Erinnerungen*, Stuttgart: Cotta, 1898, 3 vols.

Bismarckbriefe, 1836-1873, ed. H. Kohl, 8th edit., Bielefeld/Leipzig: Velhagen & Klasing, 1900, 484 pp.

Bismarcks Briefe an den General Leopold von Gerlach, ed. H. Kohl, Berlin: Häring, 1896, 378 pp.

Bismarcks Briefwechsel mit dem Minister Freiherrn von Schleinitz, 1858-61, Stuttgart: Cotta, 1905, 186 pp.

Briefe Otto von Bismarcks an Schwester und Schwager, 1843-1897, ed. H. Kohl, Leipzig: Dieterich, 1915, 171 pp.

Booth, John, *Persönliche Erinnerungen an den Fürsten Bismarck*, Hamburg: Richter, 1899, 81 pp.

Brauer, Arthur von, *Im Dienste Bismarcks*, ed. H. Rogge, Berlin: Mittler & So., 1936, 438 pp.

Bülow, Bernhard von, *Deutsche Politik*, Berlin: Reimar Hobbing, 1916, 359 pp.

Busch, Moritz, *Tagebuchblätter*, Leipzig: Grunow, 1899, 3 vols.

Crispi, Francesco, *Memoirs*, London: Hodder & Stoughten, 1912, 3 vols.

Dewitz, Hermann von, *Von Bismarck bis Bethmann*, Innerpolitische Rückblicke eines Konservativen, Berlin: Konservative Schriftenvertriebsstelle, 1918, 110 pp.

Fürst Bismarcks Briefe an seine Braut und Gattin, ed. H. v. Bismarck, Stuttgart: Cotta, 1900, 598 pp.

Gerlach, Ernst Ludwig von, *Aufzeichnungen aus seinem Leben und Wirken, 1795-1877*, ed. J. v. Gerlach, Schwerin/Meck.: Bahn, 1903, 2 vols.

Holstein, Friedrich von, *Lebensbekenntnis in Briefen an eine Frau*, ed. H. Rogge, Berlin: Ullstein, 1932, 357 pp.

Hugenberg, Alfred, *Streiflichter aus Vergangenheit und Gegenwart*, 2nd edit., Berlin: August Scherl, 1927, 311 pp.

Hohenlohe-Schillingsfürst, Chlodwig zu, *Denkwürdigkeiten*, ed. F. Curtius, Stuttgart/Leipzig: Deutsche Verlags-Anstalt, 1906, 2 vols.

Hutten-Czapski, Bogdan von, *Sechzig Jahre Politik und Gesellschaft*, Berlin: Mittler & So., 1936, 568 pp.

Im Ring der Gegner Bismarcks, Denkschriften und politischer Briefwechsel Franz von Roggenbachs ;mit Kaiserin Augusta und Albrecht von Stosch, 1865-1896, Deutsche Geschichtsquellen des 19. Jahrhunderts, vol. 35, ed. J. Heyderhoff, 2nd edit., Leipzig: Koehler & Amelang, 1943, 453 pp.

Keim, August, *Erlebtes und Erstrebtes*, Hanover: Ernst Letsch, 1925, 280 pp.

Keudell, Robert von, *Fürst und Fürstin Bismarck*, Stuttgart: Spemann, 1901, 497 pp.

Komierowski, Roman, *Koło Polskie w Berlinie, 1875-1900*, Poznań: Dziennik Poznański, 1905, 343 pp.

Lucius von Ballhausen, Robert, *Bismarck-Erinnerungen*, Stuttgart/Berlin: Cotta, 1920, 589 pp.

Radziwiłł, Marie, *Briefe vom deutschen Kaiserhof, 1889-1915*, Berlin: Ullstein,

1936, 376 pp.

Raschdau, Ludwig, *Unter Bismarck und Caprivi*, Erinnerungen eines deutschen Diplomaten aus den Jahren 1885-1894, Berlin: Mittler, 1939, 381 pp.

Schlözer, Kurd von, *Letzte römische Briefe, 1882-1894*, ed. L. v. Schlözer, Stuttgart: Deutsche Verlags-Anstalt, 1924, 222 pp.

Scholz, Adolf von, *Erlebnisse und Gespräche mit Bismarck*, ed. W. v. Scholz, Stuttgart/Berlin: Cotta, 1922, 150 pp.

Schweinitz, Hans Lothar von, *Briefwechsel*, Berlin: Reimar Hobbing, 1928, 398 pp.

_____, *Denkwürdigkeiten*, Berlin: Reimar Hobbing, 1927, 2 vols.

Seeckt, Hans von, *Aus meinem Leben*, ed. F. v. Rabenau, Leipzig: Hase & Koehler, 1941, 640 pp.

Stein, August, *Es war alles ganz anders*, Frankfurt/Main: 1922, 227 pp.

Tiedemann, Christoph von, *Sechs Jahre Chef der Reichskanzlei unter dem Fürsten Bismarck*, 2nd edit., Leipzig: Hirzel, 1910, 504 pp.

Tirpitz, Alfred von, *My Memoirs*, New York: Dodd, Mead, 1919, 2 vols.

Vom jungen Bismarck, Briefwechsel mit Gustav Scharlach, Weimar: Duncker, 1912, 139 pp.

Waldersee, Alfred von, *Briefwechsel*, ed. H. O. Meisner, Stuttgart: Deutsche Verlags-Anstalt, 1928, 2 vols.

_____, "Briefwechsel zwischen Chef des General-Stabes Waldersee und Militär-Attaché Yorck von Wartenburg, 1885-1894," *Historisch-politisches Archiv zur deutschen Geschichte des 19. und 20. Jahrhunderts* 1(1930):133-192 (ed. H. O. Meisner)

_____, *Denkwürdigkeiten*, ed. H. O. Meisner, Stuttgart/Berlin: Deutsche Verlags-Anstalt, 1925, 2 vols.

Wedel, Erhard von, *Zwischen Kaiser und Kanzler*, Leipzig: Koehler & Amelang, 1943, 216 pp.

Whitman, Sidney, *Fürst von Bismarck*, Persönliche Erinnerungen, Stuttgart: Deutsche Verlags-Anstalt, 1902, 241 pp.

Wilhelm II, *Ereignisse und Gestalten, 1878-1918*, Leipzig: Koehler, 1922, 308 pp.

D. Literature

Aal, Arthur, *Das preussische Rentengut*, Seine Vorgeschichte und seine Gestaltung in Gesetzgebung und Praxis, Münchner Volkswirtschaftliche Studien, #43, Stuttgart: Cotta, 1901, 170 pp.

Altkemper, Johannes, *Deutschtum und Polentum in politisch-konfessionaler Bedeutung*, Leipzig: Duncker & Humblot, 1910, 252 pp.

Bachem, Karl, *Vorgeschichte, Geschichte, und Politik der deutschen Zentrumspartei*, Cologne: Bachem, 1927, 3 vols.

Baske, Siegfried, "Praxis und Prinzipien der preussischen Polenpolitik vom Beginn der Reaktionszeit bis zur Gründung des Deutschen Reichs," *Forschungen zur Osteuropäischen Geschichte* 9 (1963): 7-268.

Behrendt, Johannes, "Die polnische Frage und das österreichisch-deutsche Bündnis 1885 bis 1887," *Vierteljahrsschrift für Politik und Geschichte* 7 (1926): 699-767.
Bełcikowska, Alicja, *Stronnictwa i związki polityczne w Polskie*, Warsaw: Dan Książki Pol., 1925, 1086 pp.
Belgard, Martin, *Parzellierung und innere Kolonisation in den sechs östlichen Provinzen Preussens, 1875-1906*, Leipzig: Duncker & Humblot, 1907, 541 pp.
Bernhard, Ludwig, *Die Polenfrage*, 3rd edit., Munich/Leipzig: Duncker & Humblot, 1920, 572 pp.
_____, *Zur Polenpolitik des Königreichs Preussen*, Berlin: Otto Liebmann, 1923, 16 pp.
_____, "Preussische Polenpolitik," *Handbuch der Politik*, vol. 2, 66. Abschnitt, Berlin/Leipzig: Walther Rothschild, 1912-3, pp. 623-633.
Bernin, Edmond, "Polonais et Prussians," *Cahiers de la Quinzaine*, serie 8, vols. 10, 12, 14. (1907)
Richard Blanke, "Bismarck and the Prussian Polish Policies of 1886," *Journal of Modern History* 45 (1973): 211-239.
_____, "The Development of Loyalism in Prussian Poland, 1886-1890," *Slavonic and East European Review* 52 (1974): 548-565.
_____, "An Era of Reconciliation in German-Polish Relations (1890-1894)," *Slavic Review* 36 (1977): 39-53.
Böckh, Richard, "Verschiebung der Sprachverhältnisse in Posen und Westpreussen," *Preussische Jahrbücher* 77 (1894): 424-436.
Böhning, Peter, *Die nationalpolnische Bewegung in Westpreussen 1815-1871*, Marburger Ostforschungen, #33, Marburg: Herder Institut, 1973, 254 pp.
Boguslawski, A. von, *Fünfundachtzig Jahre Regierungspolitik in Posen und Westpreussen*, Berlin: Gose & Tetzlaff, 1901, 92 pp.
Bornkamm, Heinrich, *Die Staatsidee im Kulturkampf*, Darmstadt: Wissenschaftliche Buchgesellschaft, 1969, 2nd edit., 85 pp.
Borowski, Stanisław, *Rozwarstwienie wsi wielkopolskij w latach 1807-1914*, Poznań: Prezydium WRN, 1962, 352 pp.
Brackmann, Albert (ed.), *Germany and Poland*, Munich: Oldenbourg, 1934, 266 pp.
Brock, Peter, "Polish Nationalism," in *Nationalism in Eastern Europe*, ed. P. Sugar & I. Lederer, Seattle: University of Washington, 1969, pp. 310-372.
Brodnicki, Bolesław, *Beiträge zur Entwicklung der Landwirtschaft in der Provinz Posen (1815-1890)*, Leipzig diss., Leipzig: Oswald Schmidt, 1893, 120 pp.
Bronkański, H., *Stowarzyszenia katolickiej Czeladzi Rzemieślniczej Kolpinga*, Poznań: Kuryer Poznański, 1892, 58 pp.
Broszat, Martin, *200 Jahre deutscher Polenpolitik*, Munich: Ehrenwirth, 1963, 269 pp.
Brüggen, Ernst von der, "Die Kolonisation in unserem Osten und die Herstellung des Erbzinses," *Preussische Jahrbücher* 44 (1879): 32-51.
Buzek, Józef, *Historya polityki narodowościowej rządu pruskiego wobec*

Polaków, Lwów: Altenberg, 1909, 569 pp.

———, *Pogląd na wzrost ludności ziem polskich w wieku 19.*, Cracow: Centralne Biuro Wydawnictw, 1915, 74 pp.

Cambridge History of Poland, vol. 2, ed. W. Reddaway, *et al.*, Cambridge: University Press, 1951, 630 pp.

Carl, Helmut, *Kleine Geschichte Polens*, Frankfurt/Main: Heinrich Scheffler, 1960, 168 pp.

Chartier, Pierre, *La colonisation allemande dans l'ancienne Pologne prussienne et ses conséquences actuelles*, Paris diss., Paris: Jouve, 1921, 151 pp.

Chociszewski, Stefan, *O wewnętrznem życiu Towarzystw Przemysłowych*, Odczyty dla polskich warstw średnich, #3, Poznań: Orędownik, 1893, 14 pp.

Chudziński, Anton, *Die polnische Frage in Preussen*, Berlin: Mittler & So., 1891, 32 pp.

Cieślak, Tadeusz, "Główne problemy historii politycznej ziem pomorskich w latach 1870-1914," *Studia i Materiały do Dziejów Wielkopolski i Pomorza* 2:1 (1956): 167-176.

———, *Przeciw pruskiej przemocy*, Warsaw: Ludowa Spółdzielnia Wydawnicza, 1959, 194 pp.

———, *Z dziejów prasy polskiej na Pomorzu gdańskim w okresie zaboru pruskiego*, Danzig: Gdańskie Towarzystwo Naukowa, 1964, 184 pp.

Conrad, J., "Grossgrundbesitz in der Provinz Posen," *Jahrbücher für Nationalökonomie und Statistik* 61 (1893): 516-542.

Conze, Werner, *Polnische Nation und deutsche Politik im ersten Weltkrieg*, Ostmittel-europa in Vergangenheit und Gegenwart, #4, Cologne/Graz: Böhlau, 1958, 415 pp.

Czartoryski, Zygmunt, *Ueber die antipolnische Politik der preussischen Regierung*, 2nd edit., Cracow: Gebethner, 1912, 230 pp.

Delbrück, Hans, *Bismarcks Erbe*, Männer und Völker, Berlin: Ullstein, 1915, 220 pp.

———, *Die Polenfrage*, Berlin: Hermann Walther, 1894, 48 pp.

Dettmer, Günther, *Die ost- und westpreussischen Behörden im Kulturkampf*, Heidelberg: Quelle & Meyer, 1958, 143 pp.

Deutscher Aufstieg, Bilder aus der Vergangenheit und Gegenwart der rechtsstehenden Parteien, ed. H. v. Arnim & G. v. Below, Berlin: Franz Schneider, 1925, 517 pp., articles on Lucius and C. v. Tiedemann.

Dix, Arthur, "Das Slaventum in Preussen," Seine Bedeutung für die Bevölkerungsbewegung und Volkswirtschaft in den letzten Jahrzehnten, *Jahrbücher für Nationalökonomie und Statistik* 70 (1898): 561-602.

Dmowski, Roman, *La question polonaise*, Paris: Armand Colin, 1909, 332 pp.

Donimirski, Antoni, "Kolonizacya niemiecka i Bank Ziemski," *Przegląd Polski* 21:4 (1887): 324-352.

Employment-seeking Emigrations of the Poles World-wide XIX and XX c., ed. C. Bobińska & A. Pilch, Zeszyty Naukowe Uniwersytetu Jagiellońskiego,

#417, Cracow: Uniw. Jagielloński, 1975, 194 pp.

Eyck, Erick, *Bismarck*, Erlenbach/Zürich: Eugen Rentsch, 1944, 3 vols.

Feldman, Józef, *Bismarck a Komisja Osadnicza*, Cracow: Nakładem Krakowskiej Spółki Wydawniczej, 1928, 34 pp.

_____, *Bismarck a Polska*, 2nd edit., Cracow: Czytelnik, 1947, 451 pp.

_____, *Problem polsko-niemiecki w dziejach*, Katowice: Wydawnictwo Instytutu Śląskiego, 1946, 171 pp.

Franz, Georg, *Der Kulturkampf*, Munich: Callwey, 1954, 355 pp.

Franz, Günther, *Bismarcks Nationalgefühl*, Leipzig/Berlin: Teubner, 1926, 125 pp.

Frauendienst, Werner, "Preussisches Staatsbewusstsein und polnisches Nationalismus. Preussisch-deutsche Polenpolitik," in *Das östliche Deutschland*, ed. Göttinger Arbeitskreis, Würzburg: Holzner, 1959, pp. 305-362.

Galos, Adam/Felix-Heinrich Gentzen/Witold Jakóbczyk, *Die Hakatisten. Ein Beitrag zur Geschichte der Ostpolitik des deutschen Imperialismus*, Schriftenreihe der Kommission der Historiker der DDR und Volkspolens, East Berlin: Deutscher Verlag der Wissenschaften, 1966, 529 pp.

Galos, Adam, "Klasy posiadające w Niemczech wobec sprawy polskiej (1894-1914)," *Przegląd Historyczny* 45 (1954): 652-690.

_____, "Tragizm Ugody; Władze pruskie a Arcybiskup Stablewski," *Przegląd Zachodni* 21 (1975): 235-256.

_____, "Utworzenie Komisji Kolonizacyjnej (1886) a sprawa wewnętrznej kolonizacji w Niemczech," *Prace Historyczne* 26 (1969): 37-55.

Ganz, Hugo, *Die preussische Polenpolitik*, Frankfurt/Main: Rütten & Loening, 1907, 96 pp.

Geffcken, Heinrich, *Preussen, Deutschland, und die Polen seit dem Untergang des polnischen Reiches*, Berlin: Vossische Buchhandlung, 1906, 168 pp.

Gehre, M., *Neue deutsche Kolonisation in Posen und Westpreussen*, Grossenhain: Starke & Sachse, 1899, 55 pp.

Geis, Robert, *Der Sturz des Reichskanzlers Caprivi*, Historische Studien, #192, Berlin: Emil Ebering, 1930, 124 pp.

Geisler, Walter, "Die Sprachen- und Nationalitätenverhältnisse an den deutschen Ostgrenzen und ihre Darstellung," *Petermanns Mitteilungen*, Ergänzungsheft #217 (1933).

Goebel, Heinz, *Die Militärvorlage 1892-3*, Münster diss., Borna/Leipzig: Noske, 1935, 79 pp.

Gothein, Georg, "Die preussische Polenpolitik," *Patria* (1909): 47-84.

_____, *Reichskanzler Graf Caprivi*, Fehler und Forderungen, #5, Munich: George Müller, 1918, 179 pp.

Grot, Zdzisław, "Koło Polskie w Berlinie," in *Wiek XIX*, Kieniewicz Festschrift, 1967, pp. 237-250.

_____, "Die Stellung der preussischen Forschrittspartei zur Minderheitenfrage," *Wissenschaftliche Zeitschrift des Schiller-Universität Jena*, 14 (1965): 225-228.

Grygier, Tadeusz, "Sprawa polska w Prusach Wschodnich w latach 1870-

1900 w oświetleniu władz pruskich," *Przegląd Zachodni* 7 (1951): 493-544.

Günzel, Walter, *Die nationale Arbeit der polnischen Presse in Westpreussen und Posen zur Zeit der Kanzlerschaft Bülows*, Leipzig diss., Łódź: Libertas, 1933, 69 pp.

Guttzeit, Johannes, *Die Geschichte der deutschen Polen-Entrechtung*, Danzig: Danziger Zeitungsverlagsgesellschaft, 1927, 323 pp.

Hagen, William, "The Impact of Economic Modernization on Traditional Nationality Relations in Prussian Poland, 1815-1914," *Journal of Social History* 6 (1973): 306-324.

_____, "National Solidarity and Organic Work in Prussian Poland, 1815-1914," *Journal of Modern History* 44 (1972): 38-64.

Hartmann, Eduard von, "Der Rückgang des Deutschtums," *Die Gegenwart* 27 (1885): 1-3, 19-22.

Hartung, Fritz, *Deutsche Geschichte, 1871-1919*, 6th edit., Stuttgart: Koehler, 1952, 446 pp.

_____, "Graf von Hutten-Czapski," *Historische Zeitschrift* 153 (1936): 548-559.

_____, "Verantwortliche Regierungen, Kabinette, und Nebenregierungen im konstitutionellen Preussen," *Forschungen zur Brandenburgischen und Preussischen Geschichte* 44 (1932): 1-45, 302-373.

Hartwig, Edgar, "Der Alldeutsche Verband und Polen," *Wissenschaftliche Zeitschrift der Schiller-Universität Jena*, 19 (1970): 251-276.

Hauser, Oswald, "Polen und Dänen im Deutschen Reich," in *Die Reichsgründung 1870/1*, ed. T. Schieder & E. Deuerlein, pp. 291-318.

Hausmann, Kurt-Georg, "Dmowskis Stellung zu Deutschland vor dem ersten Weltkrieg," *Zeitschrift für Ostforschung* 13 (1964): 56-91.

Heckel, Johannes, "Die Beilegung des Kulturkampfes in Preussen," in *Das blinde, undeutliche Wort "Kirche"*, gesammelte Aufsätze, ed. S. Grundmann, Cologne: Böhlau, 1964, pp. 454-571.

Held, Walter, *Caprivi und Bismarck*, Leipzig diss., Leipzig: Gebr. Junghans, 1931, 48 pp.

Herzfeld, Hans, *Johannes von Miquel, Sein Anteil am Ausbau des Deutschen Reiches bis zur Jahrhundertwende*, Detmold: Meyer, 1938, 2 vols.

History of Poland, 1795-1918 section by Stefan Kieniewicz and Henryk Wereszycki, Warsaw: Polish Scientific Publishers, 1968, 783 pp.

Höhn, Reinhard & Helmut Seydel, "Der Kampf um Wiedergewinnung des deutschen Ostens—Erfahrungen der preussischen Ostsiedlung, 1886-1914," in *Festgabe für Heinrich Himmler*, Darmstadt: Wittich, 1941, pp. 61-174.

Hoetzsch, Otto, "Nationalitätenkampf und Nationalitätenpolitik in der Ostmark," in *Deutsche Ostmark*, Lissa: Eulitz, 1913, 633 pp.

_____*Osteuropa und der deutsche Osten*, Königsberg/Pr.: Ost-Europa, 1934, 431 pp.

Hubrich, Eduard, "Zur preussisch-polnischen Sprachenfrage," *Beiträge zur Erläuterung des deutschen Rechts* 48 (1904): 570-590.

Jablonowski, Horst, *Die preussische Polenpolitik von 1815 bis 1914*, Göttinger Arbeitskreis, #69, Würzburg: Holzner, 1964, 20 pp.

Jackowski, Tadeusz, *Bauernbesitz in der Provinz Posen im 19. Jahrhundert,* Leipzig diss., Leipzig: Veit, 1913, 154 pp.

Jaffé, Moritz, *Die Stadt Posen unter preussischer Herrschaft,* Schriften des Vereins für Sozialpolitik, #119:2, Leipzig: Duncker & Humblot, 1909, 453 pp.

Jakóbczyk, Witold, "The First Decade of the Prussian Settlement Commission's Activities (1886-1897)," *Polish Review* (1972): 3-13.

_____, Kolonizatorzy i Hakatyści," *Annales Universitatis Mariae Curie-Skłodowska Lublin* 29 (1974): 193-199.

_____, *Patron Jackowski,* Poznań: Uniw. Poznański, 1938, 334 pp.

_____, *Studia nad dziejami Wielkopolski w 19. weiku,* Dzieja pracy organicznej, Poznań: Państwowe Wydawnictwo Naukowe, 1959-67, 3 vols.

_____, "Towarzystwo Oświaty Ludowy w Poznanie 1872-8," *Roczniki Historyczne* 23 (1957): 581-605.

_____, "Z dziejów ruchu robotniczego w Poznaniu," *Studia Poznańskie* 9 (1953): 376-402.

_____, "Z dziejów walki o ziemię na poraniczu," *Przegląd Zachodni* 17 (1961): 25-52.

Jeismann, Karl-Ernst, *Das Problem des Präventivkrieges im europäischen Staatensystems.* Mit besonderem Blick auf die Bismarckzeit, Freiburg: Karl Aller, 1957, 200 pp.

Kalkstein, Teodor, *Der Grossgrundbesitz gegenüber der Rentengütergesetzgebung,* Ein Beitrag zur Parzellierungspraxis, Poznań: Kuryer Poznański, 1892, 53 pp.

Kaminski, Lotte, *Auseindersetzungen um die polnische Frage zur Zeit der Reichskanzlerschaft des Fürsten zu Hohenlohe-Schillingsfürst,* Hamburg diss., Hamburg: 1938, 70 pp.

Kardorff, Siegfried von, *Wilhelm von Kardorff,* Ein nationaler Parlamentarier im Zeitalter Bismarcks und Wilhelms II, Berlin: Mittler & So., 1936, 384 pp.

Karpiński, Antoni, "Niemiec arcybiskupem gnieźno-poznańskim," *Niepodległość* 2 (1930): 363-366.

Keyser, Erich (ed.), *Der Kampf um die Weichsel,* Untersuchungen zur Geshichte des polnischen Korridors, Stuttgart: Deutsche Verlags-Anstalt, 1926, 175 pp.

Kieniewicz, Stefan, *Historia Polski, 1795-1918,* Warsaw: Państwowe Wydawnictwo Naukowe, 1970, 611 pp.

Kissling, Johannes, *Die Geschichte des Kulturkampfes im Deutschen Reich,* Freiburg: Herder, 1911-1916, 3 vols.

Klanowski, Tadeusz, *Germanizacja gimnazjów w Wielkim Księstwie Poznańskim i opór młodzieży polskiej w latach 1870-1914,* Poznań: Mickiewicz Univ., 1962, 199 pp.

Klessmann, Christoph, *Polnische Bergarbeiter im Ruhrgebiet 1870-1945* Kritische Studien zur Geschichtswissenschaft, #30, Göttingen: Vandenhoeck & Ruprecht, 1978, 306 pp.

Knötel, Paul, *Die Geschichte der Provinz Posen,* Kattowitz: Gebr. Böhm,

1911, 151 pp.

Koch, Friedrich, *Bismarck über die Polen*, Berlin: Ostmarkenverein, 1913, 150 pp.

Koehl, Robert, "Colonialism inside Germany," *Journal of Modern History* 25 (1953): 255-272.

Kohn, Hans, *Die Welt der Slawen*, vol. I: Die West- und Südslawen, Frankfurt/Main: FIscher, 1960, 302 pp.

Kohte, Wolfgang, "Die staatliche Ansiedlungspolitik im deutschen Nordosten (1886-1914)," *Studien zum Deutschtum im Osten* 8 (1971): 219-240.

———, "Volkstum und Wirtschaft des preussischen Ostens im 19. Jahrhundert," *Deutsche Wissenschaftliche Zeitschrift für Polen* 29 (1935): 231-260.

———, "Zur Volkstumsentwicklung Posens und Westpreussens im deutschen Wirtschaftsgefüge des 19. Jahrhunderts," *Deutsche Zeitschrift für Wirtschaftskunde* 3 (1938): 172-187.

Korth, Rudolf, *Die preussische Schulpolitik und die polnischen Schulstreiks. Ein Beitrag zur preussischen Polenpolitik der Aera Bülow*, Marburger Ostforschungen, #23, Würzburg: Holzner, 1963, 184 pp.

Kozicki, Stanisław, *La Pologne depuis le Congrès de Vienne (1815-1915)*, Paris: Agence Polonaise, 1916, 93 pp.

———, *The Social Evolution of Poland in the 19th Century*, London: Hodder & Stoughton, 1918, 40 pp.

Kozłowski, Jerzy/Bolesław Grześ/Aleksandr Kramski, *Niemcy w Poznańskiem wobec polityki germanizacyjnej, 1815-1920*, ed. L. Trzeciakowski, Poznań: Instytut Zachodni, 1976, 472 pp.

Krasuski, Jerzy, *Kulturkampf*, Poznań: Wydawnictwo Poznańskie, 1963, 271 pp.

———, "Zagadnienie polskie w publicystyce Hansa Delbrücka (1887-1917)," *Przegląd Zachodni* 14:1 (1958): 64-81.

Krausnick, Helmut, *Holsteins Geheimpolitik in her Aera Bismarck, 1886-1890*, 2nd edit., Hamburg: Hanseatische Verlags-Anstalt, 1942, 381 pp.

Krische, Paul, *Die Provinz Posen, Ihre Geschichte und Kultur unter besonderer Berücksichtigung ihrer Landwirtschaft*, Stassfurt: Weicke, 1907, 318 pp.

Krüger, Karl Heinz, *Die Konservativen und die Politik Caprivis*, Rostock diss., 1937, 82 pp.

Krysiak, F., *Hinter den Kulissen des Ostmarkenvereins, Aus den Geheimakten der preussischen Nebenregierung für die Polenausrottung*, Poznań: Selbstverlag, 1919, 274 pp.

Książka jubileuszowa Dziennika Poznańskiego, 1859-1909, Poznań: Dziennik Poznański, 1909, 304 pp.

Księga pamiątkowa PPS, Warsaw: "Robotnik," 1923, 264 pp.

Kubiak, Stanisław, *Ruch socjalistyczny w Poznaniu, 1872-1890*, Poznań: Wydawnictwo Poznańskie, 1961, 232 pp.

Kucner, Alfred, "Polityka 'Koła Polskiego' w Berlinie w erze Kanclerza Capriviego," *Nauka i Sztuka* 3 (1947): 42-76.

Kucharski, N., *Jubileuszowe sprawozdanie z czynności 25cioletniej Tow-*

arzystwo Przemysłowego w Śremie, Poznań: Kuryer Poznański, 1896, 73 pp.

Kuhn, Walter, "Die geschichtliche Stellung des Warthe- und Weichseldeutschtums im Wandel der Zeiten," in *Heimat im Herzen: Wir von der Weichsel und Warthe*, ed. E. Wittek, Salzburg: Akademischer Gemeinschaftsverlag, 1950, 405 pp.

Kulczycki, John, "Social Change in the Polish National Movement in Prussia before World War I," *Nationalities Papers* 4 (1976): 17-53.

Kunkel, Adolf, "Der Posener Marcinkowski-Verein für Unterrichtshilfe," *Vierteljahrsschrift für Sozial- und Wirtschaftsgeschichte* 16 (1922): 148-167.

Kusztelan, Rus, Ks. *Patron Augustyn Szamarzewski*, Poznań: Gebr. Winiewicz, 1918, 205 pp.

Land, Hanne-Lore, *Die Konservativen und die preussische Polenpolitik, (1886-1912)*, Berlin diss., 1963, 153 pp.

Laubert, Manfred, *Deutsche und Polen im Wandel der Geschichte*, Breslau: Deutschnationaler Verband Mittelschlesien, 1921, 32 pp.

―――, *Das Heimatrecht der Deutschen in Westpolen*, Die Entwicklung des deutschen Anteils an der Bevökerung und dem Grundbesitz in den an Polen abgetretenen Gebieten, Bromberg: 1924, 35 pp.

―――, *Die preussische Polenpolitik, 1772-1914*, 3rd edit., Schriften des Instituts für Deutsche Ostarbeit, Cracow: Burgverlag, 1944, 244 pp.

Lehmann, Hartmut, "Bodelschwingh und Bismarck," *Historische Zeitschrift* 208 (1969): 607-626.

Lemberg, Eugen, *Nationalismus*, 2nd edit., Reinbek: 1967, 2 vols.

―――, "Zur Geschichte der deutschen Volksgruppen in Ost-Mitteleuropa," *Zeitschrift für Ostforschung* 1 (1952): 321-345.

Lorenz, Friedrich, *Die Geschichte der Kaschuben*, Berlin: Reimar Hobbing, 1926, 172 pp.

Lorenz, Friedebert, *Die Parteien und die preussische Polenpolitik, 1885-6*, Halle diss., Halle: Eduard Klinz, 1938, 119 pp.

Luczak, Czesław, *Położenie ekonomiczne rzemiosła wielkopolskiego w okresie zaborów*, Poznań: Polskie Towarzystwo Historyczne, 1962, 159 pp.

―――, *Życie gospodarczo-społeczne w Poznaniu, 1815-1918*, Poznań: Wydawnictwo Poznańskie, 1965, 291 pp.

Lüdicke, Reinhard, *Die preussischen Kultusminister und ihre Beamten im Jahrhundert des Ministeriums, 1817-1915*, Stuttgart: Cotta, 1918, 169 pp.

Mai, Joachim, *Die preussisch-deutsche Polenpolitik 1885-7*, East Berlin: Rütten & Loening, 1962, 232 pp.

Marchlewski, Julian, *Pisma wybrane*, Warsaw: Książka i Wiedza, 1956, 2 vols.

―――, *Zur Polenpolitik der preussischen Regierung*, East Berlin: Dietz, 1957, 112 pp.

Marczewski, Jerzy, *Narodowa Demokracja w Poznańskiem 1900-1914*, Warsaw: Państwowe Wydawnictwo Naukowe, 1967, 430 pp.

Marten, Wacław, *Sprawozdanie jubileuszowe z czynności Towarzystwa* przemysłowego w Poznaniu, 1848-1898, Poznań: Dziennik Poznański, 1898, 42 pp.

Maschke, Erich, "Deutschland und Polen im Wandel der Geschichte," *Neue Jahrbücher für Wissenschaft und Jugendbildung* 12 (1936): 219-323, 354-366.

Massow, Wilhelm von, *Die deutsche innere Politik unter Kaiser Wilhelm II*, Stuttgart/Berlin: Deutsche Verlags-Anstalt, 1913, 342 pp.

_____, *Polennot im deutschen Osten*, 2nd edit., Berlin: Duncker, 1907, 427 pp.

Meisner, Heinrich Otto, *Der Reichskanzler Caprivi*, 2nd edit., Darmstadt: Wissenschaftliche Buchgesellschaft, 1969, 84 pp.

Meyer, Enno, "Die Polen im preussischen Staat von 1815 bis 1914," in *Deutschland und Polen*, ed. H. Fechner, Würzburg: Holzner, 1964, pp. 47-67.

Mitscherlich, Waldemar, *Die Ausbreitung der Polen in Preussen*, Leipzig: Hirschfeld, 1913, 295 pp.

_____, *Der Einfluss der wirtschaftlichen Entwicklung auf den ostmärkischen Nationalitätenkampf*, Leipzig: Hirschfeld, 1910, 48 pp.

_____, "Irrtümer über das wirtschaftliche Vordringen der Polen," *Jahrbuch für Gesetzgebung, Verwaltung und Volkswirtschaft im Deutschen Reich* 35,4 (1911): 51-89.

_____, "Die polnische Boykottbewegung in der Ostmark und ihre Aussichten," *Ibid.*, 35,3 (1911?: 31-65.

Morsey, Rudolf, "Bismarck und der Kulturkampf," *Archiv für Kulturgeschichte* 39 (1957): 232-270.

Moysett, Henri, "La politique de la Prusse et les Polonais," *Revue des Deux Mondes* 48 (1908): 108-138, 519-550.

Müller, Helmut, *Die polnische Volksgruppe im Deutschen Reich, Ihre Stellung in Verfassung und Verwaltung seit 1871*, Warsaw: Selbstverlag, 1941, 207 pp.

Müller, Leonhard, *Nationalpolnische Press, Katholizismus, und der katholische Klerus (1896-99)*, Breslau: Müller & Seiffert, 1931, 223 pp.

Narkiewicz, Olga, *The Green Flag*, Polish Populist Politics, 1867-1970, London: Croom Helm, 1976, 313 pp.

Neveux, J.-B., "Les Polonais et 1871," *Revue d'Histoire Moderne et Contemporaine* (1972): 308-316.

Neubach, Helmut, *Die Ausweisungen von Polen und Juden aus Preussen 1885-6*, Wiesbaden: Otto Harrassowitz, 1967, 293 pp.

_____, "Eduard von Hartmanns Bedeutung für die Entwicklung der deutschpolnischen Verhältnisse," *Zeitschrift für Ostforschung* 13 (1964): 106-159.

Neumann, Friedrich, "Germanisierung oder Polonisierung," *Jahrbücher für Nationalökonomie und Statistik* NF 7 (1883): 457-463.

Nichols, J. Alden, *Germany after Bismarck, The Caprivi Era, 1890-4*, Cambridge/Mass.: Harvard University Press, 1958, 404 pp.

Nichtweiss, Johannes, *Ausländische Saisonarbeiter in der Landwirtschaft der östlichen und mittleren Gebieten des Deutschen Reiches*, East Berlin: Röt-

Bibliography

ten & Loening, 1959, 289 pp.

Niklewski, Zdzisław, *Rolnik. Landwirtschaftliche Einkaufs—und Absatzvereine im Verbande "Związek Spółek Zarobkowych" für Posen und Westpreussen in ihrem Wesen und ihrer Entwicklung,* Heidelberg diss., Merseburg: Friedrich Stollberg, 1915, 69 pp.

Nowakowski, Tadeusz, *The Radziwiłłs,* New York: Delnorte, 1974, 325 pp.

Ohnesseit, Wilhelm, *Fünfunddreissig Jahre Deutscher Ostmarkenverein,* Berlin: Thormann & Goetsch, 1929, 19 pp.

Oppen, Dietrich von, "Deutsche, Polen, und Kaschuben in Westpreussen, 1871-1914," *Jahrbuch für die Geschichte Mittelund Ostdeutschlands* 4 (1955): 157-223.

Ostdeutscher Volksboden, Aufsätze zu den Fragen des Ostens, ed. W. Volz, Breslau: Ferdinand Hirt, 1926, 387 pp.

Ostland, Jahrbuch für ostdeutsche Interessen, vol. 1 (1912).

Die Ostmark, Einführung in die Probleme ihrer Wirtschaftsgeschichte, ed. W. Mitscherlich, Aus Natur und Geisteswelt, #351, Leipzig: Teubner, 1911, 153 pp.

Pabisz, Jerzy, "Wyniki wyborów do Parlamentu Związku Północnoniemieckiego i Parlamentu Rzeszy Niemieckiej na terenie Śląsku w latach 1867-1918," *Studia i Materiały z Dziejów Śląsku* (1966): 186-383.

Pastor, Ludwig, *August Reichensperger,* Freiburg: Herder, 1899, 2 vols.

Pater, Mieczysław, *Centrum a ruch polski na Górnym Śląsku (1879-1893),* Opole: Śląsk, 1971, 316 pp.

Perdelwitz, Richard, *Die Posener Polen, 1815-1914,* Ein Jahrhundert grosspolnischer Ideengeschichte, Schneidemühl: Comenius, 1936, 128 pp.

Pfeiffer, Hans, *Der polnische Adel und die preussische Polenpolitik von 1863 bis 1894,* Jena diss., Würzburg: Richard Mayr, 1939, 97 pp.

Piwarski, Kazimierz, "Stosunki polsko-niemieckie w okresie 1795-1939," *Sobótka* 5 (1950): 48-50.

Polen, Entwicklung und gegenwärtiger Zustand, Bern: Haller, 1918, 1039 pp.

Polen und Deutschland, Geschichtlicher Ueberblick, Göttingen: Göttinger Arbeitskreis, 1949, 40 pp.

Poschinger, Heinrich von, "Aus den Denkwürdigkeiten Wilhelm von Kardorffs," *Deutsche Revue* 33,2 (1908): 152-160.

Pragier, Adam, *Królewsko-pruska Komisja Kolonizacyjna, 1886-1918,* 1920, 64 pp.

Puhle, Hans-Jürgen, *Agrarische Interessenpolitik und preussischer Konservatismus im wilhelminischen Reich (1893-1914),* Schriftenreihe des Forschungsinsstituts der Friedrich-Ebert-Stiftung, Hanover: Literatur und Zeitgeschehen, 1966, 364 pp.

Puttkamer, Albert von (ed.), *Staatsminister von Puttkamer,* Ein Stück preussischer Vergangenheit, 1828-1900, Leipzig: Koehler, 1928, 212 pp.

Puttkamer, Karl von, *Die Misserfolge in der Polenpolitik,* Berlin: Karl Curtius, 1913, 29 pp.

Quante, Peter, "Die Bevölkerungsentwicklung der preussischen Ostprovinzen im 19. und 20. Jahrhundert," *Zeitschrift für Ostforschung* 8 (1959): 481-499.

Rakowski, Kazimierz, *Walka w obronie narodowości polskiej pod berłem pruskim*, Warsaw: Gebethner & Wolff, 1925, 72 pp.

Randow, Albert von, "Die Landesverweisungen aus Preussen und die Erhaltung des Deutschtums an der Ostgrenze," *Jahrbuch für Gesetzgebung, Verwaltung und Volkswirtschaft im Deutschen Reich* 10 (1886): 91-125.

"Le régime politique et administrativ dans la Pologne prussienne," *Encyclopédie Polonaise*, vol. 4,1, Fribourg/Lausanne: 1918, 518 pp.

Rek, Tadeusz, *Ruch ludowy w Polsce*, 2nd edit., Warsaw: Wydawnictwo Ludowe, 1947, 3 vols.

Retinger, J. H., *The Poles and Prussia*, (n.d., n.p.) 16 pp.

Rhode, Arthur, *Die Geschichte der evangelischen Kirche im Posener Land*, Marburger Ostforschungen, #4, Würzburg: Holzner, 1956, 263 pp.

Rhode, Gotthold (ed.), *Die Geschichte der Stadt Posen*, Neuendettelsau: Freimund, 1953, 318 pp.

Rich, Norman, *Friedrich von Holstein*, Cambridge: University Press, 1965, 2 vols.

Richter, Günter, *Friedrich von Holstein—ein Mitarbeiter Bismarcks*, Historische Studien, #397, Lübeck/Hamburg: Matthiesen, 1966, 188 pp.

Richter, Kurt, *Der Kampf um den Schulgesetzentwurf des Grafen Zedlitz-Trützschler vom Jahre 1892*, Halle diss., Halle: Eduard Klinz, 1934, 119 pp.

Röhl, John, "The Disintegration of the Kartell and the Politics of Bismarck's Fall from Power, 1887-90," *Historical Journal* 9 (1966): 60-89.

_____. "A Document of 1892 on Germany, Prussia, and Poland," *Historical Journal* 7 (1964): 143-9.

_____, *Germany without Bismarck*, London: 1967.

Rogmann, Heinz, *Die Bevölkerungsentwicklung im preussischen Osten in den letzten 100 Jahren*, Berlin: Volk & Reich, 1937, 269 pp.

Rose, William, *The Rise of Polish Democracy*, London: Bell, 1944, 253 pp.

Rosenbaum, L., *Beruf und Herkunft der Abgeordneten zu den deutschen und preussischen Parlamenten, 1847 bis 1914*, Frankfurt/Main: Sociëtats-Druckerei, 1923, 78 pp.

Rosenberg, Hans, *Grosse Depression und Bismarckzeit*, Veröffentlichungen der Historischen Kommission zu Berlin, #24, Berlin: Walter de Gruyter, 1967, 301 pp.

Rosenthal, Harry, "The Election of Archbishop Stablewski," *Slavic Review* 28 (1969): 265-275.

_____, *German and Pole*, National Conflict and Modern Myth, Gainesville: University Presses of Florida, 1976, 175 pp.

_____, "Germans and Poles in 1890: Possibilities for a New Course," *East European Quarterly* 5 (1971).

_____, "Nation or Class: the Bund der Landwirte and the Poles," *Australian Journal of Politics and History* 19 (1973): 200-204.

_____, "National Self-Determination: the Example of Upper Silesia," *Journal of Contemporary History* 7 (1972): 231-241.

_____, "Poles, Prussians, and Elementary Education in Nineteenth-Century Posen," *Canadian-American Slavic Studies* 7 (1973): 209-218.

_____, "The Problem of Caprivi's Polish Policy," *European Studies Review* 2 (1972): 255-264.

_____, "The Prussiasn View of the Pole," The Significance of the Year 1894, *Polish Review* (1972): 13-20.

_____, "Rivalry between 'Notables' and 'Townspeople' in Prussian Poland: the First Round," *Slavonic and East European Review* 49 (1971): 68-79.

_____, "Tactics and National Unity in Prussian Poland: the Necessary Disunities," *East Central Europe* 1 (1974): 65-70.

Ross, Ronald, *The Beleaguered Tower*, South Bend: Univ. of Notre Dame, 1976, 218 pp.

Rothfels, Hans, *Bismarck, der Osten, und das Reich*, 2nd edit., Stuttgart: Kohlhammer, 1962, 295 pp.

_____, "Die Nationsidee in westlicher und östlicher Sicht," in *Osteuropa und der deutsche Osten*, Reihe 1, #3, Cologne: Rudolf Müller, 1956, 29 pp.

_____, *Ostraum, Preussentum und Reichsgedanke*, Königsberger Historische Forschungen, #7, Leipzig: Hinrich, 1935, 256 pp.

Rubinsztejn, Helena, *Polityka imperializmu niemieckiego na polskich zeimiach zachodnich na przełomie 19. i 20. wieków*, Warsaw: Książka i Wiedza, 1955, 289 pp.

Sarrazin, Hermann, *Die Entwicklung der Preise des Grund und Bodens in der Provinz Posen*, Halle diss., Halle: 1897, 78 pp.

Schieder, Theodor, *Das Deutsch Reich von 1871 als Nationalstaat*, Wissenschaftliche Abhandlungen der Arbeitsgemeinschaft für Forschung des Landes Nordrhein-Westfalen,#20, Cologne/Opladen: Walter, 1961, 182 pp.

_____, "Nationalstaat und Nationalitätenproblem," *Zeitschrift für Ostforschung* 1 (1952): 161-181.

_____, "Das Problem des Nationalismus in Osteuropa," in *Osteuropa und der deutsche Osten*, Reihe 1, #3, Cologne: Rudolf Müller, 1956, 29 pp.

Schinkel, Friedrich, *Polen, Preussen, und Deutschland*, Die polnische Frage als Problem der preussisch-deutschen Nationalstaatsentwicklung, Breslau: Korn, 1931.

Schleier, Hans & Gustav Seeber, "Zur Entwicklung und Rolle des Antisemitismus in Deutschland von 1871-1914," *Zeitschrift für Geschichtswissenschaft* 9 (1961): 1593-1597.

Schmidt, Martin, *Graf Posadowsky*, Halle diss., Halle: Klinz, 1935, 173 pp.

Schmidt-Volkmar, Erich, *Der Kulturkampf in Deutschland, 1871-1890*, Göttingen: Musterschmidt, 1962, 387 pp.

Schmitz, Hans Jakob, *Geschichte des Netze-Warthelandes*, Leipzig: Hirzel, 1941, 324 pp.

Schneider, Hagen, "Die Darstellung Polens in Schulgeschichtsbüchern des Kaiserreiches," *Internationales Jahrbuch für Geschichts- und Geographieunterricht* 16 (1975): 164-214.

Schofer, Lawrence, "Patterns of Worker Protest: Upper Silesia, 1865-1914," *Journal of Social History* 5 (1972): 447-463.

Schröder, E., *Ein Tagebuch Wilhelms II (1888-1902)*, Breslau: Schlesische

Verlagsanstalt, 1903, 421 pp.

Schultz-Klinken, Karl-Rolf, "Preussische und deutsche Ostsiedlungspolitik von 1886 bis 1945; ihre Zielvorstellungen, Entwicklungsphasen und Ergebnisse," *Zeitschrift für Agrargeschichte und Agrarsoziologie* 21 (1973): 198-215.

Schulz, Gerhard, "Deutschland und der preussische Osten," *Kritische Studien zur Geschictswissenschaft* 11 (1974): 86-103.

Schumacher, Bruno, *Geschichte Ost- und Westpreussens*, Göttinger Arbeitskreis, Würzburg: Holzner, 1957, 402 pp.

Sering, Max, *Arbieterfrage und Kolonisation in den östlichen Provinzen Preussens*, Berlin: Paul Parey, 1892, 28 pp.

———, *Die innere Kolonisation im östlichen Deutschland*, Schriften des Vereins für Sozialpolitik, #61, Leipzig: Duncker & Humblot, 1893, 330 pp.

Slavenas, Julius, "The Polish Parliamentarians in the North German Reichstag, 1867-1870," *Polish Review* 19 (1974): 71-76.

Sobkowiak, Valerian, *Józef Chociszewski*, Gniezno: Lech, 1937, 161 pp.

Spandowski, Franz, *Genossenschaftliche Probleme in dem "Verband der Erwerbs- und Wirtschaftsgenossenschaften der Provinzen Posen und Westpreussen,"* Freiburg diss., Poznań: St. Adalbert, 1915, 147 pp.

Spandowski, Paweł, *Towarzystwa przemysłowe*, Polnische Gewerbevereine im Rahmen der Entwicklung eines polnischen gewerblichen Mittelstandes, Poznań: Św. Wojciech, 1909, 143 pp.

Spatz, M., *Die Kampforganisationen Neu-Polens*, Munich: Lehmann, 1910, 78 pp.

Stade, Paul, *Das Deutschtum vs. die Polen in Ost- und Westpreussen nach den Sprachzählungen von 1861, 1890, und 1900*, Berlin diss., Berlin: Ebering, 1908, 45 pp.

Stern, Leo, *Die zwei Traditionen der deutschen Polenpolitik und die Revolution von 1905-7 im Königreich Polen*, East Berlin: Rütten & Loening, 1961, 81 pp.

Stolberg-Wernigerode, Otto zu, *Die unentschiedene Generation*, Munich: Oldenbourg, 1968, 488 pp.

Stumpfe, E., *Polenfrage und Ansiedlungskommission*, Berlin: Dietrich Reimer, 1902, 262 pp.

Supan, A., "Die Nationalitäten der preussischen Monarchie nach der Zählung von 1890," *Petermanns Mitteilungen* 40 (1894): 160-165.

Swart, Friedrich, *Diesseits und jenseits der Grenze*, Das deutsche Genossenschaftswesen im Posener Land und das deutsch-polnische Verhältnis bis zum Ende des zweiten Weltkrieges, Leer: Rautenberg & Möckel, 1954, 231 pp.

———, "Die preussische Ansiedlungskommission," *Schmollers Jahrbuch für Gesetzbegung, Verwaltung und Volkswirtschaft im Deutschen Reich* 65,4 (1941): 73-100.

Symmons-Symonolewicz, Konstantin, *Nationalist Movements*, Meadville/Pa.: Maplewood, 1970, 91 pp.

Szembek, Alexander, *Les associations économiques des paysans polonais sous* la domination prussienne, Lille/Paris/Brugge: Desclée, de Brouwer, & Co., 1909, 461 pp.

Szołdrski, Jan, *Die landwirtschaftliche Entwicklung der Provinz "Grossherzogtum Posen" (1772-1900)*, Munich diss., Poznań: Dziennik Poznański, 1903, 191 pp.

Szymański, Roman, *Znaczenie handlu ludowego*, Odczyty dla polskich warstw średnich, #5, Poznań: Orędownik, 1893, 13 pp.

"Territoire et population de la Pologne," *Encyclopédie Polonaise*, vol. 2, Lausanne: Impriméries Réunies, 1920, 865 pp.

Thiel, H., "Verhandlungen der letzten Jahre über innere Kolonisation und ihr förderliche Rechtsformen im preussischen Landtage, dem kgl. preussischen Landesoekonomie-Kollegium, und der Zentral-Moorkommission," in *Zur inneren Kolonisation in Deutschland*, Schriften des Vereins für Sozialpolitik, #32, Leipzig: Duncker & Humblot, 1886, pp. 45-123.

Tims, Richard, *Germanizing Prussian Poland, The HKT Society and the Struggle for the Eastern Marches in the German Empire, 1894-1919*, 2nd edit., New York: AMS Press, 1966, 312 pp.

Tirrell, Sarah, *German Agrarian Politics after Bismarck's Fall*, New York: Columbia University Press, 1951, 354 pp.

Tomaszewski, Władysław, *Bank Związku Spółek Zarobkowych (1886-1910), Pamiętnik za pierwsze 25 lat istnienia*, Poznań: Gebr. Wieniewicz, 1911, 128 pp.

———, *Die Entwicklung der polnischen Erwerbs- und Wirtschaftsgenossenschaften in den Provinzen Posen, Westpreussen, und Schlesien, 1861-1912*, Poznań: Gebr. Winiewicz, 1913, 32 pp.

Toporowski, Lorraine, "The Origins of the National Democratic Party, 1886-1903: a Study in Polish Nationalism," Columbia diss., 1973.

Trzeciakowski, Lech, *Kulturkampf w zaborze pruskim*, Poznań: Wydawnictwo Poznańskie, 1970, 318 pp.

———, *Polityka polskich klas posadających w Wielkopolski w erze Capriviego*, Poznań: Univ. im. Mickiewicza, 1960, 157 pp.

———, "Polskie ugrupowania politicznie zaboru pruskiego wobec Niemiec 1871-1918," *Dzieje Najnowsze* 4 (1972): 25-47.

———, "The Prussian State and the Catholic Church in Prussian Poland 1871-1914," *Slavic Review* 26 (1967): 618-637.

———, *Walka o polskość miast poznańskiego na przełomie XIX i XX wieku*, Poznań: 1964, 237 pp.

Trziński, Juliusz, *Russisch-polnische und galizische Wanderarbeiter im Grossherzogtum Posen*, Münchener Volkswirtschaftliche Studien, #79, Stuttgart/Berlin: Cotta, 1906, 145 pp.

Tümmler, Hans, "Die preussische Polenpolitik in der Provinz Posen vom Wiener Kongress bis zum Ausbruch des Weltkrieges," *Vergangenheit und Gegenwart* 29 (1939): 578-590.

Ullmann, Eduard, "Zur preussisch-deutschen Polenpolitik von 1885 bis 1887," *Jahrbuch für die Geschichte der Sozialistischen Länder Europas* 8 (1964): 463-474.

Vallentin, Wilhelm, *Westpreussen seit den ersten Jahrzehnten dieses Jahrhunderts*, Beiträge zur Geschichte der Bevökerung in Deutschland, ed. F. Neumann, Tübingen: Laupp, 1893, 225 pp.

Wahl, Adalbert, *Deutsche Geschichte 1871-1914*, Stuttgart: 1926-36.

Wäber, Alexander, *Preussen und Polen*, Munich: Lehmann, 1907, 391 pp.

Wajda, Kazimierz, "Robotnicy rolni w Prusach na przełomie XIX i XX wieku zaostrzenie ustawodawstwa," *Kwartalnik Historyczny* 75 (1968): 23-40.

Waldhecker, Paul, "Ansiedlungskommission und Generalkommission," *Jahrbuch für Gesetzbegung, Verwaltung, und Volkswirtschaft im Deutschen Reich* 21 (1897): 202-227.

Wandycz, Piotr, *The Lands of Partitioned Poland, 1795-1918*, A History of East Central Europe, vol. 7, Seattle: Univ. of Washington Press, 1974, 431 pp.

Warschauer, Adolf, *Deutsche Kulturarbeit in der Ostmark*, Erinnerungen aus vier Jahrzehnten, Berlin: Reimar Hobbing, 1926, 324 pp.

Weber, Max, "Der Nationalstaat und die Volkswirtschaftspolitik," in *Gesammelte Politische Schriften*, 3rd edit., ed. J. Winckelmann, Tübingen: Mohr, 1971, pp. 1-25.

Wegener, Leo, *Der wirtschaftliche Kampf der Deutschen mit den Polen um die Provinz Posen*, Poznań: Joseph Jolowicz, 1903, 319 pp.

Wehler, Hans-Ulrich, *Das Deutsche Kaiserreich 1871-1918*, Deutsche Geschichte, Band 9, Göttingen: Vandenhoeck & Ruprecht, 2nd edit., 1975, 275 pp.

_____, "Die Polenpolitik im deutschen Kaiserreich 1871-1918," *Politische Ideologien und Nationalstaatliche Ordnung*, Festschrift Theodor Schieder, ed. W. Mommsen & K. Kluxen, Munich: 1968, pp. 297-316.

_____, *Sozialdemokratie und Nationalstaat*, Marburger Ostforschungen, #18, Würzburg: Holzner, 1962, 281 pp.

Wendel, Hermann, *Preussische Polenpolitik in ihren Ursachen und Wirkungen*, Berlin: Vorwärts, 1908, 86 pp.

Wendt, Hans, *Bismarck und die polnische Frage*, Halle: Max Niemeyer, 1922, 98 pp.

Wereszycki, Henryk, *Historia polityczna Polski w dobie popowstaniowej 1864-1918*, Warswa: Instytut Pamięci Narodowej, 1948, 374 pp.

Wertheimer, Mildred, *The Pan-German League, 1890-1914*, Columbia diss., New York: 1924, 256 pp.

Wichardt, Hans-Jürgen, "Die Polenpolitik Preussens und die Vereins- und Versammlungsfreiheit in der Rechtsprechung des kgl. preussischen Oberverwaltungsgerichts," *Zeitschrift für Ostforschung* 27 (1978): 67-78.

Widdern, Cardinal von, *Polnische Eroberungszüge im heutigen Deutschland und die deutsche Abwehr*, Lissa: Oskar Eulitz, 1913, 152 pp.

Wiegand, Berthold, *Die anti-deutsche Propaganda der Polen, 1890-1914*, Danzig: Danziger Verlags-Gesellschaft, 1940, 152 pp.

Wielkopolanin, *Walka ekonomiczno-rasowa w Poznańskiem*, Cracow: Anczyca, 1898, 133 pp.

Winiarski, Bohdan, *Les institutions politiques et administrativs en Pologne* au 19. siècle, Paris: Picart, 1921, 271 pp.

Witten, M. von, *Unsere Ostmark*, Lissa: Ebbecke, 1907, 56 pp.

Witting, Richard, *Ostmarken-Probleme*, Berlin: Puttkamer & Mühlbrecht, 1907, 78 pp.

Ein Wort zu ernster Stunde an die deutschen Mitbürger von einem polnischen Bürger, Poznań: Kuryer Poznański, 1893, 24 pp.

Wurzbacher, Gerhard, "Studien über den Wandel der sozialen und völkischen Struktur eines Landkreises im pommerisch-westpreussischen Grenzraum zwischen 1773 und 1937," *Zeitschrift für Ostforschung* 2 (1953): 190-207.

Wydarzenia wrzesińskie w roku 1901, ed. Z. Grot, Poznań: Wydawnictwo Poznańskie, 1964, pp. 11-43.

Wybitni Wielkopolanie 19. wieku, ed. W. Jakóbczyk, Poznań: Wydawnictwo Poznańskie, 1959, 2 vols.

Young, Anne, "Bismarck's Policy toward the Poles," Chicago diss., 1951.

Załuski, Bronisław, *Spółki zarobkowe i gospodarcze w Poznańskiem i w Prusach zachodnich*, Warsaw: Gebethner & Wolff, 1921, 283 pp.

Zarnowski, Janusz, "Les événements de 1871 dans la pensée politique et l'historiographie polnaises," *Revue d'histoire Moderne et Contemporaine* (1972): 337-344.

Zechlin, Egmont, *Staatsstreichpläne Bismarcks und Wilhelms II, 1890-4*, Stuttgart/Berlin: Cotta, 1929.

Zeender, John, *The German Center Party, 1890-1906*, Philadelphia: APS, 1976, 125 pp.

Zimmermann, Kazimierz, "Bank Przemysłowców" in Posen, Poznań: St. Adalbert, 1907, 148 pp.

Zitzlaff, Franz/Fritz Vosberg/Karpiński, *Preussische Städte im Gebiete des polnischen Natinoalitätkampfes*, ed. L. Bernhard, Schriften des Vereins für Sozialpolitik, #119:1, Leipzig: Duncker & Humblot, 1909, 202 pp.

Zwanzig Jahre alldeutscher Arbeit und Kampf, ed. Alldeutscher Verband, Leipzig: Dieterich, 1910, 467 pp.

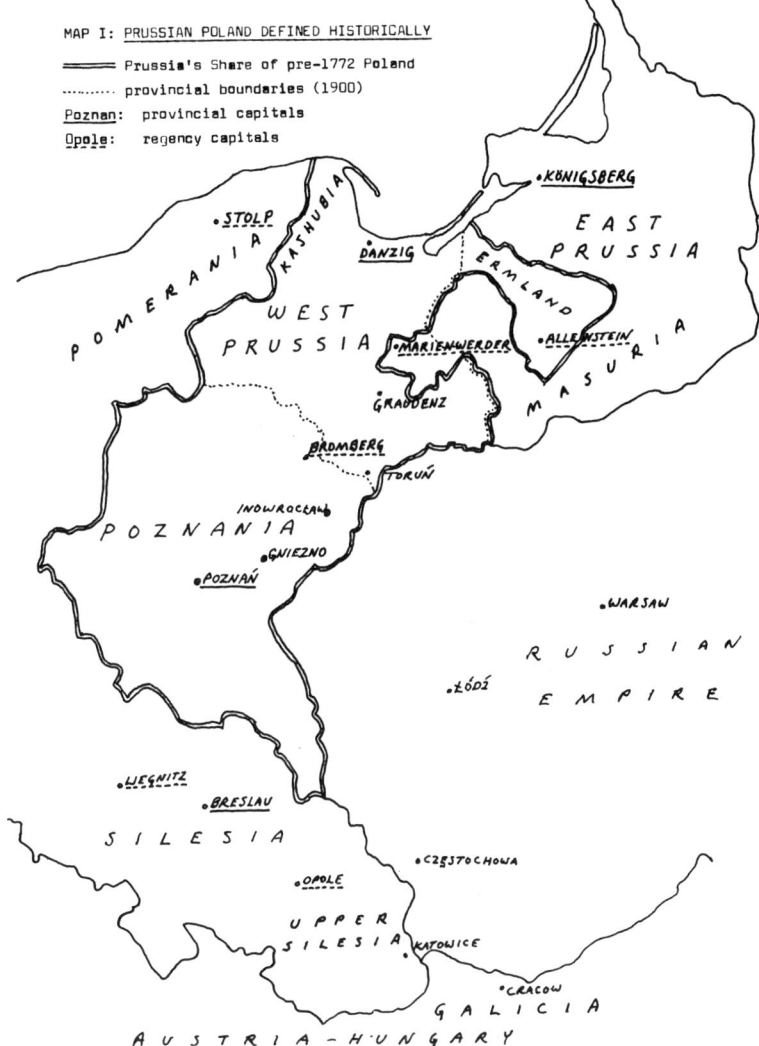

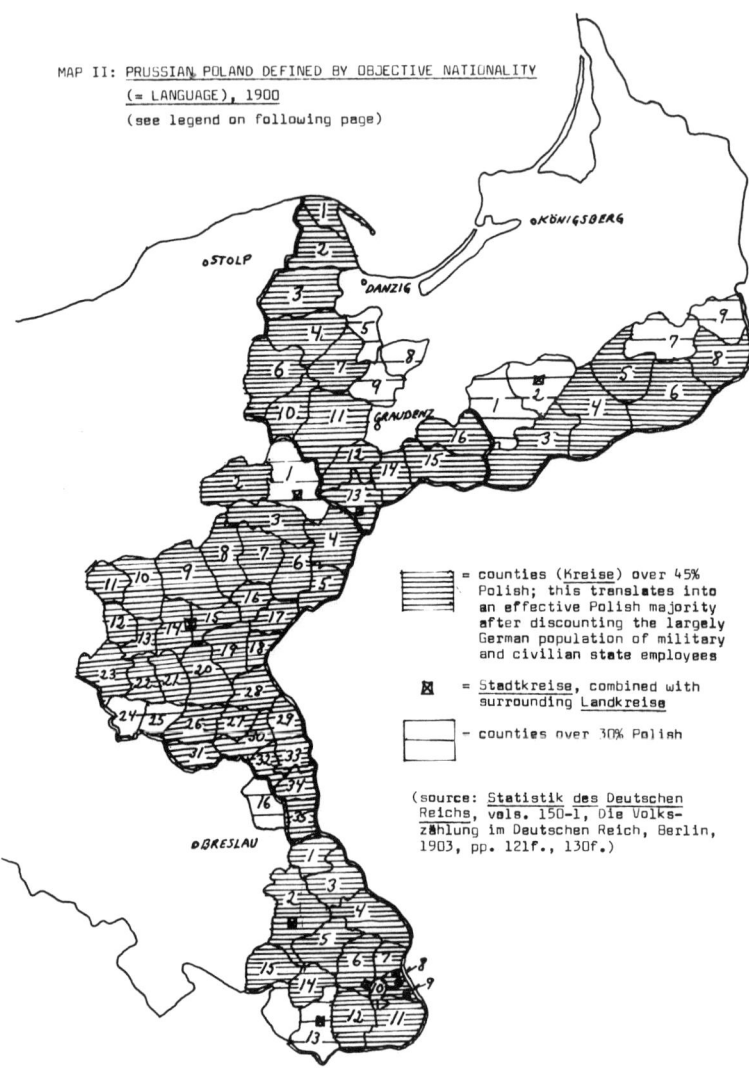

East Prussian counties:
(more than 45% Polish-speaking:)
3. Nidzica/Neidenburg
4. Szczytno/Ortelsburg
5. Mrągowo/Sensburg
6. Pisz/Johannisburg
8. Ełk/Lyck

30-45% Polish-speaking:
1. Osterode/Ostróda
2. Allenstein/Olsztyn
7. Łötzen/Giżycko
9. Treuburg/Olecko

West Prussian counties:
more than 45% Polish-speaking:
1. Puck/Putzig
2. Wejherowo/Neustadt
3. Kartuzy/Karthaus
4. Kościerzyna/Berent
6. Chojnice/Konitz
7. Starogard Gd./Pr. Stargard
10. Tuchola/Tuchel
11. Świecie/Schwetz
12. Chełmno/Culm
13. Toruń/Thorn
14. Wąbrzeźno/Briesen
15. Brodnica/Strasburg
16. Lubawa/Löbau

30-45% Polish-speaking:
5. Dirschau/Tczew
8. Stuhm/S₂tum
9. Marienwerder/Kwidzyn

Poznanian counties:
more than 45% Polish-speaking:
2. Wyrzysk/Wirsitz
3. Szubin/Schubin
4. Inowrocław/Hohensalza
5. Strzelno/Strelno
6. Mogilno
7. Żnin/Znin
8. Wągrowiec/Wongrowitz
9. Oborniki/Obornik
10. Szamotuły/Samter
11. Międzychód/Birnbaum
12. Nowy Tomyśl/Neutomischel
13. Grodzisk Wlkp./Grätz

14. Poznań/Posen West
15. Poznań/Posen East
16. Gniezno/Gnesen
17. Witkowo
18. Września/Wreschen
19. Środa Wlkp./Schroda
20. Śrem/Schrimm
21. Kościan/Kosten
22. Śmigiel/Schmiegel
23. Babimost/Bomst
26. Gostyń/Gostyn
27. Koźmin/Koschmin
28. Jarocin/Jarotschin
29. Pleszew/Pleschen
30. Krotoszyn/Krotoschin
31. Rawicz/Rawitsch
32. Udolanów/Adelnau
33. Ustrów Wlkp./Ostrowo
34. Ostrzeszów/Schildberg
35. Kępno/Kempen

30-45% Polish-speaking:
1. Bromberg/Bydgoszcz
24. Fraustadt/Wschowa
25. Lissa/Leszno

Silesian counties:
more than 45% Polish-speaking:
1. Kluczbork/Kreuzburg
2. Opole/Oppeln
3. Olesno/Rosenberg
4. Lubliniec/Lublinitz
5. Strzelce Op./Gr. Strehlitz
6. Toszek-Gliwice/Tost-Gleiwitz
7. Tarnowskie Góry/Tarnowitz
8. Bytom-Chorzów/Beuthen-Königshütte
9. Katowice/Kattowitz
10. Zabrze/Hindenburg
11. Pszczyna/Pless
12. Rybnik
14. Koźle/Cosel
15. Prudnik/Neustadt

30-45% Polish-speaking:
13. Ratibor/Racibórz
16. Gross Wartenberg/Syców

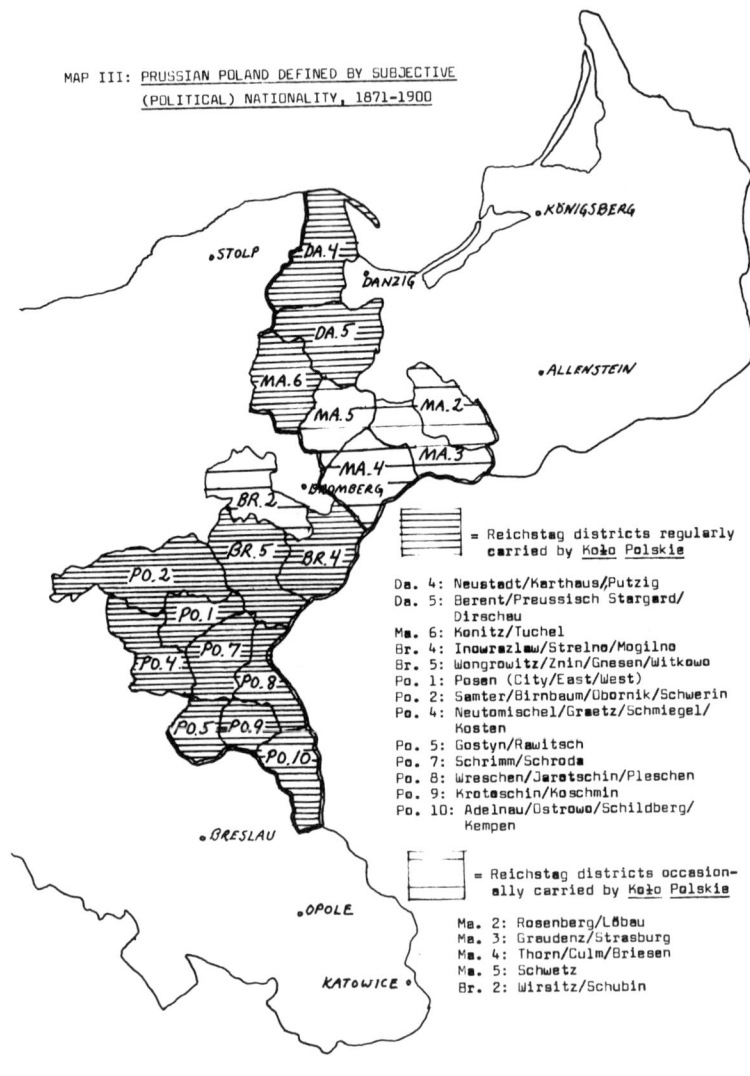

Index

Achenbach Resolution (1886) - 59
agrarians, German, and Poles - 97, 164-5, 181, 191, 223
Agricultural Bank for Poznania - 11
alien workers - 43, 127-8
Altenstein, Karl v., Prussian Culture Minister - 2
Alvensleben Convention (1863) - 8, 13
Andrzejewski, Józef - 226-7
anti-clericalism, Polish - 27
anti-Semitism - 40-1, 47-8, 51, 162-4, 219
Army, German, and Poles - 82-3, 123, 197-8
Army Bill of 1893 - 154-8

Balicki, Zygmunt - 216-7
Ballestrem, Franz v. - 165
Bennigsen, Rudolf v. - 61
Berlepsch, Hans v., Prussian Trade Minister - 137
Bismarck, Otto v., German Chancellor - 7-11, 17-25, 30-1, 40, 44, 47, 50-1, 55, 64-86, 110-1, 113-4, 121-2, 147-9, 180-1, 185-6, 211
Bosse, Robert, Prussian Culture Minister - 139-40, 151-2, 157, 165-7, 178-80, 187-8, 190, 192-4, 196, 199-201, 209-10, 213, 221
boycotts, Polish - 104, 163
Bronsart v. Schellendorf, Paul, Prussian War Minister - 83, 122
Brüggen, Ernst v. der - 45
Bülow, Bernhard v., German Chancellor - 191, 230-1
Bund der Landwirte - 165, 224

Caprivi, Leo v., German Chancellor - 121-7, 131-3, 135-41, 147-53, 157, 165-7, 170, 209
Catholic Section of the Prussian Culture Ministry - 18, 20
Catholics, German, and Poles - 56, 71, 196-7
Cegielski, Stefan - 103, 107, 111, 149, 155-6, 160, 225-6
censure of expulsion measure by Reichstag (1886) - 51, 59
Center Party, German, and Poles - 28-9, 30, 32, 50, 56, 69, 76-7, 97-8, 156, 165, 221-3
Central Economic Society - 5, 23, 161
Chłapowski, Franciszek - 77, 227
Chrzanowski, Bernard - 219-21, 225-9
Church, Catholic, in Poznania - 19-20, 25-7, 78-81, 159-62, 196-7
civil service, Prussian, and Poles - 82, 197-8
clergy, Polish - 26, 83, 100, 108, 196, 225
colonization of Germans - 46, 57-8, 62, 129, 137, 186-92
confiscation of Polish estates - 57, 231-2
co-op movement, Polish - 26, 107-9, 129-30, 154, 211-3
counties, redivision of - 82
courts, Prussian, and Poles - 24, 78, 195, 231
Czarliński, Leon - 94, 112, 128, 133, 136, 155-6, 158, 189, 209, 214, 224, 227

Delbrück, Hans - 185
demographic trends - 41-2, 44, 106, 185
Dinder, Julius, Archbishop of Gniezno-Poznań - 79-81, 131
Dispositionsfonds - 199-200

Dmowski, Roman - 216-9
Dobrowolski, Franciszek - 27, 158-9
Dziennik Poznański - 102-3, 128, 134-5, 138, 151, 155, 158, 167-8, 209-10, 215, 224, 227

Eastern Marches Association (*Ostmarkenverein*) - 180-4, 199, 232
economic background, Poznanian - 42-3
Eichorn, Johann, Prussian Culture Minister - 3
Eulenburg, Botho zu, Prussian Minister-President - 129, 137, 139, 151, 166, 188
Eulenburg, Friedrich v., Prussian Interior/Culture Minister - 12, 20-1, 23-5, 110
expulsion of Polish aliens - 21, 47-50, 94
"extermination" (*ausrotten*) - 30, 45, 82

Falk, Adalbert, Prussian Culture Minister - 22-4, 26
farm workers in Prussian Poland - 47-9, 72, 127-8, 190-1
Flottwell, Eduard v. - 2, 60
Francis Joseph, Austrian Emperor - 215
Franco-Prussian War (1870-1) and Poles - 20
Frederick I, German Emperor - 113-4
Frederick William III, Prussian King - 1
Frederick William IV, Prussian King - 3
Fund for Estate Management (*Güterbetriebsfonds*) - 2, 60-2

Galicia, and Prussian Poland - 3, 84, 94-5, 109, 111, 215, 232
Gazeta Grudziązka - 219
Gazeta Toruńska - 95, 101, 115, 152, 158, 228
General Commission (Bromberg) - 128-9, 186-8, 191
German Empire of 1871, and Poles - 12, 28
Germania (Cologne) - 65, 98
"Germanization" - 2, 11, 45, 55, 63
Germans in Prussian Poland - 46, 126, 138, 149-50, 180-1, 185, 199-200
Germans, Settlement Commission purchases from - 69-70, 137, 186, 188-9
Gołuchowski, Agenor - 109

Goniec Wielkopolski - 111, 134, 153-4, 156, 227
Gossler, Gustav v., Prussian Culture Minister - 46-7, 58, 62-3, 67, 74-82, 84, 114, 124-5, 127, 130-1, 170
Gossler, Henrich v., Prussian War Minister - 190

Hammerstein, Wilhelm v., Prussian Agriculture Minister - 187-90
Hansemann, Adolf - 180
Hartmann, Eduard v. - 45-6
Hebungspolitik - 200-2
Heyden, Wilhelm v., Prussian Agriculture Minister - 137
Hohenlohe-Schillingsfürst, Chlodwig z., German Chancellor - 177-9, 183, 187-8, 192, 196-9, 210
Holstein, Friedrich v. - 139
Horn, Karl v., Poznamian *Oberpräsident* - 12, 18
Huene, Center Party leader - 165, 222
Hugenberg, Alfred - 150, 183
Hutten-Czapski, Bogdan - 100, 110, 127, 138, 168, 177, 182, 210

Insurrection of 1863, Polish - 6, 8-9

Jackowski, Maximilian - 102, 161, 164, 211, 214
Jażdżewski, Ludwik - 27-8, 30, 77, 79, 113, 122, 131, 133, 136, 152, 155-6, 160, 163, 168, 181, 185, 209-10, 222-3, 225
Jews in Prussian Poland - 40-1, 44, 49-50, 73, 106

Kalkstein, Teodor - 96
Kalnoky, Gustav v., Austro-Hungarian Foreign Minister - 69
Kaltenborn, Hans v., Prussian War Minister - 157
Kantak, Kazimierz - 12, 25, 29, 31, 77, 99, 110-1
Kardorff, Wilhelm v. - 66
Kashubes/Kashubia - 31-2, 71, 99
Kennemann, Hermann v. - 180
Ketteler, Archbishop of Mainz - 20, 79
Knapowski, Stanisław - 104, 162-3, 211
Köller, Ernst v., Prussian Interior

Postęp - 104, 134, 152, 156, 159, 160-1
press, Polish - 31, 99, 104-5, 114-5,
    134-5, 155, 229
Preussische Kasse (Co-op Bank) - 212-4
Progressive Party, and Poles - 50, 56,
    69, 73, 156, 164-5, 223, 227
Przegląd Poznański - 219-20
Przegląd Wszechpolski - 2126-7
Puttkamer, Robert v., Prussian Interior
    Minister - 25, 41, 47-9, 58, 64, 66,
    77, 82, 85, 114

Rabski, Władysław - 219-20
Radziwiłł family - 20, 110, 127
Radziwiłł, Antoni - 1-2
Radziwiłł, Ferdynand - 112, 126, 138,
    214, 225
Recke, Prussian Interior Minister - 183,
    195, 199, 232
Rentengüter - 61-4, 66, 128-9, 186-8
Rheinbaben, Georg v., Prussian Interior
    Minister - 189, 230
Russia, German relations with - 69,
    121-2, 148
Russian Poland - 109, 138-9

Schmoller, Gustav - 61
Schönstedt, Prussian Justice
    Minister - 195, 197, 230
Scholz, Adolf v., Prussian Finance
    Minister - 75
school policy, Prussian, in Prussian
    Poland - 20-1, 58, 74-8, 84, 130-1,
    140, 157-8, 165-7, 192-4, 231
Seeckt, Gen. Richard v. - 123
self-government, provincial, in
    Poznania - 23
Settlement Commission
    (Ansiedluggskommission) - 65-7,
    70-3, 96, 100, 128-9, 136-7, 185-92,
    210, 212, 231
Settlement Law of 1886 - 46, 60-9, 136,
    152, 184-5
Seyda, Marian - 229
Skarżyński, Witold - 110-1, 223
Social Democratic Party, German, and
    Poles - 50, 69, 97, 222, 224
socialism, Polish - 112, 224
Stablewski, Florian, Archbishop of
    Gniezno-Poznań - 93-4, 97-8, 110-2,
    125, 131-3, 135-6, 138, 148, 152,
    159-60, 166-7, 196-7, 210-1, 221, 227
Straż - 232
Studt, Konrad v., Prussian Culture
    Minister - 230
Szamarzewski, Augustyn - 107
Szymański, Roman - 42, 101-5, 108,
    115, 152-3, 159, 161-4, 170, 180,
    211, 214-5, 220-1, 223, 225-6, 228-9

Tiedemann, Christoph v. - 46, 56-7,
    62-5, 83-4, 130
Tiedemann, Heinrich v. - 149, 180
towns in Prussian Poland - 43-4, 73
trade schools, Prussian,-and Poles -
    77-8, 194
trade treaties with foreign states, and
    Poles - 164, 167-8
Treitschke, Heinrich v. - 40

Union Bank (Bank Związku) - 107, 213
Upper Silesia - 32, 43, 76-7, 101, 112,
    125, 165, 169, 221-2

Victoria, German Empress - 113, 137-8

Waldersee, Gen. Alfred v., - 121-2,
    150
Wawrzyniak, Piotr - 154, 168, 210-1,
    214
Wilamowitz-Moellendorff, Hugo v.,
    Poznanian Oberpräsident - 136, 149,
    166, 182-4, 187, 190, 193-4, 196-8,
    200
William I, German Emperor - 26, 50,
    58, 82
William II, German Emperor - 126-7,
    132, 138, 141, 147, 151-3, 157-8, 170,
    190, 195, 210
Windthorst, Ludwig - 28, 50-1, 165

"Young-Poland" - 219-20, 228

Zedlitz-Trützschler, Robert v.,
    Prussian Culture Minister - 66, 72, 78,
    100, 125-6, 130-1, 136, 138-9
Żółtowski, head of Central Economic
    Association - 154, 211, 225

Index

Minister - 182-3
Koło Polskie (Polish Party) - 26-7, 30, 77, 93-4, 97-8, 101-5, 111, 115, 133-4, 136, 140, 152-5, 163-5, 166-9, 211, 214-5, 221-9
Komierowski, Roman - 149, 210
Kopp, Archbishop of Breslau - 127, 132
Korfanty, Wojciech - 222, 228
Kościelski, Józef - 111-3, 115, 132, 135-7, 140-1, 149, 153-4, 158, 168-9, 210, 232
Kraszewski, Józef - 27, 42
Kreuzzeitung - 167
Kulerski, Wiktor - 219, 223-4, 228
Kuryer Poznański - 80, 94-5, 97, 99, 133-6, 151, 155, 159, 167, 210, 227
Kusztelan, head of Bank Związku - 169, 211

Land Bank (Bank Ziemski) - 94-6, 128, 188, 212
land ownership, Polish in Prussian Poland - 67-8, 189, 192
Ledówski, Archbishop of Poznań-Gniezno - 12, 22, 25-7, 78-81, 134, 149, 157, 160
Leonhardt, Prussian Justice Minister - 11
liberalism, German and Poles - 13, 97
Liga Polska/Liga Narodowa - 216
"Long Depression" (1873-1896) - 41, 57
loyalism, Polish - 109-15, 124, 131-6, 147, 150-3, 158, 169-70, 210-1
Lucius, Robert, Prussian Agriculture Minister - 63-5, 67-8, 71
Łyskowski, Ignacy - 49

Manteuffel, Otto v., Prussian Minister-President - 4
Marcinkowski, Karol - 5
Masuria - 32
May Laws (1873) and Poles - 22, 26
Miarka, Karol - 76
middle classes, Polish - 56-7, 85, 102-4, 106-9, 150, 201, 213, 229-30
Mierosławski, Ludwik - 3
Miłkowski, Zygmunt - 216
Miquel, Johannes, Prussian Finance Minister - 61-2, 66, 68, 137, 178-9, 186-9, 196, 198-201, 213-4, 229
Motty, Mieczysław - 226-7

Mühler, Prussian Culture Minister - 20

National Democracy, Polish - 215-22, 228-9, 232
nationalism, Polish - 5-6, 31-3, 98-9, and preface
nationalism, German - 39, 44-5, and preface
National Liberals, and Poles - 58, 61, 63, 66, 128
"National Solidarity," - 5, 27, 100, 102-4, 111, 154-5, 160-1, 210
Neue Freie Presse (Vienna) - 69
Niegolewski, Władysław - 25, 27, 29, 111
nobility, Polish - 5-6, 57, 68, 83, 94-104, 113, 124, 215
North German Confederation of 1867 and Poles - 12
Nowa Reforma (Cracow) - 94

"official language" regulations - 24, 28, 30, 194-5, 231
Orędownik - 101, 134, 152-3, 159, 160-2, 209, 227-9
Organic Work - 5, 25, 106-9, 219

Pan-German League - 150, 181-2
Papacy - 19, 56, 78-9
parcelling efforts, Polish - 96, 137, 186, 212-3, 231
partition of Poznania, discussion of - 3, 82
peasant organizations, Polish - 161, 213-4
peasantry, Polish - 6, 68, 71, 83-4, 186, 189
People's Party (Partia Ludowa)/Populists - 154-6, 158, 162-4, 168-9, 197, 211, 214-5, 219-29
Polonization of Germans - 17-8
Polish language in the schools - 22, 78, 80-1, 84, 130-1, 151, 166-7, 193, 231
Popławski, Jan - 216-7
population growth rates - 42-4
Posadowsky, Arthur v., German Treasury Secretary - 46, 84-5, 178-9, 187, 190-1, 199-201
Posener Zeitung - 131, 133, 223

WITHDRAWN